INCOME AND WELFARE
IN THE UNITED STATES

INCOME AND WELFARE IN THE UNITED STATES

James N. Morgan, *University of Michigan*

Martin H. David, *University of Wisconsin*

Wilbur J. Cohen, *University of Michigan*

Harvey E. Brazer, *University of Michigan*

with the assistance of
Norma Meyers *and* **Barbara Baldwin**

A STUDY BY THE SURVEY RESEARCH CENTER
INSTITUTE FOR SOCIAL RESEARCH
UNIVERSITY OF MICHIGAN

McGraw-Hill Book Company, Inc.
New York   San Francisco   Toronto   London

PREFACE

In contrast to the general prosperity of the last decade is the plight of a group of families with small and inadequate incomes. The paucity of material available on the causes of poverty and dependency, and the need for studying poverty in a framework of the welfare and economic security of the nation generally, brought about this study.

The study of poverty and dependency requires knowledge of the distribution of earned incomes, and the redistribution of available real incomes through public and private transfers, taxes, and public provision of services such as education. In addition, it requires an understanding of dynamics—the persistence or change in levels of welfare of individuals within their lifetimes and from one generation to the next.

Within this broad explanation, it is then possible to examine the low income units carefully, comparing them with those whose economic position is satisfactory, and assessing the possibility that they will solve their problems in this generation or the next.

The process of income determination is studied not just for the poor but for a cross section of the United States population. Improved data on income is developed in order that the descriptive material on income distribution can be more precise. Major forms of nonmoney income are estimated. Families are separated into adult units to isolate the economic benefits of living with relatives. Income adequacy is assessed, relative to a standard of need for each family.

The determination of family income is viewed as a sequential process, with each component of income, once determined, combining with other factors to affect later components. Some components of income, such as labor force participation of wives, have been intensively studied elsewhere, but never before has the whole set been analyzed for the same representative cross section sample. The analysis is more detailed than any previously attempted. It attempts to explain the details of income, rather than merely explaining the shape of the distribution.

The use of variables and hypotheses from several branches of the behavioral sciences makes the model of income determination more complete and more realistic. The use of psychological and sociological variables takes account of the fact that decisions which affect income are not made solely on economic grounds. Personality measures, measures of mobility and family background, and variables which describe the community in which the family lives complement the economic data about earnings, income, and economic well-being. In order to make such a rich body of data understandable, each component of income is related simultaneously to a whole set of explanatory factors.

With the model of income determination completely described, it is possible to examine the economic situation of two disadvantaged groups, the poor and the disabled.

The impact of some major redistributional mechanisms on the distribution of income is examined. Public and private transfers in the form of pensions, welfare, social security, philanthropy, income taxes, property taxes, and the benefits of free public education are analyzed. Public policy relies on public support, hence some attention is paid to attitudes toward public programs and toward private family responsibilities.

Since education is a major determinant of income, the transmission of education over three generations is studied. As with income, education levels are related simultaneously to a variety of factors. In the analysis of education, these factors reflect availability of educational facilities, economic ability to invest in education, and motivation. Parents' plans for the education of today's children are also analyzed along with the implications of these plans for the future demand for educational facilities.

Large scale social research is a group undertaking, its total quality depending upon the quality of many individual contributions. A great many people aided or inspired this research project in one way or another. Funds from the Ford Foundation allowed Kenneth Boulding to start a Faculty Seminar on Income Maintenance during which this study was conceived. The members of that seminar included scholars from several disciplines, and its secretary was Martin David. In particular, Prof. Richard Musgrave made clear the need for better information about the effects of various redistributive mechanisms, and Prof. Patricia Rabinowitz pointed out the need for more adequate information about the background and potentials of low income families.

An advisory committee proved especially helpful in the design of the study and the analysis of data. Professor Musgrave served in that capacity after his move from Ann Arbor prevented closer collaboration. Other members of the Advisory Committee were Mrs. Selma Goldsmith, Prof. William Haber, Prof. Lawrence R. Klein, Mrs. Helen Lamale, Mrs. Ida Merriam, Mr. Herman Miller, Mrs. Selma Mushkin, Prof. Guy Orcutt.

A number of other people provided suggestions, not all of which we had the good sense to utilize but all of which we appreciated.

Other members of the Economic Behavior Program of the Survey Research

Center gave generously of their time and counsel, particularly Profs. George Katona and John B. Lansing.

During most of the period in which the study was carried out, all four authors were at the University of Michigan with various connections in the Institute for Social Research, the Department of Economics, the School of Social Work, and the Institute of Public Administration. The Survey Research Center is a part of the Institute for Social Research. Many members of the Institute made important contributions to the study. We are indebted to Charles Cannell and Morris Axelrod for aid in the design of the questionnaire and supervision of the field procedure, to Irene Hess and Leslie Kish for supervision of the sampling design and procedures, to Doris Muehl for aid in the development of codes and supervision of the content analysis, and to John Sonquist and Keith Mather for data processing including the reprogramming of the multivariate analysis for the IBM 704. The contributions of Norma Meyers and Barbara Baldwin extended far beyond the usual research assistance into substantive contributions, writing descriptions of the procedures, and editing.

The major financial support came from the Ford Foundation. Additional grants from the Office of Education and the Office of Vocational Rehabilitation provided for special analyses of education and disability.

The Authors

TABLE OF CONTENTS

PART I

Income, Welfare, and Public Policy

Chapter 1

INCOME, WELFARE, AND PUBLIC POLICY—A SUMMARY AND SOME IMPLICATIONS

Issues relating to the distribution of income and the improvement of the general welfare have perplexed the "guardians of the State" from time immemorial. Pericles, in his famous Funeral Speech said: "Wealth to us is not mere material for vainglory but an opportunity for achievement; and poverty we think it no disgrace to acknowledge but a real degradation to make no effort to overcome." [1]

Significant efforts have been made over many decades in the United States to overcome poverty and to create opportunities for achievement. This process has been especially noticeable during the past twenty-five years when the extent of low incomes has been diminished, the level of educational attainment has risen, and mobility has been facilitated.

In the United States poverty has declined markedly in recent decades. The same development is reported in Great Britain. A reduction in poverty has gone hand in hand with economic growth. This has occurred in free-enterprise America, semisocialist England, communist Russia, and in Canada, West Germany, and the Scandinavian countries. The political and economic systems of these countries do not seem to be prime determining factors.

But economic growth in itself does not eradicate poverty. Other elements seem necessary: a broad program of education; income maintenance and health programs to meet basic needs; an equitable and efficient tax system; and a constant effort to achieve and maintain optimum use of resources and manpower.

The United States has arrived at the point where poverty could be abolished easily and simply by a stroke of the pen. To raise every individual and family in the nation now below a subsistence income to the subsistence level would cost about $10 billion a year. This is less than 2 per cent of the gross national

[1] Quoted from Alfred Zimmern, *The Greek Commonwealth*, 4th ed. (New York: Oxford University Press, 1924), p. 204.

3

product. It is less than 10 per cent of tax revenues. It is about one-fifth of the cost of national defense.

The fiscal requirement involved in abolishing poverty is the least troublesome aspect of the problem. This was not always so. There was a time when the abolition of poverty would have been impossible or would have involved such a gigantic redistribution of income that the basic character of the economy would have had to be changed. This is no longer true. Yet some reluctance to begin the attack on poverty persists. There are those who believe that poverty is a spur to progress, that it encourages individual incentive and thrift, and that it must be a penalty for laziness, error, or failure.

We do not subscribe to this brand of morality or economics which attempts to perpetuate beliefs of the seventeenth century in the twentieth and twenty-first centuries.

The Biblical statement, "Yea have the poor with you always" is taken by some as a universal rule rather than a simple historical view backwards. There are those who, believing firmly in *laissez faire,* are convinced that if government does something for poor people it will only make them more dependent.

However, the more possible it is to eliminate the *causes* of poverty, the less serious the whole discussion of incentives versus adequacy becomes. Hence a major objective of public policy in the United States is to shift from the short run alleviation of poverty to a longer run set of programs for the elimination of dependency. The intensified urgency for increasing the rate of economic growth makes it even more important that public policy focus on making individuals more productive and hence not dependent upon welfare or philanthropy. However, sound public policy must be based on facts, not surmises. It is essential to know how much poverty and dependency exists today, what causes it, and what the problems may be in eliminating it in the future.

The current level of economic welfare and independence of any family is a result of the forces impinging on that family, of its background and situation, and of its decisions and actions. The way in which a family acts in any situation depends to some extent upon the motivation and attitudes of the family members, as well as upon the possibilities open to them.

If factors which determine family income are subject to change, then the raising of substandard incomes through public policy appears possible. It is important to discover that family income is affected by factors such as physical disabilities, geographic mobility, education, attitude toward hard work and achievement motivation, as well as by such unchangeable characteristics as age and sex. The former things are subject to change, some in the short run, such as physical condition and attitudes; others like achievement motivation and education may require a generation or two.

At the same time, the discovery of attitudes incongruent with a present or predictable future situation forecasts future public problems. A major form of intrafamily aid consists of providing housing and food for dependent relatives; yet most people are opposed to having parents live with their grown children. A belief in and legal enforcement of relatives' financial responsibility for the aged persists while public programs and geographical separation makes such financial help less and less likely. Parents' desires for higher education for their children, coupled with an egalitarian feeling that aid to students should be general and not restricted to those with ability or need, may lead to vast demands for public support to higher education.

There is a unity and overreaching purpose to the research reported here. Factors affecting the present distribution of income and welfare, and changes in income from one generation to the next, provide the essential background for a discussion of the problems and possibilities for elimination of dependency in the long run as well as the abolition of poverty in the short run.

The Present Distribution of Income

The first section of this book analyzes each of the components that make up the level of current family income, as it is affected by the characteristic skills and backgrounds of the individuals, the situations they face, and the attitudes and motives they bring to bear in making choices. Individuals' motives are shown to join with situational and background factors in determining labor force participation, hours worked, and hourly earnings of both the head and wife, home production, the providing of housing for relatives, and philanthropy. Families also have earnings from capital, particularly the returns from investment in a home; these earnings are also studied.

A better understanding of the processes by which the incomes of families are determined is essential. Chapters 2–15 provide such an analysis in more detail and with a broader selection of explanatory variables than has ever been attempted before. The findings in these chapters make it clear that family income is at least in part the result of the decisions of the individuals in the family, not merely something determined by society or by the decisions of entrepreneurs and government. Even the head's hours and earnings seem to result in part from his own decisions. More important, the wife's earnings, and the economics of living with relatives, clearly allow the family some flexibility in adapting to circumstances.

To the extent that outside forces affect income, the data indicate that, while advantages may cumulate to produce very high incomes, it frequently takes only one disadvantage such as low education, disability, or membership in a minority racial group to produce very low income.

One explanatory factor looms above the others in importance in determining family income: the level of formal education of the head and his wife. The measurable economic value of education to the individual, in the form of increased earnings, represents only part of the social value of that education, which includes also the noneconomic benefits to the individual and to others. It is useful, however, to determine what the direct measurable economic benefits are.

Some have argued that educational differences exaggerate the effect of education itself, because the more highly educated came from higher income families, are more highly motivated, and have greater native intelligence. The data in this study attempt to take account of some of these intercorrelations, and to derive a net or "pure" effect of education. Even the net effect proves to be so powerful that it reinforces the popular notion that better education is the one sure path to economic advancement.

Transfer Payment

Of course, not all the family's income is earned by its labor and capital. Some income is the result of redistribution through public and private transfer systems and through taxation and public expenditure. Transfer income, income which is not earned currently, is distributed through several types of programs. The largest group is public transfer programs. These may be contributory, such as social security and unemployment compensation, where the recipient or his employer has contributed to the program, or noncontributory, such as public welfare and old age assistance, if the funds are provided entirely by someone other than the recipient.

In addition, some transfers come from private organizations, such as private pensions, or from individuals. Regular and irregular contributions from persons outside the family, as well as philanthropic contributions, are part of redistributive income.

The distinction between outside forces and the family's own decisions and adjustments breaks down when the redistribution of income is examined. Even when the focus is on transfer payments, nearly nine-tenths of the transfers today are in systems to which the individual contributes either directly or indirectly through his employer. In addition, most of them are involuntary.

More important, the predominance of contributory transfers means that most of them are transfers of funds across time, for the same individual, rather than between individuals at a point in time. Consequently, they are far less redistributive than the term "transfers" would imply. It is only the relatively small ($3 billion) noncontributory transfers like welfare payments which are clearly redistributive in the long run, and clearly directed only at those who would otherwise be in dire economic circumstances. These transfers are discussed in Chapter 13.

The evaluation of the data on transfer payments is facilitated by assessing people's attitudes about one form of them, unemployment compensation. The most important finding about people's attitudes toward the level of compensation payments was not that so many favored higher payments, but that those with more unemployment experience were most likely to argue their inadequacy.

Public transfers amounted to some $25 billion in 1959, and private pensions another $2 billion. But private charity and aid to friends and family amounted to at least $21 billion including the free food and housing provided to relatives.

Private philanthropy adds its redistribution to that accomplished by the regular transfers of social security, pensions, welfare, and other public programs. The United States is a wealthy country, one whose laws favor philanthropy more than most, and one whose traditions of mutual aid are strong. Chapter 18 documents the vast extent of private philanthropy, and explains some of the differences between families in the type and extent of their giving. Attitudes toward responsibility for relatives and toward living with relatives indicate a continuation of the long term trend toward the separation of complex families, but a persistence of some feeling of responsibility for one's own extended family. These phenomena are described in Chapters 14 and 18.

Poverty

In spite of extensive transfers and philanthropy, there remain families with low incomes relative to their needs. By including nonmoney incomes, and relating a comprehensive measure of income to the estimated budget needs of the family, it is possible to identify more accurately a series of groups with increasingly inadequate incomes. A group falling below a selected standard of adequacy was selected in Chapter 16. This group was subdivided according to characteristics which help account for their poverty, allowing the reader to see how many people might be made independent and self-sustaining, and how many are so old or otherwise handicapped that only their poverty can be eliminated, not their dependency.

Much poverty has already been eliminated, some by transfers, some by increasing levels of employment and of economic independence. The data make it clear that the immediate elimination of the remaining poverty is well within the means of Federal, state, and local governments.

The disabled are one of the larger and more challenging groups high in dependence on others. The analysis in Chapter 17 is based on self-reports of disability and on extent of work limitation and indicates that there are a substantial number affected by disabilities and describes the economic impact of disability upon those involved. Surprisingly little aid from either government or relatives goes to the disabled. It seems clear that complexities of laws and aid programs for the disabled together with low levels of benefits combine to minimize the benefits that this group receives. A choice of public policies between reducing the dependency of the disabled through rehabilitation, or reducing their poverty by more adequate income maintenance to the possible detriment of rehabilitation, must be made.

Property Taxes and Public Schools

Even the advanced analysis of earned incomes, and of public and private transfer systems, takes no account of the redistributive effects of taxes other than the Federal income tax, or of government expenditures. It was possible in this study to examine only one tax and one kind of government expenditure: the property tax and public school expenditures. They were selected taxes or benefits because they are loosely linked with one another, and be-because they appear more redistributive and in a clearer manner than most cause of the importance of public education in the long-run elimination of dependency and increase in economic growth. Property taxes are the major source of local government revenue, and are more often a subject of controversy than other forms of tax. Chapter 19 shows that properly evaluated property taxes are much less inequitable or regressive than has been supposed. Expenditures on public education currently benefit those with the most children in public schools, of course, but the benefit to each family during its lifetime, in a country where almost everyone gets married and has children, and most children go to public school, is obviously rather widespread. Inequality in the form of differences in expenditure per pupil is far smaller and far less correlated with family income than one might think, when school districts or counties are compared. If there is substantial inequality in the quality of education provided, it must come either from differences within small areas, e.g., through discrimination, or from forces other than the level of expenditures, such as the anti-intellectual culture of schools in low-income areas. At the same time, differences do exist, and programs for reducing still further the inequality of opportunity that results, are clearly in the national interest.

Inequality—The Distribution of Welfare

The over-all results of the process of distribution and redistribution of income are summarized in Chapter 20 where an index measure of inequality is estimated for nuclear units and for families, and before and after account is taken of nonmoney income and of transfers. Despite the reputed insensitivity of the measure used, vast differences appear, depending upon the specifications of the unit and of the income measure.

A complete assessment of the distribution of welfare must take account of leisure. Chapter 21 does not attempt either to value leisure or to distinguish between voluntary and involuntary leisure. It does, however, show that families with higher money and nonmoney incomes spend more hours in earning these incomes. To the extent that these represent voluntary differences, then, income measures exaggerate the inequality in welfare. Those with high incomes have less leisure and are not so much better off as one might think. The analysis dramatizes the difficulties of cross-cultural comparisons or intertemporal comparisons, if the correlations between income and work hours, or the extent to which leisure is voluntary, differ.

The Dynamics of Change

Having described and explained the current distribution of income and welfare, the study proceeds to examine further the dynamics of the process of income determination. Variables representing the past had already been used in explaining current incomes. Chapter 22 examines the interrelationships between various kinds of mobility or change, and finds them remarkably independent. Little evidence of a mobility syndrome exists, and hence changes (in place of residence, religion, occupation, education) must be motivated by many and varied things in addition to the desire to advance economically. Education, which appeared to have the most effect on earnings, is shown in Chapter 23 to have a powerful effect on occupational advancement, job security, and income stability as well.

Hence, it is clear that formal education is the major dynamic mechanism by which economic level is passed on from one generation to the next, or by which intergenerational change takes place. Chapters 24 and 25 examine the forces which have determined the education of the heads of the spending units, and the completed education of their children. As always, the truth is less dramatic than the opposing conjectures made without facts. Within a persistent trend for each generation to get more education than the last, and in spite of a powerful effect of the education of the father, mother, and grandfather, on the education of the children, there remains a substantial amount of mobility in both directions. Hopefully some of these changes represent a selective process by which the more able receive more education so that their talents can be put to work most effectively.

The Future Demand for Education

Parents' aspirations for educating their children provide information both on the immediate future demand for educational facilities, and on potential changes from one generation to the next. Chapter 26 shows that the transmission pattern has not changed much. Differential aspirations between girls and boys are small, indicating a narrowing of the educational differences of the past. More important, the chapter shows expectations for sending children to college, particularly to state colleges, in far greater numbers than the past record illustrates. The details of these plans in Chapter 28 and the attitudes toward public support in Chapter 29 would indicate a burgeoning demand for higher education without either substantial private provision for its cost or general popular support for more tax aid. Many parents expect their children to pay part of their college expenses. Most people feel that, if there is to be tax support for college students, it should go to all students rather than only to those who demonstrate need or ability. The implication is that the pressure on public funds in support of higher education will be substantial. However, no groundswell of opinion favoring such tax support directly appears to exist. When the children in question reach college age, the voters will either have to support the public expenditures, revise their expectations about their children's education, or provide substantially more direct financial support for that education than they are currently planning.

Planning and Provision for the Future

Financial planning for the future appears to be relatively short run. Few families have any idea what the future will bring, or are voluntarily providing for their own retirement beyond what social security and company pensions, plus their own home, will provide.

Implications for Public Policy

Poverty and dependency still exist in this country. The former can be eliminated, but it is the elimination of dependency which is the great goal of public policy. The elimination of poverty through direct assistance still is hampered by those who believe that such programs reduce incentive on the part of the recipients, and thus make it even more difficult to combat dependency. If the primary goal of public policy is the elimination of dependency and its causes rather than the short-run alleviation of poverty, these objections regarding human motivation and incentive can be overcome more easily.

Hence, a discussion of the major programs for the elimination of dependency appears in order. Some of them are short-run programs with an immediate return; others will take a generation before the benefits appear. All of them will not only provide a sound base for the permanent elimination of some poverty, but will simplify the problem of eliminating the remaining poverty, stimulate economic growth, and provide the unmeasurable benefits of independence and self-respect and self-reliance upon which a democracy relies so heavily.

1. Rehabilitation of the disabled requires a shift from concentration on levels of benefits and incentives to work, toward focus on vocational and physical rehabilitation, guidance and counseling, more effective employment services, and perhaps more sheltered workshops. The resources devoted by states and the Federal government are clearly inadequate. Most disabled people have had no contact with facilities that could help them.

2. Fuller employment and the elimination of discrimination based on prejudice would contribute greatly to the independence of nonwhite persons, women, teen-agers, and some of the aged.

3. Facilitation of movement of capital, plant, and, above all, labor, would reduce the inflationary pressures of nearly full employment, and get workers out of areas where intermittent or chronic dependency is likely. Here again,

a focus on movement, retraining, subsidy for the risk of trying a new area or a new job, would appear more productive than a focus on eligibility or on "incentive to work."

4. Above all, since education has proven to be the crucial nexus in inter-generational change, the long-run elimination of dependency hinges most upon reducing the drop-outs, and increasing the quality of education. Given the diversity of the ability and willingness of states and local areas to provide adequate public education, it appears that Federal funds may be necessary for school construction, teachers' salaries, and student scholarships. For talented students, even high school scholarships to reduce financial pressures may be called for. A major problem will be to educate the public to the reasons for restricting student aid to those with both ability and need, or at least to those with ability.

Even after allowing for many other interrelated factors, education remains as a powerful determinant of productivity and earnings. Here, the cost of education is an investment in human capital that will pay for itself:

Again, if an educated person can earn more, on the average, than an un-educated person, the chances are that he is worth more to the country. In that case, the cost of his education is an investment that will earn more than its cost.

If the question is asked, as it will be, who will do the rough work of the country if everyone is educated, the answer is that we will have to pay more to get the rough work done. That is the aim and purpose of the whole plan, which is to abolish mass poverty. It will be accomplished if the lowest paid workers will all get higher wages. Thin out the numbers that can do only rough, or cheap, work, increase the numbers that are able to fill the positions that are harder to fill and are therefore well paid, and you have started a movement toward equality without a revolution or the use of force. It will accomplish what communism can never do by violence or fraud.[2]

5. If attitudes and personality dispositions also affect people's behavior in earning a living, should not public policy be concerned with them too? In the short run, it appears that those who work hardest are more likely to feel that hard work, rather than luck or help from friends, is the surest path to success. Certainly anything that could strengthen the belief in an orderly, fair world would appear to lead to more work and more self-reliance. Unemployment, discrimination, failure to deal with depressed areas and industries and inadequate protection against the risks of disability, major illness, or techno-logical obsolescence of skills, are thus costly in their own right to those affected and doubly costly in their effect on the attitudes of others.

More enduring personality dispositions like achievement motivation can be changed, if the theory is correct, only over generations through early training

[2] Thomas Nixon Carver, "A Conservative's Idea on Economic Reform," *The Quarterly Journal of Economics*, LXXIV (November, 1960), 536–542. Used with permission of the Harvard University Press.

of children in independence and self-reliance. Hopefully, increased self-reliance of the parents, achieved through elimination of many sources of their dependence, will lead to such independence training of their children, and a new and more independent generation.

It is beyond the scope of this book to spell out the details of the legislation or policies that would appear most effective in achieving the elimination of dependency and the maximum productivity of the population. The criteria for such details clearly must be to allow as much personal freedom as possible, so that people may choose leisure or work, consumption or more education for their children, but to reward and facilitate mobility, adjustment, added training, and other requirements of progress. It is clear that many unsolved problems remain. The proof of the viability and the justice of a relatively free enterprise democracy depends at least in part on our ability to solve these problems.

PART II

Determinants of Family Income

Chapter 2

PREVIOUS WORK AND BACKGROUND

Theory and evidence go hand in hand in the advancement of knowledge. Economic theory developed early, and proceeded with relatively slim factual backing until the development of statistical data. Within the last half century advance in the type of data available has occurred through the development of scientific surveys of representative samples of the population.

The most dramatic innovation was in methods of producing representative samples of human populations, using area probability methods. Less dramatic but still important were methods of eliciting information from individuals, and quantifying and analyzing their replies. Early studies such as those of Frederic LePlay and Charles Booth focused on the living conditions of the lower classes. It was not until World War II that representative samples of broad populations began to be used, and then largely to provide evidence as to the extent of unemployment, or consumption habits as a base for cost of living indexes.[1]

Cross-section survey data provide information that cannot be collected in any other way. Aggregate estimates of income divided by the number of families describe the average family income, but only surveys can show how many people have incomes below any given level. More important, surveys can tell who these families are, how they see the future, whether they have other sources of support.

Such information allows the investigator to infer what the causes of differences are, and what the possibilities for change may be. Hence, one can go beyond description and interpretation into analysis and even prediction.

[1] For an annotated bibliography see Faith Williams and Carle C. Zimmerman, *Studies of Family Living in the United States and Other Countries: An Analysis of Material and Method,* U.S. Department of Agriculture, Miscellaneous Publication No. 223 (December, 1935).

For a later work see James N. Morgan, "A Review of Recent Research on Consumer Behavior," in *Consumer Behavior,* Vol. III, Lincoln Clark (ed.) (New York: Harper & Brothers, 1958), pp. 93–219; for case studies of recent surveys, see International Labour Office, *Family Living Studies, A Symposium* (Geneva: International Labour Organization, 1961).

The early focus, however, was largely on description and evaluation. Those interested in the effects of the industrial revolution wanted to know what the life of the factory worker was like. Those interested in broader analysis of economic systems wanted to know what the distribution of income in general was like, and whether it was changing.

The present study continues both the interest in the conditions of life, and that in the factors affecting the distribution of income.

Economists have long been interested in detailed information about incomes of individuals and families. A brief summary of the main streams of research and writing in this area will serve to indicate the diversity of interests and purposes, and to put the present research in proper perspective. The reader concerned only with new findings may prefer to omit this chapter and skip to Chapter 3.

The most important difference in interest has been between an attempt at deductive explanation for differences in individual earning rates on the one hand, and a focus on description and evaluation of the inequality in the distribution of total family incomes on the other. To go from individual wage rates to family incomes, one must deal with unemployment, moonlighting. extra earners, living with relatives, income from capital, and transfer incomes. Until the present work, little had been done by way of such reconciliation.

Common to all studies of distribution, however, is a concern with means of measuring inequality. This chapter will start with a discussion of the measurement of inequality, then proceed to brief summaries of (*a*) the search for explanations of the distribution of earnings, (*b*) the relation of such explanations to explanations of the share of national income going to labor, (*c*) normative assessments of the distribution of family incomes, (*d*) income redistribution and its relation to problems of optimal resource allocation, (*e*) income distribution as a determinant of aggregate consumption, (*f*) lifetime incomes and their relation to the value of human capital, and finally (*g*) recent interest in family income as a dependent variable subject to human decisions. The chapter concludes with a brief statement of how the present study presses forward several of these lines of inquiry.

The Measurement of Inequality

The distribution of income, whether individual wages or total family income, can be described in tables, but for comparing two distributions one needs a summary measure. Since one of the most interesting qualities of a distribution is its departure from equality, a measure of inequality is called for. Such a measure should be independent of the units for which income is measured, so that one can compare different countries, or different periods of time.

Inequality is presumably a measure of the distance from perfect inequality toward perfect equality. With perfect equality, everyone has the same, and there is zero variance. With perfect inequality, one unit has all the income, but the variance depends on how much that income is. A measure of inequality should then depend on both the variability of incomes and their mean, and should vary from zero with perfect equality to one with perfect inequality. The Lorenz coefficient of inequality, or the Gini index as it is sometimes called, has come to be generally accepted as the best single measure of inequality.[2] The measure and its related descriptive Lorenz curve are described in Chapter 20.

Sometimes, however, simpler measures which focused more on the very top of the distribution were still used, such as the share of aggregate income going to the top 1 per cent, or the top 5 per cent of receiving units. Increasing availability of data allowed comparative studies of changes in income distribution over time.[3]

Of course, new data frequently lead to new methodological and theoretical discussion. The comparative studies led to methodological discussions about the definition of income, the population to be included, and the unit of analysis. Critics pointed out that the distribution of wage and salary incomes of heads of families differed from a distribution of family incomes. The possibility that apparent changes in inequality over time might be distorted by differential

[2] J. Aitchison and J. A. C. Brown, "On Criteria for Descriptions of Income Distribution," *Metroeconomica,* VI (December, 1954), 88–107;

Mary Jean Bowman, "A Graphical Analysis of Personal Income Distribution in the United States," *American Economics Review,* XXXV (September, 1945), 608–628;

Maurice E. G. Kendall, *The Advanced Theory of Statistics,* Vol. 1 (London: Charles Griffin & Co., Ltd., 1945), especially pp. 145–155;

W. S. Woytinsky, *Earnings and Social Security in the United States* (Washington, D.C.: Social Science Research Council, 1943), especially Appendix;

Dwight B. Yntema, "Measures of Inequality in the Personal Distribution of Wealth and Income," *Journal of the American Statistical Association,* 28 (December, 1933), 348–361.

[3] Selma P. Goldsmith, "Changes in the Size Distribution of Income," *American Economic Review,* XLVII, *Papers and Proceedings* (May, 1957), 504–518;

Simon Kuznets, *Shares of Upper Income Groups in Income and Savings* (New York: National Bureau of Economic Research, 1953);

Harold Lydall and John B. Lansing, "A Comparison of the Distribution of Personal Income and Wealth in the United States and Great Britain," *American Economic Review,* XLIX (March, 1959), 43–67;

Horst Mendershausen, *Changes in Income Distribution During the Great Depression* (New York: National Bureau of Economic Research, 1946);

Herman P. Miller, *Income of the American People* (New York: John Wiley & Sons, Inc., 1955);

James N. Morgan, "Review of Kuznets," *Review of Economics and Statistics,* XXXVI (May, 1954), 237–239;

Mary W. Smelker, "Shifts in the Concentration of Income," *Review of Economics and Statistics,* XXX (August, 1948), 215–222.

importance of capital gains, free public services, nonmoney income, or changes in the composition of the population, was discussed.[4]

Other writers pointed out that one-year incomes do not provide a measure of the inequality or even the distribution of lifetime incomes, since incomes vary from year to year and, more important, vary systematically over the lifetime of the worker. Attempts were made to estimate the distribution of lifetime incomes from cross-section data.[5] Such estimates depend heavily on both strong assumptions and upon somewhat variable sample survey data.

The Search for Explanations

Early studies by Pareto, who was partly misled by the use of an insensitive measure, using logarithms of both income and units, seemed to show remarkable similarity in the inequality in distribution of incomes measured for different countries and historical periods. Theorists, looking for macrocosmic explanations of this similarity, hypothesized that perhaps a combination of persistent differences in people's abilities, and in society's needs for a variety of workers accepting different amounts of responsibility would always produce similar inequalities in rewards.[6] One writer even suggested that inequality could not get beyond certain bounds without precipitating a revolution or a civil war.[7] Discussions attempting to explain inequality concentrated on factors affecting individual earnings as distinct from family incomes. However, a recent paper by one of the authors of this book shows that distributions of family incomes are also affected substantially by extra earners, less than a full year's work, and other factors.[8]

[4] Robert J. Lampman, "Recent Changes in Income Inequality Reconsidered," *American Economic Review*, XLIV (June, 1954), 251–268;

Lee Soltow, "The Distribution of Income Related to Changes in the Distribution of Education, Age, and Occupation," *Review of Economics and Statistics*, XLII (November, 1960), 450–453.

[5] Robert Solow, "Some Long-run Aspects of the Distribution of Wage Income," (Abstract) *Econometrica*, 19 (July, 1951), 333–334;

Robert Summers, *An Econometric Investigation of the Lifetime Size Distribution of Average Annual Income*, Cowles Foundation Discussion Paper No. 9 (New Haven: Cowles Foundation, 1956).

[6] R. Gilbrat, *Les inégalities économiques* (Paris: Recueil Sirey, 1931);

Benoit Mandelbrot, "Paretian Distributions and Income Maximization," *Quarterly Journal of Economics*, LXXVI (February, 1962), 57–85;

Vilfredo Pareto, *Cours d'économique politique*, Vol. 2 (Paris: F. Pichou, 1897);

E. C. Rhodes, "The Pareto Distribution of Incomes," *Economica*, NS XI (February, 1944), 1–11.

[7] Harold T. Davis, *The Analysis of Economic Time Series* (Bloomington, Indiana: The Principia Press, 1941), p. 435.

[8] James N. Morgan, "The Anatomy of Income Distribution," *Review of Economics and Statistics*, XLIV (August, 1962);

See also Jacob Mincer, "Labor Supply, Family Income, and Consumption," *American Economic Review*, L (May, 1960), 574–583.

At a more detailed level of analysis, the question arose of why the earnings of individuals were distributed in such a skewed fashion if ability were normally distributed among individuals. Some argued that there were barriers to economic mobility from one noncompeting economic group to another.[9] Others argued that the extreme incomes were temporary, especially the very high ones, so that individual's incomes, if averaged over a number of years, might form a nearly normal distribution.[10] Numerous writers have discussed the accumulation of assets that earn income, and analyzed the effects of investing in education and training on the distribution of income.[11]

More recently it has been argued that control over productive assets, a major source of income, is great for those who can borrow money, but that lenders will not lend to those who seem to have less native ability. For the latter group the expected return may be zero, or negative, even though some might make money. Hence the greater ability of some is magnified by their access to borrowed funds and the resulting leverage.[12]

Finally, if high productivity and earnings result from the possession of particular combinations of skills, such combinations might be distributed in a skewed fashion even though each component was normally distributed.[13]

Some economists have attempted to set up mathematical models with some

[9] Frank W. Taussig, *Principles of Economics,* 2 vols. (New York: The Macmillan Company, 1911), Chapter 47, especially p. 134.

[10] Solow, *Econometrica,* 19, 333–334.

[11] Paul C. Glick and Herman P. Miller, "Educational Level and Potential Income," *American Sociological Review,* XXI (June, 1956), 307–312;

Herman P. Miller, "Annual and Lifetime Income in Relation to Education, 1939–1959," *American Economic Review,* L (December, 1960), 962–986;

Jacob Mincer, "Investment in Human Capital and Personal Income Distribution," *Journal of Political Economy,* LXVI (August, 1958), 281–302;

H. S. Houthakker, "Education and Income," *Review of Economics and Statistics,* XLI (February, 1959), 24–28;

Arthur C. Pigou, *Economics of Welfare,* 3d ed. (London: Macmillan & Co., Ltd., 1929), p. 648ff.;

Theodore W. Schultz, "Investment in Human Capital," *American Economic Review,* LI (March, 1961), 1–17.

[12] Stanley Lebergott, "The Shape of the Income Distribution," *American Economic Review,* XLIX (June, 1959), 328–347;

Thomas Mayer, "The Distribution of Ability and Earnings," *Review of Economics and Statistics,* XLII (May, 1960), 189–195.

[13] C. H. Boissevain, "Distribution of Abilities Depending upon the More Independent Factors," *Metron,* 13 (1939), 49–58;

A. D. Roy, "The Distribution of Earnings and of Individual Output," *Economic Journal,* LX (September, 1950), 489–506;

Joseph J. Spengler, "Changes in Income Distribution and Social Stratification," *American Journal of Sociology,* 59 (1953), 247–259;

Hans Staehle, "Ability, Wages, and Income," *Review of Economics and Statistics,* XXL (February, 1943), 77–87.

a priori theoretical justification, which would produce income distributions comparable to those found empirically.[14]

Explanation of the Distribution According to Function Performed

A related, but essentially separate, stream of investigation has attempted to explain the relative importance of wages, interest, rent, and profits; that is, the distribution of income according to the function performed.

After all, one part of the explanation of differences in individual income distributions between countries, or changes in such distributions over time, might be found in changing demands for labor relative to those for land or capital. From Ricardo on, a discussion continued as to the effects of increased population on a fixed land area, or increased capital relative to the labor supply, on relative levels of wages, interest and rents, and on the share of the national income going to labor.[15]

An increased demand for labor would presumably reduce unemployment, drive up the wages of unskilled workers, and increase labor incomes relative to the incomes from capital or land which were concentrated in the hands of a few. The extent to which one factor could merely substitute for another without changing relative rewards was dignified with the name "the elasticity of substitution," but the theoretical discussions and the descriptive statistics have remained relatively unconnected. The present study adds little to this area of theory or statistics, except that it points out the fact that in the present century, in contrast to the early nineteenth century, most families not only earn income derived from labor but also benefit from capital income. Therefore, factor shares no longer imply distinctions among social and economic groups to the extent that was typical of the last century.

---

[14] Carlos C. Classon, "Some Social Applications of the Doctrine of Probability," *Journal of Political Economy,* VII (March, 1899), 204–239;

Maurice Fréchet, "Noveaux essais d'explication de la repartition de revenus," *Revue de l'institut international de statistique,* XIII (1945), 16–32;

Milton Friedman, "Choice, Chance, and Personal Distribution of Income," *Journal of Political Economy,* LXI (August, 1953), 277–290;

R. Gilbrat, *Les inégalities économiques* (Paris: Recueil Sirey, 1931);

R. S. G. Rutherford, "Income Distributions, a New Model," *Econometrica,* 23 (July, 1955), 277–294;

Solow, *Econometrica,* 19, 333–334.

[15]Edward F. Denison, "Income Types and the Size Distribution," *American Economic Review,* XLIV, *Papers and Proceedings* (May, 1954), 254–269;

George Garvey, "Functional and Size Distributions of Income and Their Meaning," *American Economic Review,* XLIV, *Papers and Proceedings* (May, 1954), 236–253;

David Ricardo, *On the Principles of Political Economy and Taxation* (London: 1817);

Lee Soltow, "Shifts in Factor Payments and Income Distribution," *American Economic Review,* XLIX (June, 1959), 395–398.

Evaluations of Distributions of Family Incomes

Interpretations of the distribution of family income in terms of human welfare required that the investigator examine income and needs jointly. Estimates of the proportion of families with inadequate incomes depend heavily upon the definition of inadequacy. Hence, such a descriptive evaluation required the development of standard family budgets or cost of living estimates for each family to which the family's actual income could be compared. These budgets were based partly on normative assumptions, partly on dietary requirements, and partly on actual recent behavior of similar families.[16] The proportions of families falling below standard were estimated. There is, of course, no fixed definition of what a minimum standard of living is, and the standard clearly moves up as average standards of living improve and society recognizes more responsibility for the welfare of its members. Later in this book some budget standards are used, but instead of any one level as minimal, a ratio of actual income to standard is used as a measure of the relative adequacy of a family's income.[17]

Income Distribution and Resource Allocation

The distribution of income relative to needs affects the way in which the economic system allocates productive resources. There are two reasons for this: first, differential rewards are presumably necessary to induce people to work where they are most needed, and to work hard; secondly, since these rewards are the main source of family income, they provide most of the purchasing power in the markets for final consumer goods. Hence, they determine what is to be produced.

Economists concerned with the functioning of a free enterprise system in allocating productive resources have attempted to divorce the discussion of the mechanisms of prices and market from the problem of the distribution of income. However, this has proved to be only a temporary convenience. In order for prices to be valid indicators of the social importance of products, and hence good guides for producers, a number of assumptions had to be made. The most important assumption was that the money which individuals had to spend should be a reasonably good indicator of the importance society would attach to their needs. The justification for a market system relies on the

[16] For references, see Chapter 16, and various publications of the Heller Committee for Research in Social Economics, Berkeley, California. A statistical approach to adjusting for family composition is provided by S. J. Prais, "Estimates of Equivalent Scales from Family Budgets," *Economic Journal,* LXIII (December, 1953), 791–810, and S. J. Prais and H. S. Houthakker, *Analysis of Family Budgets* (Cambridge: Cambridge University Press, 1955).

[17] Martin David, "Welfare, Income, and Budget Needs," *Review of Economics and Statistics,* XLI (November, 1959), 393–399.

assumptions that earned incomes are a fair measure of the value of the individual's contribution to production and that human needs are adequately represented by dollars available to spend.[18] This is another area in which the present study contributes little, except to provide some attitudinal data on the extent to which families implicitly endorse present mechanisms for redistributing incomes.

Income Redistribution

For reasons of both equity and proper guidance in the allocation of resources, most societies have an array of mechanisms for redistributing income: progressive taxes, free public services, subsidies, minimum wages, social security, and other income maintainance programs. A complete assessment of the effects of the total redistributing mechanism is difficult but it has been attempted.[19]

Income Distribution as a Determinant of Aggregate Consumer Expenditures

Economists concerned with full employment or inflation have been interested in the effects of redistribution of income on aggregate expenditures. Careful investigation, however, revealed that only if there were substantial curvatures in the effect of income on consumption, i.e., substantial differences in the proportion of an extra dollar that would be spent on consumption goods at high and at low incomes, would income redistribution have much effect on aggregate expenditures.[20]

[18] A. P. Lerner, *The Economics of Control* (New York: The Macmillan Company, 1944);

J. V. de Graaff, *Theoretical Welfare Economics* (Cambridge: Cambridge University Press, 1957).

[19] Alan T. Peacock (ed.), *Income Redistribution and Social Policy* (London: Jonathan Cape, Ltd., 1954);

Richard A. Musgrave, "The Incidence of the Tax Structure and Its Effects on Consumption," *Tax Policy for Growth and Stability,* Joint Committee Print of the U.S. Joint Economic Committee, 84th Cong., 1st. Sess. (November 9, 1955).

[20] Harold Luball, "Effects of Income Redistribution on Consumers' Expenditures," *American Economic Review,* XXXVII (March, 1947), 157–170;

Lloyd Metzler, "Effects of Income Redistribution," *Review of Economics and Statistics,* 25 (February, 1943), 49–57;

Richard A. Musgrave and Mary S. Painter, "The Impact of Alternative Tax Structures on Personal Consumption and Saving," *Quarterly Journal of Economics,* LXII (August, 1948), 475–499;

For a dramatic, if oversimplified, statement of one way the effects of inequality may depend on what caused the inequality, see Milton Friedman, *A Theory of the Consumption Function* (Princeton: Princeton University Press, 1957).

Distribution of Lifetime Incomes, and the Value of a Man

Both for assessing welfare, and for explaining standards of consumption expenditures, one year's income may be inadequate. Earnings are affected by both short-run fluctuations and lifetime patterns. When the whole family is considered, these problems are accented by the extra earners who enter and leave the labor market at various stages in the family life cycle. For individuals, estimates of lifetime incomes based on cross-section data have been made.[21] Such data, discounted and adjusted for some minimal cost of maintenance, throw light on the economic value of a man, and on the economic cost of accidents, disability, or mental illness, and on the economic value of investment in education.[22]

The treatment of human beings as capital assets is frequently useful in interpreting the effects of migration or in discussing population policy. One author has argued that in some underdeveloped countries, at some rates of interest, the value of a new-born child is negative.[23]

Family Income as a Result of Family Decisions

A final and most recent focus of interest in incomes and income distribution pursues the old question of what determines family incomes and their distribution, but introduces the decisions and behavior of the individuals themselves to help explain these incomes.[24]

In poorer countries, income may well be a predetermined variable, even for the family as a whole, fixed by the limitations of available jobs and by cultural restrictions. In this country, high levels of economic activity, a wide range of jobs open to women, and a short working week which makes a second job possible, allow people to affect their own incomes by the decisions they make. Higher incomes also make the choice of whether or not to live with

[21] Herman P. Miller, *American Economic Review,* L, 962–986, and references cited therein.

See also Robert Summers, *An Econometric Investigation of the Lifetime Size Distribution of Average Annual Income.*

[22] Gary Becker, "Evidence of Underinvestment in Education," *Papers and Proceedings, American Economic Review,* L (May, 1960), 346–359;

Rashi Fein, *Economics of Mental Illness* (New York: Basic Books, 1958);

Burton Weisbrod, *The Nature and Measurement of the Economic Benefits of Improvement* (unpublished Ph.D. dissertation, Northwestern University, 1958);

Theodore W. Schultz, *American Economic Review,* LI, 1–17.

[23] Stephen Enke, "Government Bonuses for Smaller Families," *Population Review,* IV (July, 1960), 47–50.

[24] See Daniel Suits, "The Determinants of Consumer Expenditure: A Review of Present Knowledge," *Impact of Monetary Policy,* vol. 10 of *Supporting Papers of the Commission on Money and Credit* (Prentice-Hall, Inc.).

relatives a genuine decision, rather than a matter of necessity, and one which will affect family income, even relative to budget standards.

Such opportunities for rational decision-making mean that family income itself is the result in part of a series of voluntary family decisions, not solely a predetermined factor that affects spending behavior. Consumption may help determine income.

In addition to the decisions which affect present income, the family also makes decisions which will affect future incomes of the parents or of the children. The future is affected by decisions about saving for retirement, moving to new jobs, whether to send the children to college, and how many children to have.

Contributions of the Present Study

Building upon this rich and diverse background of interest in income and its distribution, the present book makes four main contributions.

First, improved data on income are developed so that the descriptive material on income distribution will be more precise. Major forms of non-money income are estimated and included. Families are separated into adult units so that the distribution of income can be shown before any benefits from living with relatives are included. The distribution of families according to their level of well-being is estimated according to income relative to a standard of need. Attention is given to the amount of time devoted to earning the income.

Second, family income and its distribution is explained by explaining each of the components. Each component is treated as the joint result of the past, the present situation, and decisions motivated by a complex of factors. Some components of income, such as labor force participation of wives, have been intensively studied elsewhere, but never before has the whole set been analyzed for the same representative cross-section sample. The logical implications of treating income as a dependent variable are thus worked out.

Third, the impact of some major redistributional mechanisms on the distribution of income is examined. Public and private transfers in the form of pensions, welfare, social security, philanthropy, income taxes, property taxes, and benefits of free public education are analyzed.

Fourth, the dynamics of income are studied both in terms of lifetime income and occupation patterns, and through intergenerational changes in education and income.

The analysis is more detailed than any previously attempted. It attempts to explain the details of income, even analyzing wage rates and hours separately, rather than explaining income as a whole. It attempts to explain individual incomes, and derive the distribution, rather than merely explaining the shape of the distribution. Finally, the explanatory factors are at least partly dynamic, with discussion of intragenerational and intergenerational changes, not merely static explanations of the present.

Chapter 3

A CONCEPTUAL FRAMEWORK
TO EXPLAIN FAMILY INCOME

The main purpose of this study has been to examine the process by which family incomes are determined and by which they change over time and from one generation to the next. An attempt has been made to create a sophisticated model of the determination of family income and to include some concepts which have not been available before.

Previous inadequacies in empirical data on income distribution have been in three areas: the measurement of income, particularly nonmoney income; the analysis of difference between individual earnings and family income; and the interpretation of income as an index of welfare or level of living.

The purpose of this chapter is to describe the ways in which these inadequacies are dealt with in this study and how new measures of income fit into and support the theoretical construct, and to describe the model for the sequential analysis of family income.

The Theoretical Construct and Its Components

The model used in this study examines the determinants of a family's income for one year. In order to do this, it takes account of past events and decisions in the experience of the family members, their present position, characteristics of the area in which they live, and their plans and outlook for the future. Different units of analysis are relevant for different components. This section presents descriptions of the various units of analysis used in the model, the income measures used, and the additional explanatory factors which augment and explain the levels of income.

Units of Analysis. Although the ultimate purpose of this model is the explanation of family income, much of the initial analysis of income components must be done using a unit more basic than the family.

Income is earned largely by individuals. Even though decisions about working may be made with the interests of the whole family in mind, the actual hours worked and the income earned are those of individuals. In order to examine these factors adequately, a nuclear unit more basic than the family was defined; this is the *adult unit*. An adult unit consists of an individual eighteen or older, his spouse if he is married, and his children under eighteen. These units are relatively stable, since their composition can change over time only by such major and infrequent events as marriage, birth of a child, divorce, death, or the arrival of an eighteenth birthday.

Adult units that live with other units, and do not keep separate finances, are called *dependent adult units*. These units are mostly children eighteen or older but still dependent, or elderly relatives who generally have no income of their own. Adult units which live in the households of others but keep separate finances are *extra adult units*. The adult unit is relevant for the analysis of earnings of heads and wives, for examining the impact of most transfer systems, and for estimating Federal income tax liability.

Spending units are the next largest unit of analysis used. A spending unit consists of all related persons who live together and pool their incomes for major items of expense. The head of the spending unit is the major earner. In this case of a married couple, the husband is always considered the head of the adult unit and of the spending unit. A spending unit may consist of one adult unit, or it may include two or more. The spending unit containing the person who owns the home or pays the rent is considered the *primary spending unit*. If any other spending units live in the same household, they are regarded as *secondary spending units*.

A *family* is composed of all the related persons who live together. This may be one adult unit, or more than one, and one or more spending units. The head of the family is the person who owns the home or pays the rent, and his adult unit is the *primary adult unit*.

Spending units and families, for whom income distributions are usually measured, can be changed by reversible, more easily made decisions, often as the result of economic pressures. These changes are described in Chapter 20.

Figure 3-1 indicates the relationships between adult units, spending units, and families.

Interviews were taken with the heads of all spending units, both primary and secondary. Information about the wives and about any dependent adults in the spendings units was elicited from the spending unit heads.

Most of the analysis of income is done for adult units who are also the heads of separate spending units (primary adult units and extra adult units). Dependent adult units were excluded from much of the analysis because data on their backgrounds and attitudes are not available. Since there is little reason to believe that dependent adult units differ behaviorally or psychologically from other adult units the results of the analysis can be extended to apply to them.

Components of Family Income. Family income is made up of many different kinds of income: income from earnings, income from capital, and transfer incomes of many varieties. Each of these in turn can be broken down into its components; for example, earned income includes earnings of the head and of his wife, and these are the result of the hours each works and the wage rate each receives.

In the analysis, annual earned incomes of individuals are separated into two components: average hourly earnings, and the number of hours worked. Each component is affected by somewhat different factors. The reason for the separation between hours and hourly earnings is that the individual probably has greater control over the number of hours he works than he has over his

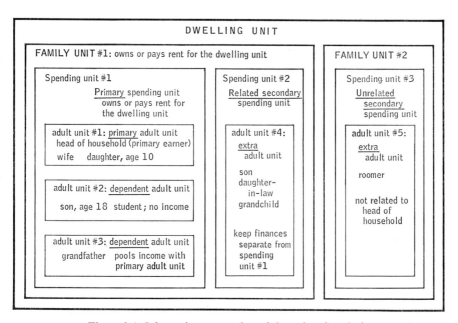

Figure 3-1. Schematic presentation of the units of analysis.

wage rate; that is, he can influence his income more by finding an extra job, working overtime, or quitting, than by successfully demanding a higher wage. In addition, time is traded for income, and time is valuable in the form of leisure. The net benefit to the worker is a complex joint result of his wages and of the amount of leisure time he has left to enjoy them. There is no discussion of whether he also gets enjoyment out of his job, but it seems likely that if two men have the same money earnings, the one who works fewer hours is generally better off.

The separation of income into wages, capital income, and transfer income also required some approximations, particularly for forms of income which result from the use of the units' labor and capital jointly, such as income from a farm or family business. These procedures are described in Appendix C; the income concepts are defined in Appendix D. A chart at the end of

Appendix D provides a schematic representation of the income definitions and their relation to one another.

Determinants of Family Income. It is possible to describe the decisions and events which affect each component of income, and to organize these factors into a sequential analysis which includes in the explanation of each component the complex of factors which explained the previous component.

In this analysis, income is treated as a dependent variable resulting from a set of interrelated decisions made by individuals or adult units. Since these decisions are not independent of one another, it is difficult to decide how to separate and analyze them. Clearly, it would be circular to use the husband's income to explain whether the wife works. The two are alternatives which must be determined jointly. If the family needs more money, the head may work longer, or the wife may work, or both.

These joint decisions are treated by making one conditional upon the other. The joint decision about the work hours of head and wife can be thought of in two alternative ways: a decision could be made about how much the head will work, and then, based on that decision and other factors, a decision about how much the wife will work. Or, alternatively, a decision could be made about whether the wife will work or how much and then, based on that decision, a choice of whether the husband should work extra hours. The over-all results will be the same statistically, whatever the order, since one can convert a joint probability into a set of conditional probability statements. However, the estimates of the effects of each explanatory factor on the two decisions will not be independent of the order in which the analysis is done. Hence, the specification of the model is important.

Figure 3-2 shows the sequence of decisions or determinants. The items in boxes are factors to be explained. They are to be explained partly by the previous items as indicated by the arrows, and partly by other factors.

The sequence of the analysis has some real-world meaning. The husband works in most families and is expected to work; hence the decision of whether the wife will work can be assumed to be made in the light of the husband's employment status. Eligibility for transfer income of many kinds depends on having a low level of income from other sources. The decision to live with others could be an alternative to working harder, but seems more likely to be a consequence of inability to earn enough to support a separate household. It is somewhat more arbitrary to consider the decision of whether to grow food at home as being made before the wife's decision of whether to work for money.

The explanatory variables used to explain income cover a wide range, including facts about the situation of the individual or the community in which he lives and attitudinal and motivational measures. Identical sets of variables were not used to explain each income component. The reasons for lack of symmetry and for the use of different factors for various steps in the analysis will be apparent from the discussion of each result.

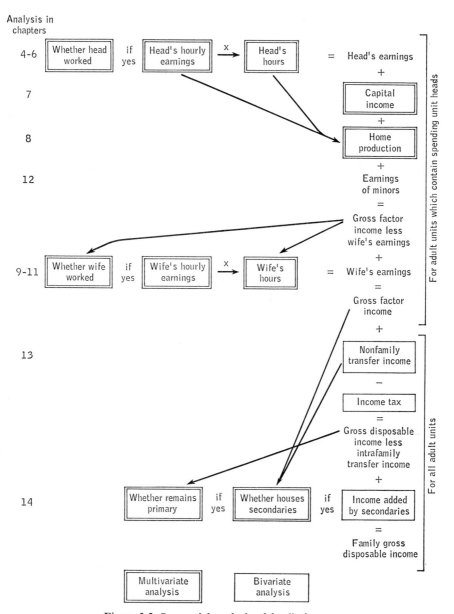

Figure 3-2. Sequential analysis of family income.

At each stage, it is not expected behavior and the results of the earlier stages which are used to help predict, but the actual behavior. Using this approach, the explanatory relationships which result can be combined to predict for an individual adult unit those decisions which culminate in family income.

The idea that income might be a result of people's desires to consume was suggested by Ruth Mack some years ago, and George Katona has spelled out a theory of the dynamic interaction between new consumption standards and new higher income standards.[1]

The Data, Their Accuracy, and Their Limitations

Within the limitations imposed by the use of a personal interview,[2] the goal of this study was to collect data which would come as close as possible to a conceptually complete measure of family income and its components, and to measure a wide range of explanatory factors. Although many of these factors could be measured only roughly, it was felt that rich but imperfect data were preferable to conceptually inadequate or incomplete measures.

Measures of Income. As mentioned in Chapter 2, little information has been available previously on the differences between individual earnings and family income. The measures of income used in this study were selected with the intention of describing and reconciling these differences.

Differences between individual earnings and family income arise for several reasons. The wife or others may work for money. There may be income from capital in the form of rent, interest, or dividends, in actual or imputed form. There may be compulsory or voluntary transfers which may add to or reduce the amount of income available for direct use by the family. Is income to be measured before or after these transfers? Most of the measures of income in current use include only some of the transfers as income. Income as defined and measured in most surveys includes regular money transfer incomes like pensions and alimony, and may be adjusted for Federal income tax liability, but irregular and nonmoney transfer incomes as well as voluntary transfer payments to others are usually omitted. All the foregoing are affected by decisions to live with other nuclear families and form a larger family unit. Since these decisions to combine units may be made as a result of economic pressures or because of a desire for higher living standards, anyone who analyzes family incomes deals with a measure that changes as the composition of the unit changes.[3] For this reason, particularly, it was deemed important

---

[1] See Ruth P. Mack, "Trends in American Consumption and the Aspiration to Consume," *American Economic Review,* XLVI (May, 1956), 55–58, and

George Katona, *The Powerful Consumer* (New York: The McGraw-Hill Book Co. Inc., 1960), especially Chapter 11, pp. 173–191.

[2] The questionnaire used for the interview is reproduced in Appendix B.

[3] Dorothy Brady, "Individual Incomes and the Structure of Consumer Units," *American Economic Review,* XLVIII (May, 1958), 269–278.

to measure the impact on income of combining adult units into larger families where one adult unit is dependent upon another.

An extensive series of questions was used to measure income, including questions on sources of money incomes which had been developed over a period of fifteen years for use by the Survey of Consumer Finances. In addition to these questions about money income, a large number of questions were asked about sources of nonmoney income. These included questions about irregular gifts and transfers received by the unit, and an estimate of any money saved by the unit through home-grown food or any home improvements or repairs done by the unit itself. Questions were asked about the amount of equity in owner-occupied housing, so that a return to that equity in the form of net rental value could be imputed. The importance of nonmoney income varies from one family to another, and it may play a significant role in determining the real level of welfare enjoyed by some families.

The use of a unit smaller than the family required estimates of the more important intrafamily transfers so that the incomes of each unit could be examined. Inquiries and estimates were made for each family concerning the value of the food and housing provided by one unit for another. Monetary transfers, transfers in the form of child care, help with housekeeping, or other goods like clothing, were disregarded because they are too difficult to estimate, and probably are small and infrequent. Appendix C explains the procedures used in estimating transfer incomes and contributions. Many of these measures, particularly the measures of nonmoney income, are unique to this study.

Some crude measure of the use of leisure time is included, but no attempt was made to put a value on leisure or to measure the differing aspects of voluntary and involuntary leisure. The question of whether people enjoy the work by which they produce real income is not considered here. A careful study of how people spend their basic resource, time, has yet to be done.

In order to analyze levels of welfare enjoyed by different units, it was necessary to devise an estimate of the family's needs which would take account of differences in family size and the differing requirements of persons of different ages. Such an estimate was calculated for each adult and each family, and the welfare level of the unit was determined by the ratio of their income to this estimate of needs. (See Chapter 16.)

Supplementary and Explanatory Measures. So that some of the many noneconomic factors which determine income could be taken into account, questions designed to elicit information providing crude measures of intelligence and motivation were asked. Standard psychological tests and batteries of attitude questions were not used because they are too cumbersome and disagreeable to be incorporated in a questionnaire sequence.

In addition to material from the personal interview, data were collected on the state, county, or local area in which the units live. The measures are rough but better than none at all. State and local data on the proportion who go to college, the amount spent per pupil in the public schools, and the proportion of the aged on government pensions were also used.

Because the income and supplementary measures presented here are so many and so varied, problems of analysis are greater than usual. The interpretation of social research data involves many conceptual difficulties concerning the meaning of the data and their relationships to basic theoretical models. Foremost among these problems is that of causal interpretation and explanation. The direction of causal relationships, or the extent to which unmeasured characteristics might affect these relationships, may be speculated upon but not proven.

In the following analyses, data on relationships are presented and suggestions are made concerning possible explanations for these relationships and their interpretations in terms of theoretical constructs such as motivation, ability, and the effects of environment. In reading interpretations of these findings, and developing the inferences, certain cautions should be kept in mind.

Some relationships reflect several causes which operate simultaneously to produce the observed effect. A nonwhite person's earnings are low because of the direct effect of racial discrimination on job opportunities, and because of the indirect effects of a poor education obtained in largely segregated schools with low standards and of a family background with less history of economic mobility than is typical of most families.

For some relationships, the direction of causation is not clear. Persistent attitudes may have determined past behavior, or past behavior may determine the attitudes expressed during the interview.

Relationships within a single cross section of the population do not indicate what is likely to happen over a period of time. Any inferences about future behavior rest on restrictive assumptions about the experiences of future generations.

Some obvious determinants of behavior cannot be measured directly in a personal interview situation. Others require so much time and care that their inclusion would preclude the measurement of other important variables. Therefore the analyses are sometimes incomplete.

Sources of Comparable Data. Some reference is made to studies which have collected information comparable to the data discussed here, but no direct comparisons are made with statistics from other studies. Many of these statistics are conceptually different from the data presented in this study, particularly since the primary purpose of this work is to examine relationships for which no other adequate data exist. The only other sources of comparable data on family incomes are the Current Population Surveys conducted by the Bureau of the Census, and the Surveys of Consumer Finances done by the Survey Research Center. These data do not generally include the nonmoney imputations that have been added to family income in this study and they do not present data for adult units or use the additional explanatory factors that have been included here.

Statistical Techniques

The sequential analysis of the components of family income is done through a series of multivariate analyses. In these analyses each income component is used as a dependent variable, and the complex of explanatory characteristics is used to predict and explain differences from one unit to another, in the form of deviations from the mean of the dependent variable.

The explanatory characteristics are correlated with one another, so that the gross relationship of each with the income measure incorporates some spurious relationship resulting from correlations through other characteristics. For example, the average incomes of education groups do not represent the true effect of education, because adults with little education are likely to be older than college graduates. Therefore, the effects of the different factors cannot be estimated by simple classification techniques. By assuming that the effects of the different factors are additive, one can use the multivariate technique to estimate the effects of each factor. Essentially the multivariate technique used here is a multiple regression procedure. The only thing new or unusual about this analysis is that instead of having variables in an equation with coefficients for each variable, the effect of belonging to each class of each characteristic is represented by a coefficient.[4] Appendix E contains a complete description of the multivariate technique. All the results which follow will present both the unadjusted and the adjusted coefficients. The unadjusted coefficients show the gross effects of each factor as measured by deviations of each subclass mean from the grand mean. The adjusted coefficients partition the explanation of the dependent variable jointly among all predictors used in the relationship. The differences between the two sets of coefficients indicate the extent to which the explanatory factors are correlated with one another, hence the extent to which the unadjusted effects represent the joint effects of several variables.[5]

In cases where it was likely that the effects of two explanatory factors might not be additive, but might interact with one another, classes were defined jointly for the two characteristics. In this case the coefficients provide an estimate of the joint effect of two factors. For instance, the effect of education on income depends heavily on age, so age-education classes were used in explaining wage rates and hours.

[4] Daniel B. Suits, "Use of Dummy Variables in Regression Equations," *Journal of the American Statistical Association,* 52 (December, 1957), 548–551.

[5] T. P. Hill calls this "bias." See "Analysis of the Distribution of Wages and Salaries in Great Britain," *Econometrica,* 27 (July, 1959), 355–381. He uses the same method of analysis, and provides a mathematical interpretation of it.

Summary

In the analysis of family income, adult units, with their backgrounds and current situations including twenty-four hours a day each to dispose of, are used. An attempt is made to unravel the complex set of interlaced decisions which determine the adult unit income. Finally the decisions that result in combining adult units to form complex families are considered, and the effect of these decisions on the distribution of family income or welfare is assessed.

The data and analyses thus bridge the gap between studies of earned incomes of individuals and distributional or welfare studies of family income. This study explores and dramatizes the difficulty in estimating long-range lifetime income: a man's economic potential consists not only of some discounted future value of his own earning stream but also of other sources of income that he might receive, minus a series of family obligations now and into the future which must be met out of this income. Indeed, a man's long-range standard of living may be more a function of his family obligations, connections, plans, and aspirations than of his own current salary. A man with a wife who works, no children, and no extended family obligations, is clearly in a different position from a man who is in the reverse situation.

The overriding purpose of this study is an explanation of why there are still low incomes and dependency after many years of high employment and general prosperity in the United States. However, one does not explain low incomes by looking only at low-income people. Part of the explanation for the continuing existence of poverty lies in the criteria which determine the adequacy of family income. How do low-income people differ from others? This question, examined in Part IV, depends on the analyses of income in Parts II and III.

The chapters which follow contain a static analysis of the determinants of an individual family's income in the previous year. One must remember that this detailed static analysis is embedded in a dynamic world, a world in which decisions of individual units interact to produce relationships among aggregates in the system and other factors that do not vary much in a single year. The market demand for labor and the prevailing wage rates are clearly variables in a complete economic system. Even conditions which are the result of long past events would be part of the variables still to be determined in a complete dynamic system that described the behavior of a man over a period of time. On the other hand, a time-slice approach may still be fitted into a dynamic model of the economy if each decision is taken as dependent only on the individual's present situation and the past. For an individual whose decisions are affected only by his own immediate past, it is possible to derive a chain of future decisions, each the result of the previous one, in a process called a Markov chain. Where these decisions are also affected by the decisions of others in the society, the resulting interdependent series of decisions can be simulated by a large-scale computer.[6] Many of the results presented here are basic building blocks which go into the development of a complete structural model of the economy, the workings of which can be examined through such simulations.

[6] This is being done by Guy Orcutt and others. For a report of their early work see Guy Orcutt and others, *Microanalysis of Socio-economic Systems* (New York: Harper & Brothers, 1961).

Chapter 4

LABOR FORCE PARTICIPATION OF SPENDING UNIT HEADS

The analysis of the forces determining family incomes begins with an explanation of which spending unit heads worked in 1959.

More people will have worked during a fifty-two week period than were working during any one week. In comparing the data presented here with those from the Census Current Population Surveys, now being released by the Bureau of Labor Statistics, this distinction between current and annual participation in the labor force must be kept in mind. Some Census data on annual work experience are also occasionally presented. The Census data are more accurate estimates for the nation. The analyses presented here make use of a wider variety of explanatory factors.

Men and single women who are able generally are expected to work; therefore, factors like age and physical condition should account for much of the variation in labor force participation of spending unit heads.[1] However, it is useful to investigate the reasons why some spending unit heads are not able to work and to discover the extent to which other factors such as inability to find a job, or lack of motivation, affect the individual's labor force participation.

A multivariate analysis with eight independent variables was used to analyze whether spending unit heads worked at any time in 1959. The head may have worked for only a short period of time in 1959.

The multivariate analysis used three predictors which measure the head's ability to work. They are self-reported physical condition of the head, age in a joint classification with education, and adult unit composition. The last combines marital status with whether there are children to care for.

---

[1] A small national sample of employed men were asked whether they thought they would work even if there were no economic necessity for it. Most of them thought they would.

Nancy C. Morse and Robert S. Weiss, "The Function and Meaning of Work and the Job," *American Sociological Review,* 20 (April, 1955), 191–198.

Three classifications associated with the head's likelihood of finding a job are: extent of unemployment in the state, race, and age and education. Labor surplus or shortage in the state is measured by the ratio of insured unemployment to total covered employment in the state. Not enough local labor markets are evaluated to permit use of a finer measure. Discrimination or other race-associated problems are indicated by race. Experience, skills, and a range of possible positions for which the person is suited are measured by a joint classification by age and education. The measure is only approximate, since some people with little education may have considerable experience, skills, or facility at locating jobs.

Finally four classifications are associated with the motivation to work, perhaps in spite of other obstacles. Need for money to take care of a wife and children is indicated by the classification by sex, marital status of head, and number of dependents. Some subgroups of the same classification were used to indicate difficulty in working because a single adult had children for whom to care.

Plans and commitments involving need for money in the future are indicated by plans to send children to college, or to provide support for relatives in the future, or both. These factors presumably increase the need for money relative to the demand for leisure.

The difference in educational level between wife and husband represents a possible disparity between the standards of living desired by the wife and the husband's ability to meet them. When the wife has more education than the head, she may expect, and exert pressure for, a higher standard of living than the husband can provide. While this pressure might have most effect on the hours worked by the head and on whether the wife works, analyzed later, it could affect whether some aged or disabled heads work. Several sociological studies have found the wife's education more highly correlated with level of living than the husband's education.[2]

Since the wife's education is highly correlated with her husband's, the use of the difference between the two, rather than the absolute levels, avoids statistical difficulties that would arise from intercorrelations among the explanatory factors.

Motivation to overcome obstacles, arising from basic personality dispositions of the head and his view of how people get ahead, are indicated by a joint distribution of a measure of need-achievement and an attitude as to whether it is lucky breaks and help from friends or hard work by which people get ahead. The hypothesis here is that only those who believe that hard work will lead to success, and have a propensity to get satisfaction from overcoming obstacles, will work even under difficulties. Motivation is a diffi-

---

[2] Robert A. Danley and Charles E. Ramsey, *Standardization and Application of a Level of Living Scale for Farm and Nonfarm Families,* Cornell University Agricultural Experimental Station, Memoir #362 (Ithaca, New York, July, 1959). This study finds correlations of .45 for wife's education and .34 for husband's education.

cult attribute to measure. The hypothesis, spelled out in more detail in Appendix C, is that three things operate in a joint fashion to spur the individual to work: high achievement motivation, belief that hard work rather than luck or help from friends leads to success, and a high value placed on the rewards of work. A combination variable was formed out of the first two factors, achievement motivation and belief that hard work pays, in case the effects of the two were more or less than additive. The third factor in the hypothesis is the importance of the money. The only available measures of the need for money are number of dependents, commitments to send children to college, and commitments to support parents. Measures of these present and future demands for money are included in the analysis.

In the mutivariate analysis of whether spending unit heads worked in 1959, the mean was .86, indicating that 86 per cent of spending unit heads worked some time during 1959. In other words, one could always predict that an individual head worked and be right 86 per cent of the time. The standard deviation was .35. The eight classifications used in the analysis accounted for 46 per cent of the variance. Thus, using the results of the multivariate analysis one can improve the prediction of whether the head worked by 46 per cent, so that the prediction would be correct 92 per cent of the time: 86 per cent, plus 6 per cent, that is, the original estimate, plus 46 per cent of the remaining 14 per cent.

Table 4-1 shows the relative importance of each of the predictor variables and its significance in explaining the participation of heads of the spending units in the labor force in 1959.

The measure of importance is a direct analogue to the beta coefficient of multiple correlation, but applies to whole sets of coefficients involved in a

TABLE 4-1

CHARACTERISTICS USED TO EXPLAIN LABOR FORCE
PARTICIPATION IN 1959
(FOR SPENDING UNIT HEADS)

Characteristics of spending unit heads	Relative importance (Beta coefficients)	Significance (F ratios)
Education and age	.482	64.53**
Adult unit composition	.361	103.42**
Physical condition	.210	81.68**
Difference in education of heads and wives	.152	21.39**
Plans to help parents or children	.065	7.83**
Extent of unemployment in states	.039	2.11
Attitude toward hard work and need-achievement score	.029	.78
Race	.009	.45

** significant at probability level of .01

characteristic, not just one subclass coefficient. The magnitudes provide a measure of the relative importance of each factor predicting the dependent variable. (See Appendix E.)

The measure of significance in Table 4-1 is an *F* test which treats the adjusted coefficients as a simple one-way analysis of variance. Clustering in the sample makes this test nonconservative so that it might be well to consider as significant only those variables with significance at the 1 per cent level. On the other hand, lack of significance should not imply rejection of a hypothesis, since the factor may be imperfectly measured, or the net effect of sample stratification and clustering may be small. The *F* ratios are approximate indicators of the likelihood that the factor is related to the dependent variable in the population.

Though the last few characteristics listed in Table 4-1 have little importance or statistical significance, they are presented to show the extent to which gross differences are explained away through intercorrelations with other variables.

In Table 4-2 and the following multivariate tables, unadjusted deviations are the differences between the subgroup means and the grand mean. For example, 86 per cent of all spending unit heads worked during 1959. For those under twenty-five with less than twelve grades of school completed, the proportion was 9 per cent higher, or 95 per cent. The adjusted deviations show the effect on the dependent variable of membership in the subgroup when other factors in the multivariate analysis are considered. Being under twenty-five and having no high school diploma raises the probability of working in 1959 by 8 per cent when adult unit composition, physical condition, and other factors are considered simultaneously.

Age and education, taken together, influence labor market participation more strongly than any other characteristic used in the analysis. The effect of age predominates. Persons who are over sixty-five are likely to be retired, a fact which is reflected in a strong negative deviation from the grand mean for that group. For this group, the age effect is largely the result of exogenous forces rather than of individual motivations and desires. Several studies show that most people retire when forced to by company rules or poor health.[3] (See Chapter 31.)

Education appears to exert a minor influence on labor force participation. Young persons with high school diplomas are somewhat more likely to find a job after finishing school than persons with less schooling. Older people with college degrees remain at work longer than those who did not finish college. Between the ages of twenty-five and sixty-four the pattern looks strikingly similar for all education groups.

The substantial differences between adjusted and unadjusted deviations for the older age groups arise because the aged are also more likely to be single

[3] Peter Steiner and Robert Dorfman, *The Economic Status of the Aged* (Berkeley: University of California Press, 1957).

or disabled. Both of these attributes are associated with less frequent labor force participation.

TABLE 4-2

LABOR FORCE PARTICIPATION IN 1959: DEVIATIONS
FOR EDUCATION AND AGE
(FOR SPENDING UNIT HEADS)

Education and age	Number of spending unit heads	Per cent of spending unit heads	Unadjusted deviations [a]	Adjusted deviations [a]
0–11 grades	1,643	52.5	(−.05)	(−.04)
Under 25	82	2.6	.09	.08
25–34	260	8.1	.11	.07
35–44	313	9.8	.10	.08
45–54	355	10.9	.08	.07
55–64	334	10.1	−.02	.01
65 and older	299	11.0	−.51	−.41
12 grades	451	15.7	(.05)	(.04)
Under 25	73	2.6	.12	.12
25–34	99	3.4	.12	.08
35–44	134	4.7	.11	.08
45–54	79	2.7	.12	.09
55–64	36	1.2	.05	.04
65 and older	30	1.1	−.70	−.54
12 grades and some college or nonacademic training	603	21.3	(.05)	(.04)
Under 25	92	3.2	.08	.09
25–34	146	5.2	.11	.08
35–44	143	5.1	.12	.09
45–54	104	3.6	.10	.09
55 and older	118	4.2	−.21	−.16
College degree	300	10.5	(−.09)	(.03)
Under 35	98	3.4	.14	.09
35–44	82	2.9	.14	.09
45–54	54	1.9	.13	.10
55 and older	66	2.3	−.06	−.06

[a] deviations from grand mean of .86
( ) Figures in brackets are weighted averages of the deviations for component age groups within each education group.

Sex and marital status are the factors which make adult unit composition a powerful predictor of labor force participation. The presence of children does not seem to affect labor force participation. This is true even when a single adult must simultaneously support and care for children.

Even when their generally advanced age is allowed for, female spending unit heads are less likely to work than are males. However, they are more likely to work than are the wives of spending unit heads. (See Chapter 9.) Less frequent labor force participation of female heads is concentrated among those who are widowed, divorced, or separated. Among female spending unit heads under sixty-five and white, 94 per cent of the single women, but only 70 per cent of those widowed, divorced, or separated, worked in 1959. The latter are more likely to have sufficient income without working. Some of this income may cease if they work.

Current Population Surveys of the United States Census give the same general results, though they give current labor force status rather than a year's work experience.[4]

In the 1957 National Survey of Old Age and Survivors Insurance Beneficiaries, it was found that 64 per cent of widowed mothers with entitled chil-

TABLE 4-3

LABOR FORCE PARTICIPATION IN 1959: DEVIATIONS
FOR ADULT UNIT COMPOSITION
(FOR SPENDING UNIT HEADS)

Adult unit composition	Number of spending unit heads	Per cent of spending unit heads	Unadjusted deviations [a]	Adjusted deviations[a]
Unmarried male heads				
No children under 18	324	11.0	−.08	−.09
Children under 18	18	0.5	.01	−.07
Unmarried female heads				
No children under 18	442	14.5	−.24	−.22
Children under 18	167	4.6	−.12	−.26
Married male heads				
No children under 18	741	26.0	−.02	.09
1 child under 18	374	13.2	.12	.08
2 children under 18	407	13.8	.12	.07
3 or more children under 18	524	16.4	.13	.07

[a] deviations from grand mean of .86

dren were employed during the survey year. Of the mothers who had not been employed just before their husbands died, more than half were employed afterward in the survey year. The more children there were, the less likely the mother was to be employed. The 64 per cent is less than the 74 per cent of single women with children employed as shown in Table 4-3, but not so much less as to indicate that the loss of social security widows' benefits has deterred very many widows from working. By working they lose only their own benefits, of course, not those for the children under eighteen.[5]

The multivariate analysis adjusts for several intercorrelations of independent variables. The single males tend to be low on the index of need-achieve-

[4] Jacob Shiffman, "Marital and Family Characteristics of Workers, March, 1960," *Monthly Labor Review,* 84 (April, 1961), pp. 355–364.

[5] *Beneficiaries Studies Note #MC-2,* Bureau of Old Age and Survivors Insurance, Social Security Administration (August, 1961 [processed]).

ment and the single females high. The proportions in the high range of the index are 21 per cent single males, 29 per cent of all spending unit heads, and 32 per cent of single females. In spite of the age differences, the single males also have less education than average, and the single females more than average. One-fourth of the single female heads with children are nonwhite. Thus, the analysis attributes to marital status part of the tendency for single persons to work less, and attributes to their other characteristics, the remainder of this tendency.

It is difficult to interpret the fact that married men are more likely to work than are single men. One hypothesis is that married men are more likely to work because of their additional responsibilities; the alternative is that working men are more likely to marry because they are able to support families. The differences are *not* due to differences in age, education, race, or the other factors used in the analysis.

The physical condition of the spending unit head is closely related to his labor force participation. The finding that one-fourth of those who reported complete disablement had worked during 1959, stems from the fact that some persons became disabled during 1959 or early 1960. The coefficients reflect the impact of self-reported disability rather than medically-defined limitations. (See Chapter 17.)

The substantial differences between unadjusted and adjusted coefficients indicate that a very large fraction of the disabled have reasons for not working

TABLE 4-4

LABOR FORCE PARTICIPATION IN 1959: DEVIATIONS
FOR PHYSICAL CONDITION
(FOR SPENDING UNIT HEADS)

Physical condition	Number of spending unit heads	Per cent of spending unit heads	Unadjusted deviations[a]	Adjusted deviations[a]
Completely disabled	115	3.7	−.62	−.35
Severely disabled	100	3.0	−.31	−.13
Moderately disabled	354	11.4	−.08	−.01
Not disabled	2,428	81.9	.05	.02

[a] deviations from grand mean of .86

other than disability. For instance, many are over sixty-five years old. The adjusted coefficients take account of this but are an *average* effect of disability assuming that the effect applies everywhere. The effect of the same physical disability may be different for those under sixty-five.

Wives who have more education than their husbands appear to induce their husbands to work. However, the major effects of this variable is offset by differences between married and single persons. The single spending unit heads here with a .08 positive adjusted deviation are the same as the first four classes in Table 4-3, all of which had negative coefficients.

TABLE 4-5

LABOR FORCE PARTICIPATION IN 1959: DEVIATIONS FOR DIFFERENCE
IN EDUCATION OF HEADS AND WIVES
(FOR SPENDING UNIT HEADS)

Difference in education of heads and wives [a]	Number of spending unit heads	Per cent of spending unit heads	Unadjusted deviations [b]	Adjusted deviations [b]
Wives have two or more levels more than heads	223	7.6	.10	−.01
Wives have one level more than heads	362	12.0	.08	−.04
Wives have same level as heads	809	26.8	.04	−.03
Wives have one level less than heads	338	12.0	.09	−.04
Wives have two or more levels less than heads	303	10.7	.09	−.04
Education of wives not ascertained	17	0.5	−.31	−.07
Unmarried spending unit heads	945	30.4	−.15	.08

[a] Levels of education are:
    none   12 grades and nonacademic training
    1–8 grades   college, no degree
    9–11 grades   college, bachelor's degree
    12 grades   college, advanced degree
[b] deviations from grand mean of .86

When other things are equal, those with plans to help parents or children are more likely to be working. The direction of causation is not clear, but it is plausible that the desire to provide such support leads some to work. The

TABLE 4-6

LABOR FORCE PARTICIPATION IN 1959: DEVIATIONS FOR PLANS
TO HELP PARENTS OR CHILDREN
(FOR SPENDING UNIT HEADS)

Plans to help parents or children	Number of spending unit heads	Per cent of spending unit heads	Unadjusted deviations [a]	Adjusted deviations [a]
Do not plan to send children to college or help parents	1,665	54.5	−.11	−.02
Plans to help parents	469	15.6	.13	.04
Plans to send children to college	533	18.3	.12	.01
Plans to send children to college and help parents	330	11.6	.13	.01

[a] deviations from grand mean of .86

alternative is that income from work allows people to make such plans. The effect of this variable is also complicated by the fact that older people are concentrated in the group with no plans, since their children are already educated and their parents are no longer living.

Extensive unemployment in the state of residence did not have a significant effect on whether spending unit heads worked, but the small deviations are in the expected direction.

TABLE 4-7

LABOR FORCE PARTICIPATION IN 1959: DEVIATIONS
FOR EXTENT OF UNEMPLOYMENT IN STATES
(FOR SPENDING UNIT HEADS)

Extent of 1958 unemployment in states	Number of spending unit heads	Per cent of spending unit heads	Unadjusted deviations [a]	Adjusted deviations [a]
Under 5.00 per cent	690	21.7	−.04	−.01
5.00–6.49 per cent	995	32.6	.02	.01
6.50–7.49 per cent	625	22.3	.02	.01
7.50–9.99 per cent	389	12.9	−.02	−.01
10.00 per cent and over	298	10.5	−.01	−.03

[a] deviations from grand mean of .86

TABLE 4-8

LABOR FORCE PARTICIPATION IN 1959: DEVIATIONS FOR ATTITUDE
TOWARD HARD WORK AND NEED-ACHIEVEMENT SCORE
(FOR SPENDING UNIT HEADS)

Attitude toward hard work and need-achievement score	Number of spending unit heads	Per cent of spending unit heads	Unadjusted deviations [a]	Adjusted deviations [a]
Hard work is equal to or more important than luck; need-achievement score is in:				
high range	714	25.1	.03	.01
middle range	1,071	36.4	.00	.00
low range	512	16.5	.00	.00
Hard work is less important than luck; need-achievement score is in:				
high range	132	4.2	.05	.01
middle range	269	8.6	−.01	−.01
low range	177	5.1	−.07	−.03
Need-achievement score not ascertained	122	4.1	−.13	−.02

[a] deviations from grand mean of .86

A measure of unemployment in 1959 rather than in 1958 might have produced significant results. Unemployment in 1958 was used because it was the latest available when the analysis was done and because there was more differentiation between states in a recession year.[6]

While the effects of the measure of need-achievement and the belief that hard work pays off were in the expected direction, they were small and were not significant.

The small difference between whites and nonwhites in the unadjusted data is reversed by the adjustments for other factors, leaving no significant difference. If there are more nonwhites than whites who are not working they must have become dependent adults more readily than whites and have disappeared from view.

TABLE 4-9

LABOR FORCE PARTICIPATION IN 1959: DEVIATIONS FOR RACE
(FOR SPENDING UNIT HEADS)

Race	Number of spending unit heads	Per cent of spending unit heads	Unadjusted deviations [a]	Adjusted deviations [a]
White	2,580	89.6	.00	.00
Nonwhite	417	10.4	−.02	.01

[a] deviations from grand mean of .86

Summary

The factors which kept spending unit heads from working were largely the mechanical effects of advanced age and disability. Only two motivational factors, difference in education of head and wife and plans requiring future income, had any significant relation with the head's labor force participation. It must be remembered, however, that small marginally significant effects of factors which can change over time may be more important than the powerful, but easily explained effects of age and other demographic factors in predicting future trends.

[6] Margaret Gordon has reported a negative correlation of −.72 between the proportion of men aged sixty-five to seventy-four in the labor force and the percentage of the civilian labor force unemployed.

Margaret S. Gordon, "Work and Patterns of Retirement," in Robert W. Kleemeier (ed.), *Aging and Leisure* (New York: Oxford University Press, 1961), p. 24.

Some of this may result from correlation of both factors with the extent of industrialization in the area, of course.

Chapter 5

HOURLY EARNINGS OF SPENDING UNIT HEADS

Hourly earnings of spending unit heads who worked during 1959 were obtained by dividing 1959 earned income by the number of hours the spending unit head worked in 1959. (See Appendix D.) Earnings of farmers and self-employed businessmen were estimated by deducting from their business or farm income 6 per cent of the value of their net assets, representing return on capital. Negative earnings result for a few farmers or businessmen who received incomes amounting to less than 6 per cent of their investments.

These data on hourly earnings differ from similar data published by the Bureau of Labor Statistics. The latter are a direct measure of amounts paid by employers, and are a more accurate indication of actual wage rates. For spending unit heads who had more than one job, and for those who changed jobs during the year, the estimate of hourly earnings presented here is an average over all jobs held during 1959. The measure is also subject to reporting errors in the spending unit heads' estimates of hours worked.[1]

The distribution of hourly earnings for all spending unit heads who worked in 1959 is as follows:

Hourly earnings	Per cent of spending unit heads who worked in 1959
$0.01–0.99; negative	16
$1.00–1.99	29
$2.00–2.99	31
$3.00–3.99	14
$4.00 or more	10
Total	100
Number of spending unit heads	2,569

[1] Most previous analysis has been on full-time weekly hours.
See Thomas A. Finegan, "Hours of Work in the United States, a Cross Sectional Analysis" (unpublished Ph.D. dissertation, University of Chicago, 1960) and references cited therein.

Again explanatory classifications designed to explain how much the head earns per hour represent one or more theoretical constructs. If the expected relation does not appear, it may be because the theory was wrong, because the characteristic measured does not represent the theoretical construct, or because the measure was imprecise.

Ability and skills should affect a person's wage rate, and in the multivariate analysis three classifications indicate differences in ability or intelligence. The interviewer's assessment of the spending unit head's ability to understand and respond to questions represents intelligence, or at least the impression of intelligence, which is important in itself.

A crude index of ability to handle school tasks is provided by a classification showing whether the person was behind his age group when he left school and his report of his grades in school.

Age and education represent a mixture of intelligence, variety of potential positions, skills, experience, and seniority.

Two further indicators of ability also represent opportunities available, and the acceptance of responsibility by the individual. The occupation of the head is in part a measure of different levels of skills and responsibility utilized. A classification of whether the person is self-employed or supervises other people indicates differing levels of responsibility.

Limited physical abilities are measured by physical condition and age.

The quality and quantity of jobs available to the individual are represented by four classifications. The proportion unemployed in the state indicates whether labor is scarce, and perhaps more highly paid.

Whether the head lives in an urban or a rural area, and the size of the population, if urban, is a rough measure of the variety of jobs available to him.

A classification by race indicates whether the individual is subject to discrimination.

Sex of the head indicates a source of possible discrimination and some differences in job preferences.

Finally four motivational determinants are included. Three aspects of motivation are implicitly measured manifestations of upward mobility. A joint classification by the need-achievement score and the belief that hard work pays off more than luck or help from friends provides a direct indicator of motivation, allowing for joint effects of the attitude and the more basic personality predisposition.

The number of states the person has lived in since taking his first regular job is presumed to measure, in its middle ranges, a manifestation of ambition. Very little movement may mean lack of ambition, while a great deal may indicate instability or irresponsibility.

Moving away from the Deep South or moving off the farm may mean movement to better job areas, where a person might earn more than someone with identical background and skill who did not move.

The characteristics in order of their importance in reducing predictive error are shown in Table 5-1.

For spending unit heads who worked in 1959, average earned income per hour was $2.29 with a standard deviation of $1.46. The 84 subclasses of 14 characteristics accounted for 34 per cent of the variance in wage rates.

TABLE 5-1

CHARACTERISTICS USED TO EXPLAIN HOURLY EARNINGS
(FOR SPENDING UNIT HEADS WHO WORKED DURING 1959)

Characteristics of spending unit heads	Relative importance (Beta coefficients)	Significance (F ratios)
Education and age	.234	10.67**
Sex	.220	188.56**
Occupation	.205	40.93**
Population of cities	.179	[a]
Urban-rural migration	.122	[a]
Movement out of Deep South	.100	7.79**
Extent of unemployment in states	.094	8.61**
Supervisory responsibility	.084	13.75**
Attitude toward hard work and need-achievement score	.067	2.91**
Race	.066	16.97**
Interviewers' assessment of ability to communicate	.061	4.83**
Geographic mobility	.056	2.44*
Physical condition	.056	4.07
Rank and progress in school	.027	0.47

** significant at probability level of .01
* significant at probability level of .05
[a] The adjusted coefficients of these two characteristics did not converge because correlation between some subgroups of the two classifications is extreme. In a regression computation the standard errors of the coefficients for the dummy variables would have been very large. Their combined contribution is still meaningful and improves the estimates of the other effects.

The level of education clearly affects wage rates. It is impossible to say whether this is a result of education itself, or of differences in the ability and intelligence required for differing levels of education.

The analysis incorporates crude measures of intelligence without substantially reducing the power of education as a predictor. Indeed, the reverse seems to be true; adjustments for education reduce the power of the other indicators of intelligence. This would indicate that skills and values acquired through education are important elements in determining wage rates. Some argue that college graduates are more likely to have parents who had the education and income to provide their children with other advantages in addition to their formal education.[2] A better-educated man may be more aware of

[2] Patricia C. Sexton, *Education and Income* (New York: The Viking Press, 1961).

opportunities and be able to select from a wider variety of jobs. Wage studies show that the same job often pays widely different wages even in the same city.

If those who start college but do not finish frequently lack the capacity to master the material, then the absence of any effect of the added education on their wage rates woud be understandable.[3]

A person's wage rate generally rises when he is between the ages of twenty-

TABLE 5-2

HOURLY EARNINGS: DEVIATIONS FOR EDUCATION AND AGE
(FOR SPENDING UNIT HEADS WHO WORKED DURING 1959)

Education and age	Number of spending unit heads	Per cent of spending unit heads	Unadjusted deviations [a]	Adjusted deviations [a]
0–11 grades	1,329	42.5	(− .39)	(−.15)
Under 25	76	2.5	$− .78	$−.52
25–34	251	7.8	− .34	−.22
35–44	297	9.5	− .27	−.09
45–54	332	10.4	− .37	−.09
55–64	269	8.5	− .29	−.04
65 and older	104	3.8	− .77	−.37
12 grades	413	14.3	(.06)	(.04)
Under 25	72	2.5	− .59	−.42
25–34	97	3.4	− .08	−.16
35–44	129	4.5	.39	.33
45–54	78	2.6	.31	.27
55–64	32	1.1	.24	.09
65 and older	5	0.2	−1.04	−.83
12 grades and some college or nonacademic training	541	19.3	(.21)	(.04)
Under 25	84	3.0	− .54	−.51
25–34	142	5.0	.27	−.04
35–44	139	5.0	.33	.19
45–54	99	3.5	.54	.36
55 and older	77	2.8	.28	.10
College graduates	286	10.0	(1.14)	(.54)
Under 35	98	3.4	.58	−.07
35–44	82	2.9	1.48	.85
45–54	53	1.9	1.84	1.27
55 and older	53	1.8	.96	.43

[a] deviations from grand mean of $2.29

( ) Figures in brackets are weighted averages of the deviations for component age groups within each education group.

[3] Dael Wolfle, *America's Resources of Specialized Talent* (New York: Harper & Brothers, 1954), pp. 314–325, 160, 162.

His findings reveal that those with "some college" have IQ's the same or lower than high school graduates, but are much more likely to have fathers in professional, semi-professional, or managerial occupations.

five and forty-four because of increased experience, seniority, and skill. After forty-five his wage rate may decline. Perhaps decreased stamina, dexterity, flexbility, and even unwillingness to change jobs for fear of losing seniority or pensions are responsible.

Age differences in a cross section do not, of course, reflect what happens to an individual over time.[4] For one thing, advancing price levels and levels of real income mean that most people have an income that continues to increase until they retire. Secondly, today's age groups represent several generations, each of which have had different experiences. Some faced depression and unemployment at a time when they would ordinarily be advancing most; some found themselves beyond the flexible age when the postwar opportunities for new and better jobs opened up.

Age and education were combined into a single characteristic in this analysis because of the possibility of nonadditive effects. Examination of the coefficients reveals that the effects are less than additive in some cases, and more than additive in others. The very young and very old with little education have low wage rates, but not as low as the assumption of two additive effects would have predicted. The middle-aged college graduates, on the other hand, have wage rates higher than one would predict by adding an average age effect to an average education effect. This may mean that disadvantages are substitutes, that is, any one operates unfavorably and the others add little further disadvantage, while advantages may be complements, each one adding more to a man's wage if it is combined with others. If this is generally true, the explanation for skewed distributions of earnings as a result of rare combinations of abilities, even when there is a normal distribution of each component of ability, would gain added credibility. (See Chapter 20.)

The females shown in Table 5-3 are heads of spending units. For an analysis of the wage rates of women, one must combine this result with the analysis of working wives presented in Chapter 10.

TABLE 5-3

HOURLY EARNINGS: DEVIATIONS FOR SEX
(FOR SPENDING UNIT HEADS WHO WORKED DURING 1959)

Sex	Number of spending unit heads	Per cent of spending unit heads	Unadjusted deviations [a]	Adjusted deviations [a]
Males	2,179	73.7	$ .13	$ .13
Females	390	12.4	−.75	−.78

[a] deviations from grand mean of $2.29

The most interesting finding in Table 5-3 is that the sex difference in hourly earnings of spending unit heads does not become smaller when other ex-

[4] Herman Miller, "Annual and Lifetime Income in Relation to Education, 1939–1959," *American Economic Review,* L (December, 1960), pp. 962–985.

planatory factors are taken into account. One economist who made crude adjustments for differences in hours worked, education, and age differences within occupations, concluded that market discrimination accounts for less than 10 per cent of the difference in annual earnings of men and women.[5] The more precise direct estimates of earning rates used here, and the multivariate adjustments for other factors, would indicate much larger sex differences unexplained by other factors. It must be remembered that the deviations in Table 5-3 are only for female spending unit heads, not all women, and of differences in earning rates, not annual earnings.

Women have a narrower range of available jobs, and less physical stamina for heavy work. They also face discrimination in some occupations. Compromise between job and family needs or failure to establish a marketable job skill could thus account for some of the observed wage differential between male and female spending unit heads.

A broad occupational classification was used in explaining earnings to avoid too much correlation with other classifications such as education. A truly comprehensive measure of occupation would require a complex classification, combining many dimensions: training, required education, skill, head versus hand work, self-employment, farming, entrepreneurial activity, supervisory activity, and others.

TABLE 5-4

HOURLY EARNINGS: DEVIATIONS FOR OCCUPATION
(FOR SPENDING UNIT HEADS WHO WORKED DURING 1959)

Occupation	Number of spending unit heads	Per cent of spending unit heads	Unadjusted deviations [a]	Adjusted deviations [a]
Professionals, managers, self-employed businessmen	589	20.8	$ .84	$ .41
Clerical and sales workers	325	12.0	− .02	.03
Blue collar workers	1,328	44.3	− .17	−.08
Farmers	190	5.0	−1.53	−.84
Not in labor force now	137	4.0	− .60	−.30

[a] deviations from grand mean of $2.29

Occupation influences earnings even after adjustment for variation in the age and education of different occupational groups. Professionals, managers, and self-employed businessmen earn more than one would expect after allowing for their educational advantages. Farmers earn even less than their generally advanced age and lower education would indicate. Thus, occupation can be interpreted as a supplemental measure of ability or perhaps as an indicator of differing opportunities available to various groups.

[5] Henry Sanborn, "Income Differences between Men and Women in the United States," (unpublished Ph.D. dissertation, University of Chicago, 1960).

Because of intercorrelations, population of cities and urban-rural migration must be considered jointly. The individuals in the last two classes of the population classification are in either the first or fourth class of the urban-rural migration variable. Moreover, rural areas encompass anything from country estates to marginal farms and an increasing proportion of small cities are not independent markets or industrial towns but suburban communities. This heterogeneity within classes is shown by Mansfield who, using 1950 Census data, found that median income was positively related to city size for isolated cities, but negatively related to city size among component cities of standard metropolitan areas. However, these are gross effects that take no account of the age, education, or occupation of the inhabitants.[6]

TABLE 5-5

HOURLY EARNINGS: DEVIATIONS FOR POPULATION OF CITIES
(FOR SPENDING UNIT HEADS WHO WORKED DURING 1959)

Population of cities	Number of spending unit heads	Per cent of spending unit heads	Unadjusted deviations [a]	Adjusted deviations [a]
Central cities of 12 largest metropolitan areas	349	12.5	$ .21	$ .20
Other cities 50,000 or more	465	16.7	.10	.08
Urban places 10,000–49,999	313	10.4	.16	.21
Urban places 2,500–9,999	473	16.3	.08	.14
Rural areas near cities	376	13.1	.37	.02
Rural areas not near cities	593	17.1	−.71	−.51

[a] deviations from grand mean of $2.29

TABLE 5-6

HOURLY EARNINGS: DEVIATIONS FOR URBAN-RURAL MIGRATION
(FOR SPENDING UNIT HEADS WHO WORKED DURING 1959)

Urban-rural migration	Number of spending unit heads	Per cent of spending unit heads	Unadjusted deviations [a]	Adjusted deviations [a]
Grew up on farms; now live:				
in rural areas	500	14.4	$−.83	$ .04
in towns 2,500–49,999	210	6.7	−.40	−.32
in cities 50,000 or more	135	4.7	.14	.21
Grew up in cities or towns; now live:				
in rural areas	449	15.1	.31	.31
in cities or towns	1,221	43.4	.21	−.09
Grew up in several places; not ascertained	54	1.8	.06	−.02

[a] deviations from grand mean of $2.29

[6] Edwin Mansfield, "City Size and Income, 1949," *Regional Income, Studies in Income and Wealth* (Princeton: Princeton University Press, 1957), pp. 271–307.

It is difficult to interpret the coefficients, though the inclusion of the two characteristics provides a better estimate of the net effects of the other characteristics used in the analysis. Nevertheless, the effect of the population of city variables does suggest higher than average wages in areas containing large population aggregates. The coefficients for urban-rural migration seem to show that moving, whether into a city or into a rural area, is associated with higher earnings.

Later analyses omitting the farmers, nonwhites, females, and retired, and then omitting also the population of city classification, produced estimates of the effects of urban-rural migration which converged. The substantial adjustments remained for other factors for those who grew up in rural areas and still live there. At least some of the adjustments are for differences in education and other factors.

One way to move up economically is to move to a place where there are more opportunities. Moving may also be regarded as an indication of ambition and flexibility. Those who moved into or out of the Deep South are now earning more than those who stayed in the same region. Those who stayed in the Deep South are worse off than those who stayed in other regions of the country. The difference between the unadjusted and the adjusted coefficients for those who grew up in the Deep South reflects adjustments for the preponderance of nonwhites and of people with low levels of formal education in these groups. Forty-three per cent of those who moved from the Deep

TABLE 5-7

HOURLY EARNINGS: DEVIATIONS FOR MOVEMENT OUT OF
DEEP SOUTH
(FOR SPENDING UNIT HEADS WHO WORKED DURING 1959)

Movement out of Deep South [a]	Number of spending unit heads	Per cent of spending unit heads	Unadjusted deviations [b]	Adjusted deviations [b]
Grew up in United States outside the Deep South; now live:				
in South	359	11.4	$ .10	$ .10
in non-South	1,458	51.2	.13	.04
Grew up in the Deep South; now live:				
in South	498	14.8	−.61	−.31
in non-South	106	3.5	−.03	.12
Grew up in foreign countries	113	4.1	.26	.19
Grew up in several regions; not ascertained	35	1.1	.28	.12

[a] The Deep South was defined to include Ga., S.C., Va., Ala., Ky., Miss., Tenn., La. (See Appendix D.)
[b] deviations from grand mean of $2.29

South and 21 per cent of those who stayed in the Deep South are nonwhites. Similarly, 77 per cent of those who moved from the Deep South, and 64 per cent of those who stayed in the Deep South did not finish high school, as compared with the over-all average of 49 per cent.

Even taking account of all the other factors, the heads who earned the most are the immigrants to the United States. They earn more than one would expect in their situation.

The hypothesis that wages might be depressed in an area with substantial unemployment clearly was not confirmed. If such an effect existed, it was more than offset by the fact that highly industrialized Northern states with high wage rates also have more unemployment. Unemployment in 1958 is appropriate in the explanation of 1959 hourly earnings, because there may be a lag in the effect of unemployment on wages.

TABLE 5-8

HOURLY EARNINGS: DEVIATIONS FOR EXTENT OF UNEMPLOYMENT
IN STATES
(FOR SPENDING UNIT HEADS WHO WORKED DURING 1959)

Extent of 1958 unemployment in states	Number of spending unit heads	Per cent of spending unit heads	Unadjusted deviations [a]	Adjusted deviations [a]
Under 5.00 per cent	563	17.8	$-.33	$-.21
5.00–6.49 per cent	878	28.8	−.09	−.01
6.50–7.49 per cent	554	19.8	.28	.14
7.50–9.99 per cent	326	10.8	.03	−.06
10.00 per cent and over	248	8.9	.28	.21

[a] deviations from grand mean of $2.29

Apparently the permanent difference between wage rates in the industrialized Northern states and other states is more important than any short-run influence of unemployment. One may even regard the wage differential as a kind of payment to workers for the greater risk of unemployment, though it is not clear that the specific jobs with less security pay higher wages.

The substantial differences between unadjusted and adjusted coefficients for supervisory responsibility result largely from the fact that those who supervise others are white, male college graduates. Nearly one-fourth of those who supervise are college graduates as against 10 per cent of the self-employed and 7 per cent of the rest. While some of the self-employed are professionals who may earn higher than average wages, many are farmers whose earnings are calculated net of the imputed return on capital in the farm, making this a heterogeneous classification for assessing wage rates.

The psychological theory behind the combination of the need-achievement score and the perception that hard work is important was that it takes both to produce outstanding effort on the part of the individual. There does seem to be a cumulative effect, but not the extreme one which might have been expected. It is possible that the question of whether people get ahead by their own hard work or by lucky breaks or help from other people did not measure subjective probabilities of the individual, but rather surface expressions of

TABLE 5-9

HOURLY EARNINGS: DEVIATIONS FOR SUPERVISORY RESPONSIBILITY
(FOR SPENDING UNIT HEADS WHO WORKED DURING 1959)

Supervisory responsibility	Number of spending unit heads	Per cent of spending unit heads	Unadjusted deviations [a]	Adjusted deviations [a]
Self-employed	446	13.5	$ .31	$ .17
Supervisors	535	19.4	.68	.21
Neither self-employed nor supervisors	1,588	53.2	−.17	−.03

[a] deviations from grand mean of $2.29

TABLE 5-10

HOURLY EARNINGS: DEVIATIONS FOR ATTITUDE TOWARD HARD WORK
AND NEED-ACHIEVEMENT SCORE
(FOR SPENDING UNIT HEADS WHO WORKED DURING 1959)

Attitude toward hard work and need-achievement score	Number of spending unit heads	Per cent of spending unit heads	Unadjusted deviations [a]	Adjusted deviations [a]
Hard work is equal to or more important than luck; need-achievement score is in:				
high range	631	22.3	$ .32	$ .12
middle range	921	31.4	.06	.01
low range	440	14.2	−.32	−.17
Hard work is less important than luck; need-achievement score is in:				
high range	120	3.9	−.04	.05
middle range	228	7.3	−.26	−.01
low range	139	4.0	−.52	−.05
Need-achievement score not ascertained	90	3.0	.01	−.16

[a] deviations from grand mean of $2.29

the virtue of hard work, or expressions of the reality faced by minorities, such as the nonwhite and Jewish populations.

It is important, however, to notice that these crude motivational measures help explain why some people earn more per hour than others, even when combined with other factors.

The unadjusted effect of the need-achievement score and attitude toward hard work conforms to the hypothesis that this motivation is important in determining a man's economic position through its effects on other things. A high level of need-achievement may lead to greater educational attainments, and greater ability to overcome physical handicaps; hence, some of the effect of need-achievement tends to be attributed to other variables such as education and physical limitation in a simultaneous multivariate analysis.

If one believed that achievement motivation determined education completely, and education determined occupation, one should look at the unadjusted deviations for achievement motivation, and perhaps reduce the adjusted deviations for occupation still further. Since these causal sequences are neither absolute, nor always clearly in one direction, these approximations must suffice.

Even allowing for other factors, whites earn 32 cents an hour more than nonwhites. Perhaps more interesting than the adjusted coefficients for wage

TABLE 5-11

HOURLY EARNINGS: DEVIATIONS FOR RACE
(FOR SPENDING UNIT HEADS WHO WORKED DURING 1959)

Race	Number of spending unit heads	Per cent of spending unit heads	Unadjusted deviations [a]	Adjusted deviations [a]
White	2,220	77.4	$ .08	$ .03
Nonwhite	349	8.7	−.69	−.29

[a] deviations from grand mean of $2.29

rate by race is the difference between the adjusted and the unadjusted coefficients. More than half of the total racial differences in wages is attributed to other things, such as level of education or occupation.[7] While these other factors may differ between whites and nonwhites as a result of prejudice, many of them represent characteristics more subject to change through social policy than is prejudice. Improved educational and job opportunities for nonwhites would reduce the wage differential, even if racial prejudice was not eliminated.

If it had been possible to adjust for the quality of the formal education received, taking account of differences in the quality of education available to nonwhites and whites, the remaining adjusted deviations for race might have been even smaller. This is in striking contrast with the sex differential, which was not reduced by any of the other factors measured in the analysis. (See Table 5-3.)

Although the adjustments for correlations with other variables such as education are substantial in Table 5-12, it is plausible that the superficial im-

[7] Morton Zeman, "A Quantitative Analysis of White-Nonwhite Income Differentials in the United States in 1939" (unpublished Ph.D. dissertation, University of Chicago, 1955).

TABLE 5-12

HOURLY EARNINGS: DEVIATIONS FOR INTERVIEWERS' ASSESSMENT
OF ABILITY TO COMMUNICATE
(FOR SPENDING UNIT HEADS WHO WORKED DURING 1959)

Interviewers' assessment of ability to communicate	Number of spending unit heads	Per cent of spending unit heads	Unadjusted deviations [a]	Adjusted deviations [a]
Spending unit heads:				
answer questions easily	2,045	70.5	$ .12	$ .04
answer questions with slight difficulty	408	12.4	−.52	−.16
answer questions with considerable difficulty	92	2.5	−.77	−.28
Not ascertained	24	0.7	.14	.28

[a] deviations from grand mean of $2.29

pression a man makes will affect the wage he can earn. This impression may, of course, result from mannerisms rather than from ability or intelligence.

The hypothesis that extreme mobility might indicate instability or irresponsibility, and hence lower wages, is not borne out by the analysis, perhaps because the classification of mobility is not detailed enough. Mobility does not mean the same thing for every head of a spending unit; some are older and have had more opportunities to move. Even after adjusting for age, however, those who have moved frequently appear to have bettered their wages in the process.

The group who has lived in four or more states contains twice as many heads who are fifty-five or older, as does the whole group of heads who worked in 1959 (42 per cent as against 21 per cent). But it contains the same pro-

TABLE 5-13

HOURLY EARNINGS: DEVIATIONS FOR GEOGRAPHIC MOBILITY
(FOR SPENDING UNIT HEADS WHO WORKED DURING 1959)

Geographic mobility	Number of spending unit heads	Per cent of spending unit heads	Unadjusted deviations [a]	Adjusted deviations [a]
Since first job, have lived in:				
one state:				
within 100 miles of present location	1,365	46.0	$−.08	$−.01
more than 100 miles of present location	293	9.8	−.07	−.13
two states	522	17.3	.11	.02
three states	181	6.2	.08	−.02
four or more states	158	5.3	.34	.19
not ascertained	50	1.5	.10	.38

[a] deviations from grand mean of $2.29

portion of college graduates (12 per cent). The adjustment in the coefficient is therefore for age differences, rather than differences in education.

The disabled clearly earn less per hour even when they work. The difference between unadjusted and adjusted deviations is due to the fact that people with more formal education report fewer physical disabilities. Some of this may be because they were asked whether they had a disability "which limits the type of work or the amount of work you can do." A manual worker might be limited by a bad back which would only irritate but not limit the work of a clerk. On the other hand, the less educated people work at more dangerous jobs and are more exposed to the hazard of injury. Indeed, evidence is accumulating that disabilities which are thought to result from job tensions are sometimes more frequent among the lower status jobs.[8]

If adjusted coefficients from Table 5-14 were used to estimate the earnings loss from disabilities, they would have to be combined with coefficients from

TABLE 5-14

HOURLY EARNINGS: DEVIATIONS FOR PHYSICAL CONDITION
(FOR SPENDING UNIT HEADS WHO WORKED DURING 1959)

Physical condition	Number of spending unit heads	Per cent of spending unit heads	Unadjusted deviations [a]	Adjusted deviations [a]
Completely disabled [b]	29	0.9	$-.44	$-.13
Severely disabled	57	1.6	-.77	-.20
Moderately disabled	276	8.9	-.41	-.22
Not disabled	2,207	74.7	.07	.03

[a] deviations from grand mean of $2.29
[b] Most of these became disabled during 1959.

Chapters 4 and 6 to reflect the lower probability of working and shorter hours which apply to the disabled. These economic effects will be analyzed in Chapter 17.

The final explanatory characteristic provides a measure that may be related to native intelligence. It proved impossible to administer even the simplest intelligence test in the questionnaire, but spending unit heads were asked whether their grades in school had been above or below average. Also from the number of grades completed and the age at leaving school, it was inferred whether or not each spending unit head had been behind his age group when he left school. Studies of high school drop-outs have indicated that they are frequently behind their grade, and have low scores on measures of achievement and intelligence.[9] Many may say their grades were average when they

[8] Stanislav V. Kasl and John R. P. French, Jr., "The Effects of Occupational Status on Physical and Mental Health," *Journal of Social Issues*, XVIII (Spring, 1962).

[9] *From School to Work* (U.S. Department of Labor, Bureau of Labor Statistics, March, 1960).

were below or slightly above average. Some will have been behind in school because of illness, demands of the family, and so forth. However, it is assumed that reports of high grades, or of grades below average, are probably correct, though incomplete, and that some of those behind their age group were having difficulty with school work.

TABLE 5-15

HOURLY EARNINGS: DEVIATIONS FOR RANK AND PROGRESS
IN SCHOOL
(FOR SPENDING UNIT HEADS WHO WORKED DURING 1959)

Rank and progress in school	Number of spending unit heads	Per cent of spending unit heads	Unadjusted deviations [a]	Adjusted deviations [a]
Grades above average	704	24.1	$ .31	$ .04
Grades average				
Not behind age group	783	26.8	− .18	−.03
1–2 years behind age group	265	8.6	− .29	.03
Grades below average				
Not behind age group	83	2.8	− .16	.03
1–2 years behind age group	57	1.7	− .58	−.10
Grades average or below				
3 or more years behind age group	137	3.6	−1.01	−.11
Progress in school cannot be measured (heads went to college, had no education, etc.)	540	18.5	.27	.00

[a] deviations from grand mean of $2.29

This combination index of "intelligence" is highly correlated with the number of grades of school completed, and hence the adjusted deviations are very much smaller than the gross effects. People in the South and in farm communities are also more likely to be behind in school, and to end up in low-wage occupations like farming. The small remaining effect of this characteristic is not significant.

Summary

The hourly earnings of spending unit heads clearly are affected most by their age and education, sex, occupation, and supervisory role, and present residence. In addition, indicators of motivation, including past mobility and present achievement motivation and belief that hard work pays off, also have a significant net relation to hourly earnings. Even after completed education was accounted for, crude proxy measures of intelligence such as ability to answer questions easily, also appear to affect earnings. The extent to which gross relations, one factor taken at a time, would exaggerate the effects of each factor has been indicated by the differences between unadjusted and adjusted coefficients.

The fact that the analysis has accounted for only 34 per cent of the variance in wage rates of heads of spending units means that there is still considerable variation in the wages of any subgroup. If more detailed and accurate measures of ability, motivation, emotional factors, and job market conditions were available this variation probably would be substantially reduced.

Table 5-16 provides the distributions of hourly earnings for age and education subgroups. While the unadjusted deviations in Table 5-2 indicate the

TABLE 5-16

HOURLY EARNINGS WITHIN EDUCATION AND AGE
(PERCENTAGE DISTRIBUTION OF SPENDING UNIT HEADS
AGED 25-64 WHO WORKED IN 1959)

	Education and age			
Hourly earnings	0–11 grades	12 grades	12 grades and some college or nonacademic training	College degree
			25–34	
$0.01–$0.99; negative	18	10	5	2
$1.00–1.99	35	31	21	19
$2.00–2.99	36	41	46	30
$3.00–3.99	8	16	20	33
$4.00 or more	3	2	8	16
Total	100	100	100	100
Number of spending unit heads	251	97	142	80
			35–44	
$0.01–0.99; negative	18	6	7	2
$1.00–1.99	29	27	22	11
$2.00–2.99	35	29	42	26
$3.00–3.99	13	25	16	25
$4.00 or more	5	13	13	36
Total	100	100	100	100
Number of spending unit heads	297	129	139	82
			45-54	
$0.01–0.99; negative	23	12	11	5
$1.00–1.99	32	23	25	11
$2.00–2.99	29	34	28	16
$3.00–3.99	10	13	22	19
$4.00 or more	6	18	14	49
Total	100	100	100	100
Number of spending unit heads	332	78	99	53
			55–64	
$0.01–0.99; negative	24	5	8	7
$1.00–1.99	29	31	18	10
$2.00–2.99	27	30	35	22
$3.00–3.99	12	24	14	14
$4.00 or more	8	10	25	47
Total	100	100	100	100
Number of spending unit heads	269	32	61	38

means for these age and education groups, Table 5-16 shows the distribution of cases which produces each mean.

Interaction Effects—Analysis of Subgroups

There remains the possibility that the effects of factors in the analysis are not additive, for instance, that the effect of education on earnings is different for females, nonwhites, and farmers, than it is for white, nonfarm men. The coefficients for subgroups offer the basis for comparison with the average and serve as an indication of the extent to which subgroups which were not analyzed have different behavior patterns from the average. To investigate

TABLE 5-17

CHARACTERISTICS USED TO EXPLAIN HOURLY EARNINGS
(FOR WHITE, MALE, NONFARMER SPENDING UNIT HEADS
WHO WORKED IN 1959)

Characteristics of spending unit heads	Relative importance (Beta coefficients)	Significance (F ratios)
Education and age	.279	8.88**
Population of cities	.170	13.19**
Occupation	.148	16.66**
Urban-rural migration	.117	6.25**
Extent of unemployment in states	.104	6.17**
Supervisory responsibility	.087	8.63**
Movement out of Deep South	.084	3.22**
Additude toward hard work and need-achievement score	.070	1.86
Geographic mobility	.066	1.99
Physical condition	.059	2.65*
Interviewers' assessment of ability to communicate	.057	2.47
Rank and progress in school	.037	0.52

** significant at probability level of .01
 * significant at probability level of .05

this, the analysis of hourly earnings was repeated for white, male, nonfarmer spending unit heads who worked during 1959.[10]

The relative importance of the predictors common to both analyses remained much the same. The race and sex variables are not shown explicitly, but their effect is accounted for by the subgroup which was selected. Omitting the farmers from the analysis reduced occupation to four groups and reduced its importance. The elimination of farmers also reduced the intercorrelation between population of city and urban-rural migration sufficiently so that all coefficients converged. Both population of city and urban-rural migration

[10] The possibility that the effect of education on earnings is different for nonwhites, and even in different regions, is supported by an analysis of Census data by C. Arnold Anderson, "Regional and Racial Differences in Relation between Income and Education," *The School Review,* 63 (January, 1955), pp. 38–45.

proved to be important with coefficients similar to those in the analysis of earnings of all spending unit heads.

The mean wage rate was higher for white, male nonfarmers than the whole sample but the standard deviation was the same. The analysis explained 23 per cent of the variance as compared with 34 per cent when it was explaining also the lower wages of women, farmers, and nonwhites. However, it is more difficult to explain differences within a more homogeneous group, and the relative precision with which this analysis explains earnings is, in fact, greater than in the earlier analysis.

A calculation from the original full-sample analysis to estimate the expected mean wage rate for the white, male, nonfarmer spending unit heads gives $2.29 plus .03 (white) plus .13 (male) plus .05 (nonfarmer), or $2.51 whereas the actual mean was $2.60. The difference between the two means indicates an interaction effect. Being a woman, a nonwhite person, or a farmer lowers the wage rate somewhat more than indicated in the previous analysis. Having the three characteristics on which the subgroup was defined results in a wage rate slightly greater than would be expected on the basis of an additive effect.

The coefficients of most of the subclasses remain substantially the same in the analysis of white, male nonfarmers, as they were in the previous analysis. Thus the interaction is limited to the wage level of the subgroup, and the differential effects of education, mobility, and other factors on hourly earnings within the group are the same for the total sample and the white, male nonfarmers.

White, male nonfarmers comprise a large proportion of the total of all spending unit heads. Thus one would expect the coefficients for this group to influence coefficients for the entire population quite strongly. Any disparity between similar coefficients in the two analyses indicates a difference in the manner in which the characteristic affects white, male nonfarmers and nonwhites, farmers, or women. The only adjusted coefficient that differs markedly is that associated with moving out of the Deep South which resulted in a rate 12 cents above expected levels for the whole sample, but 7 cents below for white, nonfarmer males; thus, it is probably the nonwhites who benefit most from moving out of the Deep South.

The coefficients for age and education shown in Table 5-18 are so highly correlated with those for the whole sample shown in Table 5-2 ($R^2 = .98$) that it must be concluded that no important interaction effects exist between age and education, on the one hand, and sex, race, or occupation, on the other hand. The assumption of additivity of effects in the multivariate analysis is a reasonable approximation.

A slight interaction appears between education and the white, male nonfarmer characteristics for the forty-five to fifty-four age group. In this age group the coefficients for those with some training beyond high school and with college degrees indicate higher hourly earnings for the subgroup than for the entire population. However, differences are unreliable because they are based on a small number of cases.

In order to test further for interaction effect between age and other factors, the analysis of hourly earnings for white, male, nonfarmer spending unit heads

TABLE 5-18

HOURLY EARNINGS: DEVIATIONS FOR EDUCATION AND AGE
(FOR WHITE, MALE, NONFARMER SPENDING UNIT HEADS
WHO WORKED IN 1959)

Education and age	Number of spending unit heads	Per cent of spending unit heads	Unadjusted deviations [a]	Adjusted deviations [a]
0–11 grades				
Under 25	54	1.9	$−1.04	$− .66
25–34	169	5.8	− .42	− .26
35–44	192	6.8	− .27	− .13
45–54	199	6.7	− .33	− .13
55–64	163	5.8	− .16	.00
65 and older	65	2.5	− .71	− .35
12 grades				
Under 25	46	1.7	− .74	− .56
25–34	70	2.6	− .21	− .22
35–44	95	3.5	.38	.34
45–54	55	1.9	.39	.26
55–64	23	.8	.29	.16
65 and older	3	.1	− .61	− .75
12 grades and some college or nonacademic training				
Under 25	46	1.7	− .58	− .67
25–34	112	4.1	.08	− .04
35–44	103	3.7	.24	.12
45–54	71	2.5	.62	.48
55 and older	51	1.9	.42	.19
College degree				
Under 35	86	3.0	.24	− .19
35–44	70	2.5	1.39	.92
45–54	43	1.5	1.92	1.50
55 and older	39	1.4	.82	.34

[a] deviations from grand mean of $2.60

who worked in 1959 was then done separately for those under thirty-five and for those thirty-five and older. These analyses considered only spending unit heads who were employed or unemployed at the time of interview. Persons who worked at some time in 1959 but retired or dropped out of the labor force before March or April of 1960 were excluded.

For the two relatively homogeneous groups, two long-term explanatory factors were added: religious preference and church attendance, and the difference in education between the head and his father. The first of these represents a dimension of social class and different attitudes toward work. The education difference presumably represents intergenerational transmission of income standards, and possibly the effects of parental standards.

The three factors which had been unimportant and not significant in the original analysis were omitted: physical condition of head, interviewers' assessment of heads' ability to communicate, and rank and progress in school. Population of city was also omitted because its effect was largely through the

TABLE 5-19

CHARACTERISTICS USED TO EXPLAIN HOURLY EARNINGS
(FOR WHITE, MALE, NONFARMER SPENDING UNIT HEADS
IN THE LABOR FORCE WHO WORKED IN 1959)

Characteristics of spending unit heads	Relative importance				Significance	
	Rank		Beta coefficients		F ratios	
	Under 35	35 and older	Under 35	35 and older	Under 35	35 and older
Education	1	1	.193	.263	3.88**	13.88**
Local labor market conditions	2	2	.183	.201	4.88**	11.35**
Age	3	7	.176	.089	22.57**	2.78**
Religious preference and church attendance	4	3	.171	.114	3.55**	3.04**
Movement out of Deep South	5	10	.160	.026	3.73**	0.19
Difference in education of heads and fathers	6	6	.135	.095	4.43**	4.23**
Attitude toward hard work and need-achievement score	7	8	.132	.081	2.12*	1.54
Urban-rural migration	8	5	.118	.096	2.03	2.59*
Supervisory responsibility	9	4	.115	.105	4.82**	7.74**
Geographic mobility	10	9	.101	.061	1.49	1.05

** significant at probability level of .01
* significant at probability level of .05

rural residence which appears in urban-rural migration. Finally, occupation was omitted because without the farmers and the retired, most of its remaining effect could be handled by the classification that indicates supervisory responsibility.

A measure of the local labor market condition was used in place of the measure of conditions in the whole state in the hope that it would be a better measure of the pressure of unemployment on wage rates.

The analysis explained 24 per cent of the variance for the spending unit heads under thirty-five and 23 per cent for those thirty-five or older. The mean for the younger heads who worked was $2.41, with a standard deviation of $1.08. For the older heads the mean was $2.82 with a standard deviation of $1.52. The relative importance of the predictors for each of the two age groups are given in Table 5-19.

There appeared some tendency for the effects of advanced education to be stronger among those thirty-five or older. This confirms the age-education interaction observed in the analysis of the total population. Table 5-20 shows the coefficients for education for each of the two age groups adjusted for detailed age, mobility, and the other factors.

Moving from an urban to a rural area appeared to be associated with higher earnings for the whole sample. In the more detailed analysis this effect appears to exist only for spending unit heads thirty-five and older. For the

TABLE 5-20

HOURLY EARNINGS: DEVIATIONS FOR EDUCATION
(FOR WHITE, MALE, NONFARMER SPENDING UNIT HEADS
IN THE LABOR FORCE WHO WORKED IN 1959)

Education [a]	Number of spending unit heads		Adjusted deviations	
	Under 35	35 and older	Under 35 [b]	35 and older [c]
1–8 grades	83	298	$−.27	$− .31
9–11 grades	135	255	−.02	− .18
12 grades	116	170	−.13	.01
12 grades and nonacademic training	60	107	−.10	− .04
College, no degree	86	107	.20	.10
College, bachelor's degree	59	101	.34	.77
College, advanced degree	15	43	.59	1.34

[a] 5 cases with no education are omitted
[b] deviations from grand mean of $2.41
[c] deviations from grand mean of $2.82

younger group, those who moved to the country are earning less. The finding applies only to nonfarmers; the implication is that rural living is made up of a bimodal distribution of older well-established people in high class rural suburbs, and younger people with earning rates less than one would expect. For both ages, moving from farms to big cities paid off in higher wages, but not moving from farms to small towns.

Migration out of or into the South appears to relate differently to wages for the older white, male, nonfarmer heads than for the younger ones. Among the young people it appears to be where the head grew up that is important, not whether he has displayed mobility by moving into or out of the South. Thus, young people who grew up in the Deep South earn about 25 cents an hour less even if they have moved out of the Deep South. Among the older people there is no significant effect, but a small group who moved out of the Deep South seems to be earning more than expected.

The new measure of local labor market conditions proved far more important in explaining wage rates than the state labor market measure which it replaced. Much of the effect of the new measure, however, reflects the low wages in areas not rated at all. These are mostly areas of low population density and not much industry. There was some tendency for wage rates of both age groups to be higher where unemployment was least. This tendency also exists at the other extreme, the very highly industrialized and unionized areas where unemployment and wages were both high. (See Table 5-21.) But wages, when adjusted for other things, appeared to be lowest in the C areas for older workers and in the E areas for younger workers.

TABLE 5-21

HOURLY EARNINGS: DEVIATIONS FOR LOCAL LABOR
MARKET CONDITIONS
(FOR WHITE, MALE, NONFARMER SPENDING UNIT HEADS
IN THE LABOR FORCE WHO WORKED IN 1959)

Local labor market conditions [a]	Number of spending unit heads		Adjusted deviations	
	Under 35	35 and older	Under 35 [b]	35 and older [c]
B	10	9	$ .40	$1.21
C	143	232	.19	.12
D	107	275	.03	.24
E	26	75	−.21	.34
F	20	55	.52	.24
Not classified	249	439	−.18	−.37

[a] Areas rated F have the worst unemployment situation; those rated B have the best. (See Appendix D.)
[b] deviations from mean of $2.41
[c] deviations from mean of $2.82

The difference in education between the head and his father is not completely free from association with the head's education, because only three levels were used to discriminate differences in education. Hence, the head with two levels more than the father must be a college graduate. The ones with less education than their fathers probably did not go to high school.

Those who finished one level more education than their fathers were earning more than expected, particularly if they were over thirty-five. The young heads who had two levels more education than their fathers were earning much less than expected on the basis of their college educations, indicating that their parents' lack of education may have been a handicap in spite of their own education. Other heads in the same classification appear to have overcome this handicap.

The final new factor in these analyses was religious affiliation and church attendance. It has an odd pattern but a significant one, which differs between the two age groups. Religious preference is classified according to major theological groups—Catholic, Protestant, and Jewish—but within the Protestants, denominations are grouped more according to their education and income levels than according to their beliefs. It happens that the higher status denominations are also more liberal theologically, and those with lower income and education levels are more Fundamentalist.[11]

Table 5-23 shows that older, infrequently attending Catholics and older regularly attending non-Fundamentalist Protestants earn more than one might expect on the basis of their other characteristics. The Fundamentalist Protestants earn less than expected.

TABLE 5-22

HOURLY EARNINGS: DEVIATIONS FOR EDUCATION DIFFERENCE
BETWEEN HEADS AND FATHERS
(FOR WHITE, MALE, NONFARMER SPENDING UNIT HEADS
IN THE LABOR FORCE WHO WORKED IN 1959)

Difference in education of heads and fathers [a]	Number of spending unit heads		Adjusted deviations	
	Under 35	35 and older	Under 35 [b]	35 and older [c]
Fathers have more levels than heads	32	71	$−.12	$−.01
Fathers have same education as heads	256	590	−.02	−.11
Fathers have one level less than heads	207	290	.14	.23
Fathers have two levels less than heads	60	134	−.34	−.02

[a] Levels are:
  0–11 grades
  12 grades
  some college
[b] deviations from mean of $2.41
[c] deviations from mean of $2.82

The direction of causation involved in the association between religion and wage rates is more difficult to determine. More than three-quarters of the spending unit heads reported that their religious preference was in the same general grouping as that of their fathers. As for attendance, fewer than one-half reported the same frequency of attendance as their fathers, but most of the change was toward less frequent attendance.

The implication is that current religious preference seems likely to represent parental and church influences. While some may change their religious

[11] Bernard Lazerwitz, "A Comparison of Major United States Religious Groups," *Journal of the American Statistical Association,* 56 (September, 1961), pp. 568–579.

Gerhard Lenski, *The Religious Factor* (New York: Doubleday & Company, Inc., 1961), and Liston Pope, "Religion and Class Structure," *Annals of the American Academy of Political and Social Science,* 256 (March, 1948), 84–91.

affiliation as their economic status changes, they are few in number. Consequently, religion remains largely an indicator of a man's past and it must be assumed that the direction of causation runs largely from religion to wage rates.[12]

There is no obvious reason for more frequent church attendance being associated with higher earnings among older Protestants, and lower earnings among young Protestants and older Catholics.

TABLE 5-23

HOURLY EARNINGS: DEVIATIONS FOR RELIGIOUS PREFERENCE
AND CHURCH ATTENDANCE
(FOR WHITE, MALE, NONFARMER SPENDING UNIT HEADS
IN THE LABOR FORCE WHO WORKED IN 1959)

Religious preference and church attendance	Number of spending unit heads		Unadjusted deviations		Adjusted deviations	
	Under 35	35 and older	Under 35 [a]	35 and older [b]	Under 35 [a]	35 and older [b]
Catholics:						
attend more than once a month	97	203	$ .14	$−.03	$ .02	$−.12
attend once a month or less	28	53	−.16	.21	−.05	.31
Fundamentalist Protestants:						
attend more than once a month	88	150	−.32	−.33	−.18	−.07
attend once a month or less	98	130	−.25	−.57	−.15	−.20
Non-Fundamentalist Protestants:						
attend more than once a month	86	192	.06	.44	−.03	.26
attend once a month or less	138	263	.11	−.08	.12	−.09
Non-Christians; not ascertained	20	94	1.10	.53	.77	.19

[a] deviations from mean of $2.41
[b] deviations from mean of $2.82

Summary

Hourly earnings of spending unit heads are affected mostly by their age, education, and occupation as representatives of skills, abilities, and acceptance of responsibilities. Earnings are also affected by the place where they live and race, representing the availability of jobs. Geographic mobility appears to

[12] Albert J. Mayer and Harry Sharp, "Religious Preference and Worldly Success," *American Sociological Review* 27 (April, 1962), 218–227;

Neil J. Weller, *Religion and Social Mobility in Industrial Society* (unpublished Ph.D. dissertation, University of Michigan, 1960).

benefit the mover somewhat. Motivation, as reflected in the rudimentary measures of need-achievement and religion, appears to affect wage rates.

On the other hand, indicators of intelligence other than formal education add nothing to the explanation of hourly earnings.

Unemployment in the state did not affect earnings as much as did the rating of the local labor market, and there the influence was partly long-run effects of high wages in industrial areas where unemployment is also greatest, and partly a depressing effect of current unemployment on current wages.

Religious preference and church attendance had powerful effects, which are different for different age groups. The age differences will require further investigation before they can be explained.

The effects of the major factors prove similar for homogeneous subgroups, excluding the farmers, nonwhites, female heads, and the retired. Hence, one need not be concerned about distortions from interaction effects. If interactions exist, they are for such small groups that they do not affect the over-all findings.

One-third of the variation in hourly earnings is accounted for by factors which relate directly to the individual—mobility and attitudes, education and achievement motivation. To this extent, the individual has some control over his wage rate.

Chapter 6

HOURS WORKED BY
SPENDING UNIT HEADS

While a man may have limited discretion as to whether he works, and at what wage rate, the most important way he can affect his own income is through the amount of time he works. Even here his freedom is constrained by the standard forty hour work week and the reluctance of employers to pay overtime or to hire people for irregular hours of work. More important, perhaps, his hours of work may be shortened involuntarily by unemployment. Conversely, many people take second jobs; others, particularly the self-employed, can set their own hours.

Very few spending unit heads worked less than a full week when they were working. Even of those who worked only a few weeks, a majority worked full weeks. Hence, the deviations from average in hours worked, which are explained in this chapter, tend to represent unemployment when they are low, and overtime or extra jobs when they are high. Two-fifths of the spending unit heads reported working more than the regular forty hour week.

Each spending unit head's estimate of the number of weeks he worked in 1959 and the average number of hours for those weeks were combined to estimate hours worked in 1959. The use of the head's estimate of average hours per week makes it likely that response error is larger than the sampling variation indicated by the standard error of the mean. No other data on hours worked are available which are strictly comparable to the data presented here. Data on average weekly, rather than annual, work hours are available in the Census—Bureau of Labor Statistics Current Population Surveys. These include both paid and unpaid employment. Comparability is further limited by the fact that the Bureau of Labor Statistics data define membership in the labor force differently than it is defined here, so that statistics on unemployment are not similar.

Some of the factors in the multivariate analysis of hours worked represent things which may motivate the worker to work more or less; others represent forces which set hours and constrain the worker's freedom in setting his own hours. The impossibility of separating the voluntary and the involuntary led to an analysis of hours as affected by both types of forces.

Constraining Factors

The constraints can be thought of in two groups: the amount of work available, or demand for this individual's work, and the worker's physical stamina and capacity for long hours of work.

Five factors measure the amount of available work. All factors except occupation were also used to predict whether the head worked.

The extent of unemployment (ratio of insured unemployment to covered employment in the state in 1958) is assumed to represent the relative condition of the job market in 1959.

The age and education of the head represent, in part, the variety of tasks he can perform and perhaps his ability to learn about new or extra job opportunities. In so far as age and education operate through their effects on his wage rate, they are already accounted for.

Race is assumed to be associated with limitations on types of work and with more frequent unemployment. It may, of course, also measure other forces.

The sex of the head is included because women have a narrower range of available jobs, being excluded, for instance, from arduous physical labor and from night jobs in some factory districts.

The occupation of the head allows for the fact that farmers and other self-employed or professional people can more easily work long hours if they wish than other workers can.

As in the analysis of whether the head worked, physical condition and age measure the individual's ability to work long hours.

Also, a single adult with children may be restricted in employment because of family responsibilities.

Motivational Factors

The motivational factors can be thought of as consisting of one major economic factor, the wage rate a man can earn, and a set of characteristics which serve as indicators of such motives as the need for money or the desire to get ahead. There are no measures of the extent to which the individual enjoys his work, which might also affect how long he worked.

The single measure of the rewards of work is the dependent variable from Chapter 5: the wage rate earned per hour. This is an average wage earned in 1959, not necessarily equal to what the person could earn by working an *extra* hour, but it should be a rough indicator of what the individual could earn if extra work were available. Hourly earnings also should be adjusted by a factor equal to head's marginal tax rate to reflect accurately the amount of take-home pay he could earn by working an extra hour.[1]

Hourly earnings also can be thought of as an indicator of the cost of leisure in terms of foregone earnings. It is not obvious that higher hourly earnings should always lead to more hours worked. As a man's wage rises, the marginal utility of the things he buys with money declines relative to the value of more leisure. He may prefer to take some of his gain in the form of more leisure, thus working less at a higher wage rate.

Six predictors other than wage rate reflect other motivations to work long hours. Perhaps the simplest motivation is having a wife and children for whom to provide. This should result in a high marginal utility of money, and is part of the classification by sex, marital status, and number of dependents. Other parts of the same classification indicate difficulty in working for single adults with children, or limited range of available jobs for female heads.

Money may also be important if there are commitments to future spending. This is indicated by a classification according to whether there are plans to send children to college, or to give more support to parents in the future.

The difference in education between head and wife indicate their relative earning ability and living standards. Differences in the wages each can earn affect the choice between the wife's working and the head's working longer hours. Secondly, the wife's education may determine the living standards of the family, but the husband's education determines his wage rate. If the wife has more education than her husband, he would have to work longer hours to achieve the desired standard of living. On the other hand, if he has more education, he can earn more per hour and may not need to work as long to meet the family's standards.

The head's religious preference and frequency of church attendance are assumed to be some indication of culture and values which may or may not stress hard work as a virtue. If Catholics are oriented toward the hereafter, the Protestants are concerned with worldly success and the prestige that goes with upward mobility, then they should behave differently in their work.[2]

If the head is an immigrant, ambitious enough to leave his native country,

---

[1] A study of 306 self-employed accountants and solicitors in England, 63 per cent of whom faced marginal tax rates greater than 50 per cent, concluded: "The chorus of complaints, vehement and eloquent, against 'penal' taxation, echoed by the great majority of respondents interviewed in the present study, was surprisingly infrequently translated into action." See George F. Break, "Income Taxes and Incentives to Work: An Empirical Study," *American Economic Review,* XLVII (September, 1957), 529–549, 548.

See also Richard Musgrave, "Adjustments in Work Effort," Chapter 2 of *The Theory of Public Finance* (New York: The McGraw-Hill Book Company, Inc., 1959), pp. 232–256, and references cited therein.

[2] See Bernard Rosen, "Race, Ethnicity, and the Achievement Syndrome," *American Sociological Review,* 24 (February, 1959), 47–60. See also Joseph Veroff and others, "Achievement Motivation and Religious Background," *American Sociological Review* 27 (April, 1962), 205–217. Also Gerhard Lenski, *The Religious Factor* (New York: Doubleday & Company, Inc., 1961).

he may be anxious to work long hours. Being foreign born may also limit the kinds of jobs he can hold. It is not clear whether this would limit or enhance opportunities to work long hours.

Finally, a high need-achievement score combined with the belief that hard work pays off more than luck or help from friends, should increase the hours of work the head does. It is assumed that the two factors work together so that the combined effect is more than either simple effect.

Religious preference and immigrant status were the only motivational factors used here, but not used to predict whether the head worked. Four types of influences are thus represented by 15 factors in 12 explanatory classifications.

Spending unit heads who worked in 1959 worked an average of 2,092 hours, or slightly over forty hours a week. The standard deviation was 797

TABLE 6-1

CHARACTERISTICS USED TO EXPLAIN HOURS WORKED
(FOR SPENDING UNIT HEADS WHO WORKED DURING 1959)

Characteristics of spending unit heads	Relative importance (Beta coefficients)	Significance (F ratios)
Adult unit composition	.291	42.38**
Education and age	.258	11.66**
Occupation	.254	56.50**
Hourly earnings	.234	23.98**
Physical condition	.115	15.44**
Plans to help parents or children	.084	8.24**
Attitude toward hard work and need-achievement score	.066	2.54*
Religious preference and church attendance	.063	2.32*
Race	.044	6.78*
Extent of unemployment in states	.032	0.90
Difference in education of heads and wives	.025	0.36
Immigration of heads and fathers	.018	0.57

** significant at probability level of .01
 * significant at probability level of .05

hours, and the standard error for the mean, about twenty hours. The 82 subclasses of the 12 predictors explained 27 per cent of the variance.

Table 6-1 provides a list of the sets of predictors used in the multivariate analysis, together with the beta coefficient as a measure of importance in reducing predictive error and the F ratio as a rough test of significance.

It is clear that constraints such as the dependents of a single person, advanced age, or low education are more powerful than such factors as the wage rate or individual motivation and desires for money. On the other hand, the motivational aspects are more important to assess and investigate since they cannot be assumed to operate in the same way that the more mechanical effects, such as advanced age, do.

The presence of children but no spouse clearly reduces the number of hours worked by women but not by men. The hours worked by single persons without children remain shorter even after adjustments for age and occupation. They are more likely to be very old or very young and they are more likely to have dropped out of the labor force even though they worked last year. The direction of causation is unclear. It is possible that the men are single because they do not work full time and cannot support a wife, or that both short hours and being single are the result of some other factor not included in the analysis.

The women spending unit heads who worked in 1959 worked substantially fewer hours than did the men, although it is not possible to determine whether this was a result of choice or limited availability of jobs. They worked more

TABLE 6-2

HOURS WORKED: DEVIATIONS FOR ADULT UNIT COMPOSITION
(FOR SPENDING UNIT HEADS WHO WORKED DURING 1959)

Adult unit composition	Number of spending unit heads	Per cent of spending unit heads	Unadjusted deviations [a]	Adjusted deviations [a]
Unmarried male heads:				
No children under 18	252	8.5	−208	−140
Children under 18	16	0.5	− 63	9
Unmarried female heads:				
No children under 18	272	9.0	−476	−485
Children under 18	118	3.4	−474	−627
Married heads:				
No children under 18	626	21.9	−− 46	88
1 child under 18	368	13.0	175	127
2 children under 18	399	13.6	261	166
3 or more children under 18	518	16.2	179	116

[a] deviations from grand mean of 2,092 hours

hours than wives who worked. (See Chapter 11.) The deviations for women increase in size after age, education, and lower hourly earnings are taken into consideration.

The effect of family responsibility on the hours worked by married heads seems clear: children lead to more work. It seems likely that heads work longer if they have more people to support.

Age and education were used in a combined set to parallel the analysis of wage rates. Other data from this study show that number of hours worked per week varies little with age. Thus much of the apparent reduction in hours worked by the very young and the very old results either from part-year work, from unemployment, or from heads who entered or left the labor force during the year rather than from part-time work.

The effect of education is not uniform. Perhaps the shorter hours of the uneducated are involuntary and those of the educated are voluntary.

Aside from the almost inevitable negative deviation for those not in the labor force in early 1960, the main conclusion connected with occupation is that the self-employed report working longer hours than the other employed. Most of the self-employed are farmers; some are professionals. The substantial adjustments for farmers presumably result from taking account of their

TABLE 6-3

HOURS WORKED: DEVIATIONS FOR EDUCATION AND AGE
(FOR SPENDING UNIT HEADS WHO WORKED DURING 1959)

Education and age	Number of spending unit heads	Per cent of spending unit heads	Unadjusted deviations [a]	Adjusted deviations [a]
0–11 grades	1,329	42.5	− 75	− 28
Under 25	76	2.5	−267	−164
25–34	251	7.8	72	46
35–44	297	9.5	69	90
45–54	332	10.4	59	106
55–64	269	8.5	−167	− 53
65 and older	104	3.8	−776	−699
12 grades	413	14.3	97	90
Under 25	72	2.5	−101	− 34
25–34	97	3.4	215	133
35–44	129	4.5	150	160
45–54	78	2.6	178	130
55–64	32	1.1	−220	− 90
65 and older	5	0.2	83	−205
12 grades and some college or nonacademic training	541	19.3	55	22
Under 25	84	3.0	−404	−376
25–34	142	5.0	134	50
35–44	139	5.0	323	224
45–54	99	3.5	185	177
55 and older	77	2.8	−234	−159
College degree	286	10.0	75	− 50
Under 35	98	3.4	−126	−312
35–44	82	2.9	280	106
45–54	53	1.9	90	45
55 and older	53	1.8	111	95

[a] deviations from grand mean of 2,092 hours

very low earning rates, while those for other white collar workers probably adjust mostly for the higher proportion of women in such jobs. The shorter hours of the blue collar workers are in large part the result of involuntary unemployment.[3]

[3] For relations of education and occupation to unemployment in 1958 see Wilbur J. Cohen, William Haber, and Eva Mueller, *The Impact of Unemployment in the 1958 Recession,* U.S. Senate Special Committee on Unemployment Problems, 86th Cong., 2d Sess., 1960, pp. 19–20ff.

TABLE 6-4

HOURS WORKED: DEVIATIONS FOR OCCUPATION
(FOR SPENDING UNIT HEADS WHO WORKED DURING 1959)

Occupation	Number of spending unit heads	Per cent of spending unit heads	Unadjusted deviations [a]	Adjusted deviations [a]
Professionals, managers, self-employed businessmen	589	20.8	202	205
Clerical and sales workers	325	12.0	5	104
Blue collar workers	1,328	44.3	− 98	−102
Farmers	190	5.0	569	306
Not in labor force now	137	4.0	−697	−635

[a] deviations from grand mean of 2,092 hours

Long working hours sometimes result from having a second job. About one in ten heads of spending units reported second jobs. There was a wide diversity as to what kind of job the second job was. Farmers were the most likely to report a second job, and their second jobs were varied. Professionals were the next most likely to have a second job, but that job was frequently also as a professional or self-employed person.

The tendency for those with higher earning rates to work fewer hours per year is strong, but appears clearly only after adjustment for other influences.

TABLE 6-5

HOURS WORKED: DEVIATIONS FOR HOURLY EARNINGS
(FOR SPENDING UNIT HEADS WHO WORKED IN 1959)

Hourly earnings	Number of spending unit heads	Per cent of spending unit heads	Unadjusted deviations [a]	Adjusted deviations [a]
None [b]	23	0.7	−426	− 82
$0.01–0.74; negative	347	8.3	195	369
$0.75–0.99	175	5.0	− 17	228
$1.00–1.49	397	12.5	−120	84
$1.50–1.99	337	12.0	74	114
$2.00–2.99	714	26.6	5	− 52
$3.00–3.99	331	12.1	− 34	−219
$4.00–4.99	130	4.8	− 70	−269
$5.00 and over	115	4.1	2	−301

[a] deviations from grand mean of 2,092 hours
[b] worked, but had no income from it (self-employed who just covered expenses)

This difference in unadjusted deviations is only about half as great as that of the adjusted deviations, however, indicating that the unadjusted deviations understate elasticity of the demand for leisure because of other factors, such as age, education, occupation, marital status, and physical condition, which affect both wage rate and hours in the same direction.

The multivariate analysis has eliminated these other causes of spurious positive correlation between wages and hours, leaving a finding that, other things being equal, higher wages are associated with shorter hours of work. Not everything that could affect both hours and wages is included in the analysis, but the finding remains highly significant.

Several interpretations of the relation between hours and earnings are possible, and they may all be partially true: people may have target incomes or standards of living, so that if they earn less per hour, they must work longer to achieve these standards.

A more complex explanation assumes that leisure is a superior good with high-income elasticity, so that the increase in real income from the higher wage rate is partly used to purchase more leisure.

As a test of whether the results were dominated by the self-employed, female heads, or those in the process of retiring, the average hours worked

TABLE 6-6

MEAN HOURS WORKED IN 1959, WITHIN HOURLY EARNINGS
(MEANS FOR ALL SPENDING UNIT HEADS WHO WORKED AND MALE
SPENDING UNIT HEADS IN LABOR FORCE, NOT SELF-EMPLOYED)

| | Hours worked in 1959 | |
| | Spending unit heads who worked | Male spending unit heads in labor force not self-employed |
Hourly earnings		
Less than $1.00	2,180	2,275
$1.00–1.49	1,972	2,247
$1.50–1.99	2,166	2,235
$2.00–2.99	2,097	2,136
$3.00–3.99	2,058	2,069
$4.00 or more	2,055	2,060

were calculated for male spending unit heads who were not self-employed and were in the labor force at the time of the interview. These averages are shown in Table 6-6. For comparison, the means for all heads who worked in 1959 were added from column 4 of Table 6-5.

For the nonretired male heads of spending units who are not self-employed the average hours worked varies from 2,275 for those making less than $1.00 an hour to 2,060 for those making $4.00 or more per hour. This confirms the multivariate relationship.

It is not surprising to find that people who report disabilities work fewer hours. The adjustment in the hours worked by the completely disabled arises because many of these people were classified as not in the labor force now. The definitional correlation between membership in this occupation class and complete disability implies that the shorter hours worked by the completely disabled are already incorporated in the coefficient for "not in the labor force." It will be easier to keep patience with these mechanically operating relationships if the reader remembers that from the point of view of estimating the net effects of the more interesting motivational variables, it is necessary first to remove the distorting effects of other more obvious factors such as extreme age or disability.

TABLE 6-7

HOURS WORKED: DEVIATIONS FOR PHYSICAL CONDITION
(FOR SPENDING UNIT HEADS WHO WORKED IN 1959)

Physical condition	Number of spending unit heads	Per cent of spending unit heads	Unadjusted deviations [a]	Adjusted deviations [a]
Completely disabled [b]	29	0.9	−683	−292
Severely disabled	57	1.6	−630	−504
Moderately disabled	276	8.9	−145	−135
Not disabled	2,207	74.7	39	31

[a] deviations from grand mean of 2,092 hours
[b] most of these became disabled during 1959

People with plans requiring money in the future, such as plans to send children to college or to support parents, work more than those with no such plans. This is true even allowing for the higher hourly earnings of people who plan to send children to college. Of course, there could be a common cause, as when those with high energy levels work more and also take on more

TABLE 6-8

HOURS WORKED: DEVIATIONS FOR PLANS TO HELP PARENTS
OR CHILDREN
(FOR SPENDING UNIT HEADS WHO WORKED DURING 1959)

Plans to help parents or children	Number of spending unit heads	Per cent of spending unit heads	Unadjusted deviations [a]	Adjusted deviations [a]
Do not plan to send children to college or help parents	1,255	41.2	−153	−60
Plan to help parents	466	15.6	− 13	− 7
Plan to send children to college	520	17.8	187	68
Plan both to send children to college and help parents	328	11.5	277	117

[a] deviations from grand mean of 2,092 hours

responsibilities. Compared with having no plans, having plans to send children to college has twice the effect of plans to support relatives, and having both types of plans seems to have an effect roughly equal to the sum of the two independent effects.

In the case of the index of need-achievement and the attitude about the relative importance of work versus luck or help from friends, all seven differences are in the expected direction. This result is hardly likely by chance. The belief in luck leads to less work for groups with the same achievement score; the higher achievement index is associated with more work within each attitude group. The effect of the index seems to be much more powerful in the group that places reliance on luck.

It is impressive that the effect of a crudely motivational measure would show up in addition to the powerful influences of demographic factors, market conditions, and custom on hours worked. The finding raises the possibility that differences in achievement motivation may affect economic progress of countries through the behavior of the masses.

TABLE 6-9

HOURS WORKED: DEVIATIONS FOR ATTITUDE TOWARD HARD WORK
AND NEED-ACHIEVEMENT SCORE
(FOR SPENDING UNIT HEADS WHO WORKED DURING 1959)

Attitude toward hard work and need-achievement score	Number of spending unit heads	Per cent of spending unit heads	Unadjusted deviations [a]	Adjusted deviations [a]
Hard work is more important than luck; need-achievement scores are in:				
high range	631	22.3	28	28
middle range	921	31.4	39	25
low range	440	14.2	10	− 29
Hard work is less important than luck; need-achievement scores are in:				
high range	120	3.9	0	18
middle range	228	7.3	−151	− 72
low range	139	4.0	−231	−181
Need-achievement scores not ascertained	90	3.0	22	73

[a] deviations from grand mean of 2,092 hours

The substantial adjustment in the coefficient for the Catholics who seldom attend church results from the fact that nearly two thirds of them have less than a high school education, and a comparatively large proportion of them are single males. The whole classification by religion and attendance, however, is not statistically significant, and can only be regarded as suggestive.

Although the differences are mostly within sampling error, the hourly earnings and hours worked of Catholics fall between those of the two Protestant groups both as to wage rates and as to hours worked. However, the pattern according to frequency of church attendance is different for the different religious groups, and also between wage rates and hours. Regularity of attendance seems to be associated with lower wages and shorter hours for Catholics, and with higher wages but shorter hours among Protestants.

On the other hand, a recent national survey found that Protestants reported

TABLE 6-10

HOURS WORKED: DEVIATIONS FOR RELIGIOUS PREFERENCE
AND CHURCH ATTENDANCE
(FOR SPENDING UNIT HEADS WHO WORKED IN 1959)

Religious preference and church attendance	Number of spending unit heads	Per cent of spending unit heads	Unadjusted deviations [a]	Adjusted deviations [a]
Catholics:				
attend more than once a month	433	15.4	− 1	− 3
attend once a month or less	112	4.0	−56	32
Fundamentalist Protestants:				
attend more than once a month	502	15.3	−38	−44
attend once a month or less	381	12.1	−66	−35
Non-Fundamentalist Protestants:				
attend more than once a month	463	15.7	29	− 6
attend once a month or less	516	17.9	96	86
Non-Christians; not ascertained	162	5.7	−98	−77

[a] deviations from grand mean of 2,092 hours

greater job satisfaction and also more problems on the job than Catholics, indicating that they were more involved with their work.[4] The same study found for all religious groups that those who reported more frequent church attendance also reported greater job satisfaction. The study presented here is not primarily concerned with the interrelationships between religion and motivation, however, and much further work remains to be done.

The effects of religious preference might, of course, work through the other variables used in the analysis, but even the unadjusted coefficients do not fit any simple hypothesis about the Protestant ethic, nor does the relation between religious preference and the index of achievement motivation. Catholics tend to be between the two main Protestant groups on the measure of need-achievement.

A more detailed study of the achievement motive on a national sample, using a more elaborate thematic apperception test measure of need-achievement, found the Catholics generally higher than the average for all Protestants on need-achievement except among upper-income groups in the Northeast.[5] Early studies by Rosen comparing religious and ethnic groups had been done among upper income groups in the Northeast, hence will require qualification.[6]

It is clear that nonwhite heads of spending units worked fewer hours in 1959 than whites, even after a substantial adjustment of the gross effects to account for the other factors such as the larger fraction of single adults with children among Negroes. The remaining difference in the adjusted residuals

[4] Gerald Gurin and others, *Americans View Their Mental Health* (New York: Basic Books, 1960), p. 244.

[5] Joseph Veroff and others, *American Sociological Review,* 27, 205–217.

[6] Bernard Rosen, *American Sociological Review,* 24, 47–60.

is probably largely explained by the differential impact of unemployment and the restricted job opportunities open to Negroes. Only if such things were accurately measured in the analysis would any motivational interpretations be feasible. The effect of race is statistically significant, though its measure of importance is smaller than that of religion.

TABLE 6-11

HOURS WORKED: DEVIATIONS FOR RACE
(FOR SPENDING UNIT HEADS WHO WORKED DURING 1959)

Race	Number of spending unit heads	Per cent of spending unit heads	Unadjusted deviations [a]	Adjusted deviations [a]
White	2,220	77.4	22	12
Nonwhite	349	8.7	−198	−104

[a] deviations from grand mean of 2,092 hours

The factors in the next three tables are not statistically significant, although they produce differences in the expected directions.

In states where unemployment was severe in 1958, spending unit heads were more likely to work shorter hours in 1959. Hourly earnings were higher in these states, perhaps as payment for the greater risk of unemployment or the result of advanced industrialization.

TABLE 6-12

HOURS WORKED: DEVIATIONS FOR EXTENT OF UNEMPLOYMENT
IN STATES
(FOR SPENDING UNIT HEADS WHO WORKED DURING 1959)

Extent of 1958 unemployment in states	Number of spending unit heads	Per cent of spending unit heads	Unadjusted deviations [a]	Adjusted deviations [a]
Under 5.00 per cent	563	17.8	56	9
5.00–6.49 per cent	878	28.8	6	10
6.50–7.49 per cent	554	19.8	−21	11
7.50–9.99 per cent	326	10.8	8	− 1
10.00 per cent and over	248	8.9	−95	−73

[a] deviations from grand mean of 2,092 hours

The most startling thing about the classification of differences in education between heads and wives is the extent to which spurious gross relationships with the head's hours were removed by the multivariate analysis.

The group of single spending unit heads was also the same as those in the first four groups in the most important predictor: adult unit composition. The added distinctions of sex of the head and presence of dependents appar-

TABLE 6-13

HOURS WORKED: DEVIATIONS FOR DIFFERENCE IN EDUCATION
OF HEADS AND WIVES
(FOR SPENDING UNIT HEADS WHO WORKED DURING 1959)

Difference in education of heads and wives [a]	Number of spending unit heads	Per cent of spending unit heads	Unadjusted deviations [b]	Adjusted deviations [b]
Wives have two or more levels more than heads	215	7.4	100	2
Wives have one level more than heads	343	11.3	147	16
Wives have the same level as heads	731	24.1	95	− 3
Wives have one level less than heads	320	11.3	107	−45
Wives have two or more levels less than heads	289	10.2	186	− 1
Education of wives not ascertained	13	0.4	−186	−33
Unmarried spending unit heads	658	21.4	−360	20

[a] levels of education are:

none	12 grades and nonacademic training
1–8 grades	college, no degree
9–11 grades	college, bachelor's degree
12 grades	college, advanced degree

[b] deviations from grand mean of 2,092 hours

TABLE 6-14

HOURS WORKED: DEVIATIONS FOR IMMIGRATION OF HEADS
AND FATHERS
(FOR SPENDING UNIT HEADS WHO WORKED IN 1959)

Immigration of spending unit heads and fathers	Number of spending unit heads	Per cent of spending unit heads	Unadjusted deviations [a]	Adjusted deviations [a]
Heads and fathers grew up in the United States	2,084	68.8	− 2	−3
Heads grew up in the United States; fathers grew up in foreign countries	372	13.2	42	−6
Heads and fathers grew up in foreign countries	113	4.1	−99	66

[a] deviations from grand mean of 2,092 hours

ently explained the fewer hours worked by unmarried heads. Conversely, where the head was married, that status accounted for the added hours worked. The original hypothesis, that the higher standards set by a wife with more education would force the head to work longer to meet those standards, is not proven, though the differences in the adjusted coefficients are in that direction.

TABLE 6-15

HOURS WORKED IN 1959 WITHIN EDUCATION AND AGE
(FOR SPENDING UNIT HEADS AGED 25–64 WHO WORKED IN 1959)

Hours worked in 1959	Education and Age			
	0–11 grades	12 grades	12 grades and some college or nonacademic training	College degree
			25–34	
Under 950	6	1	2	6
950–1,849	19	14	9	20
1,850–2,149	38	40	56	34
2,150–2,549	16	23	14	20
2,550–3,149	14	14	14	12
3,150 or more	7	8	5	8
Total	100	100	100	100
Number of spending unit heads	251	97	142	81
			35–44	
Under 950	5	5	0	0
950–1,849	20	10	9	11
1,850–2,149	35	48	38	44
2,150–2,549	17	13	23	16
2,550–3,149	16	20	20	20
3,150 or more	7	4	10	9
Total	100	100	100	100
Number of spending unit heads	297	129	139	82
			45–54	
Under 950	5	7	3	2
950–1,849	21	9	10	15
1,850–2,149	41	45	46	50
2,150–2,549	12	10	19	13
2,550–3,149	14	21	14	16
3,150 or more	7	8	8	4
Total	100	100	100	100
Number of spending unit heads	332	78	99	53
			55–64	
Under 950	11	5	15	2
950–1,849	22	33	9	18
1,850–2,149	40	37	42	27
2,150–2,549	15	18	16	24
2,550–3,149	9	7	11	19
3,150 or more	3	0	7	10
Total	100	100	100	100
Number of spending unit heads	269	32	93	39

There may be two reasons why the net effect is small. Differences in education between head and wife are negatively correlated with the head's education, that is, when the wife had two levels more, the husband probably did not graduate from high school. A wife with more education may have higher standards of living, but is also likely to go to work herself to achieve them. This pattern appears in the analysis of whether the wife worked (Chapter 9) but the relationship is not statistically significant. The fact that pressures for more income can lead either to the head's working longer hours, or to the wife's working, is a general problem, but it is particularly acute when the motivating factor, the wife's better education, also facilitates a solution through the wife's work.

The spending unit heads who grew up in foreign countries worked longer hours, as expected, although not significantly so. Their unadjusted hours were less than average, but adjustments for the facts that they are generally older, more likely to be in manual occupations, at both extremes on the educational scale, and more than twice as likely to be Catholic or non-Christian, reveal that they actually work more than one would expect.

Multivariate analysis has required concentration on averages of hours worked. The distribution of hours, for two of the more important characteristics of the analysis—age and education—are shown in Table 6-15.

In every age-education group, the largest proportion works a standard full year. The differences that have been explained are largely the result of differing proportions who work less than a full year or more than a full year. The short hours are more likely to be involuntary than are the above-average ones.

The effect of age and education through the three multivariate analyses of spending unit heads' earnings is summarized in Table 6-16. Annual earnings for each age and education group are estimated by combining the adjusted deviations for the probability of working, the wage rate, and the number of hours worked.

TABLE 6-16

ESTIMATED ANNUAL EARNINGS [a] WITHIN AGE AND EDUCATION
(FOR SPENDING UNIT HEADS)

Education	Under 35	35–44	45–54	55 and older
0–11 grades	$3,882	$4,512	$4,497	$2,570
12 grades	4,177	5,546	5,404	2,755
12 grades and nonacademic training or some college	3,857	5,456	5,712	3,234
College degree	3,754	6,557	7,303	4,759

[a] Estimated by combining adjusted deviations for probability of working, wage rate, and hours worked. These estimates are free of effects of differences in the other factors used in the multivariate analyses. The averages are for all spending unit heads, including those who did not work in 1959.

Summary

The hours worked by the spending unit head are affected both by mechanical characteristics such as having dependents to care for or being disabled, and by motivational factors such as plans to help children or the parents, need-achievement index and attitude toward hard work, and hourly earnings. From the economist's point of view the most interesting finding is the strong negative relation between the wage reward or price of leisure and the number of hours worked. Perhaps there is something to the notion that people take some of their increased income in the form of leisure.

Chapter 7

CAPITAL INCOME

Capital income is a return on investments in financial and physical assets. The average spending unit received $278 in interest, dividends, rent, and other returns on monetary investments, and another $435 as an imputed return on investment in an owner-operated farm, or business, or an owner-occupied home, for a total of $713 capital income. The imputed income was estimated by taking 6 per cent of the unit's equity in its home, farm, or business. In the case of a farm or business, the remaining income, positive or negative, was taken as a return to labor.

Capital tends to be accumulated over the working life of a spending unit. Moreover, a longer span of life provides more exposure to the possibility of inheriting capital. This effect is so strong that it appears even in a cross-section, where the younger people receive much higher incomes when they were at equivalent ages. Table 7-1 shows this pattern.

Since monetary and real capital are close substitutes for one another, this analysis deals only with total capital income. It is useful to keep in mind, however, that the bulk of capital income is primarily a return on investment in owner-occupied homes. Only a small fraction of spending units own businesses or farms or substantial stock equities and bonds. Only among spending units with heads sixty-five and older is the money return from investments greater than the imputed return. Pensions and annuities of retired persons are not included. They were treated as transfer income rather than capital income.

Capital income is not the result of current decisions in the way current wage income is, but results from a series of past decisions and events. The multivariate analysis of capital income employs variables describing some of the decisions and events that affect the unit's past ability to accumulate capital.

Assets may have been inherited. The amount inherited is used as an explanatory factor regardless of when the inheritance took place. This ignores earnings and capital appreciation possible if the money was invested. An inheritance received in 1920, which might have tripled in size through investment, is treated the same as one received in 1958. Conversely, the 1920 inheritance might have been spent, leaving nothing. Since inheritances are used as an explanatory factor, the other factors can be thought of as explaining income from capital accumulated through the spending unit's own efforts to save.

Taken as an indication of earning ability, more education means greater past income and increases possible savings. Also, education is an explanatory factor with possible motivational implications. People with more education may plan more and accumulate capital more effectively.

Emergencies such as extended unemployment can wipe out a family's savings, so one explanatory factor used is the head's employment experience during the previous five years.

TABLE 7-1

MEAN REAL CAPITAL INCOME AND ITS TWO MAIN COMPONENTS,
WITHIN AGE OF HEADS
(FOR SPENDING UNITS)

Age of heads	Number of spending units	Mean amount of money income (interest, dividends, rent)	Mean imputed income (return on investment in farm, business, or own home)	Mean real capital income
Under 25	264	$ 12	$ 24	$ 36
25–34	586	53	203	256
35–44	672	182	478	660
45–54	594	298	663	961
55–64	484	516	619	1,135
65 and older	397	615	449	1,064
All	2,997	$278	$435	$ 713

Age is included because older people have had more years over which to accumulate capital and financial assets, and are more likely to have inherited assets.

Some families are in financial difficulties from the beginning and never have an easy period during which they can accumulate assets. As one indicator of this, the age of head at the birth of his first child is used. If the children began arriving before the family could accumulate household goods and some savings, the financial pressures might have prevented accumulating any capital. If there had been an extended period without children during which both head and wife could work, substantial savings might have been possible.

The multivariate analysis accounted for 19 per cent of the variance in capital incomes. Table 7-2 gives the relative importance and the significance of each predictor used in the analysis.

Mean capital income for a spending unit was $713. However, the standard deviation was $1,581, indicating extreme skewness.

TABLE 7-2

CHARACTERISTICS USED TO EXPLAIN REAL CAPITAL INCOME
(FOR SPENDING UNITS)

Characteristics of spending units heads	Relative importance (Beta coefficients)	Significance (F ratios)
Recent unemployment experience	.249	76.58**
Amount inherited by spending units	.221	25.88**
Age	.173	18.48**
Education	.169	15.12**
Age at the birth of first child	.072	3.20**

** significant at probability level of .01

Despite the fact that recent unemployment experience was the most important variable in the analysis, there seems to be little ground for the assumption that unemployment experience is associated with low capital income. Differences between the groups which have and have not experienced unemployment are rather slight. The effect of this variable is due almost entirely to the residual category, "not employed by others," which includes self-employed businessmen and farmers, as well as retired persons.

TABLE 7-3

REAL CAPITAL INCOME: DEVIATIONS FOR RECENT
UNEMPLOYMENT EXPERIENCE OF HEADS
(FOR SPENDING UNITS)

Recent unemployment experience of heads	Number of spending units	Per cent of spending units	Unadjusted deviations [a]	Adjusted deviations [a]
Unemployed now	151	4.3	$-462	$-343
Employed now:				
unemployed during last five years	381	12.9	-503	-318
not unemployed during last five years	1,428	50.0	-255	-257
Not employed by others: self-employed businessmen, farmers, retired persons, and others not in the labor force	1,037	32.8	602	562

[a] deviations from grand mean of $713

Since most retired persons are sixty-five or older, and have had a longer time over which to accumulate assets, they are more likely to have large capital incomes. Forty per cent of spending unit heads in the category, "not employed by others," are sixty-five or older, compared with 15 per cent of the total sample. Nearly 90 per cent of persons over sixty-five are not in the labor force. The inclusion of these persons in the group, "not employed by others," may account for some of the adjustments in the coefficients for age for persons over sixty-five.

The major effect of this variable comes from the self-employed business-men and farmers. By definition these persons have some capital invested in their businesses or farms. Capital income was imputed on the basis of their own estimates of their net capital investment. Capital income of these groups may have been exaggerated somewhat by an imperfect allowance for business or farm debt in estimating capital investment, or by the assumption of a 6 per cent return on invested capital. However, it is reasonable to expect that self-employed persons have more capital income than do those who are employed by others. The fact that adjustments for the other factors like age are small suggests that there is a real effect of self-employment on capital

TABLE 7-4

REAL CAPITAL INCOME: DEVIATIONS FOR AMOUNT INHERITED
(FOR SPENDING UNITS)

Amount inherited by spending units	Number of spending units	Per cent of spending units	Unadjusted deviations [a]	Adjusted deviations [a]
None	2,418	80.4	$-162	$- 99
$1–449	77	2.5	- 60	-168
$450–949	46	1.6	-106	-122
$950–4,949	201	6.8	564	358
$4,950–9,949	99	3.4	852	516
$9,950–24,949	67	2.3	1,226	699
$24,950 or more	28	1.0	3,521	2,899
Not ascertained	61	2.0	201	- 22

[a] deviations from grand mean of $713

income. Other data show that the self-employed, particularly business owners, have a much higher propensity to save.[1]

Inheritance clearly accounts for some major differences in capital income, even though only a fifth of the spending units report having received any inheritance. While it is precarious to make estimates of aggregates or shares from small sample data, it is clear that a substantial share of aggregate capital income can be attributed to inheritances. Since an inheritance often includes real property such as housing, a considerable share of the capital income produced by inheritances may be imputed rental income.

Advancing age allows time to accumulate capital assets and increased rights to capital income. The dramatic adjustments which occur as a result of the other predictors result largely from the fact that older people also are more likely to have received inheritances. The proportion who have received

[1] See James N. Morgan, "The Structure of Aggregate Saving," *Journal of Political Economy,* 56 (December, 1951), 528–534.

an inheritance increases from 8 per cent of the youngest groups to 41 per cent of the oldest group. The downward adjustments for the aged, and the previous downward adjustments for those with inheritances, represent the removal of the spurious elements or correlation from these two related predictors. The aged are also included in the subgroup "not employed by others" of the variable describing unemployment experience. The adjustments for being over sixty-five must be considered in combination with the large positive deviation for the retired that is shown in Table 7-3.

TABLE 7-5

REAL CAPITAL INCOME: DEVIATIONS FOR AGE OF HEADS
(FOR SPENDING UNITS)

Age of heads	Number of spending units	Per cent of spending units	Unadjusted deviations [a]	Adjusted deviations [a]
Under 25	264	8.9	$-671	$-456
25–34	586	19.5	−455	−284
35–44	672	22.5	− 49	− 20
45–54	594	19.2	239	293
55–64	484	15.3	405	323
65–74	269	9.9	497	124
75 and older	128	4.7	44	−376

[a] deviations from grand mean of $713

The powerful association between education and capital income probably results both from the higher income earned by those with more education and from the tendency for the more highly educated to do more planning and take more thought for the future.

TABLE 7-6

REAL CAPITAL INCOME: DEVIATIONS FOR EDUCATION OF HEADS
(FOR SPENDING UNITS)

Education of heads	Number of spending units	Per cent of spending units	Unadjusted deviations [a]	Adjusted deviations [a]
None	56	1.5	$-451	$-708
1–8 grades	972	29.9	−148	−293
9–11 grades	615	21.1	− 89	27
12 grades	451	15.7	− 9	144
12 grades plus nonacademic training	263	9.4	− 64	− 16
College, no degree	340	11.9	153	191
College, bachelor's degree	225	7.9	370	308
College, advanced degree	75	2.6	1,144	936

[a] deviations from grand mean of $713

The difference between the adjusted and unadjusted coefficients results from correlations of education with age and with inheritances. (See Table 7-7.) Adjustment for their generally advanced ages lowers the capital income estimate for those with little education. Likewise, their higher probability of having received inheritances lowers the estimate for those with college degrees.

TABLE 7-7

AGE OF HEADS AND INHERITANCES WITHIN EDUCATION OF HEADS
(FOR SPENDING UNITS)

Education of heads	Per cent of spending unit heads who are 55 and older	Per cent of spending units who received inheritances	Per cent of spending units who inherited $9,950 or more
None	76	7	0
1–8 grades	49	18	2
9–11 grades	24	16	2
12 grades	15	16	2
12 grades plus nonacademic training	17	25	5
College, no degree	22	25	5
College, bachelor's degree	21	27	9
College, advanced degree	26	33	14

TABLE 7-8

REAL CAPITAL INCOME: DEVIATIONS FOR AGE OF HEADS
AT BIRTH OF FIRST CHILD
(FOR SPENDING UNITS)

Age of heads at birth of first child	Number of spending units	Per cent of spending units	Unadjusted deviations [a]	Adjusted deviations [a]
No children	751	25.7	$−144	$−100
Under 18	67	1.7	−457	−398
18–19	143	4.3	−481	−225
20–24	814	26.7	−131	− 7
25–29	665	22.8	157	122
30–39	488	16.5	373	109
40 or older	69	2.3	119	− 83

[a] Deviations from grand mean of $713

The last, and least powerful predictor of capital income is a classification according to the age of the head of the spending unit at the time his first child was born. The data seem to confirm the hypothesis that early arrival of children is associated with less accumulation of capital by the family, even when adjustments are made for differences in age, education, inheritances, and unemployment experience.

It may be that there are other intergenerational differences which cannot be assessed in a single cross-section survey. For instance, earlier marriage and earlier ages at the arrival of the first child may change the pattern of life-time accumulation so that most accumulation occurs after the children have grown up and left home. In a former generation early arrival of children may have meant lack of planning, hardship, and difficulty in getting ahead in the world; more recently it may have been purposive, subsidized by the parents of the young family or by the GI Bill, and made possible by prosperous times and high early salaries. Within the group who had their first child early, there may be some older people for whom this was a real handicap, and some younger people for whom it will not be.

The over-all impact of capital income on the distribution of income in a cross-section is of two contradictory sorts. Older people and farmers have substantial capital incomes. Both groups have relatively low total incomes. Thus, for the entire cross-section the lower the total income below $5,000, the larger fraction of it tends to be from capital. Above $5,000 the tendency of higher income people to accumulate capital leads to a situation where capital income is also a larger proportion of total income among the very high income spending units.

Capital Income and Achievement Motivation

A crucial motivational variable was omitted from the multivariate analysis of capital income: the index of achievement motivation. Leaving out farmers and self-employed businessmen, who have a special requirement to accumulate capital and for whom the estimate of capital income is rather tenuous, the remaining spending units were divided into groups according to their age and education. Each age-education group has had a different income level and a different span of years during which to accumulate capital. Table 7-9 shows that within each group, however, there is a strong relationship between need-achievement score and capital income.

Could this be spurious? It is doubtful that substantial correlations of both need-achievement and capital income with age or education remain. It is possible that the causation goes the other way. Success, indicated by large capital income, might make a man more sensitive to differences between different occupations, and make success more salient in evaluating them. It is even possible, though the personality theory denies it, that basic person-ality dispositions can be changed by the experience of success or failure. The correlation remains interesting, and certainly one possible explanation is that individuals high in achievement motivation accumulate more capital.

Summary

The accumulation of capital is a vital part of the process of providing for retirement, for education of children, for emergencies, and for upward mobility.

TABLE 7-9

MEAN CAPITAL INCOME WITHIN OCCUPATION, AGE, EDUCATION, AND NEED-ACHIEVEMENT SCORES OF HEADS (FOR SPENDING UNITS)

| Need-achievement scores | Retired | Not farmers, self-employed businessmen or retired | | | | | | Nonretired farmers | Nonretired self-employed businessmen |
| | | 18-34 | | | 35 or older | | | | |
		0-11 grades	12 grades	Some college	0-11 grades	12 grades	Some college		
High range	$1,587 (65)	$110 (71)	$117 (80)	$249 (100)	$553 (206)	$691 (106)	$1,415 (120)	$1,835 (35)	$2,280 (63)
Middle range	1,217 (145)	90 (142)	118 (110)	182 (92)	461 (405)	664 (169)	1,094 (118)	1,928 (84)	1,729 (75)
Low range	950 (66)	79 (94)	100 (47)	147 (35)	402 (246)	514 (59)	761 (39)	1,784 (68)	1,590 (35)
All [a]	$1,197 (303)	$ 89 (318)	$113 (240)	$204 (232)	$459 (892)	$648 (341)	$1,170 (295)	$1,897 (192)	$1,937 (184)

[a] includes those for whom need-achievement score was not ascertained
( ) number of cases

Capital accumulations and therefore capital income are related to inheritances, and even taking inheritances into account are related to the age and education of the head of the spending unit, whether he is a self-employed farmer or businessman, and his age at the time his first child was born. Finally, within nonentrepreneurial groups according to age and education, there is a strong relation between an index of achievement motivation and capital income.

Chapter 8

HOME PRODUCTION AS A SOURCE OF INCOME

The income from capital, explained in Chapter 7, contained some nonmoney income in the form of imputed return on investments in one's own home. This chapter deals with another major nonmoney component of earned income: the value of the labor put into productive use around the home.[1]

As in the national income estimates, a measure of the net value of home-grown food was attempted. An estimate of the net value of home improvements done by occupants is also included. The measure excludes, just as national accounts do, estimates of the value of the housekeeping and child care functions of the housewife. These services have recently been valued at $3,000 a year, so they are not negligible.[2]

Two types of home production were valued in this study: home-grown food and home additions and repairs done by the unit itself. Income from these activities was estimated by asking people how much money they felt they had saved by doing the work themselves. In this way it was possible to avoid estimates that included the cost of materials, or activities which were not really productive. A broad definition of production as a creation of utility might include growing roses as well as growing radishes. On the other hand, the main purpose was to achieve some comparability between spending units, and for this purpose the crucial home production is that which is a substitute for something which would otherwise have to be purchased.

Some 50 per cent of spending units reported saving something by growing their own food or making additions or repairs on their own houses. On the average these spending units reported that they saved $370 in 1959.

[1] A German study of farmers and agricultural workers relied upon amounts of home produce, multiplied by a fraction of their market price. See Peter Deneffe and Margot Englemann, "Die Lebenshaltung von Bauern und Landarbeitern," *Wirtschaft und Statistik* (Stuttgart, Statistisches Bundesamt) NS 9 (Ocober, 1957), 514–521.

[2] Marie G. Gage, The Work Load and Its Value for 50 Homemakers in Tompkins County, New York (unpublished Ph.D. dissertation, Cornell University, 1960).

The factors affecting the value of home production fall into three groups representing the ability and opportunity, the desire or motivation, and opportunity costs of alternatives.

Seven predicting characteristics were used to measure some dimensions of *ability* to work around the home. Hours worked by the head provide an index of the hours left for work at home, and of the marginal utility of the leisure that home production would absorb. Hours worked by wives were not included since the model places them later in the sequence of income determination.

Adult unit composition indicates whether there are two adults present and whether there are also children to be taken care of. The presence of children may facilitate home production by keeping an adult home and by increasing motivation. Where there is a single adult, a man may find it easier to repair the house than a woman would.

The age and physical condition of the head indicate something about his physical stamina.

The head's occupation should affect his ability and energy for home work. If he does heavy physical work all day he may not want to re-roof his house evenings and weekends, though he may do it because of other financial pressures. These influences may be in addition to the time demands of his occupation which have already been indicated by hours worked. Alternatively, persons who do skilled manual work may have more of the skills requisite for doing work at home.

The range of possible productive activities around the home may depend on the ability of the head to devise and carry out do-it-yourself projects himself. Education may be a help in this; therefore, education level was included.

Population of city tests the hypothesis that living in a small town or in the open country may provide more opportunity for growing one's own food, as compared with living in the city. This is not an optimal classification, however, since it does not take into account the distance of the local community from the nearest large metropolitan area.

Another set of characteristics describes the motivation of the spending unit to save money by doing things around the house. Population of city, in addition to providing opportunity differences, may also represent differences in the local culture and tradition that make it respectable and expected behavior to grow food, do home canning, or repair one's own house. Also in small towns or open country, there may be no one else available to repair the house. Similarly, regional differences in the social expectations may affect home production.

The presence of a large family, indicated by adult unit composition, may induce money-saving activities because of financial pressures.

The combination of a high need-achievement score and the belief in hard work as a path to success should lead to more home production.

Whether a person owns his own home or rents affects his willingness to invest his time and material costs in home improvement.

Thirdly, there are classifications which indicate barriers to working around the house in the form of opportunity costs, that is alternative, more profitable uses of time. The head's wage rate is the best measure of what he might earn if he spent more time at his major occupation where his comparative advantage is greatest. Not everyone can find extra work, of course, and not all extra work pays the wage rate of the regular job.

The occupation of the head is related to opportunities to get ahead professionally or earn more money by putting in more time on the job rather than painting the house. Farmers and self-employed businessmen have clear possibilities, whereas white collar workers may have few chances to work more hours.

Population of cities may indicate variations in the availability of extra jobs. Larger cities should offer a wider range of extra jobs which compete with home production. If there is less home production in larger cities, it may be because of more alternative job opportunities, or fewer opportunities for home production, or less local cultural and traditional inspiration for doing it oneself.

Table 8-1 gives the measures of importance and significance for the 10 explanatory classifications.

TABLE 8-1

CHARACTERISTICS USED TO EXPLAIN MONEY SAVED
BY HOME PRODUCTION
(FOR SPENDING UNITS)

Characteristics of spending unit heads	Relative Importance (Beta coefficients)	Significance (F ratios)
Housing status	.201	66.12**
Adult unit composition	.123	7.07**
Population of cities	.098	6.29**
Hourly earnings	.090	a
Education	.077	2.77**
Region	.068	5.05**
Hours worked per week	.054	a
Age	.052	1.48
Occupation	.038	1.18
Attitude toward hard work and need-achievement score	.033	0.59

** significant at probability level of .01

a The adjusted coefficients of these two characteristics did not converge for heads who did not work in 1959. In a regression computation the standard errors of the coefficients for the dummy variable representing these two subclasses would have been very large.

The mean amount saved by home production for all spending units was $182 with a standard deviation of $404, indicating extreme skewness. The 10 characteristics accounted for 10 per cent of the variance. This results in part from the irregularity of home additions and repairs; they are not made every year. An estimate of home production over a longer period of time would have been more stable, but subject to greater memory errors. The fact that only 10 per cent of the variance was explained also suggests that there are other important determinants of this kind of activity which were not measured or used. Thirty-seven spending units were excluded from the analysis because the amount of their home production was not ascertained.

People who own their own homes save more money by doing home additions or repairs themselves, or by growing some of their own food. Nearly two-thirds of all home owners saved something by home production, as compared with one-third of nonowners. Home owners who saved something report savings that average $428, compared to $178 for renters, and $327 for those who neither own nor rent, mostly related secondary units and tenant farmers. The differences probably arise from the fact that home owners are more likely to want to invest their own time and money in improving their homes and are also more likely to have plots available for growing food.

TABLE 8-2

MONEY SAVED BY HOME PRODUCTION: DEVIATIONS
FOR HOUSING STATUS
(FOR SPENDING UNITS)

Housing status	Number of spending units	Per cent of spending units	Unadjusted deviations [a]	Adjusted deviations [a]
Own homes	1,657	56.5	87	70
Pay rent	962	32.1	−122	−102
Neither own nor rent	341	10.4	− 94	− 64

[a] deviations from grand mean of $182

Married couples with children save most through home production. Even after adjusting for their tendency not to own a home, single men without children engage in less home production than would be expected. Single females do less, even if they have children.

In the smaller towns and rural areas, it was assumed that more space would be available for gardening, and that fewer specialists in home additions and repairs would be available. The results shown in Table 8-4 confirm the expectations, except for the urban places of 2,500–9,999. Perhaps these are areas where nearby farms provide both cheap food and cheap labor for making home repairs. Alternatively, many such towns are located within the confines of metropolitan areas and thus do not differ from the large central cities.

Another consideration in deciding whether to engage in home improvement work or hire someone else to do it is the fact that when income is earned

TABLE 8-3

MONEY SAVED BY HOME PRODUCTION: DEVIATIONS FOR COMPOSITION
OF HEADS' ADULT UNITS
(FOR SPENDING UNITS)

Composition of heads' adult units	Number of spending units	Per cent of spending units	Unadjusted deviations [a]	Adjusted deviations [a]
Unmarried male heads of spending units:				
no children under 18	308	10.4	$-110	$-57
children under 18	18	0.6	49	95
Unmarried female heads of spending units:				
no children under 18	441	14.4	-138	-80
children under 18	165	4.6	- 93	-42
Married heads of spending units:				
no children under 18	743	26.2	9	- 2
1 child under 18	370	13.0	35	15
2 children under 18	399	13.6	76	47
3 or children under 18	516	16.2	112	68

[a] deviations from grand mean of $182

by the homeowner at his job and paid to the painter, both the painter and the
homeowner must pay income taxes on their earnings. Since they each are taxed
at a rate of at least 20 per cent, approximately 40 per cent of the home-
owner's earnings go for taxes. If he does the work himself, the real income
which he earns is not taxed at all.

The higher wage a man can earn, the more one might expect him to work
for that wage and pay others for his food and home repairs. Yet the reverse

TABLE 8-4

MONEY SAVED BY HOME PRODUCTION: DEVIATIONS
FOR POPULATION OF CITIES
(FOR SPENDING UNITS)

Population of cities	Number of spending units	Per cent of spending units	Unadjusted deviations [a]	Adjusted deviations [a]
Central cities of the 12 largest standard metropolitan areas	398	14.1	$-78	$-46
Cities 50,000 and over, exclusive of the central cities of the 12 largest standard metroplitan areas	545	19.5	-52	-21
Urban places 10,000–49,999	359	11.9	- 4	16
Urban places 2,500–9,999; urbanized places not included in above codes	562	19.1	-16	-33
Rural areas near cities	409	14.3	56	12
Rural areas not near cities	687	20.1	83	67

[a] deviations from grand mean of $182

effect appears. The most home production takes place in spending units whose heads command the higher hourly wage rates. Adjustments for education, sex, and age reduce the effect somewhat but do not eliminate it. Apparently those most in need of this extra income are least likely to produce it. The same people who earn high wages apparently also supplement them more with home production.

TABLE 8-5

MONEY SAVED BY HOME PRODUCTION: DEVIATIONS FOR HOURLY
EARNINGS OF HEADS
(FOR SPENDING UNITS)

Hourly earnings of heads	Number of spending units	Per cent of spending units	Unadjusted deviations [a]	Adjusted deviations [a]
None	448	14.5	$-72	$-70[b]
$0.01–0.74; negative	331	7.9	− 7	−17
$0.75–0.99	170	4.8	−40	3
$1.00–1.49	394	12.5	−29	15
$1.50–1.99	335	11.9	−22	1
$2.00–2.99	710	26.5	16	5
$3.00–3.99	327	12.0	61	28
$4.00–4.99	130	4.8	130	98
$5.00 and over	115	4.1	38	7

[a] deviations from grand mean of $182
[b] Because the spending unit heads who have no earnings also have no hours worked (Table 8-8) the coefficients for these two categories did not converge. The net effect of not working is to decrease home production by $27 (−$70 + $43).

People with college degrees produce less at home; those who went beyond high school but did not finish college do the most. Those with nonacademic training beyond high school are more likely to have training and skills necessary for home improvement work. Those with some college but no degree, might have ambitions to raise their standards of living beyond what their incomes allow.

By the nature of the multistage sample used, sampling errors for regional estimates are larger than other sampling errors, that is, more affected by clustering of the sample. Hence the regional differences may well be a chance phenomenon. It is possible that the high level of home production in the Northeast might result from a mixture of the following: no large supply of very cheap labor one can hire for work around the house, high prices for produce because of the nearness of metropolitan markets, a tradition of self-reliance, and perhaps fewer second jobs for those who might prefer to earn more money and purchase the food or home improvements.

The South differs radically in most of these respects: cheap labor and lower food prices. The Midwest perhaps offers more employment opportunities for second jobs, and jobs for wives, to compete with home production,

TABLE 8-6

MONEY SAVED BY HOME PRODUCTION: DEVIATIONS
FOR EDUCATION OF HEADS
(FOR SPENDING UNITS)

Education of heads	Number of spending units	Per cent of spending units	Unadjusted deviations [a]	Adjusted deviations [a]
None	55	1.5	$−112	$−17
1–8 grades	955	29.5	− 10	− 2
9-11 grades	606	20.8	4	− 5
12 grades	445	15.6	− 8	−10
12 grades plus nonacademic training	262	9.4	67	62
College, no degree	338	11.8	23	33
College, bachelor's degree	224	7.8	− 34	−48
College, advanced degree	75	2.6	− 50	−98

[a] deviations from grand mean of $182

TABLE 8-7

MONEY SAVED BY HOME PRODUCTION: DEVIATIONS FOR REGION
(FOR SPENDING UNITS)

Region	Number of spending units	Per cent of spending units	Unadjusted deviations [a]	Adjusted deviations [a]
Northeast	635	23.0	$ 11	$ 42
North Central	849	29.2	0	− 9
South	1,030	31.4	−15	−30
West	446	15.4	13	15

[a] deviations from grand mean of $182

but the next classification throws some doubt on the hypothesis that employment hours and home production compete.

Ignoring the group which did not work at all, there is some tendency for those who work longer hours to engage in more home production as well; the result is not significant but fits with other impressions of the complementary relationship between home production and other economic activity.

A sizable proportion of the persons who work the longest hours are farmers: 13 per cent of people who worked more than forty-eight hours a week and 17 per cent of those who worked sixty hours or more, are classified as farmers, tenant farmers, or sharecroppers. For these people growing their own food involves the use of some of their job skills, and may be a part of the regular work routine, rather than an additional activity as it is for non-farm families. Also, farm families are more likely to have land available for food production than are most nonfarm families.

While the effect is not clearly significant, the two age groups with more home production than expected are the young families and those who have

TABLE 8-8

MONEY SAVED BY HOME PRODUCTION: DEVIATIONS
FOR HOURS WORKED PER WEEK BY HEADS
(FOR SPENDING UNITS)

Hours worked per week by heads	Number of spending units	Per cent of spending units	Unadjusted deviations [a]	Adjusted deviations [a]
Did not work	441	14.3	$−71	$ 43 [b]
10–19 hours	49	1.5	−98	−69
20–34 hours	97	3.0	−64	−39
35–40 hours	1,248	43.7	7	− 4
41–48 hours	434	14.3	1	−19
49–59 hours	324	10.7	41	0
60 hours or more	280	9.0	70	13
Not ascertained	87	2.5	−13	−24

[a] deviations from grand mean of $182
[b] Because the spending unit heads who have no earnings also have no hours worked the coefficients for these two categories did not converge. The net effect of not working is to decrease home production by $27 (−$70 + $43).

just retired. The first group is starting housekeeping, and the second has more available time and a reduced income.

TABLE 8-9

MONEY SAVED BY HOME PRODUCTION: DEVIATIONS FOR AGE OF HEADS
(FOR SPENDING UNITS)

Age of heads	Number of spending units	Per cent of spending units	Unadjusted deviations [a]	Adjusted deviations [a]
18–24	264	8.9	$−114	$−19
25–34	578	19.3	17	14
35–44	661	22.2	59	20
45–54	585	19.0	19	− 6
55–64	479	15.1	− 17	−14
65–74	266	9.8	− 20	10
75 and older	127	4.7	−111	−71

[a] deviations from grand mean of $182

The occupational groups accustomed to manual work appear more likely to engage in home production, particularly the farmers. The differences are small, however, and nonsignificant after adjustment for the effects of other factors. One can argue that it is being a farmer, rather than working long hours on the job, that leads to home production, and that the assumptions behind the multivariate statistical process violate reality.

The measure of achievement motivation and of the perception that hard work pays produced only small, nonsignificant residuals which are more often opposite to the predicted direction than in agreement with it. Other classifications which are associated with this one did not take over the credit because even the unadjusted differences are erratic. Table 8-10 and Table 6-10 seem to indicate that achievement motivation manifests itself in harder work on the main job or in taking second jobs rather than in home production.

This analysis has been of total home production. Table 8-12 presents a summary of the two components of home production. The table shows the

TABLE 8-10

MONEY SAVED BY HOME PRODUCTION: DEVIATIONS
FOR OCCUPATION OF HEADS
(FOR SPENDING UNITS)

Occupation of heads	Number of spending units	Per cent of spending units	Unadjusted deviations [a]	Adjusted deviations [a]
Professionals, managers, self-employed businessmen	584	20.7	$ 32	$− 4
Clerical and sales workers	324	12.0	− 55	−34
Blue collar workers	1,711	57.0	− 9	5
Farmers and farm managers	179	4.7	133	40
Not in labor force now	162	4.6	− 32	0

[a] deviations from grand mean of $182

TABLE 8-11

MONEY SAVED BY HOME PRODUCTION: DEVIATIONS FOR ATTITUDE
TOWARD HARD WORK AND NEED-ACHIEVEMENT SCORE OF HEADS
(FOR SPENDING UNITS)

Attitude toward hard work and need-achievement score of heads	Number of spending units	Per cent of spending units	Unadjusted deviations [a]	Adjusted deviations [a]
Hard work is equal to or more important than luck; need-achievement score is in:				
high range	712	25.0	$ 5	$− 2
middle range	1,063	36.2	7	2
low range	499	16.0	13	5
Hard work is less important than luck; need-achievement score is in:				
high range	131	4.2	18	30
middle range	263	8.5	−52	−29
low range	173	5.1	− 1	23
Need-achievement score not ascertained	119	4.0	−53	−27

[a] deviations from grand mean of $182

proportions engaging in food production and home improvement, and the average amounts by which spending unit income is increased within groups according to the gross disposable income of the spending unit. Low income units tend to save modest amounts by growing food while upper income

TABLE 8-12

HOME PRODUCTION BY TYPE, WITHIN GROSS DISPOSABLE INCOME OF SPENDING UNITS
(PERCENTAGE DISTRIBUTION AND MEANS FOR SPENDING UNITS)

Gross disposable income of spending units	Number of spending units	Per cent who had:			Mean amounts saved by all		
		Home grown food	Home improvements	Either or both (Home production)	Home grown food	Home improvements	Either or both (Home production)
Under $500	47	23	27	45	$36	$ 33	$ 69
$500–999	126	26	16	35	51	22	73
$1,000–1,999	410	27	19	38	48	25	73
$2,000–2,999	395	25	23	38	35	45	80
$3,000–4,999	688	20	35	45	40	77	117
$5,000–7,499	687	20	54	59	31	154	185
$7,500–9,999	357	22	58	65	56	293	349
$10,000–$14,999	208	18	59	65	55	367	422
$15,000 and over	79	14	45	48	33	277	310
All spending units	2,997	21	41	51	$40	$140	$182

units save substantial sums of money by doing their own home maintenance and repair work. This results partly from the fact that more of them are home owners, and partly from the fact that they have more money to invest in home improvements. Clearly considerations other than rational comparisons of alternative employment opportunities must have been involved, since these upper income units must have better earning opportunities in their jobs, and it is doubtful that they have more manual skills.

Home production adds about the same proportional supplement to gross disposable income at all levels except the two extremes, namely 3 to 4 per cent. It does not tend to offset differences in money income, or to make the distribution of welfare any more equal.

Summary

The multivariate analysis did not explain much of the variation between spending units in their creation of income through home production. Many of the significant effects were relatively obvious ones, such as housing status; others, such as hourly earnings, did not support the hypotheses. In particular the positive relation between the head's wage rate and his home production, and the low levels of home production in the South and North Central regions, require further explanation. Over-all, home production adds only $182 per spending unit to income, and spending unit heads were probably more likely to exaggerate than to understate this number.

Negative expected home production estimates are possible for subgroups such as aged female renters living in large Southern cities, indicating that these explanatory characteristics are less than additive, that is, that depressing effects are really substitutes for one another.

Chapter 9

LABOR FORCE PARTICIPATION OF WIVES

Seven out of ten spending units heads are married and 38 per cent of their wives earned some income in 1959. The wife's contribution to spending unit income can be explained by explaining whether there is a wife, whether she worked in 1959, how much she earned per hour, and how many hours she worked.

To explain whether there is a wife present is somewhat beyond the scope of this study. Data collected in this survey indicate that middle aged, better educated men with higher achievement motives are most likely to have wives. Others have developed more precise models of the demographic composition than can be undertaken here.[1]

Whether the Wife Worked during 1959

Thirty-eight per cent of the wives of spending unit heads earned some income during 1959. In this study, concern is not with current labor force status, but with whether the wife earned any money during the previous year. The distinction is important for women, since they tend to enter and leave the labor force frequently. Current Population Survey data show 31 per cent of wives in the labor force in March, 1959, but 42 per cent having worked at some time during 1958.[2] Data from the *Monthly Labor Review* indicate that between April, 1951 and April, 1961 the number of married women in the labor force increased by 4.2 million, roughly doubling the proportion of married women working, and accounting for about 45 per cent of the total increase in the labor force.

[1] Guy Orcutt and others, *Microanalysis of Socioeconomic Systems* (New York: Harper & Brothers, 1961), pp. 75–95.

[2] Jacob Shiffman, "Family Characteristics of Workers," *Special Labor Force Reports*, No. 7, U.S. Bureau of Labor Statistics (1960), pp. A-7, A-17.

The earnings of the head, capital income, and the real income from home production have already been explained. Using the spending unit's income if the wife did not work and there was no transfer income, one can visualize the spending unit looking over its situation and deciding whether the wife should work, and how much.

Other data show that the proportion of wives working has more than doubled since 1940, and that the increase has been particularly great among older women.[3] Korbel, Long, Orcutt, Rosett, and Sobol have done complex analyses of labor force participation of women and of wives.[4] Without detailed comparisons, which would be imperfect in any case, it can be said that their findings are similar to those presented here, but make use of fewer explanatory factors. Professor Rosett's complex analysis used earnings relative to the husband's wage rate as the dependent variable rather than labor force participation, and took account of the fact that the dependent variable could not be negative. The explanatory factors he used which this study does not use were financial data, the coefficients of which were not highly significant, or not significant at all.

Dr. Sobol's dissertation found one significant factor which is not used here: whether the wife had worked before marriage. She also found that the wife's education seems relevant only if there are children under six at home, a finding which is difficult to reconcile with the results of this study, but also difficult to check adequately. She used a sample that excluded Negroes and prescaled the classifications in order to use numerical regression routines. She excluded pregnant women from the main analysis, treating them separately. Her analysis explained about 16 per cent of the variance.

A study of 427 married women in St. Paul found labor force participation of wives related to the family income less the wife's earnings, only in families where the wife was under thirty years old, and related to the presence of children under six only where the wife was between thirty and forty. The only other factors found significant were number of children and two others which are partly circular: employment of the wife during the previous five years and the wife's attitude toward working.[5]

[3] U.S. Department of Labor, *Handbook on Women Workers,* Bulletin 275 (1960); also Shiffman, *Special Labor Force Reports,* No. 7, pp. 27–29.

[4] John Korbel, "A Decision-Unit Model for the Labor Force" (unpublished Ph.D. dissertation, Harvard University, 1959); Clarence D. Long, *The Labor Force Under Changing Income and Employment* (Princeton: Princeton University Press, 1958); Guy Orcutt and others, *Microanalysis of Socioeconomic Systems: A Simulation Study;* Richard Rosett, "Working Wives: An Economic Study," *Studies in Household Economic Behavior* (New Haven: Yale University Press, 1958), pp. 51–101; Marion Gross Sobol, "Correlates of Present and Expected Future Work Status of Married Women" (unpublished Ph.D. dissertation, University of Michigan, 1960).

For a summary of other studies, see Alva Myrdal and Viola Klein, *Women's Two Roles* (London: Routledge & Kegan Paul, Ltd., 1956), pp. 78ff.

[5] See Thomas A. Mahoney, "Factors Determining the Labor Force Participation of Married Women," *Industrial and Labor Relations Review,* 14 (July, 1961), 563–577.

The ten characteristics used to explain labor force participation of wives fall into four groups. The analysis parallels that used for labor force participation of spending unit heads as far as possible.

Three classifications provide measures of the wife's ability to work. The first is a classification of race and age of children. The presence of children at home makes it difficult for the wife to work. There may be problems in making suitable arrangements for child care, and the cost of such care may be prohibitive.

It is possible that race is relevant here as well, since nonwhite women often hold jobs such as housework, which can be scheduled to fit with their family needs.[6] Race and presence of children would have a joint effect on the wife's ability to work if housing discrimination forced combining households, thus increasing the possibility that someone else would be at home to care for the children. The second and third classifications of ability to work are age and physical condition of the wife. Advanced age and physical disabilities would make it difficult for her to work.

Four classifications describe the kinds of jobs available to the wife. The wife's age and education should affect the range of jobs open to her and rates of pay available to her. A rate of pay was not used directly, since potential earnings of nonworking wives are not known. The extent of unemployment in the state shows the condition of the job market and the competition for jobs. The race component of the "race and age of children" classification should be related to the kinds of jobs available. The "population of city" classification should be related to the variety of jobs available. Statistical studies show that female labor force participation rates are high in areas where there are industries that employ high proportions of females. The direction of causation is unclear here. A measure of this aspect of industry mix was not available.[7]

Five characteristics serve as proxy indicators of motivation and the need for the extra income the wife can earn. Head's and wife's gross factor income, excluding the wife's earnings, indicates the level at which the unit can live without depending on transfers or on the wife's work. The presence of children, again in the classification with race, means additional dependents to be cared for. Also, the income instability of many nonwhites may add pressure to have an extra earner. Plans to send children to college, or to provide support for parents in the future, may require the extra income the wife can provide, although the causation may go the other way: commitments may be undertaken because they can be met. The frequency with which the head is

[6] U.S. Department of Labor, *The Economic Situation of Negroes in the United States,* Bulletin S-3 (October, 1960), p. 13. See also Elizabeth Herzog, *Children of Working Mothers,* U.S. Department of Health, Education and Welfare, Children's Bureau Publication 382 (1960), and references cited therein.

[7] See Nedra Bartlett Belloc, "Labor-Force Participation and Employment Opportunities for Women," *Journal of the American Statistical Association,* 45 (September, 1950), 400–410.

unemployed should affect the spending unit's economic security and the need for added income and an extra earner.

A difference in education between the head and his wife may produce pressures on the wife to work in order to bring the spending unit level of living up to standards consonant with her education. The head with his lesser education and earning power may find it difficult to meet this standard with his earnings. Where the wife has less education than her husband, she may not be able to secure a job consonant with her husband's status and is more likely to be satisfied with what he earns. There is some sociological evidence that the wife tends to set the standards of the family.[8]

Although it was assumed that all spending unit heads who were able were expected to work, this assumption is not valid for wives. The husbands' attitude toward wives working distinguishes groups which differ in their basic feeling about wives working. The husband who feels it is good for a wife to work is more likely to encourage her to work than the husband who feels the wife's place is in the home.

A measure of need-achievement and attitude toward hard work was not available for wives.

Table 9–1 indicates how the multivariate analysis related these ten classifications to the probability that the wife worked during 1959.

TABLE 9-1

CHARACTERISTICS USED TO EXPLAIN LABOR FORCE
PARTICIPATION IN 1959
(FOR SPENDING UNIT WIVES)

Characteristics of spending unit wives	Relative importance (Beta coefficients)	Significance (F ratios)
Age and education	.287	19.87**
Race and age of children	.281	38.09**
Attitude of heads toward wives working	.162	9.04**
Gross factor income of heads and wives, excluding wives' earnings	.157	6.61**
Plan to help parents or children	.080	5.15**
Population of cities	.078	2.94*
Extent of unemployment in states	.071	3.04*
Difference in education of heads and wives	.065	2.04
Physical condition	.063	3.19*
Frequency of unemployment of heads	.063	1.37

** significant at probability level of .01
 * significant at probability level of .05

Both age and education affect the wife's tendency to work, with youth and extra education each apparently inducing more wives to work. This is true

[8] This hypothesis is suggested by C. Arnold Anderson, "Employment, Occupation, and Socio-economic Status of Swedish Wives in Relation to Occupation and Status of Husbands," *Statistisk Tidskrift*, 6 (1957), pp. 3–15.

after taking account of the presence of preschool or school-age children and other factors. Age and education are classified jointly, since their effect might be more or less than additive. They appear, however, to have a simple additive effect, except for the extreme effect of advanced age.

Education increases the earnings a woman can expect on her job, and increases the tendency for wives to work. It is doubtful that the age differences are pure effects of advancing age. More likely two things are involved: some women drop out while their children are young, and then find it unnecessary, or difficult, to return to work. Secondly, some of the age differences are the result of a tendency for each generation of wives to look more favorably

TABLE 9-2

LABOR FORCE PARTICIPATION IN 1959: DEVIATIONS
FOR AGE AND EDUCATION
(FOR SPENDING UNIT WIVES)

Age and education	Number of spending unit wives	Per cent of spending units	Unadjusted deviations [a]	Adjusted deviations [a]
Under 30:				
0–11 grades	184	5.8	.04	.08
12 grades	221	7.9	.12	.17
some college	82	2.8	.22	.25
30–44:				
0–11 grades	349	11.2	.01	.02
12 grades	323	11.3	.00	.04
some college	127	4.4	.03	.11
45–64:				
0–11 grades	367	12.0	−.09	−.16
12 grades	162	5.8	−.02	−.07
some college	96	3.4	.12	.06
65 and older	138	5.0	−.26	−.31
Education not ascertained	10	0.3	.02	.08

[a] deviations from grand mean of .38

on working than the last. In a period of rapid change, it is not possible to know whether any generation will really repeat the age-work patterns of the previous one.

Nonwhite wives are more likely to be working, even taking account of the presence of children, and the other factors in the analysis such as age and education, the husband's attitude, his unemployment experience, and the spending unit factor income net of the wife's wages. The inference is that it is not just the need for income that makes the difference, nor the husband's acceptance of the idea, that results in a higher proportion of Negro women working. On the other hand, the racial difference is greatest when there are school children.

The presence of school children clearly discourages white wives from working more than it does nonwhites. When the youngest child is six or older, and likely to be in school, nonwhite wives are 17 per cent more likely to work than are white wives, and only 3 per cent less likely than if they did not have any children at home.

It is interesting that the adjustments for other factors actually increased the divergence between whites and nonwhites in many instances. This would indicate that the effects of other factors, such as the frequency of unemployment of the spending unit head, or his attitude toward wives working, or the low income of the unit, would have been exaggerated had not race and the presence of preschool children been simultaneously considered.

TABLE 9-3

LABOR FORCE PARTICIPATION IN 1959: DEVIATIONS
FOR RACE AND AGE OF CHILDREN
(FOR SPENDING UNIT WIVES)

Race and age of children	Number of spending unit wives	Per cent of spending units	Unadjusted deviations [a]	Adjusted deviations [a]
White:				
no children	685	24.6	.01	.13
children under 6	643	22.0	−.06	−.18
all children 6–17	500	17.3	.02	.01
Nonwhite:				
no children	68	2.0	.14	.22
children under 6	112	2.7	.05	−.12
all children 6–17	51	1.3	.23	.18

[a] deviations from grand mean of .38

Results of other studies of the effects of children on female labor force participation are difficult to compare; Rosett's because his dependent variable is more complicated than mere participation, and Orcutt's because he includes single women, 18 interaction classes involving the presence of children at home, and excludes race.[9]

Having children at home clearly does not keep *all* mothers from working. What do these working mothers, or families with a single working adult, do about child care? One-sixth of them put the children in nursery or playschool. One-eighth have someone else in the dwelling unit who can care for the child: an older child, or a grandparent, or other relative. The largest group, however, has someone outside the home who takes care of the children, and about half the time this person is a relative.

About half these spending units with children under six but with all adults working did not pay anything for child care. A majority of the rest paid less

[9] Rosett, *Studies in Household Economic Behavior*, pp. 75–76; Orcutt and others, *Microanalysis of Socioeconomic Systems*, pp. 226–227.

than $50 a month for child care.[10] It seems reasonable to suppose, however, that where the wife does not work, it may be partly because child care would be more costly than it is for those who do work.

The husband's feelings about wives working are clearly related to his wife's working.[11] This is particularly true when the husband feels strongly about it. Some part of this relationship may follow from the husband's acceptance of the fact that his wife does or does not work and extension of his own situation to others. However, if the wife's participation in the labor force were largely determined by economic and demographic facts, and then reflected in the husband's attitudes, the attitude and the wife working would be more closely related than it is.

TABLE 9-4

LABOR FORCE PARTICIPATION IN 1959: DEVIATIONS FOR ATTITUDE OF HEADS TOWARD WIVES WORKING [a]
(FOR SPENDING UNIT WIVES)

Attitude of heads toward wives working	Number of spending unit wives	Per cent of spending units	Unadjusted deviations [b]	Adjusted deviations [b]
Favorable	288	9.0	.22	.18
Favorable with qualifications	409	14.0	.05	.01
Ambivalent	92	3.2	−.02	−.03
Unfavorable with qualifications	302	10.4	−.05	−.03
Unfavorable	532	18.4	−.11	−.08
Depends on the situation	374	12.9	−.01	.00
Do not know	12	0.4	.01	.04
Not ascertained	50	1.6	−.01	.07

[a] The question was: "There are many wives who have jobs these days. Do you think it is a good thing for a wife to work, or a bad thing, or what? Why do you say so?"
[b] deviations from grand mean of .38

What reasons do husbands give for their attitudes about whether wives should work? The predominant favorable reason is that the extra income is needed, useful, or desirable. Nineteen per cent of all husbands, and 63 per cent of the husbands who say it is good for wives to work, talk in terms of supplementary income, raising the family standard of living.

Allied to this, 4 per cent of the husbands and 6 per cent of those who said it was good for wives to work mentioned the security aspects of the

[10] For additional detail on the care of children whose mothers work, and on the effects on the children and on family life see Henry C. Lajewski, "Working Mothers and Their Arrangements for Care of Their Children," *Social Security Bulletin,* 22 (August, 1959), 8–13; Herzog, *Children of Working Mothers.*

[11] For a study of women's attitudes, see Hortense M. Glenn, "Attitudes of Women Regarding Gainful Employment of Married Women" (unpublished Ph.D. dissertation, Florida State University, 1958).

wife's income; that is, her income would be essential if the husband was disabled, unemployed, or dead.

Very few mentioned the use of the wife's skills. The second most frequent reason why wives should work was that they would get bored staying at home, would not have enough to keep them busy. Seven per cent of all husbands and 16 per cent of the husbands most in favor of wives working said this.

The negative reasons mostly concerned neglect of children, or of the wife's role as a homemaker. Twenty-seven per cent of husbands mentioned neglect of the children, and 40 per cent of the husbands who said it was bad for wives to work mentioned neglect of children. General statements about woman's role, or a husband's responsibility for supporting his wife, were given by 15 per cent of husbands, and by 38 per cent of the husbands most opposed to wives working. A much smaller group mentioned more specific neglect of housework or home management.

Finally, there were 8 per cent, 17 per cent of those most opposed, who said that working women take jobs away from men. The belief that there is a fixed number of jobs or a total wage fund apparently still persists among a minority in the country.

It is interesting to note that 60 per cent of the husbands whose wives were not working said their wives could find jobs if necessary.

When asked why their wives could find jobs, husbands referred mostly to the skills, training, experience, or seniority of their wives; and second to local conditions, such as the fact that there were jobs available. The reasons husbands gave for their wives' inability to work, excluding cases where the wife was over sixty-five, referred mostly to the wives' physical condition or poor health. Thirteen per cent of all husbands who said their wives could not work, and 24 per cent of those who had a wife under sixty-five who could not work, mentioned lack of skills or experience and seniority. Only 8 per cent of those who said their wives could not work mentioned local conditions and availability of jobs.

Discussions of the working wife by academicians tend to concentrate on the wife's emotional and psychological needs for financial independence and recognition, whereas field studies have frequently concluded that the economic motive was the main reason wives worked.[12] This study cannot resolve this issue since it does not measure the wives' attitudes toward working. However, the level of husbands' and wives' other income exerts a powerful effect on the proportion of wives' working. This income measure includes heads' earnings and real capital income of heads and wives. The higher the income without the wife working, the less likely she is to work.

The apparent exception to this is a very small group of spending units in which there was no factor income other than the wives', and it is possible

[12] Sobol, "Correlates of Present and Expected Future Work Status of Married Women," pp. 41–43.

that the adjustments for other characteristics were inadequate here. In 50 per cent of these units, the wife was sixty-five or older. These older units are likely to have retirement income which was not included in the estimate of income available to units if the wives did not work. For most adult units the consideration of transfer income as supplementary to and determined by earned income is appropriate. Only for the small proportion of adult units who are entitled to retirement income are the results of the sequential analysis distorted by the analysis of transfer incomes at a later point in the seqeunce than the analysis of earned incomes.

TABLE 9-5

LABOR FORCE PARTICIPATION IN 1959: DEVIATIONS FOR HEADS' AND WIVES' GROSS FACTOR INCOME, EXCLUDING WIVES' EARNINGS
(FOR SPENDING UNIT WIVES)

Heads' and wives' gross factor income, excluding wives' earnings	Number of spending unit wives	Per cent of spending units	Unadjusted deviations [a]	Adjusted deviations [a]
None	17	0.6	−.24	−.06
$1–499; negative	70	2.2	−.07	.06
$500–999	103	3.0	−.08	.04
$1,000–1,999	193	5.1	.03	.07
$2,000–2,999	178	4.9	.04	.07
$3,000–4,999	403	14.2	.07	.06
$5,000–7,499	547	20.3	.02	.01
$7,500–9,999	277	10.1	−.02	−.04
$10,000–$14,999	177	6.3	−.08	−.11
$15,000 or more	94	3.2	−.19	−.25

[a] deviations from grand mean of .38

The last of the clearly significant factors is plans to send children to college, or to help parents in the future. It operates in the expected way with

TABLE 9-6

LABOR FORCE PARTICIPATIONS IN 1959: DEVIATIONS FOR PLANS TO HELP PARENTS OR CHILDREN
(FOR SPENDING UNIT WIVES)

Plans to help parents or children	Number of spending unit wives	Per cent of spending units	Unadjusted deviations [a]	Adjusted deviations [a]
Do not plan to send children to college or help parents	957	32.0	−.04	−.04
Plan to help parents	316	10.6	.10	.03
Plan to send children to college	480	16.5	.00	.02
Plan to send children to college and help parents	306	10.8	.02	.06

[a] deviations from grand mean of .38

more wives working in units that have plans than in units that have no plans. The combination of both kinds of plans seems to have an effect slightly more than the sum of two separate effects.

The direction of causation is, of course, unclear. Perhaps wives who are working are more likely to make plans and undertake obligations for the future. A more appealing, but equally conjectural, inference is that the desires embodied in plans induce the wife to work.

The hypothesis that women would be more likely to work in densely populated areas where a wider variety of jobs are available is not completely borne out by Table 9-7. It is in the middle sized cities that the most wives work. However, many of these cities are suburbs of larger cities. The relationship between the wives working and distance from the nearest large city might be more orderly.

TABLE 9-7

LABOR FORCE PARTICIPATION IN 1959: DEVIATIONS
FOR POPULATION OF CITIES
(FOR SPENDING UNIT WIVES)

Population of cities	Number of spending unit wives	Per cent of spending units	Unadjusted deviations [a]	Adjusted deviations [a]
Central cities of 12 largest metropolitan areas	246	8.9	.01	−.03
Other cities 50,000 or more	332	12.2	.00	−.01
Urban places 10,000–49,999	230	7.9	.07	.07
Urban places 2,500–9,999	398	13.9	.04	.05
Rural areas near cities	328	11.5	−.06	−.03
Rural areas not near cities	525	15.5	−.03	−.02

[a] deviations from grand mean of .38

The effects of the job market in the state are small, but as expected; substantial unemployment makes it less likely that the wife will work because

TABLE 9-8

LABOR FORCE PARTCIPATION IN 1959: DEVIATIONS FOR EXTENT
OF UNEMPLOYMENT IN STATES
(FOR SPENDING UNIT WIVES)

Extent of 1958 unemployment in states	Number of spending unit wives	Per cent of spending units	Unadjusted deviations [a]	Adjusted deviations [a]
Under 5.00 per cent	467	15.2	−.03	−.05
5.00 per cent to 6.49 per cent	664	21.9	.05	.04
6.50 per cent to 7.49 per cent	431	15.5	−.01	.01
7.50 per cent to 9.99 per cent	266	8.9	−.04	−.03
10.00 per cent and over	231	8.4	−.01	−.01

[a] deviations from grand mean of .38

fewer jobs are available. The lower participation in states with very little unemployment may reflect the fact that these are largely farm states.

Wives with more education than their husbands are more likely to work, even after adjusting for their age and actual amount of education; wives with less education than their husbands are less likely to work. This is consonant with the notion that the wife sets the living standards for the family, and the husband's ability to meet them without the wife working usually depends on the relation of his education to hers. The differences are so small that this crude test does not show statistical significance, but all the differences are in the expected direction, an event unlikely to arise by chance if there were really no effect.

TABLE 9-9

LABOR FORCE PARTICIPATION IN 1959: DEVIATIONS FOR DIFFERENCE IN EDUCATION OF HEADS AND WIVES
(FOR SPENDING UNIT WIVES)

Difference in education of heads and wives [a]	Number of spending unit wives	Per cent of spending units	Unadjusted deviations [b]	Adjusted deviations [b]
Wives have two or more levels more than heads	223	7.6	.11	.05
Wives have one level more than heads	363	12.0	.06	.04
Wive have the same level as heads	809	26.8	−.03	−.01
Wives have one level less than heads	338	12.0	−.03	−.02
Wives have two or more levels less than heads	303	10.7	−.04	−.04
Education of wives not ascertained	23	0.8	−.13	−.10

[a] levels of education are:

none	12 grades and nonacademic training
1–8 grades	college, no degree
9–11 grades	college, bachelor's degree
12 grades	college, advanced degree

[b] deviations from grand mean of .38

Disabilities of the wife, as reported by her husband, affect whether she worked, but were relatively rare. The substantial adjustments for the other factors largely take account of the fact that disabled wives are usually old.

The last and least important of the predictors of the wife's labor force participation was the frequency with which her husband experiences unemployment. The effect seems to differ from expectations, with more wives' working where the husband was subject to short spells of unemployment and fewer wives' working when the husband was frequently unemployed. However, the number of wives in both groups is small.

The data do not test precisely the hypothesis that a temporarily low husband's income is more likely to induce the wife to work than a permanently

TABLE 9-10

LABOR FORCE PARTICIPATION IN 1959: DEVIATIONS
FOR PHYSICAL CONDITION
(FOR SPENDING UNIT WIVES)

Physical condition	Number of spending unit wives	Per cent of spending units	Unadjusted deviations [a]	Adjusted deviations [a]
Completely disabled	21	0.7	−.33	−.19
Severely disabled	30	0.9	−.14	−.07
Moderately disabled	104	3.5	−.14	−.09
Not disabled	1,904	64.8	.01	.01

[a] deviations from grand mean of .38

low one. That hypothesis implies an interaction effect between income and the frequency of the husband's unemployment.[13] The lack of any relationship between wives working and heads' reported unemployment experience, even when the extent of unemployment in the state is also taken into account, implies that the wife's working is largely dominated by factors other than short-run emergencies created by her husband's unemployment.

TABLE 9-11

LABOR FORCE PARTICIPATION IN 1959: DEVIATIONS FOR FREQUENCY
OF UNEMPLOYMENT OF HEADS
(FOR SPENDING UNIT WIVES)

Frequency of unemployment of heads	Number of spending unit wives	Per cent of spending units	Unadjusted deviations [a]	Adjusted deviations [a]
Frequent	108	3.3	.03	−.01
Occasional	37	1.2	.09	.01
Short spells only	32	1.1	.09	.07
Infrequent	699	24.7	.04	.01
Never	407	14.3	.02	.01
Entered labor force recently	4	0.2	.34	.29
Not ascertained	158	5.4	.05	.05
Retired or self-employed	614	19.7	−.10	−.04

[a] deviations from grand mean of .38

The Wife's Work History

It is of interest to examine the number of years worked by wives according to their background and the demands of their family, since wives can make substantial contributions to family income if they work. The 1959 employment experience is presumably a part of a larger cycle of periods of employ-

[13] Jacob Mincer, "Labor Force Participation of Married Women," Report on Conference of National Bureau of Economic Research to be published by Princeton University Press.

ment which are determined by the wife's career plans, her husband's lifetime income pattern, and her family responsibilities.

The characteristics which explain number of years worked fall into groups similar to those used to explain 1959 labor force participation of wives. Some characteristics, such as income and population of cities, were used to explain 1959 labor force participation but are not appropriate in the explanation of years worked. They pertain to the present situation of the family rather than to its situation during the years when the wife might have worked.

The first group of characteristics represents the wife's ability to work. Age, of course, determines the maximum number of years that she could possibly have worked. Present physical condition may be related to years worked if there has been no recent change. Number of children of all ages indicates family responsibilities which may have interfered with the wife's working.

Race and education would affect the types of jobs and the range of pay available to the wife. Race, as shown in the earlier analysis, is also related to less economic security and greater need for a second earner in the family.

Again, the head's attitude toward wives working distinguishes groups with different feelings about wives having jobs.

Table 9-12 shows the characteristics used in the analysis and their relative importance and significance.

TABLE 9-12

CHARACTERISTICS USED TO EXPLAIN THE NUMBER OF YEARS WORKED
(FOR SPENDING UNIT WIVES)

Characteristics of spending unit wives	Relative importance (Beta coefficients)	Significance (F ratios)
Age	.367	55.15**
Number of living children of the head	.238	34.79**
Attitude of heads toward wives working	.128	5.75**
Race	.112	30.82**
Education	.091	2.54**
Physical condition	.068	3.79**

** significant at probability level of .01

The average number of years worked by wives for whom estimates were given was 7.50; the standard deviation was 8.50, indicating a slightly skewed distribution. A few married women have worked most of their adult lives and many women have never worked. The mean also reflects the age distribution of the sample. Differing generations probably will have had different lifetime work histories as customs and employment opportunities have changed in the past decades. Many young women will continue to work after their marriages while many women over fifty-five have never worked. If young married women who enter the labor force in future years also continue to work the pattern shown in this cross-section will change and the average number of years worked will rise.

The multivariate analysis accounts for .19 of the population variance. Added years during which a wife could have worked increase the number of years the average wife has worked. The increase is less than proportionate to the increase in age, presumably because older women are less likely to be working now and because older women grew up at a time when it was less customary for women to work.

TABLE 9-13

NUMBER OF YEARS WORKED: DEVIATIONS OF AGE
(FOR SPENDING UNIT WIVES)

Age	Number of spending unit wives	Unadjusted deviations [a]	Adjusted deviations [a]
Under 25	228	−4.41	−6.13
25–34	507	−2.42	−2.49
35–44	527	.42	.71
45–54	378	3.17	3.14
55–64	224	3.07	3.41
65–74	109	1.84	3.14
75 and older	24	−3.60	−1.46

[a] deviations from grand mean of 7.50 years

Some wives may have worked because they could not have children; some may have had few or no children because they preferred to work. Whichever is the case there is a net difference of nearly seven years in the work experience of women who did not have children and those who had five or more. Because heads of poor families have more children, it is clear that their wives will tend to spend less time in the labor force than other wives. This variable represents the number of living children of the head; in a few cases his present wife may not have raised them all, or her children by a previous marriage may be excluded if they are not presently in the spending unit.

TABLE 9-14

NUMBER OF YEARS WORKED: DEVIATIONS FOR NUMBER
OF LIVING CHILDREN
(FOR SPENDING UNIT WIVES)

Number of living children	Number of spending unit wives	Unadjusted deviations [a]	Adjusted deviations [a]
None	274	3.34	3.79
One	391	.95	1.34
Two	511	− .14	− .30
Three or four	569	−1.39	−1.36
Five or more	252	−2.19	−3.19

[a] deviations from grand mean of 7.50 years

The direction of causation in Table 9-15 is not clear. The husband may be rationalizing his own situation, but it is also possible that his attitude helped determine how much his wife worked. There is a difference, in the expected direction, of nearly five years in the net effects of extreme attitudes of the husband about wives working.

The multivariate adjustment results in part from the fact that heads of spending units with attitudes favorable toward wives working are likely to have fewer children than those who disapprove of wives working. Whether the head's attitude influences family size rather than conversely remains conjectural. The head may have planned to have a small family so that his wife could work, or a small family may have influenced his attitude about wives working.

TABLE 9-15

NUMBER OF YEARS WORKED: DEVIATIONS FOR ATTITUDE
OF HEADS TOWARD WIVES WORKING
(FOR SPENDING UNIT WIVES)

Attitude of heads toward wives working	Number of spending unit wives	Unadjusted deviations [a]	Adjusted deviations [a]
Favorable	277	2.95	2.15
Favorable, with qualifications	398	.03	.07
Ambivalent	90	.39	.26
Unfavorable, with qualifications	291	− .58	− .27
Unfavorable	523	−1.46	−1.28
Depends on the situation	365	.60	.60
Do not know	11	−1.38	−2.88
Not ascertained	42	−1.73	−1.07

[a] deviations from grand mean of 7.50 years

Nonwhite wives worked more than whites. The low and unstable incomes of their husbands and the instability of family bonds among nonwhites are possible explanations of the difference, but it is rather difficult to interpret this finding without more data on the employment and family history of nonwhite wives and their husbands.[14]

The relation between the wife's education and her work experience is not systematic, even after substantial adjustments for the effects of other factors such as age and race. However, when education groups are combined to correspond with the classification in Table 9-2, a slight tendency emerges for better educated wives to work longer.

Though the wife's education bears an ambiguous relationship to the number of years she has already worked, it appears to be extremely relevant to

[14] For one year data and analysis of unemployment rates for Negroes, see John Hope II, "The Problem of Unemployment as It Relates to Negroes," *Studies in Unemployment*, U.S. Senate, Special Committee on Unemployment Problems, 86th Cong., 2d Sess. (1960), pp. 173–224.

TABLE 9-16

NUMBER OF YEARS WORKED: DEVIATIONS FOR RACE
(FOR SPENDING UNIT WIVES)

Race	Number of spending unit wives	Unadjusted deviations [a]	Adjusted deviations [a]
White	1,787	− .24	− .28
Nonwhite	210	2.74	3.20

[a] deviations from grand mean of 7.50 years

her ability to find a job if she is not working. About three-fourths of the husbands whose wives were not working and had training beyond high school reported that their wives could find work. If the wife had only a high school diploma, two-thirds reported that she could find work, and if the wife had less than high school education, less than a third gave this response.

TABLE 9-17

NUMBER OF YEARS WORKED: DEVIATIONS FOR EDUCATION
(FOR SPENDING UNIT WIVES)

Education	Number of spending unit wives	Unadjusted deviations [a]	Adjusted deviations [a]
None	17	1.74	1.07
1–8 grades	486	.42	− .50
9–11 grades	455	.27	.53
12 grades	508	− .92	− .22
12 grades and nonacademic training	203	.35	.61
College, no degree	197	− .36	− .36
College, bachelor's degree	101	1.53	.81
College, advanced degree	12	5.83	3.89
Not ascertained	18	−5.05	−5.58

[a] deviations from grand mean of 7.50 years

In spending units where the wife was working at the time of interview, the head was more likely to report that the wife would continue work for less than three years if she had college training than if she had less education. The difference in attitude may reflect the greater ease with which women with college training can enter and leave the labor force. The correlation may also reflect the greater economic security of the women with college training, most of whose husbands also have college training.

Wives with disabilities worked fewer years in the past. Interpretation of this variable is complicated by the fact that present physical condition is being related to work history. In cases where the wife's physical condition has recently changed, there is no basis for relating it to the number of years she has worked.

TABLE 9-18

NUMBER OF YEARS WORKED: DEVIATIONS FOR PHYSICAL CONDITION
(FOR SPENDING UNIT WIVES)

Physical condition	Number of spending unit wives	Unadjusted deviations [a]	Adjusted deviations [a]
Completely disabled	20	2.04	−1.41
Severely disabled	30	−2.65	−4.34
Moderately disabled	101	.50	− .84
Not disabled	1,846	− .01	.13

[a] deviations from grand mean of 7.50 years

Summary

The two preceding analyses of wives working give consistent results. Younger women, women with no children, nonwhite women, women whose husbands favor wives working, and women with no disabilities are more likely to have worked in 1959 or for a number of years in the past. The effect of education was not consistent; better educated wives were more likely to have worked in 1959, but only a slight indication of the same pattern appeared for number of years worked. In addition to the variables which were used in both analyses, two additional predictors were significantly related to 1959 labor force participation. Women whose families had low income from sources other than the wives' earnings and those who have plans for sending children to college or helping parents in the future were more likely to have worked in 1959.

In both analyses there remains a great deal of unexplained variation, associated with idiosyncratic factors and with wives' attitudes and motivations which were not measured.

Chapter 10

HOURLY EARNINGS OF WORKING WIVES

Considering only the wives who work, the next multivariate analysis assesses the factors that determine their hourly earnings. The multivariate analysis uses two kinds of explanatory characteristics: one describes the wife's background, skills, training, experience, and the amount of responsibility she is willing to undertake; the other represents conditions in the job market.

Population of city, extent of unemployment, and race indicate the labor market conditions the wife faces. Population of city is used because large metropolitan areas provide more job opportunities, and are more likely to provide jobs for persons with special skills or unusual schedules. Also, wage levels tend to be higher in large urban areas. The extent of unemployment in the state indicates whether there is a labor surplus which keeps wages down and reduces the variety of jobs to choose from. It also tells whether the state was a farm state or an industrial state. Race is used on the assumption that nonwhite women have a more limited and lower paying range of jobs available to them. However, it is not possible to determine how much of the difference results from differences in the quality of education and how much from discriminatory restrictions on nonwhites.

The remaining predictors measure characteristics of the wife's ability, stamina, and experience, which should affect wage rates. Her age and education provide a measure of physical stamina through the age classification, and a measure of ability, intelligence, and potential skills through the education classification.

The number of years worked indicates experience and seniority.

Occupation provides some measure of the degree of responsibility and of ability required in her job.

Physical condition tells whether there are any disabilities that would reduce productivity on the job or limit the kinds of work she can do.

As in all these analyses, the predictors are not all at the same level in the causal process, and one can argue that the simultaneous adjustments are not justifiable. For instance, the age, education, and work experience of the wife affect her occupation, but not the reverse. It is a legitimate question whether occupation brings to bear additional dimensions, such as the acceptance of responsibility, rather than simply taking credit for something which is really the result of education or experience. Causal relations among explanatory variables imply that the effects of some variables may be somewhat larger than indicated by the adjusted deviations.

The importance and significance of the characteristics used to explain hourly earnings of wives are given in Table 10-1.

TABLE 10-1

CHARACTERISTICS USED TO EXPLAIN HOURLY EARNINGS
(FOR SPENDING UNIT WIVES WHO WORKED DURING 1959)

Characteristics of spending unit wives	Relative importance (Beta coefficients)	Significance (F ratios)
Occupation	.305	13.79**
Number of years worked	.289	12.38**
Age and education	.189	3.71**
Population of cities	.112	2.60*
Physical condition	.090	2.80*
Extent of unemployment in states	.082	1.74
Race	.040	1.66

** significant at probability level of .01
 * significant at probability level of .05

The mean hourly wage rate for working wives was $1.43, which compares closely with the mean wage rate of $1.54 for working female spending unit heads. The standard deviation for working wives was $.88. The seven classifications, with forty-four subclasses, account for 26 per cent of the variance in the population.

Occupations which require more skill, education, or independent responsibility seem to give higher rewards. This is true even after taking account of the wife's age and education, race, and work experience. Female operatives seem to make more than clerical and sales workers, perhaps because they are doing a man's job. The low wages of wives who are managers has no obvious explanation, but the group is so small that the difference is well within sampling error.

These results compare roughly with the effect of occupation on spending unit heads' hourly earnings. The findings are not completely comparable since a classification of self-employment and supervisory responsibilities supplemented the occupation measure for heads.

It is clear that experience and seniority affect earning rates of wives, even after taking account of age and education. Age and education adjust the seniority effect roughly for differences in potential earnings that might affect

TABLE 10-2

HOURLY EARNINGS: DEVIATIONS FOR OCCUPATION
(FOR SPENDING UNIT WIVES WHO WORKED IN 1959)

Occupation	Number of spending unit wives	Per cent of spending units	Unadjusted deviations [a]	Adjusted deviations [a]
Professionals	88	3.2	$ .76	$ .58
Managers	15	0.5	.09	−.10
Self-employed businesswomen	15	0.5	.13	.12
Clerical and sales workers	310	11.3	−.01	−.05
Skilled workers	17	0.6	.09	.03
Semiskilled workers	135	4.7	.03	.07
Unskilled workers	183	5.6	−.47	−.33
Not ascertained	10	0.3	.14	.84

[a] deviations from grand mean of $1.43

the wife's decision to remain in the labor force. It is still possible, however, that there is some reverse causation here; that is, women who find they can earn more stay in the labor force longer.

TABLE 10-3

HOURLY EARNINGS: DEVIATIONS FOR NUMBER OF YEARS WORKED
(FOR SPENDING UNIT WIVES WHO WORKED DURING 1959)

Number of years worked	Number of spending unit wives	Per cent of spending units	Unadjusted deviations [a]	Adjusted deviations [a]
1–2	100	3.5	$−.37	$− .38
3–5	156	5.4	−.20	− .18
6–10	191	6.7	.00	− .02
11–15	111	3.8	.23	.23
16–19	45	1.6	.53	.42
20 or more	131	4.5	.28	.28
Not ascertained how many years	35	1.1	−.40	− .18
Not ascertained whether worked [b]	4	0.1	−.68	−1.28

[a] deviations from grand mean of $1.43
[b] inconsistently coded

The education of the wife clearly affects her ability to earn, even after taking account of occupation, years of experience, physical condition, and so forth. Education measures basic intelligence, accumulation of skills, and the persistence which was required to pass each level. It also serves to make it easier to enter some occupations; some of the effects that the symmetrical analysis attributes to occupation could be attributed to the education that permitted entry into the occupation, rather than to the occupation itself.

Before age sixty-five there is no apparent uniform effect of age on the earnings of wives after adjustment for length of work experience. If any-

TABLE 10-4

HOURLY EARNINGS: DEVIATIONS FOR AGE AND EDUCATION
(FOR SPENDING UNIT WIVES WHO WORKED DURING 1959)

Age and education	Number of spending unit wives	Per cent of spending units	Unadjusted deviations [a]	Adjusted deviations [a]
Under 30				
0–11 grades	75	2.4	$−.44	$−.18
12 grades	110	4.0	−.14	.07
some college	47	1.7	.21	.22
30–44				
0–11 grades	132	4.5	−.08	−.04
12 grades	121	4.3	.03	.00
some college	51	1.8	.46	.13
45–64				
0–11 grades	109	3.5	−.24	−.20
12 grades	59	2.1	.17	−.03
some college	48	1.7	.83	.42
65 and older	17	0.6	−.25	−.29
Education not ascertained	4	0.1	−.45	−.51

[a] deviations from grand mean of $1.43

thing, there is a tendency for the least educated to be making the most when they are between thirty and forty-five, and for the highly educated to make most when they are past forty-five.

The tendency for wages of spending unit heads to be higher in larger cities also exists for their wives, though the differences are small, except in very large cities and rural areas. Whether the wage difference results from differences in costs of living, in standards of living, in the particular kinds of jobs, or in some other factor such as unionization is difficult to say. It does not result from any concentration in the cities of more educated women in more professional occupations, since education, occupation, and other factors have already been taken into account.

TABLE 10-5

HOURLY EARNINGS: DEVIATIONS FOR POPULATION OF CITIES
(FOR SPENDING UNIT WIVES WHO WORKED IN 1959)

Population of cities	Number of spending unit wives	Per cent of spending units	Unadjusted deviations [a]	Adjusted deviations [a]
Central cities of the 12 largest metropolitan areas	95	3.5	$ .21	$ .19
Other cities 50,000 or more	127	4.6	.07	.03
Urban places 10,000–49,999	105	3.6	−.04	−.03
Urban places 2,500–9,999	169	5.9	.05	.04
Rural areas near cities	104	3.7	.00	−.05
Rural areas not near cities	173	5.4	−.23	−.14

[a] deviations from grand mean of $1.43

It should surprise no one that wives for whom a disability is reported are less likely to work and earn less than average per hour if they do work. The differences are significant but not very important in the whole population. Few wives with disabilities worked.

TABLE 10-6

HOURLY EARNINGS: DEVIATIONS FOR PHYSICAL CONDITION
(FOR SPENDING UNIT WIVES WHO WORKED IN 1959)

Physical condition	Number of spending unit wives	Per cent of spending units	Unadjusted deviations [a]	Adjusted deviations [a]
Completely disabled	1	0.0	$−.38	$−.34
Severely disabled	7	0.2	−.87	−.73
Moderately disabled	26	0.9	−.24	−.20
Not disabled	739	25.6	.02	.01

[a] deviations from grand mean of $1.43

The amount of unemployment in the state in 1958 has an effect on the wife's wages similar to the one it had on whether she worked at all. Perhaps different reasons underlie the depressing effects of very high and very low unemployment. Extensive unemployment may be associated with lower wages because the wives who can find jobs go to work at low wages to supplement family incomes. Very little unemployment may be associated with lower wages because the nonindustrial states with few good jobs for women and generally lower wage rates have the least registered unemployment. The first of these is a short run phenomenon, and the second is a long run one.

It is interesting to note that in states with heavy unemployment heads earn higher wage rates but wives lower ones. This is consistent with the preceding hypothesis.

The last and least important characteristic in explaining how much working wives earned per hour was race. An over-all difference of 61 cents an

TABLE 10-7

HOURLY EARNINGS: DEVIATIONS FOR EXTENT OF UNEMPLOYMENT
IN STATES
(FOR SPENDING UNIT WIVES WHO WORKED DURING 1959)

Extent of 1958 unemployment in states	Number of spending unit wives	Per cent of spending units	Unadjusted deviations [a]	Adjusted deviations [a]
Under 5.00 per cent	160	5.3	$−.11	$−.10
5.00–6.49 per cent	286	9.6	−.01	.02
6.50–7.49 per cent	157	5.7	.15	.11
7.50–9.99 per cent	89	3.0	−.07	−.02
10.00 per cent and over	81	3.1	.03	−.06

[a] deviations from grand mean of $1.43

hour was reduced to 11 cents by differences in age, education, work experience, and type of job. This reduction does not necessarily mean that race is unimportant. The poor education that restricts the job opportunities of nonwhites can be attributed to race as the basic predetermining condition. Table 10-8 suggests that potential reduction of actual differences in earnings could be accomplished by providing more and better education for nonwhites as well as removing job discrimination based on color alone.

TABLE 10-8

HOURLY EARNINGS: DEVIATIONS FOR RACE
(FOR SPENDING UNIT WIVES WHO WORKED IN 1959)

Race	Number of spending unit wives	Per cent of spending units	Unadjusted deviations [a]	Adjusted deviations [a]
White	659	23.7	$ .03	$ .01
Nonwhite	114	3.0	−.27	−.10

[a] deviations from grand mean of $1.43

Summary

Some of the differences in the hourly earnings of wives are the effects of education, job experience, occupation, and the place where the family lives. The highly educated wife with extended experience in a professional occupation might be expected to make $2.85 an hour, about as much as a female spending unit head in the same position.

The over-all average hourly earnings of working wives ($1.43) are not much lower than those of female spending unit heads who worked ($1.54). However, differences in the age and education levels of the two groups may mean that some discrepancies in wage rates do occur between comparable subgroups, if wives receive lower wages for the same jobs, or are forced into lower-paying occupations than female heads at the same age and education levels. For this reason, it is interesting to compare average hourly earnings of wives and female spending unit heads according to age and education groups. Table 10-9 indicates, except for slight variations for young and middle-aged women with college degrees, little discrimination exists because of marital status.

Direct comparisons of factors affecting earnings of heads and of wives are difficult. Different explanatory factors were used, because they seemed appropriate or not in the two cases. A striking finding of this chapter is the small difference in hourly earnings between white and nonwhite wives. This results partly from the use of a more detailed occupational classification, which absorbs more of the racial differences, in so far as they operate through exclusion from certain types of jobs. The use of more detailed occupation groups does not account for the apparently lower effect of education and

TABLE 10-9

HOURLY EARNINGS WITHIN AGE AND EDUCATION (MEANS FOR SPENDING UNIT WIVES AND FEMALE SPENDING UNIT HEADS)

	Age							
	Under 30		30–44		45–64		65 and older	
Education	Wives	Female heads	Wives	Female heads	Wives	Female heads	Wives	Female heads
0–11 grades	$.99		$1.35		$1.19			
		$1.28		$1.15		$1.19		
	(75)	(18)	(132)	(59)	(109)	(92)		
12 grades; 12 grades plus nonacademic training	1.29		1.46		1.60		$1.14	
		1.47		1.74		1.77		$1.04
	(110)	(40)	(121)	(33)	(59)	(39)	(17)	(22)
Some college; college degree	1.59		1.89		2.26			
		1.86		2.33		2.29		
	(47)	(22)	(51)	(23)	(48)	(37)		

( ) number of spending units

age on the earnings of wives, however, because the unadjusted deviations are also smaller.

The direct comparisons of average hourly earnings presented in Table 10-9 and Table 10-4 are more relevant than comparisons of the adjusted deviations in comparing single females with working wives. For comparing wives with husbands, Table 10-4 can be compared with Table 5-2. It is clear that women, whether wives or not, earn less than men in the same age and education group.

Chapter 11

HOURS WORKED BY WORKING WIVES

Thirty-eight per cent of working wives worked all year, and three-fourths worked a thirty-five hour week or more when they were working.[1] In general, variations among wives as to hours worked represent voluntary or involuntary unemployment rather than overtime or second jobs. As with spending unit heads, it is assumed that there is some latitude for a wife to determine how many hours she works.

TABLE 11-1

DISTRIBUTION OF NUMBER OF HOURS WORKED PER YEAR
(PERCENTAGE DISTRIBUTION FOR SPENDING UNIT WIVES
WHO WORKED DURING 1959)

Number of hours worked per year	Per cent of spending unit wives who worked in 1959
1–949	36
950–1,849	26
1,850–2,149	30
2,150–2,549	5
2,550–3,049	2
3,050 or more	1
Total	100
Number of spending unit wives	773

Explanatory classifications fall into two groups. One represents barriers keeping the wife from working and the other measures incentives and motives encouraging working.

As in the analysis of whether wives work, four of the classifications in whole

[1] These estimates are reasonably close to the more precise Census, Bureau of Labor Statistics estimates of work experience of married women in 1959, which show 32 per cent of working wives worked at full-time jobs for 50 to 52 weeks, and another 33 per cent worked at part-time jobs, some of them presumably all year, but not many. See Jacob Shiffman, "Marital and Family Characteristics of Workers, March, 1960," *Monthly Labor Review* (April, 1961, Reprinted as "Special Labor Force Report No. 13," Table 3).

or part serve as indicators of barriers to working. Physical disabilities of the wife may affect her ability to work full time. The wife's age may indicate her stamina relative to the physical demands of the job, and her education may indicate whether less physically demanding jobs are available to her, or indeed whether any jobs are available. A classification of race and whether there are preschool or school children at home indicates whether child care would be needed if the wife worked full time. Nonwhites may also be restricted in the range of jobs available, yet if they do cleaning and housework, they are more likely to be able to adjust their work hours so they can care for their children too. The congested housing of nonwhites and perhaps acceptance of the needs of working mothers might make it easier for nonwhites to find inexpensive child care arrangements. A negative attitude on the part of the husband about working wives might reduce the wife's work hours without keeping her from working altogether.

Six of the classifications indicate motives or incentives to work. The wife's hourly earnings measure the direct monetary reward, probably even the marginal reward for extra hours. There is evidence in many surveys that many women say they work almost solely for the money and that they would not work if they did not have to.[2] The education of the wife may reflect the fact that women with formal education can find interesting jobs where part of the reward is the appeal of the job itself.

(The following factors were also used to predict whether wives worked.) Frequency of unemployment of the head, an indicator of financial insecurity in the spending unit, should indicate the pressure on the wife to provide both current income and security through full-time work. Head's and wife's gross factor income less the wife's earnings represents the marginal utility of money, the ease with which the family could get along without wages from the wife. Plans to help parents or children should increase the need for money and the wife's willingness to work long hours. Race may affect incentives, if nonwhite wives feel the need to make up for their husband's lower job security.

The eight classifications accounted for 14 per cent of the variance in the population; the analysis explains less of the variability of wives' hours than of heads' hours. Apparently noneconomic forces are more important in determining how much wives will work. The average hours worked by working wives was 1,345, and the standard deviation was 824 hours.

Having children at home reduces the number of hours the wife works and the probability that she will work at all, which was studied in Chapter 9. The net effect of having preschool children at home is to reduce hours of white working wives to 502 hours less than those with no children, and to reduce the hours of nonwhite working wives to only 238 less than nonwhite wives with

[2] Marion Gross Sobol, "Correlates of Present and Expected Future Work Status of Married Women" (unpublished Ph.D. dissertation, The University of Michigan, 1960), and references therein.

no children. Having all children in school made much less difference—143 hours for whites, 71 hours for nonwhites. Thus the hypothesis about the effect of children is borne out as well as the hypothesis about the smaller effect of children for nonwhites.

TABLE 11-2

CHARACTERISTICS USED TO EXPLAIN HOURS WORKED
(FOR SPENDING UNIT WIVES WHO WORKED DURING 1959)

Characteristics of spending unit wives	Relative importance (Beta coefficients)	Significance (F ratios)
Race and age of children	.271	13.20**
Hourly earnings	.234	6.15**
Gross factor income of spending units less wives' earnings	.140	1.96*
Age and education	.139	1.74
Attitude of heads toward wives' working	.125	2.01*
Frequency of unemployment of heads	.096	1.18
Physical condition	.062	1.15
Plans to help parents or children	.056	0.94

** significant at probability level of .01
* significant at probability level of .05

On the other hand, nonwhite wives, who were more likely to be working, worked fewer hours. This may be due to the fact that a large proportion of nonwhite women workers are employed as domestic and other service workers. In 1960, 60 per cent were so employed, compared with 25 per cent of all

TABLE 11-3

HOURS WORKED: DEVIATIONS FOR RACE AND AGE OF CHILDREN
(FOR SPENDING UNIT WIVES WHO WORKED IN 1959)

Race and age of children	Number of spending unit wives	Per cent of spending units	Unadjusted deviations [a]	Adjusted deviations [a]
White:				
No children	267	9.6	226	226
Children under 6	197	7.1	−303	−276
Children 6–17	195	7.0	101	83
Nonwhite				
No children	34	1.0	−184	−155
Children under 6	48	1.2	−345	−393
Children 6–17	32	0.8	−183	−226

[a] deviations from grand mean of 1,345 hours

women workers. Almost two-thirds of the nonwhite women workers in service occupations were domestic workers. Sixty-five per cent of all domestic workers worked only part time.[3]

[3] *The Economic Situation of Negroes in the United States,* Bulletin S-3, U.S. Department of Labor (Washington, 1960), Table 11, p. 12;

Combining analyses of labor force participation, wage rates, and hours shows that nonwhite wives are about 10 per cent more likely to work, make about 10 cents less per hour, and work about 240 hours less per year than white wives.

Very low and very high hourly earnings are associated with a reduction in the number of hours worked. The low-paying jobs may be largely part time jobs not subject to the minimum wage laws, while high paying ones may include some substitute teachers or women who work only during critical rush periods. However, the number of wives with high hourly earnings is too small to allow intensive analysis.

TABLE 11-4

HOURS WORKED: DEVIATIONS FOR HOURLY EARNINGS
(FOR SPENDING UNIT WIVES WHO WORKED IN 1959)

Hourly earnings	Number of spending unit wives	Per cent of spending units	Unadjusted deviations [a]	Adjusted deviations [a]
None [b]	5	0.2	−510	−460
$0.01–0.74; negative	99	3.1	−104	− 44
$0.75–0.99	114	3.7	−380	−318
$1.00–1.49	294	10.2	− 25	− 7
$1.50–1.99	113	4.2	271	223
$2.00–2.99	103	3.7	297	237
$3.00–3.99	30	1.1	− 16	−111
$4.00–4.99	11	0.4	−117	−263
$5.00 or more	4	0.1	−676	−857

[a] deviations from grand mean of 1,345 hours
[b] worked but had little or no income from it, e.g., self-employed who just covered expenses

Working wives tend to work fewer hours if the other factor income of the unit is either high or low. The association of shorter hours with low factor income is difficult to explain. The coefficients are adjusted for race and age, but not for occupation of the head or size of city. It is possible that some of the wives who work short hours, even though the other income is low, are farm wives who find it possible to work only during certain seasons.

The effect of age and education on hours worked is reduced by the association of age and education with hourly earnings, another predictor of hours worked. For example, the shorter hours worked of the young, poorly educated wives may be partly attributed to their low hourly earnings.

The adjusted deviations show a complex age-education effect that is clearly not the additive effect of the two. Wives with more education work longer hours, even taking account of the fact that they earn more per hour. The one exception to this is the group between thirty and forty-four with some college

1960 Handbook of Women Workers, Bulletin 275, U.S. Department of Labor (Washington, 1960), Table 26, p. 51.

TABLE 11-5

HOURS WORKED: DEVIATIONS FOR HEADS' AND WIVES' GROSS FACTOR
INCOME EXCLUDING WIVES' EARNINGS
(FOR SPENDING UNIT WIVES WHO WORKED IN 1959)

Heads' and wives' gross factor income excluding wives' earnings	Number of spending unit wives	Per cent of spending units	Unadjusted deviations [a]	Adjusted deviations [a]
None	3	0.1	−161	130
$1–499; negative	24	0.7	−257	−185
$500–999	35	0.9	− 49	− 58
$1,000–1,999	74	2.1	− 28	36
$2,000–2,999	66	2.1	63	262
$3,000–4.999	175	6.4	38	79
$5,000–7,499	220	8.2	12	− 17
$7,500–9,999	102	3.7	− 39	− 82
$10,000–14,999	55	1.9	27	−180
$15,000 or more	19	0.6	−152	−300

[a] deviations from grand mean of 1,345 hours

training, a group which may feel more strongly about staying home with young children. The multivariate adjustment takes account of the presence of children but not of the possibility that their influence interacts with the mother's education and with the husband's income. Dr. Sobol's analysis indicates that such an interaction exists.[4]

Adjusted deviations by age and education for whether the wife worked,

TABLE 11-6

HOURS WORKED: DEVIATIONS FOR AGE AND EDUCATION
(FOR SPENDING UNIT WIVES WHO WORKED IN 1959)

Age and education	Number of spending unit wives	Per cent of spending units	Unadjusted deviations [a]	Adjusted deviations [a]
Under 30				
0–11 grades	75	2.4	−458	−297
12 grades	110	4.0	− 26	− 10
Some college	47	1.7	48	73
30–44				
0–11 grades	132	4.5	27	21
12 grades	121	4.3	82	99
Some college	51	1.8	− 46	46
45–64				
0–11 grades	109	3.5	35	− 39
12 grades	59	2.1	143	7
Some college	48	1.7	234	171
65 and older	17	0.6	− 12	−168
Not ascertained	4	0.1	−584	−151

[a] deviations from grand mean of 1,345 hours

[4] Sobol, "Correlates of Present and Expected Future Work Status of Married Women."

wage rate, and number of hours can be combined to estimate the annual earnings contributed by wives according to the average age and education of the wife. All these are net effects, taking account of many other factors affecting wages or hours or the decision to work. Multiplying these together, it appears that the average wife's contribution has three different age patterns depending on her education: peaked in the middle, declining consistently, or lowest during middle age.

TABLE 11-7

ESTIMATED ANNUAL EARNINGS WITHIN AGE AND EDUCATION [a]
(FOR SPENDING UNIT WIVES)

Education	Age			
	Under 30	30–44	45–64	65 and older
0–11 grades	$ 603	$ 760	$ 353 ⎫	
12 grades	1,101	867	503 ⎬	94
Some college	1,474	1,063	1,234 ⎭	

[a] Estimated by combining adjusted deviations for whether worked, wage rate, and hours worked. These estimates are free of effects of differences in the other factors used in the multivariate analyses. The averages are for all spending unit wives, including those who did not work.

Wives seem to work somewhat shorter hours when the husband does not think it is a good idea for wives to work but the effects are somewhat erratic.

TABLE 11-8

HOURS WORKED: DEVIATIONS FOR ATTITUDE OF HEADS
TOWARD WIVES' WORKING
(FOR SPENDING UNIT WIVES WHO WORKED IN 1959)

Attitudes of heads toward wives' working	Number of spending unit wives	Per cent of spending units	Unadjusted deviations [a]	Adjusted deviations [a]
Favorable	171	5.5	141	146
Favorable, qualified	171	6.0	93	15
Ambivalent	32	1.1	33	− 23
Unfavorable, qualified	98	3.4	− 27	60
Unfavorable	143	5.1	− 99	− 82
Depends	136	4.9	−122	− 96
Do not know	4	0.1	327	209
Not ascertained	18	0.6	−365	−338

[a] deviations from grand mean of 1,345 hours

It was originally thought that wives would work more if their husbands were subject to unemployment, the accompanying insecurity, and lower income. Even before husband's earnings are accounted for, however, no such relationship appears. Indeed, the small group with infrequent short spells of unemployment where the wife was most likely to work is the one where she tends to work the fewest hours. If economic insecurity does drive the wife to work and to work longer hours, a better measure of this insecurity than the reported unemployment experience of the husband is needed to demonstrate the effect.

TABLE 11-9

HOURS WORKED: DEVIATIONS FOR FREQUENCY
OF UNEMPLOYMENT OF HEADS
(FOR SPENDING UNIT WIVES WHO WORKED IN 1959)

Frequency of unemployment of heads	Number of spending unit wives	Per cent of spending units	Unadjusted deviations [a]	Adjusted deviations [a]
Frequent	41	1.4	−124	− 63
Occasional	15	0.6	73	30
Short spells only	16	0.5	−223	−366
Infrequent	291	10.4	20	14
Never	167	5.8	− 89	− 57
Entered labor force recently	3	0.1	7	−317
Not ascertained	69	2.3	156	152
Retired or self-employed	171	5.6	34	24

[a] deviations from grand mean of 1,345 hours

Physical disabilities reduce hours worked as well as the tendency to work and the wage rate. The lack of importance and significance results from the fact that there were very few cases of disabled wives who worked during 1959.

TABLE 11-10

HOURS WORKED: DEVIATIONS FOR PHYSICAL CONDITION
(FOR SPENDING UNIT WIVES WHO WORKED IN 1959)

Physical condition	Number of spending unit wives	Per cent of spending units	Unadjusted deviations [a]	Adjusted deviations [a]
Completely disabled	1	0.0	−345	−868
Severely disabled	7	0.2	−277	−195
Moderately disabled	26	0.9	−238	−211
Not disabled	739	25.6	11	10

[a] deviations from grand mean of 1,345 hours

Plans involving a commitment of future income, which were associated with the wife's participation in the labor force, do not have the expected effects on hours worked. The fewest hours are worked by those with plans both to send children to college and to support parents in the future. Perhaps such commitments drive wives to work even when they can only work part time. In estimating the average hours worked for all wives, however, the extra proportion of wives who worked will more than offset the reduced hours among this group.

TABLE 11-11

HOURS WORKED: DEVIATIONS FOR PLANS TO HELP PARENTS
OR CHILDREN
(FOR SPENDING UNIT WIVES WHO WORKED IN 1959)

Plans to help parents or children	Number of spending unit wives	Per cent of spending units	Unadjusted deviations [a]	Adjusted deviations [a]
Do not plan to send children to college or help parents	321	10.9	42	−30
Plan to help parents	149	5.1	134	67
Plan to send children to college	181	6.3	− 79	37
Plan to send children to college and help parents	122	4.4	−149	−59

[a] deviations from grand mean of 1,345 hours

With some of the factors affecting the wife's earnings explained, it is useful to look at their over-all impact on the spending unit. For this purpose, a final table shows the distribution of wives' contribution according to the spending unit's factor income without the wife's income.

Table 11-13 is not intended to explain why wives work or the level of their incomes, but to describe the impact of wives' earnings on the distribution of income. It is clear that wives' earnings do not make the distribution of income much more nearly equal. Where the head's income is very low, the head is probably retired, but the wife is also likely to be old and to earn little or nothing. Where the head's earnings are relatively high, the wife is somewhat less likely to work but if she works she earns more, perhaps because both she and her husband are more highly educated. Where the head's earnings are very high, of course, the wife is still less likely to work.

Thus a major reason why a wife works and works long hours is because the spending unit income would otherwise be low. However, the impact of wives' earnings is not limited to spending units where the heads earn the least. Other

TABLE 11-12

NET COMBINED EFFECTS OF PLANS ON WIVES' WORK
(FOR ALL SPENDING UNIT WIVES)

Plans to help parents or children	Expected probability of working	Expected hours worked (adjusted)	Product (average hours per spending unit)
Do not plan to send children to to college or help parents	.34	1,315	447
Plan to help parents	.41	1,412	579
Plan to send children to college	.40	1,382	553
Plan to send children to college and help parents	.44	1,286	566

TABLE 11-13

EARNINGS OF SPENDING UNIT WIVES WITHIN HEADS' AND WIVES' GROSS FACTOR INCOME OF SPENDING UNIT EXCLUDING WIVES' EARNINGS

(PERCENTAGE DISTRIBUTION OF SPENDING UNITS WITH WIVES PRESENT)

Earnings of spending unit wives	Heads' and wives' gross factor income excluding wives' earnings						All spending units with wives present
	Under $1,000	$1,000– 2,999	$3,000– 4,999	$5,000– 7,499	$7,500– 9,999	$10,000 and over	
None	71	59	55	60	64	73	62
$1–499	9	10	7	9	8	7	8
$500–999	6	7	7	5	4	2	5
$1,000–1,999	5	11	10	5	6	2	7
$2,000–2,999	3	7	9	5	4	5	6
$3,000–4,999	5	4	11	13	10	6	9
$5,000 and more	0	1	1	2	3	4	2
Not ascertained	1	1	0	1	1	1	1
Total	100	100	100	100	100	100	100
Number of spending units	190	371	403	547	277	271	2,059

factors such as the age and education of the couple produce some positive correlation between the head's and wife's earnings.

Summary

The analysis of hours worked by wives explained less of the population variance than was explained by the analysis for heads. This indicates that noneconomic factors are more important in determining the hours worked by the wife than by the head.

The restraint of children at home, in a classification with race, had the most important effect on hours worked. Race was an important determinant as well; nonwhite wives, who are more likely to be working, worked substantially fewer hours than white wives. This may result from the fact that many nonwhite wives work in service occupations, where the proportion of part-time jobs is high.

Wage inducements also clearly affect the number of hours the wife works, as does the unit's gross factor income less the wife's earnings.

Combining the Results of Three Analyses

It is important to notice that there are differences between the impact of the same factors on hours worked, and their impact on whether the wife worked at all.

Where the same classification was used in each subsection of the analysis, it is possible to combine its effect on whether the wife works, wage rate, and total hours worked, to estimate its net effects, taking account of the other factors, on the contribution per spending unit of the wife's earnings.

Even if the classification is used for only two of the three parts, its effect can be assessed by using the average for the third. For instance, the adjusted effects of having plans to help children, combining effects on participation and on hours, added 106 hours of wives' work per year per spending unit. Assuming that such plans did not affect the wife's wage rate, this 106 hours multiplied by the *average* wage of $1.43 suggests that such plans result in an average contribution of additional income by the wife of 106 × $1.43 or $152 per year. This is not the difference between average wife's income in units with and without plans to send children to college. Rather, it is an estimate of the net effect of these plans taking account of many other factors.

In view of the attention which has been given to labor force participation of wives, it is important to note that many of the factors used in this analysis had quite different effects on whether the wife worked, her wage rate, and the number of hours she worked during the year.

Chapter 12

ADDITIONAL COMPONENTS OF SPENDING UNIT'S EARNINGS

In addition to income earned by the spending unit head, by his wife, or by their capital, a few small amounts of earned income accrue to spending units. These should be taken into account before the analysis of unearned or transfer incomes.

Six per cent of spending units have children under eighteen who earn money. The amounts reported are generally small, as is shown in Table 12-1.

TABLE 12-1

EARNINGS OF CHILDREN UNDER 18
(PERCENTAGE DISTRIBUTION OF SPENDING UNITS)

Earnings of children under 18	Per cent of spending units
None	94
$1–499	4
$500–999	1
$1,000 or more	1
Total	100
Number of spending units	2,997

Spending units also contain dependent adults, adults other than the spending unit head and his wife, who may have earned income. Not enough descriptive data was available for dependent adult units to permit detailed analysis of their gross factor incomes similar to the analysis done for spending unit heads and wives. However, it seems reasonable to assume that gross factor income of dependent adult units are affected by factors similar to those described in Chapters 4 through 11. The mean gross factor income of all dependent adult units was slightly over $600. Forty-seven per cent of the dependent units had gross factor income.

Nearly half of the dependent adult units are headed by a housewife, often a widow. About one-third are either currently working or looking for work.

Dependent adult unit heads are mostly quite young or quite old. Only one-fifth of them are between thirty-five and sixty-four compared with nearly three-fifths of the spending unit heads. Fifty-four per cent of all dependent adult unit heads are under thirty-five and 25 per cent are sixty-five or older. The young ones presumably are living with their parents only temporarily until they finish school or until they are financially able to maintain their own households.

Since the heads of dependent adult units were not interviewed very little else is known about them. Their transfer incomes are known; hence, the remainder of the analysis of transfer incomes and of the effects of combining of households will use all adult units and treat dependent adult units as separate units.

Chapter 13

TRANSFER INCOME AND ATTITUDES TOWARD TRANSFERS

If people had only the income they currently earned, many would lack the minimum amount necessary to take care of themselves. To make up for this deficiency, there has developed a complex system of transfer incomes, incomes which are not earned currently by the recipient.

Transfer incomes are classified in this analysis both according to whether the individual contributed to a program that provided them and according to whether they came from a private source or a public agency. Social security, unemployment compensation, and veterans pensions are included in public contributory transfers. Public noncontributory transfers cover welfare, old age assistance, free medical care, and other aid from public and private institutions. Nongovernmental pensions, alimony, and regular or irregular support from persons outside the immediate family are included in nonpublic transfers.

Components of Transfer Income

It may be useful first to list the major components of transfer income, together with the proportion of adult units who receive each of them. The reader must note that the analysis has shifted from the spending unit basis of Chapters 4 through 11, to an adult unit basis. Dependent adult units are considered as separate units. Only 23 per cent of dependent adult units received nonfamily transfer payments compared with 40 per cent of all adult units. The mean payments of such income to dependent adult units is $195.

It is possible that spending unit heads failed to report some transfer incomes, particularly aid which was irregular or hard to value, and perhaps welfare which some might not want to admit receiving. However, a test was made using the same interview schedule with 51 known welfare recipients in a single county. Even with interviewers somewhat less well-trained than the regular Survey Research Center interviewers, there was surprisingly little

142

failure to report such income. In 47 interviews, only two respondents failed to report welfare income.[1]

The size distribution of transfer incomes of various types cannot be estimated accurately from these data since so few people receive any one type. More than half of the yearly transfer payments to adult units are less than $1,000, however. There is no need for examining some of them further, since

TABLE 13-1

PER CENT RECEIVING COMPONENTS OF NONFAMILY
TRANSFER INCOME AND MEAN AMOUNTS
(FOR ADULT UNITS)

Components of nonfamily transfer income		Per cent receiving	Means for all adult units
Public contributory transfers		20	$177
Veterans benefits	6		
Unemployment conmpensation	5		
Social security	11		
Public noncontributory transfers		11	65
Welfare	4		
Free medical care	8		
Gifts from institutions	2		
Nonpublic transfers		19	165
Private retirement pensions	6		
Alimony, regular support from individuals	2		
More than $50 in gifts from individuals	12		
Total nonfamily transfers		40	$407
Number of adult units		3,396	3,396

it is known that certain transfers go to the disabled, the aged, the blind, the widowed, or the retired. Most of these programs have means tests or earning limits. Contributory transfers such as unemployment compensation, social security, and veterans benefits are already well studied.[2] Concern here is less with assuring a detailed picture of all transfer programs, and more with describing the welfare impact of the transfers for which reasonably good measures are available.

Public Noncontributory Transfers. The public noncontributory transfers such as public welfare and free medical care involve a wider variety of pro-

[1] Martin David, "Validity of Income from Welfare Reported by a Sample of Families Receiving Assistance," *Journal of the American Statistical Association* (forthcoming).

[2] See issues of *Social Security Bulletin;* Reports of the President's Commission on Veterans Pensions (Bradley Commission); Reports of the Special Committee on Unemployment Problems, U.S. Senate, 86th Cong., 2d. Sess.

For a study of the redistributive effects of the government in the United States, through taxes, transfers, and the benefits of government expenditures, see Alfred H. Conrad, "Redistribution through Government Budgets in the United States, 1950," *Income Redistribution and Social Policy* (ed.) Alan T. Peacock (London: Jonathan Cape, Ltd., 1954), pp. 178–267.

grams and less is known about them. The 11 per cent of all adult units who received public noncontributory transfers received an average of $586.

Adult units headed by people sixty-five and older are more likely to receive such transfers with 16 per cent receiving them.

Nonwhites are twice as likely to receive public noncontributory transfers as whites. The mean amount received by the 20 per cent of nonwhites who got such transfers was also above average, $833. Fourteen per cent of adult units headed by females, the majority of them older widows, receive such transfers. They, too, receive more than the average amount, $746.

Adult unit heads who are disabled and not working are the most likely to be receiving public noncontributory transfers. The 35 per cent for disabled who are not working is followed by 22 per cent of housewives, 16 per cent of retired, and 13 per cent of unemployed. The recipients are also largely those with little education.

Public welfare, which goes to 4 per cent of all adult units, goes to 15 per cent of those with less than $1,000 in factor income, 12 per cent of nonwhites, 8 per cent of those headed by women, 22 per cent of those with no education, and 29 per cent of the disabled who are not working.

When people were asked whether they had ever received welfare or other government aid, nearly 10 per cent reported that they had. However, many of them were recalling the distant past, including the Depression of the thirties.

About 8 per cent of all adult units reported receiving free medical care during 1959. The age group reporting free medical care most frequently was the twenty-five to thirty-four year olds. Free medical care was also reported more frequently than average by the nonwhites for whom the proportion was 11 per cent, and by 17 per cent of the disabled who are not working. The disabled may be covered by workmen's compensation and think of this as free medical care.

Nonpublic Transfers. Alimony and regular support payments from individuals, a substantial amount where they occur, were reported by only 2 per cent of adult units. Private retirement pensions were reported by 6 per cent. More than $50 in gifts from individuals outside the household were reported by 12 per cent. Over-all, irregular gifts are the most frequent and the largest among people over sixty-five years old, and least frequent among the middle aged. Most of the gifts received were food and clothing from relatives living in another dwelling.

Total Nonfamily Transfers. A clear picture of the extent to which transfer incomes accrue to those whose other incomes are low is provided in Table 13-2. Adult units with less than $2,000 from earnings and capital income are most likely to receive transfer income and receive high payments. The 30 per cent of adult units with gross factor incomes of less than $2,000 receive 59 per cent of nonfamily transfer income.

Although nonfamily transfers tend to go to low-income adult units, substantial amounts accrue to units that are otherwise modestly well off. Although the proportions receiving nonfamily transfer income decrease steadily as gross factor income rises, the mean payments to eligible adult units are high at both ends of the gross factor income distribution. The high mean payments to upper income adult units probably represent largely contributory transfers such as pensions for which the adult units made substantial contributions in previous years.

TABLE 13-2

PER CENT RECEIVING NONFAMILY TRANSFER INCOME AND MEAN
AMOUNT OF NONFAMILY TRANSFER INCOME WITHIN GROSS
FACTOR INCOME
(FOR ADULT UNITS)

Gross factor income	Number of adult units	Per cent of adult units	Per cent receiving non-family transfer income	Mean non-family transfer income for recipients
None	311	9	53	$1,260
$1–499; negative	291	7	63	1,194
$500–999	252	6	66	1,322
$1,000–1,999	359	8	59	1,389
$2,000–2,999	287	7	49	824
$3,000–4,999	531	17	37	858
$5,000–7,499	617	21	31	753
$7,500–9,999	354	12	22	510
$10,000–14,999	273	9	22	739
$15,000 and over	121	4	20	1,458
All adult units	3,396	100	40	$1,021

In general, the details of transfer incomes are about what one might expect with one exception—they are not so redistributive as might have been expected. If one considers that a substantial fraction of transfer incomes involved earlier contributions, it is obvious that the amount of income redistribution among individuals through transfer incomes is relatively small in any one year. Contributory transfer programs largely redistribute income in time, from the earning years to the retirement years, for instance.[3] These programs are far more important than the other transfer systems which redistribute income between people, largely between those able to pay and those unable to support themselves.

Once the data in Chapters 4 through 12 have been used to predict components of gross factor income for an adult unit, the components can be combined. The resulting estimate of gross factor income can be used, together with Table 13-2, to estimate transfer income for the unit. The third column of Table 13-2 gives the probability of a unit in each income group having

[3] Paul Samuelson, "An Exact Consumption-Loan Model of Interest with or without the Social Contrivance of Money," *Journal of Political Economy*, LXVI (December, 1958), 467–482.

transfer income and the fourth column gives the average amount for those units which have it.

Public Contributory Transfers. There has been much disagreement about the proper level of support for those on relief. Many have championed the idea that only the deserving poor should be helped. There have been suggestions that too liberal benefits would result in people not trying to find work. However, as standards of living have risen, definitions of minimal and too liberal benefits have also risen.

Similar questions arise even with contributory programs, where part or all the cost is covered out of contributions from those who will or may benefit. The contributory aspect of such a program frees it from the necessity for being at a bare maintenance of subsistence level, but not from questions about the effects of benefits on incentives.

Unemployment Compensation: Experience and Attitudes

A question about unemployment compensation benefits was used to determine attitudes about benefit levels because there has been much discussion about those benefits, the incentive to look for employment appears variable and subject to influence, and the system is sometimes not thought of as contributory. In this chapter attitudes held by spending unit heads who work for others or are unemployed toward unemployment compensation payments are analyzed.

This is not a discussion of the problem of defining a standard of adequacy, nor of assessing the importance of incentives. Nor is it intended that the views of the people should be taken directly as a basis for public policy. The analysis focuses more on the differences in people's attitudes about the adequacy of unemployment compensation than on the average response, which is a function of the particular questions asked. Many people have no knowledge nor experience with the unemployment compensation system, others are so likely to benefit from it that they have a personal stake in its provisions.

Although only 4 per cent of all spending unit heads were unemployed at the time they were interviewed in March and April, 1960, and only 5 per cent had received unemployment compensation in 1959, the program of unemployment insurance has a broader impact on families than these small percentages indicate.[4] In the five years prior to the interview slightly over one-fifth of all spending unit heads in the labor force had been unemployed. For each of these spending units, the provisions of unemployment insurance are of a vital interest.

[4] Wilbur J. Cohen, William Haber, and Eva Mueller present data on the effects of unemployment during the 1958 recession on work experience, atitudes, and finances which supplement the material presented here. See Wilbur J. Cohen and others, *The Impact of Unemployment in the 1958 Recession,* U.S. Senate, Special Committee on Unemployment Problems, 86th Cong., 2d. Sess., 1960.

TABLE 13-3

UNEMPLOYMENT EXPERIENCE
(PERCENTAGE DISTRIBUTION OF SPENDING
UNIT HEADS IN THE LABOR FORCE)

Unemployment experience	
Unemployed at the time of the interview	5
Unemployed in the previous five years	16
Not unemployed during the five-year period	79
Total	100
Number of spending unit heads	1,960

Table 13-4 shows that many of those who were unemployed during this period never received benefits while one in eight exhausted their benefit payments.

Spending unit heads who were not unemployed also have an interest in the provision of unemployment insurance programs, since unemployment insurance is a protection against a potential financial risk for these families. For this reason all spending unit heads who were either unemployed or working for

TABLE 13-4

EXPERIENCE WITH UNEMPLOYMENT COMPENSATION
(PERCENTAGE DISTRIBUTION OF SPENDING UNIT HEADS WHO WERE
UNEMPLOYED DURING THE FIVE-YEAR PERIOD PRIOR
TO THE INTERVIEW)

Unemployment compensation experience		Per cent of spending unit heads who where unemployed during the five-year period prior to the interview
Received benefits		63
Received compensation for the entire period of unemployment	50	
Exhausted benefits	13	
Did not receive benefits		35
Ineligible	18	
Did not apply	8	
Other reasons	9	
Not ascertained whether received benefits		2
Total		100
Number of spending unit heads		532

someone else were asked whether they thought unemployment compensation payments should be higher, lower, or about the same.

Thirty-six per cent were in favor of higher payments; 29 per cent were in favor of present benefit levels; 3 per cent were in favor of a reduction in benefits. The fact that 32 per cent had no opinion is an indication that a substantial group of workers are poorly informed about unemployment compensation programs or uninterested in them.

The reasons which workers gave for preferring different levels of benefits fell quite clearly into two groups, according to whether the head felt that benefits ought to be higher or not.

Persons who felt that benefits ought to be increased referred primarily to their feeling that benefits are generally inadequate or that benefits are too small for a large family. Statements such as "when the cost of living keeps going up, the payments should get higher, too," and "with kids, you just can't live on what they pay," reflect this attitude.

Persons who approved of present levels of benefits reported that the amounts were adequate. One respondent who felt that payments were reasonable said: "Unemployment compensation is intended to tide a worker from one job to the next—all I feel that it should take care of is subsistence."

Those who felt benefit levels are too high referred most often to the disincentive of high benefits. One respondent, who felt payments should be lower, stated that: "The more they pay, the more unemployment there is." Another person said: "I know some men don't even look for a job—they can get better money just staying home." A second reason given by some who felt that payments should be the same or lower was that increasing benefits would raise taxes.

Determinants of Attitudes toward Unemployment Compensation Benefits

Table 13-5 indicates that workers hold differing views on the adequacy of unemployment compensation benefits. It seems relevant to ask to what extent their attitudes are influenced by past experience with the program and by other characteristics. Four groups of influences seemed appropriate in explaining the attitudes. Perhaps the most obvious variables are measures of the head's own experience with unemployment and unemployment compensation. Here one would expect that if benefit levels are inadequate, workers who had received benefits and workers who had been denied benefits would be likely to support higher compensation benefits.

A second group of variables indicate the economic circumstances of the spending unit. Those units with a high income, savings, and few dependents may be more likely to feel that present benefits are adequate than those families who must cut their living standards or go on welfare to meet their needs during unemployment.

Local economic conditions and the extent of unemployment during recessions may also influence attitudes. If a high proportion of workers become unemployed during a period of slack, even the workers who remain employed may be more aware of any inadequacies in benefit payments than if unemployment affects only a small fraction of the workers in the area. This would lead one to suspect that workers in areas with least stable employment would be more likely to favor increasing benefits than would workers in areas

TABLE 13-5

FEELINGS ABOUT LEVEL OF UNEMPLOYMENT COMPENSATION
PAYMENTS AND REASONS
(PERCENTAGE DISTRIBUTION OF SPENDING UNIT HEADS
WHO WORK FOR OTHERS OR ARE UNEMPLOYED)

Reasons	Unemployment compensation payments should be: [a]		
	Higher [b]	Same	Lower
Payments are generally inadequate	82	2	0
Payments are inadequate for some people	8	1	0
Payments are adequate	0	51	3
High payments destroy incentive to work	3	33	73
Payments are too high	0	1	10
Normative, moral reasons	4	6	7
Reasons involving taxes	1	5	7
Other reasons	6	5	6
Do not know; not ascertained	2	8	2
Per cent of spending unit heads who work for others or are unemployed	36	29	3

[a] The question was: "Do you think unemployment compensation payments should be higher, lower, or the same as they are now? Why do you say so?"
[b] Columns add to more than 100 per cent because some spending unit heads mentioned more than one reason.

of stable employment. Local economic conditions were measured by the average proportion of workers who were unemployed during 1958 in the state. The measure gives an indication of the extent of labor surplus during a moderate recession and could be expected to influence attitudes toward level of benefits. Attitudes toward government responsibility for seeing that people who want jobs can find them have been shown to be related to the unemployment experience in the county several years previously.[5]

A fourth group of variables describe the head's affiliations with organizations that might take a stand on unemployment compensation or related issues. Union membership, political preference, and perhaps religious affiliation would be relevant here.

The remaining variables indicate where the head lives and whether he moved into that area from a different part of the country.

Since each spending unit head was referring to the level of unemployment compensation benefits in his state, a measure of the adeqacy of benefits in the state was included. A variable describing the proportion of unemployment compensation claimants exhausting benefits was used to adjust for differences between states in the adequacy of benefits. A more direct indication of benefit adequacy, such as the average benefit for a family of a given size, was not available at the time of the survey.

[5] Angus Campbell and others, *The American Voter* (New York: John Wiley & Sons, Inc., 1960), pp. 382–384.

For purposes of the multivariate analysis it was necessary to scale the attitudes reported in Table 13-5. The relatively clear differentiation in reasons given by persons advocating higher, lower, and the same levels of benefits made it seem reasonable to use a single linear scale for the dependent variable. The responses were scored:

Higher	2
Same	0
Lower	−2

The mean for the scaled attitude was 0.94, about halfway between "same" and "higher." The standard deviation was 1.18.

In some ways the analysis proved disappointing. The explanatory variables accounted for only 10 per cent of the variance in attitudes toward level of benefits, in spite of the fact that persons who expressed no opinions on benefit levels, were excluded from the analysis.

Table 13-6 shows the importance and significance of the twelve variables included in the analysis. Only five were both significant and important in explaining attitudes held.

TABLE 13-6

CHARACTERISTICS USED TO EXPLAIN FEELINGS ABOUT LEVEL OF
UNEMPLOYMENT COMPENSATION PAYMENTS
(FOR SPENDING UNIT HEADS WHO WORK FOR OTHERS
OR ARE UNEMPLOYED)

Characteristics of spending unit heads	Relative importance (Beta coefficients)	Significance (F ratios)
Earning potential	.210	8.24**
Religious preference	.132	2.89**
Extent of unemployment in states	.123	5.66**
Frequency of unemployment	.117	3.41**
Labor union membership	.081	4.91**
Movement out of Deep South	.080	1.91
Adult unit composition	.077	1.27
Gross disposable income	.067	0.75
Experience with unemployment compensation in past five years	.065	2.11
Political preference	.056	0.94
Urban-rural migration	.054	0.87
Per cent of claimants exhausting unemployment compensation in states	.019	0.13

** significant at probability level of .01

Earning potential displays several highly significant differences in attitudes toward benefits. Negative deviations for college people indicate that they tend to think present benefit levels are adequate. Positive deviations for noncollege people show that those over thirty-five favor increases in benefit levels slightly more than the younger group. The nonwhite group reports about

TABLE 13-7

FEELINGS ABOUT LEVEL OF UNEMPLOYMENT COMPENSATION
PAYMENTS: DEVIATIONS FOR EARNING POTENTIAL
(FOR SPENDING UNIT HEADS WHO WORK FOR OTHERS
OR ARE UNEMPLOYED)

Earning potential	Number of spending unit heads	Unadjusted deviations [a]	Adjusted deviations [a]
Nonwhites	195	.26	.21
White farmers	4	−.89	−.94
White nonfarmers, under 35			
0–11 grades	166	.21	.12
12 grades	133	−.17	−.16
Some college	111	−.48	−.42
White, nonfarmers, 35 or older			
0–11 grades	394	.25	.23
12 grades	194	−.07	−.06
Some college	144	−.52	−.39
Not ascertained	6	.47	.52

[a] deviations from grand mean of 0.94

the same opinions as older high school dropouts; this is not surprising, since the majority of nonwhite spending unit heads are over thirty-five and have not graduated from high school. In general the groups most exposed to the threat of unemployment are most in favor of increasing benefits.

Religious groups in Table 13-8 are ordered according to the average level of income and education of their members. However, only the unadjusted

TABLE 13-8

FEELINGS ABOUT LEVEL OF UNEMPLOYMENT COMPENSATION
PAYMENTS: DEVIATIONS FOR RELIGIOUS PREFERENCE
(FOR SPENDING UNIT HEADS WHO WORK FOR OTHERS
OR ARE UNEMPLOYED)

Religious preference	Number of spending unit heads	Unadjusted deviations [a]	Adjusted deviations [a]
Baptist	312	.20	.05
Fundamentalist Protestant other than Baptist	141	.04	−.01
Roman Catholic	334	.04	.05
Lutheran	81	−.11	−.03
Non-Christian; non-Jewish	6	−.18	−.04
Non-Fundamentalist Protestant other than Lutheran, Presbyterian, and Episcopalian	296	−.17	−.14
Presbyterian	77	−.25	−.07
Jewish	30	.44	.76
Episcopalian	35	−.58	−.35
None; not ascertained	35	.31	.18

[a] deviations from grand mean of 0.94

TABLE 13-9

FEELINGS ABOUT LEVEL OF UNEMPLOYMENT COMPENSATION
PAYMENTS: DEVIATIONS FOR EXTENT OF UNEMPLOYMENT
IN STATES
(FOR SPENDING UNIT HEADS WHO WORK FOR OTHERS
OR ARE UNEMPLOYED)

Extent of 1958 unemployment in states	Number of spending unit heads	Unadjusted deviations [a]	Adjusted deviations [a]
Under 5.00 per cent	211	.03	.10
5.00–6.49 per cent	476	−.15	−.15
6.50–7.49 per cent	332	−.05	−.05
7.50–9.99 per cent	167	.21	.22
10.00 per cent and over	161	.28	.21

[a] deviations from grand mean of 0.94

deviations for religious preference can be interpreted as effects of income and education, since these variables are included separately in the analysis. The adjusted deviations must be associated with differences in religious groups other than differences in education and income.

Except for the Jewish group, unadjusted deviations show that the higher the average income and education of the group, the less the members think unemployment compensation benefits should be raised. The Jewish group, in spite of its high average income and education, shows more concern with better benefits for the unemployed than any other group.

Jewish spending unit heads are most likely to favor increasing benefits while Episcopalians are most likely to feel present benefits are adequate. The Jews have a long history of philanthropy within their own group and in general. The factors which lead to the highly significant adjusted differences between religious groups are not clear.

TABLE 13-10

FEELINGS ABOUT LEVEL OF UNEMPLOYMENT COMPENSATION
PAYMENTS: DEVIATIONS FOR FREQUENCY OF UNEMPLOYMENT
(FOR SPENDING UNIT HEADS WHO WORK FOR OTHERS
OR ARE UNEMPLOYED)

Frequency of unemployment	Number of spending unit heads	Unadjusted deviations [a]	Adjusted deviations [a]
Frequent	137	.33	.13
Occasional	41	.41	.21
Short spells only	36	.37	.09
Infrequent	648	.05	.05
Never	363	−.33	−.21
Entered labor force recently	28	−.21	.12
Not ascertained	94	.26	.19

[a] deviations from grand mean of 0.94

TABLE 13-11

FEELINGS ABOUT LEVEL OF UNEMPLOYMENT COMPENSATION
PAYMENTS: DEVIATIONS FOR LABOR UNION MEMBERSHIP
(FOR SPENDING UNIT HEADS WHO WORK FOR OTHERS
OR ARE UNEMPLOYED)

Labor union membership	Number of spending unit heads	Unadjusted deviations [a]	Adjusted deviations [a]
Members	458	.22	.10
Nonmembers	886	−.13	−.06
Not ascertained	3	1.06	1.27

[a] deviations from grand mean of 0.94

Residents of states with very heavy or very light unemployment during the 1958 recession favor increased benefits more than residents of states in which insured unemployment ran 5.00–7.49 per cent. The favorable attitude of residents of states with little insured unemployment is difficult to understand, unless it is because these are farm states with lower than average benefits. The remaining areas deviate from the average in much the manner that one would expect, with residents of high unemployment areas favoring higher compensation.

The unemployment frequency of the head had the expected effect. Those who were more frequently unemployed indicated that benefits should be higher.

Union members were more likely to favor increased benefits than nonmembers. The multivariate adjustment reduces the effect of union member-

TABLE 13-12

FEELINGS ABOUT LEVEL OF UNEMPLOYMENT COMPENSATION
PAYMENTS: DEVIATIONS FOR MOVEMENT OUT OF DEEP SOUTH
(FOR SPENDING UNIT HEADS WHO WORK FOR OTHERS
OR ARE UNEMPLOYED)

Movement out of Deep South	Number of spending unit heads	Unadjusted deviations [a]	Adjusted deviations [a]
Grew up in United States outside the Deep South, now live:			
in South	154	−.02	.10
in non-South	787	−.06	−.04
Grew up in the Deep South, now live:			
in South	258	.13	.10
in non-South	79	.31	.12
Grew up in foreign countries	60	−.01	−.28
Grew up in several regions; not ascertained	9	.21	.37

[a] deviations from grand mean of 0.94

TABLE 13-13

FEELINGS ABOUT LEVEL OF UNEMPLOYMENT COMPENSATION
PAYMENTS: DEVIATIONS FOR ADULT UNIT COMPOSITION
(FOR SPENDING UNIT HEADS WHO WORK FOR OTHERS
OR ARE UNEMPLOYED)

Adult unit composition	Number of spending unit heads	Unadjusted deviations [a]	Adjusted deviations [a]
Unmarried male heads:			
No children under 18	143	−.19	−.22
Children under 18	7	.06	−.25
Unmarried female heads:			
No children under 18	123	−.05	.02
Children under 18	55	.08	.05
Married heads:			
No children under 18	308	.02	−.01
1 child under 18	201	.06	.11
2 children under 18	218	.03	.07
3 or more children under 18	292	.00	−.02

[a] deviations from grand mean of 0.94

ship because union members are less educated and more likely to report
unemployment.

The pattern of coefficients for movement out of the Deep South does not
support either the hypothesis that there are regional differences in attitudes
nor that mobility affects attiudes toward benefit levels.

No tendency appears for those with more dependents to favor higher
unemployment compensation benefits.

TABLE 13-14

FEELINGS ABOUT LEVEL OF UNEMPLOYMENT COMPENSATION
PAYMENTS: DEVIATIONS FOR GROSS DISPOSABLE INCOME
(FOR SPENDING UNIT HEADS WHO WORK FOR OTHERS
OR ARE UNEMPLOYED)

Gross disposable income	Number of spending unit heads	Unadjusted deviations [a]	Adjusted deviations [a]
None	1	−.94	−1.15
$1–499; negative	15	.43	.37
$500–999	26	.05	− .06
$1,000–1,999	101	.30	.20
$2,000–2,999	141	.06	.04
$3,000–4,999	337	.02	− .01
$5,000–7,499	420	.05	.03
$7,500–9,999	190	−.11	− .09
$10,000–14,999	91	−.32	− .10
$15,000 and over	25	−.45	− .16

[a] deviations from grand mean of 0.94

TABLE 13-15

FEELINGS ABOUT LEVEL OF UNEMPLOYMENT COMPENSATION
PAYMENTS: DEVIATIONS FOR EXPERIENCE WITH UNEMPLOYMENT
COMPENSATION IN PAST FIVE YEARS
(PER CENT OF SPENDING UNIT HEADS WHO WORK FOR OTHERS
OR ARE UNEMPLOYED)

Experience with unemployment compensation in past five years	Number of spending unit heads	Unadjusted deviations [a]	Adjusted deviations [a]
Have not been unemployed	921	−.11	−.02
Have been unemployed:			
Received compensation	291	.37	.12
Did not receive compensation	129	.00	−.16
Not ascertained whether received compensation	6	−.34	−.36

[a] deviations from grand mean of 0.94

The effect of income is not significant and somewhat erratic, but in general persons with higher incomes are more likely to favor maintaining present benefits.

Those heads who received unemployment compensation are more likely to favor increasing benefits than those who did not, but the differences here are extremely small. Curiously the unemployed who did not receive benefits are less inclined to increase benefits than those who were never unemployed.

Differences in attitudes of Republicans and Democrats largely disappear when adjusted for differences in education, income, and labor union membership.

The urban-rural migration pattern suggests that some differences in attitudes may exist between those who grew up on a farm and those who grew

TABLE 13-16

FEELINGS ABOUT LEVEL OF UNEMPLOYMENT COMPENSATION
PAYMENTS: DEVIATIONS FOR POLITICAL PREFERENCE
(FOR SPENDING UNIT HEADS WHO WORK FOR OTHERS
OR ARE UNEMPLOYED)

Political preference	Number of spending unit heads	Unadjusted deviations [a]	Adjusted deviations [a]
Strongly Democratic	331	.16	.03
Not very strongly Democratic	332	.07	.00
Independent	318	−.03	.05
Not very strongly Republican	209	−.22	−.15
Strongly Republican	110	−.23	.00
Other; not ascertained	47	.09	.06

[a] deviations from grand mean of 0.94

TABLE 13-17

FEELINGS ABOUT LEVEL OF UNEMPLOYMENT COMPENSATION
PAYMENTS: DEVIATIONS FOR URBAN-RURAL MIGRATION
(FOR SPENDING UNIT HEADS WHO WORK FOR OTHERS
OR ARE UNEMPLOYED)

Urban-rural migration	Number of spending unit heads	Unadjusted deviations [a]	Adjusted deviations [a]
Grew up on farms, now live:			
in rural areas	176	−.01	−.12
in towns 2,500–49,999	108	.07	−.06
in cities 50,000 or more	74	−.01	−.15
Grew up in cities or towns, now live:			
in rural areas	247	−.07	.01
in cities or towns	716	.01	.04
Grew up in several places; not ascertained	26	.05	.00

[a] deviations from grand mean of 0.94

up in towns or cities. The latter group is more likely to favor increasing benefits.

The per cent of claimants in the state exhausting unemployment benefits had no significant relation to attitudes of people in that state, once differences in rates of unemployment were considered.

TABLE 13-18

FEELINGS ABOUT LEVEL OF UNEMPLOYMENT COMPENSATION
PAYMENTS: DEVIATIONS FOR PER CENT OF CLAIMANTS
EXHAUSTING UNEMPLOYMENT COMPENSATION IN STATES
(FOR SPENDING UNIT HEADS WHO WORK FOR OTHERS
OR ARE UNEMPLOYED)

Per cent of claimants exhausting unemployment compensation in states	Number of spending unit heads	Unadjusted deviations [a]	Adjusted deviations [a]
Under 25.0 per cent	371	−.07	.02
25.0–29.9 per cent	209	.04	−.02
30.0–34.9 per cent	298	−.11	.02
35.0–39.9 per cent	239	.13	.00
40.0 per cent and over	230	.11	−.04

[a] deviations from grand mean of 0.94

Summary

The distribution of transfer incomes shows the great importance of contributory systems, and systems where the benefits depend in part on the previous economic status of the person. Transfer incomes are not so much a force for redistribution as one might have supposed. Most of the redistribution is between points of time for the same individuals, as when a man pays premiums when he is working but receives benefits when he is unemployed or retired.

Among those who are working for someone else and subject to unemployment, there is a preponderance of opinion in favor of increased unemployment compensation benefits. Those most likely to become unemployed, the uneducated, those with recent unemployment experience, and those most likely to suffer from unemployment—the married and the older—were most in favor of increased benefits. A sizable proportion of spending unit heads were unable to give an opinion on the adequacy of unemployment benefits, indicating a rather widespread lack of information about the program.

Chapter 14

THE ECONOMICS OF LIVING WITH RELATIVES

One of the ways in which a needy adult unit improves its living standard is by living with relatives, and a major way an adult unit helps its relatives is by sharing its home with them. These living arrangements may offer advantages to both the host and the guest adult units. One unit may provide some financial support in addition to housing for the other unit; the dependent unit may care for children or help with housework. Along with these benefits, such living arrangements usually necessitate sacrifices of privacy and independence on the part of both units.

Attitudes toward Relatives' Living Together

As a measure of general attitudes toward relatives' living together, the following question was asked: "Some older people move in with their children —others try hard to keep a separate household even when it means pinching pennies. Do you think it is a good idea or a bad idea for older people to live with their children? Why is that?" Since the question was asked only of spending unit heads, attitudes of dependent adults, who are receiving family aid, were not obtained. Attitudes of wives were not obtained either but wives' attitudes are less likely to differ greatly from the heads' attitudes.

Nearly two-thirds of all spending unit heads are opposed to having aged parents live with their children. They see this arrangement as disadvantageous largely to the children or to both generations, although some persons mentioned disadvantages to older people as well. Differences in views and attitudes of the two generations accounted for many of the reasons why people see disadvantages in having the generations live together. "The old do not understand the young," said one man, "and the young do not understand the old or the young."

Most heads cited conflicts between the two groups: "Old people are pretty hard to get along with"; "The parents and the children try to boss each other

158

and when they live with you there's always fighting." "It takes a pretty big house to hold two women," said one man, and another felt that "a kitchen is only big enough for one."

Those who saw the disadvantages to older people of living with younger people cited noise from young children and loss of familiar surroundings as reasons. One older woman felt that "you still want to be independent, even though you're old."

Those spending unit heads who favored having older people live with their children were most concerned about providing care for the parents: "It's a good thing to have them with you so you can see after them."

A few spending unit heads reported advantages to the children or both generations, such as the unemployed head who said: "The old folks might get a pension or something, so they could help you out."

People most able to provide support for relatives are most opposed to it. Older people with some college education are eleven to one against it. White

TABLE 14-1

REASONS FOR ATTITUDE TOWARD OLDER PEOPLE LIVING
WITH THEIR CHILDREN WITHIN ATTITUDE
(PERCENTAGE DISTRIBUTION OF SPENDING UNIT HEADS)

Attitude toward Older People Living with Their Children

Reasons [a]	Favorable	Favorable, qualified	Depends	Unfavorable, qualified	Unfavorable	All spending unit heads [b]
Advantages for older people	38	16	4	0	0	5
Advantages for children or for both generations	16	7	2	0	0	2
Children ought to care for parents	33	21	4	2	0	5
Other advantages	4	3	1	0	0	1
Disadvantages for older people	1	5	8	17	15	12
Disadvantages for children or for both generations	2	9	17	64	80	60
Parents ought not to depend on children; normative answers	0	3	3	5	5	4
Other disadvantages	0	1	0	3	3	2
No reasons given	12	40	67	15	3	16
Number of spending unit heads	280	163	288	369	1,788	2,997

[a] Columns add to more than 100 per cent because some spending unit heads gave more than one reason.

[b] Includes 109 spending unit heads whose feelings about parents living with children were not ascertained. The question was: "Some older people move in with their children. Others try to keep a separate household even if it means pinching pennies. Do you think it's a good idea or a bad idea for older people to live with their children? Why is that?"

TABLE 14-2

ATTITUDES TOWARD OLDER PEOPLE LIVING WITH THEIR CHILDREN WITHIN EARNING POTENTIAL
(PERCENTAGE DISTRIBUTION OF SPENDING UNIT HEADS)

Attitude toward older people living with their children	Retired	Nonretired nonwhite	Nonretired white farmers	Earning potential						All spending unit heads [a]
				Nonretired white nonfarmer						
				18–34			35 or older			
				0–11 grades	12 grades	College	0–11 grades	12 grades	College	
Favorable	4	25	6	10	9	6	7	5	5	8
Favorable, qualified	5	9	3	7	6	3	4	5	3	5
Depends	6	12	8	12	10	14	8	9	11	10
Unfavorable, qualified	6	9	12	14	14	18	13	13	13	12
Unfavorable	71	40	70	51	59	57	65	65	65	61
Not ascertained	8	5	1	6	2	2	3	3	3	4
Total	100	100	100	100	100	100	100	100	100	100
Number of spending unit heads	312	378	170	250	220	211	759	365	314	2,997

[a] includes 18 spending unit heads for whom earning potential was not ascertained

farmers are ten to one against it. Even among nonwhites, who are most favorable to it, there is still a majority opposed to having older people living with their children. Among the white nonfarmer population who have generally higher incomes, those with more education and those who are somewhat older are more likely to oppose having older people live with their relatives.

Neither the head's frequency of church attendance nor his religious preference affect his attitude toward living with relatives. The non-Fundamentalist Protestants, liberal denominations whose members have more education and income, are somewhat more opposed to having older people live with their children. This may be largely an income effect, however.

Living in a Relatives' Home

This chapter considers the decision of adult units to live together. The analysis is divided into two parts: first, the adult units' decisions to live alone or to move into relatives' homes, and second, the decision of adult units which live alone about whether to invite relatives to live in their homes. A third part of the chapter examines income and financial needs the secondary units add when they move in.

The adult units being housed by relatives are divided into two groups in this sample. One group, the dependent adult units, keep no separate finances. In most surveys, these people are not counted separately but are treated as extra adults in some other spending unit or family. Dependent adult units tend to be very young or very old, to be single, and to have very little income. The other group, related secondary spending units, keep separate finances and have some income of their own but live with relatives, who own the home or pay the rent, usually their parents or children. These units also tend to be at the extremes of the age groups, but, by definition, have more income. They must have an income of $15 a week or more to qualify as separate spending units.

The factors associated with becoming an extra adult unit are analyzed by assigning a value of one to units which live within relatives' homes, and a value of zero to units who live in their own homes. A multivariate analysis then becomes a discriminant analysis maximizing the ability to predict whether a unit will live in a relative's home.

The multivariate analysis of factors associated with living in a relative's dwelling uses largely economic or physical factors, plus a few classifications which may serve as proxy measures of cultural influences.

The factors used to explain living with relatives fall into two general categories: those which measure economic and physical needs of the unit, and those which measure preferences and cultural differences.

The needs of the unit are measured by five factors. The adult unit's gross disposable income minus any intrafamily transfer income describes the unit's financial ability to take care of itself without living with relatives. Physical condition of the head indicates whether the unit might need to live with another unit in order to obtain nursing care and other aid. Age is used because both ends of the distribution contain persons most likely to live with relatives. Young people may not leave home after their eighteenth birthdays because they are still in school, or because they can provide needed help around the house, or because they want to accumulate some assets before trying to establish separate households. Older people may live with relatives because they need care or company or economic help.

The composition of the unit is described by the "stage in the family life cycle" variable. Married couples with children are probably most likely to want the independence and need the space that a separate home provides. Single persons are most likely to need companionship, and can be accommodated most easily in another's home. Sex of the adult unit head was used to see whether males are more likely than females to live alone.

Three variables were used to reflect cultural variations and differences in preferences for combining households. Region was used since it might reflect differences in the willingness of families to combine households in different regions of the country. It might also measure geographical differences in housing arrangements.

Race was used because there may be racial differences if discrimination forces units to combine in limited available housing, or if there is greater incidence of broken homes among nonwhites who compensate by combining households.

The remaining measure related to cultural differences attempts to measure variations in public preferences for government support of aged persons. The average old age assistance payments per inhabitant of a state indicate the level of public resources available to needy older people.

The relative importance and significance of the classifications used to explain living with relatives are shown in Table 14-3.

TABLE 14-3

CHARACTERISTICS USED TO EXPLAIN LIVING IN A RELATIVE'S HOME
(FOR ADULT UNITS)

Characteristics of adult units	Relative importance (Beta coefficients)	Significance (F ratios)
Stage in life cycle	.391	141.14**
Gross disposable income minus net intrafamily transfers	.378	175.89**
Age of heads	.164	33.11**
Physical condition of heads	.063	5.86**
Region	.058	8.28**
Old Age Assistance payments per inhabitant in states	.057	4.80**
Race	.035	9.05**
Sex of heads	.013	1.25

** significant at probability level of .01

The mean of the dependent variable was .17, indicating that 17 per cent of adult units were living in a relative's home; the standard deviation was .38. The multivariate analysis accounted for 54 per cent of the population variance. The simple demographic and financial facts in the first two predictors obviously accounted for most of the differences. Marital status and income account for most of the variations in whether adult units live with relatives.

Unmarried persons without children are more likely to be living with relatives. These single people are also more likely to be very young or very old. Correlation with age, the third most important predictor, accounts for some of the reduction in the adjusted coefficients for single people. Single people also have lower incomes. For married couples, presence of children seems to have no added deterrent effect on living with relatives.

TABLE 14-4

LIVING IN A RELATIVE'S HOME: DEVIATIONS FOR STAGE
IN LIFE CYCLE
(FOR ADULT UNITS)

Stage in life cycle	Number of adult units	Per cent of adult units	Unadjusted deviations [a]	Adjusted deviations [a]
Unmarried heads under 45				
No children under 18	495	14.4	.53	.32
Married, wives under 45				
No children under 18	212	6.6	−.13	−.11
Children under 6	733	21.4	−.16	−.12
Children 6–17	352	10.7	−.17	−.09
Married, wives 45 or older				
Children under 6	26	0.7	−.17	−.06
Children 6–17	199	5.8	−.17	−.09
No children under 18	546	17.1	−.16	−.07
Unmarried heads 45 or older				
No children under 18	623	18.1	.13	.08
Unmarried				
Children under 18	210	5.2	.00	.01

[a] deviations from grand mean of .17

Almost no one lives in a relative's house if he has an income of $5,000 or more. But most of these people are also married and middle aged; hence, the multivariate analysis attributes about one-half the effect to these other characteristics. However, 70 per cent of the adult units with incomes under $1,000 live with relatives, but these people are largely single and either very young or very old. Therefore, the adjusted effect of low incomes is reduced somewhat.

Even with the life cycle classification's age division at forty-five, there remains a substantial tendency for adult units where the head is under twenty-five to live with relatives. Adjusting for income and marital status and age division in the life cycle classification removes most of the remaining age effect, however. This appears a reasonable outcome implying that only

TABLE 14-5

LIVING IN A RELATIVE'S HOME:
DEVIATIONS FOR GROSS DISPOSABLE INCOME
MINUS NET INTRAFAMILY TRANSFERS
(FOR ADULT UNITS)

Gross disposable income minus net intrafamily transfers	Number of adult units	Per cent of adult units	Unadjusted deviations [a]	Adjusted deviations [a]
Less than $1,000	539	13.8	.53	.35
$1,000–1,999	462	11.0	.06	.01
$2,000–2,999	402	10.9	.02	−.01
$3,000–4,999	693	21.9	−.07	−.07
$5,000–7,499	672	22.4	−.14	−.08
$7,500–9,999	346	11.2	−.17	−.08
$10,000 or more	282	8.8	−.17	−.07

[a] deviations from grand mean of .17

TABLE 14-6

LIVING IN A RELATIVE'S HOME: DEVIATIONS FOR AGE OF HEADS
(FOR ADULT UNITS)

Age of heads	Number of adult units	Per cent of adult units	Unadjusted deviations [a]	Adjusted deviations [a]
Under 25	434	12.5	.44	.15
25–34	631	18.6	−.03	.03
35–44	694	20.6	−.11	−.03
45–54	624	17.9	−.11	−.03
55–64	517	14.5	−.09	−.05
65–74	317	10.2	−.01	−.04
75 or older	179	5.7	.12	−.01

[a] deviations from grand mean of .17

among the very young is there combining of households that cannot be accounted for by low income or the lack of a spouse or children.

People who are disabled are less likely to be living in a relative's home than those who are not disabled. This fits with the finding that the disabled receive surprisingly little help from relatives, whether from intrafamily transfers of remittances. (See Chapter 17.) The disabled tend to be older, to have a home of their own.

There is more combining of households in the West and less in the South than one would expect on the basis of other characteristics. It is also interesting that the adjustments for other factors worked in opposite directions in these two regions. There was less combining of households in the South in spite of more low income people. And there was more combining of households in the West in spite of the fact that there are more middle-aged people with adequate incomes. Perhaps the migration from South to West, leaving

TABLE 14-7

LIVING IN A RELATIVE'S HOME:
DEVIATIONS FOR PHYSICAL CONDITION OF HEADS
(FOR ADULT UNITS)

Physical condition of heads	Number of adult units	Per cent of adult units	Unadjusted deviations [a]	Adjusted deviations [a]
Completely disabled	139	3.8	.00	−.04
Severely disabled	108	2.9	−.05	−.09
Somewhat disabled	286	8.2	−.09	−.04
Disabled, but work not limited	30	0.9	−.17	−.05
Disabled, limitation not ascertained	75	2.0	.19	.04
Not disabled	2,758	82.2	.01	.01

[a] deviations from grand mean of .17

relatively more housing, particularly rental housing, in the South and a shortage in the West, accounts for this.

TABLE 14-8

LIVING IN A RELATIVE'S HOME: DEVIATIONS FOR REGION
(FOR ADULT UNITS)

Region	Number of adult units	Per cent of adult units	Unadjusted deviations [a]	Adjusted deviations [a]
Northeast	734	23.6	.02	.01
North Central	964	29.3	.01	.01
South	1,200	31.8	−.02	−.03
West	498	15.3	−.01	.03

[a] deviations from grand mean of .17

Apparently residents of states which dispense higher than average amounts of Old Age Assistance are less likely to live with relatives. This variable can be

TABLE 14-9

LIVING IN A RELATIVE'S HOME: DEVIATIONS FOR OLD AGE
ASSISTANCE PAYMENTS PER INHABITANT IN STATES
(FOR ADULT UNITS)

Old Age Assistance payments per inhabitant in states	Number of adult units	Per cent of adult units	Unadjusted deviations [a]	Adjusted deviations [a]
Less than $5.00	476	14.6	.00	.01
$5.00–7.49	831	24.7	.04	.02
$7.50–9.99	685	20.7	.01	.01
$10.00–14.99	657	18.0	−.03	−.01
$15.00–20.99	656	19.6	−.02	−.02
$21.00 and over	91	2.4	−.07	−.10

[a] deviations from grand mean of .17

interpreted as distinguishing states where Old Age Assistance is a well-known and possibly easily accessible means of support for older people. It is possible that in some states feelings against relatives' responsibility result in less combining of households and more reliable on Old Age Assistance.

Nonwhites live with relatives less frequently than whites if their low incomes and concentration in the South are accounted for. These significant findings attribute to other factors effects that are usually assumed to be the results of segregation and racial discrimination in housing.

TABLE 14-10

LIVING IN A RELATIVE'S HOME: DEVIATIONS FOR RACE
(FOR ADULT UNITS)

Race	Number of adult units	Per cent of adult units	Unadjusted deviations [a]	Adjusted deviations [a]
White	2,887	88.8	−.01	.00
Nonwhite	509	11.2	.05	−.04

[a] deviations from grand mean of .17

More women than men live with relatives, but the differences can be attributed completely to their unmarried state, extreme age, and low income. A female spending unit head is, by definition, unmarried.

TABLE 14-11

LIVING IN A RELATIVE'S HOME: DEVIATIONS FOR SEX OF HEADS
(FOR ADULT UNITS)

Sex of heads	Number of adult units	Per cent of adult units	Unadjusted deviations [a]	Adjusted deviations [a]
Male	2,552	76.5	−.06	.00
Female	844	23.5	.21	−.01

[a] deviations from grand mean of .17

Table 14-12 shows that even with the inclusion of contributions from relatives, including free food and rent, the adult units with the lowest welfare position are most likely to live with relatives. Living with relatives may alleviate some poverty but does not put very many adult units in a really comfortable economic position, unless imputations from intrafamily transfers are substantially underestimated.

Half of the adult units who live with relatives are below seven-tenths of the budget standard compared with 13 per cent of other adult units.

Providing Housing for Relatives

This section deals only with primary adult units, that is, units which live in their own homes. It examines the factors which account for decisions about whether or not to invite relatives to live with them. Such acts would,

TABLE 14-12

PROPORTION LIVING IN RELATIVES' HOMES
WITHIN ADULT UNIT WELFARE RATIO
(FOR ADULT UNITS)

Adult unit welfare ratio [a]	Number of adult units	Per cent in group living in relatives' homes	Percentage distribution of adults living in relatives' homes
Under 0.5	522	51	33
0.5–0.6	387	34	18
0.7–0.8	293	24	11
0.9–1.0	309	16	9
1.1–1.2	287	11	6
1.3–1.5	390	10	8
1.6–2.0	542	9	9
2.1 and over	666	5	6
All adult units	3,396	17	100

[a] ratio of adult unit gross disposable income to a budget standard. (See Appendix C and Chapter 16.) The ratio is a measure of the adequacy of income to meet the unit's needs. A ratio of 1.0 indicates an income equal to the estimated need.

in most cases, provide greater benefit to the relatives than to those who provided the housing for them.

The explanatory classifications in the multivariate analysis can be interpreted in several ways. Classifications may be associated with the physical ability to care for relatives and with ease in absorbing relatives into the household, with the head's willingness to accept the responsibility, with the unit's financial ability to provide for others, and with the likelihood that there would be relatives needing help and willing to accept it.

One of the crucial explanatory factors, whether there are living relatives, is indicated only by the number of living children. Clearly, an adequate explanation also requires knowledge of living parents, siblings, and so forth.

The ease with which a family could absorb secondaries and the likelihood that the family would have very young or very old relatives are indicated by age of head. Middle aged persons might be able to support relatives more easily than older persons would be able to support them. Middle aged persons also would be more likely to have needy relatives. Stage in life cycle indicates whether there is a wife at home to help care for relatives or children who might make it more difficult to care for relatives. There is also the possibility that males and females may differ in their willingness to house relatives.

Financial ability to provide for relatives is indicated by gross factor income, transfer income, and education. The sum of gross factor income and transfer income describes current income, while education represents past or potential income. Existence of needy relatives is indicated by the number of living children, geographic mobility, and race. Geographic mobility is assumed to be important, since there is more chance that the head still lives near his parents or his children if he has not moved much. Race may be important if discrimination and income instability induce living together.

A favorable attitude toward housing relatives is indicated by the family head's attitude toward older people living with their children, his attitude toward government responsibility for the aged, his religious preference and church attendance, and where the head of the family grew up. The latter will be important if there are geographic differences in the acceptance of relatives' living together.

The multivariate analysis of factors associated with housing attempts to discriminate between the 17 per cent of the primary adult units which house relatives and the 83 per cent which do not. The 13 explantory classifications with a total of 85 subclasses accounted for 12 per cent of the variance. The previous multivariate analysis of which units become secondary units was much more effective. This indicates that the variables studied describe dependent relatives but fail to distinguish supporting relatives with any great certainty. As in the earlier analysis, the mean was .17, and the standard deviation was .38.

TABLE 14-13

CHARACTERISTICS USED TO EXPLAIN HOUSING RELATIVES
(FOR FAMILY HEADS)

Characteristics of family heads	Relative importance (Beta coefficients)	Significance (F ratios)
Stage in life cycle	.263	27.40**
Number of living children	.215	16.27**
Attitude toward older people living with their children	.158	13.18**
Gross factor income of heads and wives	.105	3.88**
Age	.097	4.97**
Nonfamily transfer income of heads and wives	.080	2.25*
Education	.075	8.91**
Attitude toward government responsibility for the aged	.073	2.81**
Geographic mobility	.045	3.21*
Background	.033	0.69
Religious preference and church attendance	.033	0.58
Race	.026	2.14
Sex	.022	1.53

** significant at probability level of .01
* significant at probability level of .05

Single persons are more likely to house relatives than married persons. Perhaps the resistance of wives to another woman in the kitchen is more important that the need for a wife to care for the relatives. Having children at home, as well as a wife, makes housing of relatives even less likely.

The more children the head has, the more likely he is to be providing

TABLE 14-14

HOUSING RELATIVES: DEVIATIONS FOR STAGE IN LIFE CYCLE
(FOR FAMILY HEADS)

Stage in life cycle	Number of family heads	Per cent of family heads	Unadjusted deviations [a]	Adjusted deviations [a]
Unmarried heads under 45				
No children	154	5.2	.05	.15
Married, wives under 45				
No children under 18	203	7.7	−.05	.02
Children under 6	720	25.6	−.10	−.13
Children 6–17	349	12.9	−.02	−.07
Married, wives 45 or older				
Children under 6	26	0.8	.22	.00
Children 6–17	199	7.0	.05	−.06
No children under 18	539	20.4	.05	.06
Unmarried, heads 45 or older				
No children	437	15.2	.04	.12
Unmarried				
Children under 18	173	5.2	.12	.11

[a] deviations from grand mean of .17

housing, although he may be housing his own parents or his wife's rather than adult children. A substantial amount of housing of relatives involves children eighteen or older who have not yet left the parental home. Yet it is meaningful to consider this as aid to others, since most of these children are capable of providing for themselves.

TABLE 14-15

HOUSING RELATIVES: DEVIATIONS FOR NUMBER OF LIVING CHILDREN
(FOR FAMILY HEADS)

Number of living children	Number of family heads	Per cent of family heads	Unadjusted deviations [a]	Adjusted deviations [a]
None	573	20.9	−.03	−.10
One	509	19.1	−.03	−.02
Two	638	23.3	−.03	−.01
Three	459	16.6	.00	.03
Four	269	9.2	.03	.06
Five	142	4.7	.06	.10
Six	74	2.2	.15	.13
Seven	45	1.4	.14	.15
Eight or more	89	2.6	.31	.33
Not ascertained	2	0.0	.50	.34

[a] deviations from grand mean of .17

Family heads who feel it is bad for older persons to live with their children are less likely to house relatives. Those who referred to personal experience include many who presently house relatives. The large positive deviation for this group is partly definitional. It is impossible to determine whether people

TABLE 14-16

HOUSING RELATIVES: DEVIATIONS FOR ATTITUDE TOWARD
OLDER PEOPLE LIVING WITH THEIR CHILDREN
(FOR FAMILY HEADS)

Attitude toward older people living with their children	Number of family heads	Per cent of family heads	Unadjusted deviations [a]	Adjusted deviations [a]
Favorable	245	7.5	.11	.09
Favorable, qualified	148	4.9	.08	.10
Depends	263	9.4	.04	.06
Unfavorable, qualified	336	12.0	.03	.02
Unfavorable	1,711	62.9	−.04	−.04
Only references to personal experience	17	0.7	.38	.37
Not ascertained	80	2.6	.12	.07

[a] deviations from grand mean of .17

The question was: "Some older people move in with their children. Others try to keep a separate household even if it means pinching pennies. Do you think it is a good idea or a bad idea for older people to live with their children? Why is that?"

who have to house their relatives accept the necessity gracefully, or whether people who previously approved of housing relatives act on their attitude.

Families with income of $7,500 to $10,000 provide the greatest relative proportion of housing for other units. Those with very high incomes, if they have needy relatives, can support them in independent homes or institutions. It is surprising that families with gross factor incomes as low as $1,000 are as likely as average to support relatives. Only those with incomes under $1,000 cannot afford to support relatives. Of course, nonfamily transfer in-

TABLE 14-17

HOUSING RELATIVES: DEVIATIONS FOR GROSS FACTOR INCOME
OF HEADS AND WIVES
(FOR FAMILY HEADS)

Gross factor income of heads and wives	Number of family heads	Per cent of family heads	Unadjusted deviations [a]	Adjusted deviations [a]
None	103	3.2	−.08	−.12
$1–499; negative	190	5.7	.00	−.09
$500–999	183	5.4	.02	−.05
$1,000–1,999	300	8.3	.05	.01
$2,000–2,999	249	7.6	.02	.00
$3,000–4,999	449	17.2	.02	.01
$5,000–7,499	585	23.8	−.03	.00
$7,500–9,999	350	13.9	.03	.06
$10,000–14,999	271	10.4	−.03	.01
$15,000 and over	120	4.5	−.02	−.02

[a] deviations from grand mean of .17

come, which might be used to support relatives, is not included in this income measure. Table 14-19 shows how transfer income affects housing of relatives.

A family with a very young or very old head is not likely to provide housing for relatives. Families with heads under thirty-five or over sixty-five either are dependents or live alone. The families with heads in the middle of the age range are most likely to have elderly parents who need help or children who are young adults and not independent.

TABLE 14-18

HOUSING RELATIVES: DEVIATIONS FOR AGE
(FOR FAMILY HEADS)

Age	Number of family heads	Per cent of family heads	Unadjusted deviations [a]	Adjusted deviations [a]
Under 25	167	5.9	−.13	−.05
25–34	541	19.3	−.09	−.04
35–44	652	23.4	−.01	.00
45–54	581	20.2	.08	.05
55–64	475	16.0	.07	.03
65–74	261	10.3	−.01	−.04
75 and older	123	4.9	.00	−.04

[a] deviations from grand mean of .17

TABLE 14-19

HOUSING RELATIVES: DEVIATIONS FOR NONFAMILY TRANSFER
INCOME OF HEADS AND WIVES
(FOR FAMILY HEADS)

Nonfamily transfer income of heads and wives	Number of family heads	Per cent of family heads	Unadjusted deviations [a]	Adjusted deviations [a]
None	1,550	56.9	.02	.02
$1–499	490	16.5	−.03	−.02
$500–999	291	9.9	.01	−.01
$1,000–1,499	195	6.6	−.05	−.06
$1,500–1,999	98	3.5	−.05	−.05
$2,000–2,999	112	4.1	−.05	−.06
$3,000–4,999	52	2.0	−.01	−.01
$5,000–7,499	5	0.2	−.17	−.10
$7,500–9,997	5	0.2	.23	.21
$9,998 and over	2	0.1	−.17	−.16

[a] deviations from grand mean of .17

When the primary adult unit relies on transfer income, it is less likely to be providing housing for relatives.

In addition to other effects, heads with more education are less likely to provide housing for relatives. Possibly educated people have looser family ties, or relatives of the well-educated are fewer in number and better able to care for themselves.

TABLE 14-20

HOUSING RELATIVES: DEVIATIONS FOR EDUCATION
(FOR FAMILY HEADS)

Education	Number of family heads	Per cent of family heads	Unadjusted deviations [a]	Adjusted deviations [a]
0–11 grades	1,567	53.6	.04	.02
12 grades	629	23.7	−.02	−.01
Some college	604	22.7	−.07	−.05

[a] deviations from grand mean of .17

There is a slight tendency for those who assign major responsibility for the aged to their relatives also to provide housing for their own relatives. Again, of course, the causation could be from the behavior to the attitude rather than conversely.

TABLE 14-21

HOUSING RELATIVES: DEVIATIONS FOR ATTITUDE TOWARD
GOVERNMENT RESPONSIBILITY FOR THE AGED
(FOR FAMILY HEADS)

Attitude of head toward government responsibility for the aged	Number of family heads	Per cent of family heads	Unadjusted deviations [a]	Adjusted deviations [a]
Relatives should have sole responsibility	773	28.9	.00	.02
Relatives should have primary responsibility; government help if necessary	827	29.7	.00	.00
Relatives and government should share responsibility	247	9.0	−.04	−.03
Government should have primary responsibility; relatives help if necessary	161	5.6	.02	.04
Government should have sole responsibility	648	21.8	−.02	−.04
Other	23	0.9	−.04	−.05
Do not know; not ascertained	121	4.1	.12	.05

[a] deviations from grand mean of .17
The question was: "If the older people don't have enough money, do you think their relatives should support them, or should the government take care of them, or what? Why do you say so?"

Moving and possibly leaving relatives behind does not seem to have any effect on the frequency of housing relatives. Persons who move may maintain close family ties; other persons may remain in one location while relatives move away.

Apparently there is nothing about growing up in the Deep South or in a small town that encourages providing housing for relatives.

TABLE 14-22

HOUSING RELATIVES: DEVIATIONS FOR GEOGRAPHIC MOBILITY
(FOR FAMILY HEADS)

Geographic mobility	Number of family heads	Per cent of family heads	Unadjusted deviations [a]	Adjusted deviations [a]
Have worked, lived in one state, less than 100 miles from present location	1,320	47.7	.01	.01
Have worked, lived in several states or more than 100 miles from present location	1,289	46.1	−.01	−.02
Never worked	191	6.2	.03	.03

[a] deviations from grand mean of .17

TABLE 14-23

HOUSING RELATIVES: DEVIATIONS FOR BACKGROUND
(FOR FAMILY HEADS)

Background	Number of family heads	Per cent of family heads	Unadjusted deviations [a]	Adjusted deviations [a]
Grew up in the Deep South: On a farm or in a small town	572	18.1	.00	−.01
In a large city or different places	100	3.4	−.03	−.01
Grew up in United States outside the Deep South: On a farm or in a small town	1,170	41.9	−.01	.00
In a large city or different places	688	26.5	.00	.02
Grew up in a foreign country	153	5.9	.04	.02
Not ascertained	117	4.2	.03	−.01

[a] deviations from grand mean of .17

Religious preference and frequency of church attendance apparently do not affect the propensity to provide housing for relatives.

After adjustments there remains a slight nonsignificant tendency for nonwhites to provide more housing for their relatives than whites do. The difference is remarkably slight considering discrimination in housing and the number of incomplete families among nonwhites.

Single females are apparently only slightly less likely to be providing housing for relatives, and not significantly so.

Income and Dependents Added by Housing Relatives

The 17 per cent of family heads who provide housing for relatives must provide added beds and places at the table. To compensate there is also added

TABLE 14-24

HOUSING RELATIVES: DEVIATIONS FOR RELIGIOUS PREFERENCE
AND CHURCH ATTENDANCE
(FOR FAMILY HEADS)

Religious preference and church attendance	Number of family heads	Per cent of family heads	Unadjusted deviations [a]	Adjusted deviations [a]
Catholics:				
Attend more than once a month	444	16.9	.02	.01
Attend once a month or less	118	4.5	.01	.01
Fundamentalist Protestants:				
Attend more than once a month	564	18.2	−.01	−.02
Attend once a month or less	416	14.0	.00	.00
Non-Fundamentalist Protestants:				
Attend more than once a month	522	19.0	−.02	−.01
Attend once a month or less	568	21.1	.00	.01
Non-Christian; not ascertained	168	6.3	.03	.02

[a] deviations from grand mean of .17

TABLE 14-25

HOUSING RELATIVES: DEVIATIONS FOR RACE
(FOR FAMILY HEADS)

Race	Number of family heads	Per cent of family heads	Unadjusted deviations [a]	Adjusted deviations [a]
White	2,402	89.4	−.01	.00
Nonwhite	398	10.6	.06	.03

[a] deviations from grand mean of .17

TABLE 14-26

HOUSING RELATIVES: DEVIATIONS FOR SEX
(FOR FAMILY HEADS)

Sex	Number of family heads	Per cent of family heads	Unadjusted deviations [a]	Adjusted deviations [a]
Male	2,265	82.4	−.01	.00
Female	535	17.6	.06	−.02

[a] deviations from grand mean of .17

income from the three-fourths of extra adult units who have income of their own. The average complex family includes 1.4 persons in its secondary adult units. The family receives an average of $1,660 money income after taxes from secondary adult units. It seems clear that housing relatives brings more extra expense than extra income. Table 14-27 shows the added income brought in by the extra units for which the primary provides housing, and the number of added people by age of the family head. Where older people provide housing it seems to be for more people and for people with larger incomes of their own.

The average primary adult unit with extra adult units in his home contributes $492 a year in food and housing to the extra adult units. This estimate is based on spending unit heads' reports of housing costs and payments between units and on estimates of food costs for families of various sizes and incomes.[1]

When extra adult units' incomes are compared to the amounts of money required to provide them with modest amounts of food and housing, it appears that 62 per cent of them have inadequate incomes. However, only 24 per cent of them are members of families whose total incomes are inadequate. According to the scale of income adequacy, 73 per cent of extra adult units improve their situation by living with relatives; only 5 per cent of them are worse off than they would be if they lived alone.

Although most of the families with extra adult units are contributing to the support of these adult units, the families enjoy about the same level of income adequacy as do families which do not house extra adult units. (See Table 14-27.)

TABLE 14-27

ECONOMIC EFFECT OF HOUSING RELATIVES WITHIN AGE OF HEAD
(FOR FAMILIES)

Age of head	Number of families	Per cent who house relatives	Per cent of extra adult units who have income	Mean disposable money income from extra unit [a]	Average number of dependents added in extra unit [a]
Under 25	167	4	( )	( )	( )
25–34	541	8	67	$1,198	1.43
35–44	652	16	67	1,244	1.37
45–54	581	25	81	1,478	1.40
55–64	475	24	81	2,203	1.36
65–74	261	16	81	2,187	1.67
75 or older	123	17	63	1,741	1.69
All families	2,800	17	76	1,660	1.43

[a] mean for all with extra adult units (including those with no income)
( ) too few cases

Sharing a home with relatives appears to be associated with poorer housing conditions. Table 14-28 indicates that housing of units which include secondary units or dependent units is more crowded than housing of units which live alone.

Table 14-29 shows two measures of housing conditions based on the

[1] U.S. Department of Agriculture, "Income and Household Size: Their Effects on Food Consumption," *Household Food Consumption Survey* (October, 1959).

TABLE 14-28

NUMBER OF PERSONS PER ROOM
WITHIN FAMILY COMPOSITION
(PERCENTAGE DISTRIBUTION OF PRIMARY ADULT UNITS)

| | Families contain primary adult units and: | | | |
Number of persons per room	No extra units	Secondary spending units; no dependent units	Dependent adult units	All primary adult units
.01–.44	34	15	21	31
.45–.74	30	44	34	31
.75–.94	14	15	14	14
.95–1.44	18	23	21	19
1.45 and more	4	3	10	5
Total	100	100	100	100
Number of primary adult units	2,312	151	337	2,800

TABLE 14-29

QUALITY OF HOUSING WITHIN FAMILY COMPOSITION
(PERCENTAGE DISTRIBUTION OF SPENDING UNITS)

| | Families contain primary adult units and: | | | |
Quality of interior	No extra units	Secondary spending units; no dependent units	Dependent adult units	All spending units
Well kept up; in good condition	57	53	44	55
Fairly well kept up; in fair condition	30	30	34	30
Not kept up; in poor condition	11	16	20	13
Not ascertained	2	1	2	2
Total	100	100	100	100
Quality of exterior				
Well kept up; in good condition	55	47	40	52
Fairly well kept up, in fair condition	31	35	38	32
Not kept up; in poor condition	13	18	22	15
Not ascertained	1	0	0	1
Total	100	100	100	100
Number of spending units	2,310	347	340	2,997

reports of the interviewers. The interviewer was asked to evaluate the interior and the exterior of the dwelling unit according to whether it was neat and well cared for, or shabby and dirty. While these judgments are, of course, subjective, and there are differences in measurement from interviewer to interviewer, they do provide some indication of the general surroundings in which the unit lives.

There are around 9 million individuals aged fifty-five and older who live in adult units where the welfare ratio is .84 or less, that is, the unit has less than 85 per cent of what it would take to meet a modest estimate of its needs. Two million of these individuals, however, live in families where the family budget ratio is .85 or higher. In other words, the number of individuals fifty-five and older whose incomes are clearly inadequate is reduced by nearly one-fourth through living with relatives.

For those aged sixty-two or older, of whom there are nearly 7 million, a similar reduction in the number falling below the level of adequacy occurs.

TABLE 14-30

MEAN GROSS DISPOSABLE INCOME WITHIN AGE
OF ADULT UNIT HEAD
(FOR ADULT UNITS AND FAMILIES)

Age of adult unit heads	Adult unit disposable income	Family disposable income
18–24	$2,602	$6,315
25–34	5,562	6,485
35–44	6,441	6,998
45–54	5,977	6,794
55–64	5,306	6,445
65–74	3,452	4,711
75 and older	1,935	3,731

Table 14-30 shows how living with relatives affects the absolute levels of family income for each age group.

Summary

Relatives' living together has become less frequent as living standards have risen in this country. Many people do not think that it is a good idea to have older people living with their children. When relatives live together, the situation can be partially explained on the basis of economic necessity, physical disability, age, race, and differences in attitudes. The over-all impact of combining households is clearly to improve the financial welfare of the secondary units, and to add greater financial burdens than extra income to the primary unit.[2] When people live with relatives, they may also contribute, that is, do housework, take care of the children, help grow food or make additions or improvements to the house. Likewise, the estimate of what they receive from the primary unit includes only food and housing and there may be more help received than that.

Of the 64.6 million adult units in this country in 1959, 11.2 per cent were dependent adult units, 6.2 per cent were financially independent related secondary spending units living in a relative's home, and another 1.9 per cent were unrelated secondary spending units living in the same dwelling with other units. Hence, nearly a fifth of the adult units had no home of their own, and could be thought of as a source of potential demand for separate housing. In other words, there were 64.6 million adult units but only 52.2 million dwelling units, leaving a potential demand for 12.4 million dwelling units if every adult unit were to have its own.

As the trend continues toward a separate dwelling for each adult unit, the distribution of family income will continue to be affected. Most units that move out will add low income units to the distribution, and reduce the family incomes of the former host units.

[2] There are several small studies in this area; see, for instance, Marvin B. Sussman, "The Help Pattern in the Middle-Class Family," *American Sociological Review,* 18 (February 1953), 22–29.

Marjorie Knoll, *Economic Contributions and Receipts of Household Members,* Memoir #350 (Ithaca, New York: New York State College of Home Economics, Cornell University, October, 1957).

Chapter 15

SUMMARY OF INCOME ANALYSES

Chapters 4 through 14 describe the over-all picture of 1959 income in the United States. Eighty-six per cent of the 57.4 million spending unit heads in the United States worked in 1959. They worked an average of 2,092 hours at an average hourly wage rate of $2.29, earning an average of $4,122. The average amount that all spending units saved by growing their own food and doing home repairs was $182. Their average income from capital, including the imputed return on their equity in their homes, was $713. Seventy per cent of the spending unit heads were married; 38 per cent of the wives worked in 1959. They worked an average of 1,345 hours at an average wage of $1.43, contributing an average of $515 to spending unit incomes. Dependent adult units added average real earnings of $66; minor children earned an average of $30.

Perhaps the most interesting thing about this information is the fact that capital income is second only to earnings of the head in its importance as a source of spending unit income. The largest component of capital income is the imputed return on the equity in the owner-occupied homes.

For an accurate assessment of adequacy of incomes, it is preferable to deal with all 64.6 million adult units in the United States, not just the independent ones who are heads of spending units. The average gross factor income for all adult units was $5,191, of which $4,560 was real earnings and $631 was income from capital. The adult unit also received $407 of transfer income from outside the dwelling. Some adult units received income from within the dwelling, but others donated equal amounts and the average is zero for all adult units. Estimated Federal income taxes averaged $612 for adult units, leaving $4,986 average gross disposable income. Out of this the average adult unit contributed $261 to churches, charities, and other individuals. This left the average adult unit with $4,725 net real income available for present consumption needs and savings.

Eighty-three per cent of all adult units live alone or with persons who are not relatives; the remaining 17 per cent live in relatives' households. Those who live with relatives bring an average of 1.4 additional people and less than

179

$1,700 gross disposable income to each family. They bring this income largely to units whose income is somewhat less than average. However, the combined incomes and the economies of living together bring the welfare positions of these complex families up to a more nearly adequate level.

Estimating Income for Particular Families

Chapters 4 through 14 reveal a great deal about family income in addition to the average size of each component; they tell something about the reasons for variation in the sizes of the components. There are many things which may be done with this information.

It is possible to see how any particular characteristic affects various aspects of the family income determination process. One can take a factor like race or age, for instance, and follow it through Chapters 4 through 14 to see how being old or nonwhite affects the labor force participation, hourly earnings, and hours of work of head and wife, their income from capital, home production, and transfers. Where the particular factor was not used, or was used in combination, some approximations are necessary. For example, being non-white makes it more likely that the head will be in the labor force and reduces his work hours by 104 hours per year and his hourly earnings by 29 cents, after allowing for other things, some of which may be partly the result of race. Being nonwhite makes his wife a few percentage points more likely to be working, but at 10 cents less per hour and some 260 hours less per year. Finally, while nonwhites are slightly more likely to be living with relatives, adjustment for other factors shows them less likely to be doing so than whites in comparable situations.

In designing the analysis, the strategy of using the most meaningful set of factors in each analysis seems more important than over-all symmetry, so that not every factor appears in every analysis. Wherever a factor is used, however, one can extend the analysis by asking what the effects might be of meaningful or expected changes in the distribution of the population according to that characteristic. For instance, there will be changes in the age distribution and the age-education distribution of the population. One can take the adjusted coefficients for age-education, which now have a weighted mean of zero, and apply the new set of weights implied by a new distribution of the population. These effects will generally be small, as those familiar with the effects of weights on index numbers can attest, but may still be useful to have in quantitative terms. Of course, one must assume that the other characteristics in the population are unchanged, or at least separable from the characteristic whose influence is being investigated, and one must assume that the same pattern of effects of that characteristic will persist in the future.

Since other things do not remain the same, ultimately it will be necessary to come to an analysis which simultaneously and dynamically takes account of the whole pattern of interrelated effects. Work is progressing in the development of large-scale simulation of economic systems using the kind of detailed information and relationships presented here.[1]

These models actually represent, in a large-scale computer, many thousand representative families, including information which allows the machine to estimate each unit's behavior for a period on the basis of the events up to that time, including the cumulative effects of what others have done and the necessity for things to add up, and for sales to equal purchases. The movements of aggregates, and the effects of changes in laws of behavior on these movements, can then be examined by letting the machine simulate historic processes. A connection is thus finally made between aggregate dynamic problems of economics, and detailed information about factors affecting the behavior of individual consumers and businessmen.

Another more immediate possibility would be to estimate for an imaginary family the components of income, labor force participation, wage rates, hours worked, capital income, income from extra adults, and so forth. Thus an estimate of net income for this family results.

For a given individual, one would use the analysis in Chapter 4 to estimate the probability that he was in the labor force in 1959, on the basis of age, sex, and the other factors used in that analysis. Given the probability, one would enter a table of random numbers to decide whether this individual was in the labor force. If so, one could use Chapter 5 to determine his expected wage rate by starting with the mean wage rate and adjusting the expected value for his age, education, race, and other characteristics. An expected number of hours of work could be similarly derived from the coefficients in Chapter 6.

The subgroup memberships combined with the coefficients of Chapter 7 would provide an expected value for the unit's capital income, and with the coefficients from Chapter 8, an expected value of its home production, if any, added to the product of wages times hours.

A probability that there is a wife and, if so, that she works can then be derived from Chapter 9. Expected values for the wife's wage rate and hours can be determined from the coefficients of Chapters 10 and 11.

After adding expected values for other earnings, and transfer incomes from Chapters 13 and 14, one can derive estimates of the probability that this unit lives with relatives and expected values for the income of the other unit if one exists. The final result is an expected value for family income.

Qualifications to the Relationships

There are three major problems which must be kept in mind in using these results. First, there is the possibility of complex interaction effects. This model of income determination is an additive one; the effect of each explanatory

[1] For a progress report see Guy Orcutt and others, *Microanalysis of Socioeconomic Systems* (New York: Harper & Brothers, 1961).

factor is assumed to be independent of the level of other factors. For example, sex is assumed to affect a spending unit head's wage rate in the same way regardless of his age, education, or other characteristics. Where reality clearly made such an assumption invalid, joint classifications were used. Age and education, religious preference, and church attendance are examples of variables which were treated in this way. Variables still remain which are not additive. This can be demonstrated by the fact that it is possible to define a particular kind of family for whom the set of formulas would predict a negative income. This is a familiar problem whenever multiple correlation techniques are used, but one which can be eliminated by appropriate statistical techniques if the group affected is sufficiently important to warrant it.

It seems likely that relationships shown for wage rates are not completely additive. Disadvantages are substitutes for one another, while advantages are complements. That is, any one of a number of disadvantages can drive a man's wage down, but having additional disadvantages can do little further damage. There is, after all, a minimum wage law. On the other hand, a combination of favorable factors may produce a rare and desired type of ability which would result in higher earnings than the model would predict.

Secondly, there is a problem of direction of causation. This is particularly important in relating attitudes and behavior. It is hoped that the attitude reflects a stable personality disposition which affects behavior. However, it is possible that the past behavior has changed the attitude.

The third problem arises from the possibility of a chain of causation where, for instance, education affects wage rate directly and also determines other factors like occupation which are related to wage rate. In such a case, using education and occupation simultaneously to explain wage rate does not reflect the complexity of the real world. It almost certainly gives too much credit to the later-stage variables like occupation. For this reason, such things as education and achievement motivation, which were probably determined before other factors, should have some precedence. There is some argument for looking at the unadjusted coefficients to assess the effect of these prior variables on the dependent variable.

Had machine facilities allowed, we might have handled this problem by using a multistage analysis of each of the dependent variables. For instance, we could have first used parental and early childhood factors to explain the dependent variables, then analyzed the residuals from this analysis against activities and events from that time to the present, and finally analyzed the residuals from that analysis against the current situational and attitudinal variables. Since some of the background factors might mediate or influence the effect of the later influences, however, they might have had to be reintroduced into the two later-stage analyses as well. It is obvious that such a procedure would have vastly complicated an already complex analysis. If the analysis were to be made more complex, it is an open question of strategy whether it would be more fruitful to allow for more interaction effects among the factors, or to take account of logical priorities in the causal process.

It is always possible, looking back over an analysis like this, to think of things that could have been done better, of variables that might have improved the explanation, and of bits and pieces that have not been explained. It appears, however, that this analysis is superior to explanations of family income based on a few variables and the use of a single dependent variable. The analysis has shown that not only economic and demographic factors, but also attitudinal, motivational, and geographic variables affect income. This method of analysis has compressed a large amount of statistical work into a small space.

Perhaps the most useful thing about this analysis is the juxtaposition of the gross and net effects of each explanatory factor. In many cases the gross relations, say between education and earning rates, have been well-known. What has not been so well-known is the extent to which any of these effects can be attributed to other factors with which the one in question is correlated. Indeed, in some cases, as with the effect of hourly earnings on hours of work, a theoretically interesting and meaningful result hidden by other intercorrelations shows up only in the adjusted deviations.

PART III

The Low Income Population

Chapter 16

POVERTY IN THE UNITED STATES

The plight of a group of families with small and inadequate incomes stands out in sharp contrast to the general prosperity enjoyed during the last decade. Because little is known about the causes of poverty, it is difficult to define remedial programs to combat it, or to determine the extent to which such programs can be effective. By studying the poor in a framework of over-all income distribution and degrees of economic well-being, their backgrounds, their attitudes and plans, and their outlooks for the future can be compared with those of the whole population. Through this process it may be possible to describe some of the factors responsible for poverty and determine whether these factors can be alleviated or eliminated through legislative programs and private concern.

In this chapter poor families are defined, and possible causes for their economic situation are examined. Records of their past earnings and descriptions of their probable futures are included in the analysis of their economic position.

In Chapter 17 the economic position of the disabled is explored. Disability may be one source of poverty and dependency which can be combated through public policy and rehabilitation programs.

This chapter describes and analyzes the problems of poor families—those whose incomes fall below a minimum standard of adequacy. The chapter describes the extent to which characteristics of the poor imply limited working ability and poor earning power in a competitive market, the possible permanence of poverty, and the degree to which it is transmitted from generation to generation. It also includes a discussion of the sources of income of poor families and the effect of transfers, particularly those provided by government income maintenance programs.[1]

[1] For other data and analyses, see U.S. Congress, Subcommittee of the Joint Committee on the Economic Report, *Low Income Families and Economic Stability, Materials on the Problem of Low Income Families,* 81st Cong., 1st Sess., 1949.

U.S. Congress, Joint Committee on the Economic Report, *Selected Government Programs which Aid the Unemployed and Low Income Families,* 81st Cong., 1st Sess., 1949.

Definition of the Poor

In order to select for study a group of "poor" families, measures of income, need, and income adequacy are required.

The Measure of Income. Gross disposable income was chosen as the most appropriate measure of income for a study of inadequacy and needs because it is a relatively comprehensive measure of the total resource flow of a family. In addition to money income, an estimate of the more important sources of income in kind is included; rental income on net equity in a home is imputed; and estimated Federal income tax liability is deducted.

The measure of income understates somewhat the resources of families who could use savings or realize capital gains; however, very few of the families with inadequate incomes have substantial savings, and it is unlikely that many had capital gains during 1959.

The Standard of Need. Family needs differ according to the size and composition of each family, and any indicator of the requirements of families must include some measure of these varying needs.[2]

The budget needs of each family and each adult unit in the sample were estimated according to data derived from a schedule prepared by the Community Council of Greater New York.[3] This schedule allows for variations in the size and composition of each unit, and for differences in food, clothing, and other requirements of persons of different ages. It also recognizes that the cost of clothing, transportation, and food is higher for persons employed outside the home than for those who are not.

An estimate of the budget requirements of each adult unit was prepared by adding the entry appropriate to each adult unit member in part I of Table 16-1 to the entry determined by the size of the unit in part II of Table 16-1. Thus, the budget costs of an adult unit containing an employed head, a housewife, and two children aged eight and eleven would equal $4,330 ($1,444 + 546 + 416 + 416 + 1,508). The estimates of the budget needs of families were calculated in the same manner as for adult units, except that entries from the rows entitled "other adults" were necessary in families where there were extra adult units.

These estimates of family budgets have several limitations. They make no provision for differences in the cost of living in different areas. The Bureau of Labor Statistics data indicate a range of about 20 per cent in the cost of

---

Robert J. Lampman, *The Low Income Population and Economic Growth,* U.S. Congress, Joint Economic Committee, Study Paper #12, 86th Cong., 1st Sess., Dec., 1959.

U.S. Congress, Subcommittee on Low-Income Families of the Joint Committee on the Economic Report, *Low-Income Families,* 84th Cong., 1st Sess., 1955.

[2] For a discussion of these measures, see Martin David, "Welfare, Income, and Budget Needs," *The Review of Economics and Statistics,* XLI (November, 1959), 393–399.

[3] *Annual Price Survey and Family Budget Costs, October 1959* (New York: The Community Council of Greater New York, December, 1959), pp. 11-12.

TABLE 16-1

SCHEDULE OF ESTIMATED ANNUAL COSTS OF GOODS AND SERVICES

I. Food, clothing, and other personal costs
   Head

	Employed or unemployed	$1,144
	Other (retired, disabled, housewife)	676

   Wife

	Employed	1,092
	Other	546

   Other adults

	Age	
Employed	18–40	1,196
	41 and older	988
Other		546

   Children

Under 6		312
6–11		416
12–15		572
16–17		676

II. Rent, utilities, and other costs

1 person in the unit	1,040
2	1,248
3	1,404
4	1,508
5	1,664
6	1,924
7	2,080
8 and more	2,184

Adapted from The Community Council of Greater New York, Budget Standard Service, *Annual Price Survey and Family Budget Costs, October, 1959.*

living between the most and least expensive of the twenty largest cities in the United States in the fall of 1959. Similar variation can be expected between large cities and rural areas.[4] However, as no systematic data on rural-urban prices differences have been collected since 1936, no adjustment was made for this bias.

The New York budget used in this study agrees fairly well with other attempts to measure the relative costs of maintaining families of different sizes.[5] The New York Council Budget is probably a low estimate of the cost of living, since it is used by private agencies in New York City as a standard for determining eligibility for assistance and free medical care. Also, the Council estimates are consistently exceeded by estimates prepared by the Bureau of Labor Statistics for New York City worker families in 1959.[6]

The Ratio of Income to Need. The ratio of gross disposable income to the

[4] See Margaret S. Strotz, "The BLS Interim Budget for a Retired Couple," *Monthly Labor Review* (November, 1960), 1141–1157; and, with Helen H. Lamale, "The City Worker's Interim Family Budget," *Monthly Labor Review* (August, 1960), 785–808.

[5] For a comparison of various estimates, see "Estimating Equivalent Incomes or Budget Costs by Family Type," *Monthly Labor Review* (November, 1960), 1197–1200, Table 2.

[6] *Monthly Labor Review* (November, 1960), 1197–1200.

estimated budget requirement was used to estimate the level of welfare enjoyed by each unit; this quantity is referred to as the *welfare ratio*. Table 16-2 shows the distribution of welfare ratios for adult units and families.

Families with inadequate incomes are defined as those whose incomes are less than nine-tenths of their budget requirements. The exact point which separates adequacy from inadequacy is, of course, a matter of judgment. Incomes were defined as inadequate when welfare ratios fell below nine-tenths in order to assure that this study's estimates of inadequate incomes would be conservative relative to the standards set by the Community Council, and to allow for some error in estimates of the cost of living in rural areas.

TABLE 16-2

ADULT UNIT AND FAMILY WELFARE RATIOS
(PERCENTAGE DISTRIBUTION OF ADULT UNITS AND FAMILIES)

Welfare ratio	Adult units	Families
0–0.4	11	6
0.5–0.6	9	7
0.7–0.8	8	7
0.9–1.0	10	10
1.1–1.2	10	10
1.3–1.5	13	14
1.6–2.0	18	21
2.1 and over	21	25
Total	100	100
Number of units	3,396	2,800

Although the income measure somewhat understates the resources of families who can supplement their income by dissaving, less than 5 per cent have liquid savings of $5,000 or more. Nearly 40 per cent do not have as much as $500 now, and have not had $500 within the last five years. The average amount of savings used in 1959 by families with inadequate incomes was about $150.

Even if families with inadequate incomes were to use all their capital on an annuity basis the added income would do little to improve their financial position. Older persons would receive higher annuity incomes from a given amount of capital because of their shorter life expectancies. Older persons also have larger capital accumulations. However, adult unit heads over sixty-five with inadequate incomes would receive an average of only $135 or .07 of their average budget requirement from investment of their capital in annuities.

For home-owning families with inadequate incomes the average equity in the home was slightly over $5,000. Though this equity appears substantial it may be of little use to a family in financial straits. Borrowing on a home is difficult and the sale of a home often yields less than the cost of rental housing.

Most of the analysis is based on the group designated as *poor families,* families with inadequate incomes who also have less than $5,000 in liquid assets.[7] According to these definitions, poor families comprise one-fifth of the nation's families.

Causes of Poverty. It is quite clear that both the family income and the number of its dependents vary in the course of the life cycle. This raises an important question concerning the interpretation of the welfare ratio for different families in the sample. For some the level of well-being indicated by the ratio may reflect a temporary situation, especially when 1959 income is not representative of the normal earnings of that family. For others the welfare index may be quite a suitable measure of long-run well-being.

The classification illustrated in Figure 16-1 was developed to distinguish families whose level of welfare is associated with long-run factors from those with temporary fluctuations of income.

For example, the aged are most likely to have stable, though low, incomes. The incomes of farmers and self-employed may rise or fall rapidly with innovations, short-term fluctuations in yield, and long-term changes in productivity.

The classification also offers a *sequential* analysis of factors which may lead to low earning power. Thus old age and retirement (category 1) are sufficient to explain low incomes; a single parent with children is somewhat more likely to be able to work regularly, although such a situation would lead to low earning power; and the residual category (7) includes families whose heads have no obvious impediment to earning income on a regular basis.

The residual group (category 7) is composed of families which meet the criteria for poor families but which exhibit none of the characteristics classified as likely causes of poverty. The heads of many of these families are unskilled seasonal workers, for whom yearly unemployment is usual. Others are widows or single females under sixty-five with no work experience, students, and a small number of housekeepers or servants who live in their employers' households and work for room and board.

For a few of the families in the residual group, students or young couples just getting started, poverty is only temporary. For most families, however, the problem of chronic poverty is serious. One such family is headed by a thirty-two year old man who is employed as a dishwasher. Though he works

[7] Other approaches to the measurement of levels of living and income adequacy are suggested in Robert A. Danley and Charles E. Ramsey, *Standardization and Application of a Level of Living Scale for Farm and Nonfarm Families,* Memoir #362 (Ithaca, New York: Cornell Agricultural Experimental Station, 1958).

See also Eleanor M. Snyder, "Measurement of the Size of the Urban Population with Chronic Low Income Status," a paper presented at the 1957 annual meeting of the American Statistical Association, September 10, 1957 (New York State Interdepartmental Committee on Low Income, 1957).

steadily and more than full time, he earned slightly over $2,000 in 1959. His wife earned $300 more, but their combined incomes are not enough to support themselves and their three children. Although the head of the family is only thirty-two, he feels that he has no chance of advancement partly because he finished only seven grades of school. The plight of this family is typical of the situations faced by many in category 7. The possibility of such families leaving the ranks of the poor is not high.

The sequential classification also sorts families into groups which are significant from the point of view of remedial legislation and government programs designated to alleviate poverty. Without major changes in the labor market, most of the aged will retire and will have little chance of returning to the labor force. Their economic problem can be eliminated if they receive an annuity sufficient to meet their needs. The economic problems of the nonwhite population may be alleviated by fair employment practices legislation.[8]

Table 16-3 indicates that significantly more of the aged, the disabled, the single parents with children, the unusually unemployed, and nonwhite persons have inadequate incomes than is the case for the remaining groups of the classification. A parellel tabulation showing the welfare index of adult units would show the same pattern, but the proportion of adult units whose incomes are inadequate would be somewhat higher. (See the last two rows of Table 16-4.) Despite the relationship between the causes of poverty shown in the sequential classification and the welfare ratio, a majority of the families in each category of the classification have incomes that meet or exceed their needs. This fact indicates that the sequential classification does not predict which families have inadequate incomes. At best the classification serves to describe a part of the family's economic problem. If a family is poor the classification tells something about the type of poverty and the chances that the family may be able to improve its situation.

[8] For additional background on families in these categories, see the following for the aged:

Henry D. Sheldon, *The Older Population of the United States* (New York: John Wiley & Sons, Inc., 1958);

P. O. Steiner and R. Dorfman, *The Economic Status of the Aged* (Berkeley: University of California Press, 1957);

Gordon J. Aldridge and Fedele F. Fauri, *A Syllabus and Annotated Bibliography on Social Welfare and the Aged,* Vol. 4, *Syllabi of Social Gerontology,* Sec. #4 (Ann Arbor: Institute of Social Gerontology: University of Michigan, 1959).

For nonwhites see:

Elton Rayack, "Discrimination and the Occupational Progress of Negroes," *Review of Economics and Statistics,* 43 (May, 1961), 209–214;

U.S. Department of Labor, *The Economic Situation of Negroes in the United States,* Bulletin S-3 (Washington: October, 1960).

For farmers see:

Buis T. Inman and John H. Southern, "Opportunities for Economic Development in Low-Production Farm Areas," *Agriculture Information Bulletin #234,* U.S. Department of Agriculture (November, 1960).

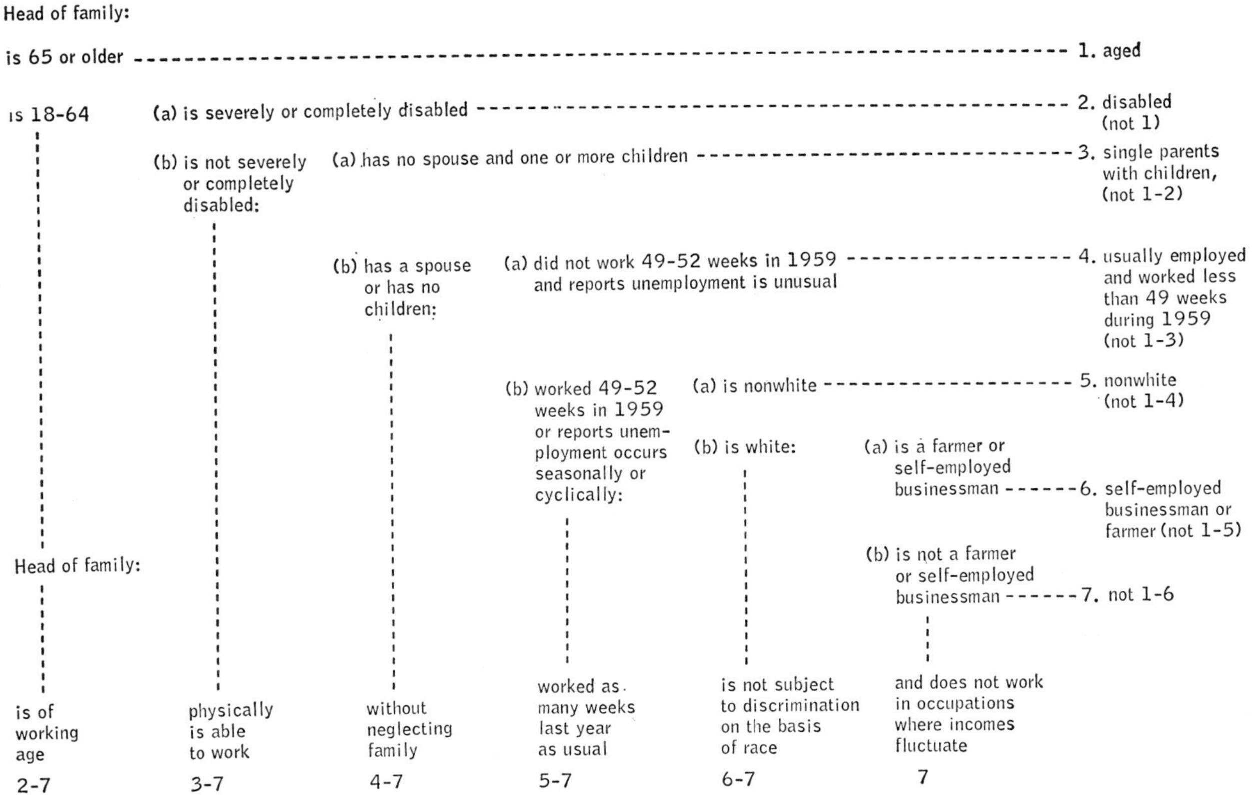

Head of family:

is 65 or older - 1. aged

is 18-64

   (a) is severely or completely disabled - 2. disabled (not 1)

   (b) is not severely or completely disabled:

      (a) has no spouse and one or more children - - - - - - - - - - - - - - 3. single parents with children, (not 1-2)

      (b) has a spouse or has no children:

         (a) did not work 49-52 weeks in 1959 and reports unemployment is unusual - - - - - - - - - 4. usually employed and worked less than 49 weeks during 1959 (not 1-3)

         (b) worked 49-52 weeks in 1959 or reports unemployment occurs seasonally or cyclically:

            (a) is nonwhite - - - - - - - - - - - - - - - 5. nonwhite (not 1-4)

            (b) is white:

               (a) is a farmer or self-employed businessman - - - - - - 6. self-employed businessman or farmer (not 1-5)

               (b) is not a farmer or self-employed businessman - - - - - - 7. not 1-6

                  and does not work in occupations where incomes fluctuate

Head of family:

is of working age	physically is able to work	without neglecting family	worked as many weeks last year as usual	is not subject to discrimination on the basis of race	and does not work in occupations where incomes fluctuate
2-7	3-7	4-7	5-7	6-7	7

Figure 16-1. Likely causes of poverty.

TABLE 16-3

FAMILY WELFARE RATIO WITHIN LIKELY CAUSES OF POVERTY
(PERCENTAGE DISTRIBUTION OF FAMILIES)

Head of family is:

Likely causes of poverty

| | 1 | 2 | 3 | 4 | 5 | 6 | 7 | |
Family welfare ratio	Aged	Disabled (not 1)	Single and has children (not 1 or 2)	Usually employed, and worked less than 49 weeks during 1959 (not 1–3)	Nonwhite (not 1–4)	Self-employed businessman or farmer (not 1–5)	Not 1–6	All families
0.0–0.8	39	46	45	27	47	21	8	20
0.9–1.2	21	22	22	25	24	17	18	20
1.3–1.6	11	7	21	26	13	13	23	19
1.7–2.2	14	16	8	13	12	16	28	21
2.3 and over	15	9	4	9	4	33	23	20
Total	100	100	100	100	100	100	100	100
Number of families	384	116	157	177	216	299	1,451	2,800
Per cent of adult units with welfare ratios of 0.8 or less	48	57	48	26	55	23	17	28
Number of adult units	496	143	194	192	279	314	1,778	3,396

TABLE 16-4

PROPORTIONS AND AGGREGATE ESTIMATES OF HEADS OF POOR FAMILIES HAVING CHARACTERISTICS RELATED TO POVERTY WITHIN LIKELY CAUSES OF POVERTY
(PROPORTIONS AND AGGREGATE ESTIMATES FOR POOR FAMILIES)

Proportions and aggregate estimates of heads of poor families having characteristics related to poverty

Likely causes of poverty	Aged	Disabled	Single and has children	Usually employed, unemployed in 1959	Nonwhite	Self-employed businessman or farmer	None of these	Per cent with other indications of poverty
1. Aged	100% 2.8 mil.	32% .9 mil.	1% .04 mil.	2% .04 mil.	22% .6 mil.	8% .2 mil.	0%	65%
2. Disabled (not 1)		100% .8 mil.	15% .1 mil.	4% .03 mil.	26% .2 mil.	17% .1 mil.	0%	62%
3. Single and has children (not 1–2)			100% 1.1 mil.	14% .1 mil.	43% .5 mil.	3% .01 mil.	0%	60%
4. Usually employed, worked less than 49 weeks in 1959 (not 1–3)				100% .9 mil.	29% .2 mil.	0%	0%	29%
5. Nonwhite (not 1–4)					100% 1.4 mil.	14% 1.4 mil.	0%	14%
6. Self-employed businessman or farmer (not 1–5)						100% 1.0 mil.	0%	0%
7. Not 1–6							100% 2.4 mil.	0%
All	2.8 mil.	1.7 mil.	1.2 mil.	1.1 mil.	2.9 mil.	1.7 mil.	2.4 mil.	

Table 16-4 presents the relationships among the categories used to classify likely causes of poverty, and shows the extent to which poor families in each group exhibit more than one characteristic associated with poverty. For poor families which belong to two or more of the groups, the problem of poverty is compounded. For example, 29 per cent of heads of poor families who experienced unusual unemployment in 1959 are also nonwhite. Forty-three per cent of the poor single parents with children are nonwhite.

Earning Power of Poor Families

To determine in what way the characteristics of poor families limit the head's ability to earn a living, labor force participation rates, wage rates, and hours worked were derived from the multivariate relationships presented in Part II. Each adjusted deviation from the analyses in Chapters 4 to 6 was weighted by the proportion of family heads with that characteristic and with inadequate incomes; the weighted coefficients were added to give the average expected rates of labor force participation, wage rates, and hours of work for the heads of families with inadequate incomes.

TABLE 16-5

WORK EXPERIENCE PROJECTIONS

	Families with inadequate incomes	All spending unit heads
Proportion who worked during 1959	73%	86%
Wage rate earned	$1.63 [a]	$2.29
Hours worked	1,852 [a]	2,092
Estimated earnings (Product of lines 1, 2, and 3)	$2,204	$4,122
Number of cases	788	2,997

[a] Calculated on the unrealistic assumption that equal rates of labor force participation apply to all groups of family heads whose incomes are inadequate. The assumption implies some downward bias in the estimated values, as aged and disabled heads that are least likely to work also have lower than average wages and hours.

Although the expected value of earnings for the heads of families whose incomes are inadequate is estimated at $2,204, the heads of these families *actually earned* an average only slightly more than $900. Both expected and actual earnings of the heads of these families fell substantially short of the national averages, and their actual earnings averaged even less than expected. The *gross disposable income* of families with inadequate incomes averaged only $1,886.

Many heads of families with inadequate incomes are aged, or poorly educated, or unskilled, or farm workers. The group includes a high proportion of female family heads, disabled persons, and families living in the South. All of these characteristics reduce the expected earning power of the group below the average estimated for all spending units, but they do not explain

TABLE 16-6

LABOR FORCE STATUS OF WIVES OF FAMILY HEADS WITHIN LIKELY CAUSES OF POVERTY
(PERCENTAGE DISTRIBUTION OF POOR FAMILIES WITH WIVES PRESENT)

	Likely causes of poverty							All poor families with wives present	All families with wives present
	Head of family is:								
	1	2	3	4	5	6	7		
Labor force status of wife	Aged	Disabled (not 1)	Single and has children (not 1 or 2)	Usually employed, and worked less than 49 weeks during 1959 (not 1–3)	Nonwhite (not 1–4)	Self-employed businessman or farmer (not 1–5)	Not 1–6		
Wife works now	16	31		19	25	12	23	20	28
Wife does not work; has worked in past	36	42	inapplicable	60	55	45	44	47	57
Wife never worked	41	20		21	20	42	32	31	14
Not ascertained	7	7		0	0	1	1	2	1
Total	100	100		100	100	100	100	100	100
Number of families	50	34		49	82	85	121	421	2,059

the very low actual earnings of the group. The difference between expected and actual earnings may reflect underlying variability in the determination of incomes. Alternatively, it may be associated with differences in ability, motivation, or other factors not adequately measured by the analyses in Part II.

Because one-third of the heads of families with inadequate incomes are women, their labor force participation rate and the hourly wage rate they can command are severely curtailed. The plight of these families is compounded by the fact that a large proportion of female heads are either aged, or single women with children for whom to care.

Even in the families which include wives, most of the responsibility for providing a living falls to the head. The presence of young children in the family, or lack of work experience on the part of the wife, commonly limit any contribution which she might make to the family income by going to work. The labor force participation of wives in poor families is well below the average for all families in which wives are present. Two-thirds of the wives of heads of poor families have had some work experience, but only one-fifth were working early in 1960. The proportion of wives working was highest among the disabled families and lowest among the families of farmers and self-employed businessmen. The wives of the latter group may help in the family business on an irregular basis even though this employment was not reported (see Table 16-6).

Permanence of Low Incomes among the Poor

Of course, one year's income is not a complete measure of the economic status of the unit. Workers suffer from unemployment in some years, not in others. The self-employed have good and bad years. However, most people have to live out of their current income, including unemployment compensation, so that current income is important. Also, the analysis of those with low incomes in this chapter takes account of imperfections in one-year income by excluding from the group for most of the analysis those with substantial assets, and by looking separately at those who were unemployed in 1959 and are not unemployed every year and those who were self-employed. The residual group of the poor thus contains no substantial number of temporarily poor.

The permanence of low incomes is inferred from a variety of findings. Data on the past earnings of the heads of the families suggest chronically low earnings. The meager assets held by the poor result from low incomes, financial disasters, or poor financial management in the past. Data on health insurance and pension rights suggest that the poor will continue to be hounded by financial difficulties, since they have little protection against future risks of poor health and involuntary retirement.

In many poor families the head has never earned enough to cover the family's present needs. (See Table 16-7.) The heads of poor families report they earned an average of $2,949 in the year in which they earned the most. Present needs of these families cost an average of $3,676. There are substantial differences in the highest earnings reported by poor families in the seven categories of the classification of likely causes of poverty. The unemployed and the farmers and self-employed businessmen report considerably higher than average past peak earnings. The level of peak earnings for those groups suggests the instability of their incomes. The peak earnings of the aged and disabled actually represent more purchasing power than the peak earnings for other groups because the aged and disabled earned their past incomes at a more distant time in the past than is true for other families.

Almost a third of the poor families in this study report that 1959 was the year in which the head earned his highest income. Both the aged and the disabled are likely to report that the head earned the most in years prior to 1959. This finding is to be expected since few of these heads worked in 1959. Since the average age of aged heads of poor families is less than seventy-five years, the frequency with which peak earnings are reported for 1941 to 1950 indicates that a substantial number of the poor who are now over sixty-five suffered from a declining income even before a normal retirement age.

The distribution of assets among poor families identified by likely causes of poverty reveals relatively clear differences in income history. The nonwhites and single parents with children have accumulated the least reserves from their past incomes. Farmers and aged persons have accumulated some assets; but even these amounts are small.

To some extent these differences in assets reflect wide differences in the average age of family heads in the groups identified by likely causes of poverty. The disabled and the businessmen and farmers with inadequate incomes are largely aged forty-five to sixty-four. Families whose heads are sixty-five and older are included in a single category by definition. More than one-third of the single parents with children and nearly half of the unemployed family heads are under thirty-five. The aged have had a lifetime to accumulated savings; many of the unemployed have just begun. If the ages of heads of families with inadequate incomes are considered, the findings in Tables 16-9 and 16-10 suggest that nonwhites with inadequate incomes have had low incomes for a longer period of time than other groups. Nonwhite families include a substantial minority whose heads are over forty-five and who have had the time to accumulate savings; yet they report less savings than any other group. This probably results largely from lack of income in past years. No matter what the interpretations of the cause of their lack of assets, it is clear that the nonwhite families whose incomes are inadequate have almost no contingency reserves to meet future crises. The situation of the disabled, single parents with children, and persons who were out of work during 1959 is little better.

Table 16-11 offers another indication of the past experience of poor

TABLE 16-7

HIGHEST INCOME FAMILY HEAD EVER EARNED WITHIN LIKELY CAUSES OF POVERTY
(PERCENTAGE DISTRIBUTION OF POOR FAMILIES WHOSE HEADS HAVE WORKED)

Highest income head ever earned	Likely causes of poverty							All poor families	All families
	Head of family is:								
	1 Aged	2 Disabled (not 1)	3 Single and has children (not 1 or 2)	4 Usually employed, and worked less than 49 weeks during 1959 (not 1-3)	5 Nonwhite (not 1-4)	6 Self-employed businessman or farmer (not 1-5)	7 Not 1-6		
$1–949	13	14	32	12	19	11	9	14	4
$950–1,949	18	24	24	20	19	10	16	18	5
$1,950–2,949	18	16	24	16	17	14	20	18	7
$2,950–4,949	10	15	11	29	25	24	27	21	22
$4,950–7,449	2	8	0	13	6	18	15	9	33
$7,450 or more	1	4	0	1	0	10	4	3	21
Not ascertained	38	19	9	9	14	13	9	17	8
Total	100	100	100	100	100	100	100	100	100
Per cent who never worked	28	13	19	0	2	0	4	12	4
Mean highest income ever earned	$2,230	2,833	1,673	3,066	2,490	4,143	3,474	2,949	
Mean budget requirement	$2,401	3,801	4,359	4,161	4,144	4,446	4,033	3,676	
Number of families	137	65	86	65	128	91	183	755	2,800

TABLE 16-8

YEAR IN WHICH FAMILY HEAD EARNED THE HIGHEST INCOME WITHIN LIKELY CAUSES OF POVERTY
(PERCENTAGE DISTRIBUTION OF POOR FAMILIES WHOSE HEADS HAVE WORKED)

| | Head of family is: | | | Likely causes of poverty | | | | | |
| | 1 | 2 | 3 | 4 | 5 | 6 | 7 | | |
Year in which head earned the highest income	Aged	Disabled (not 1)	Single and has children (not 1 or 2)	Usually employed, and worked less than 49 weeks during 1959 (not 1-3)	Nonwhite (not 1-4)	Self-employed businessman or farmer (not 1-5)	Not 1-6	All poor families	All families
1959	7	16	59	41	50	22	37	32	51
1958	1	7	1	22	10	10	10	8	9
1956–1957	1	10	13	16	10	19	14	11	10
1951–1955	10	18	12	12	9	11	17	13	10
1946–1950	15	16	2	0	7	18	6	9	6
1941–1945	18	16	6	6	3	11	5	9	5
Before 1941	16	7	0	0	5	2	3	6	3
Not ascertained	32	10	7	3	6	7	8	12	6
Total	100	100	100	100	100	100	100	100	100
Per cent who never worked	28	13	19	0	2	0	4	12	4
Number of families	137	65	86	65	128	91	183	755	2,800

201

TABLE 16-9

AMOUNT OF SAVINGS WITHIN LIKELY CAUSES OF POVERTY
(PERCENTAGE DISTRIBUTION OF POOR FAMILIES)

				Likely causes of poverty					
	1	2	3	4	5	6	7		
				Head of family is:					
Amount of savings [a]	Aged	Disabled (not 1)	Single and has children (not 1 or 2)	Usually employed, and worked less than 49 weeks during 1959 (not 1-3)	Nonwhite (not 1-4)	Self-employed businessman or farmer (not 1-5)	Not 1-6	All poor families	All families
$1,000–5,000	23	6	1	5	1	10	8	10	26
$500–1,000	9	5	3	3	4	6	7	6	14
Has none or less than $500 now:									
$500 or more in past 5 years	11	14	5	12	7	10	10	10	18
Less than $500 in past 5 years	45	31	50	36	41	37	36	41	28
Amount in past 5 years not ascertained	5	38	37	40	44	33	38	29	10
Amount now not ascertained	7	6	4	4	3	4	1	4	4
Total	100	100	100	100	100	100	100	100	100
Number of families	137	65	86	65	128	91	183	755	2,800

[a] savings of the spending unit containing the head of the family

TABLE 16-10

MEAN AMOUNT OF NET EQUITY IN HOME OR FARM, WITHIN LIKELY CAUSES OF POVERTY (FOR POOR FAMILIES)

Likely causes of poverty	Number of families	Proportion of each group who are home owners	Mean amount of net equity in home or farm
Head of family is:			
1. Aged	137	50	$ 3,300
2. Disabled (not 1)	65	53	3,600
3. Single and has children (not 1 or 2)	86	20	1,000
4. Usually employed, and worked less than 49 weeks during 1959 (not 1–3)	65	29	1,900
5. Nonwhite (not 1–4)	128	23	1,200
6. Self-employed businessman or farmer (not 1–5)	91	77	12,000
7. Not 1–6	183	37	4,300
All poor families	755	41	3,800

families. Families with unemployed or disabled heads used up a significant amount of savings during 1959. The amounts used are a small but useful addition to their incomes. Farmers and businessmen dissaved somewhat less; nonwhites and single parents with children reported almost no dissaving. Perhaps the unemployed and disabled became poor in the recent past and were able to maintain their living standard somewhat by living on savings.

TABLE 16-11

MEAN AMOUNT OF SAVINGS USED IN 1959,[a] WITHIN LIKELY CAUSES OF POVERTY (FOR POOR FAMILIES)

Likely causes for poverty	Number of families	Proportion in group who used savings in 1959	Mean amount of savings used in 1959
Head of family is:			
1. Aged	137	30	$119
2. Disabled (not 1)	65	24	182
3. Single and has children (not 1 or 2)	86	12	24
4. Usually employed, and worked less than 49 weeks during 1959 (not 1–3)	65	30	160
5. Nonwhite (not 1–4)	128	14	24
6. Self-employed businessman or farmer (not 1–5)	91	26	125
7. Not 1–6	183	23	185
All poor families	755	23	$120

[a] savings and liquid assets of spending units which contain family heads

TABLE 16-12

HOSPITALIZATION INSURANCE COVERAGE WITHIN LIKELY CAUSES OF POVERTY
(PERCENTAGE DISTRIBUTION OF POOR FAMILIES)

	Likely causes of poverty								
	Head of family is:								
	1	2	3	4	5	6	7		
Hospitalization insurance [a]	Aged	Disabled (not 1)	Single and has children (not 1 or 2)	Usually employed, and worked less than 49 weeks during 1959 (not 1–3)	Nonwhite (not 1–4)	Self-employed businessman or farmer (not 1–5)	Not 1–6	All poor families	All families
Everyone in the spending unit is covered	21	21	25	60	39	27	36	32	63
Someone in the spending unit is covered	3	8	12	1	8	3	5	5	6
No one in the spending unit is covered	74	67	63	38	51	70	58	62	30
Coverage not ascertained	2	4	0	1	2	0	1	1	1
Total	100	100	100	100	100	100	100	100	100
Number of families	137	65	86	65	128	91	183	755	2,800

[a] coverage for spending units containing heads of families

Poor families have little protection against the costs of illness. Only one-third of the families in this group have hospitalization insurance which covers the entire spending unit containing the head of the family; three-fifths have no insurance whatever. This contrasts with the 63 per cent of the national population who have hospitalization coverage for the entire spending unit.

Poor families are similarly disadvantaged by lack of rights to public and private retirement pensions. Among poor families, only those whose heads are usually employed but who worked less than 49 weeks during 1959 are more completely covered by social security than the national population. In the case of private pensions a similar finding holds.

TABLE 16-13

PUBLIC AND PRIVATE PENSION COVERAGE
(PERCENTAGE DISTRIBUTION OF POOR FAMILIES AND ALL FAMILIES
WHOSE HEADS ARE 30 AND OLDER AND NOT RETIRED)

Pension coverage	Social security and other government pensions [a]		Private pensions and annuities [b]	
	Poor families	All families	Poor families	All families
Covered	84	93	11	40
Not covered; coverage not ascertained	16	7	89	60
Total	100	100	100	100
Number of families	453	1,967	453	1,967

[a] includes only family heads
[b] includes family heads and wives

Clearly short-run cash deficiencies and temporary loss of earning power are not the sole explanation for the economic difficulties of poor families; their difficulties also develop from inadequate long-term protection against those contingencies which are likely to curtail further their incomes in the future.

For persons fifty-five and older, the question of resources for the future is particularly critical. The incidence of both illness and unemployment increases for that age group, and the availability of a cushion of savings or insurance is important. Table 16-14 shows the welfare ratio of families which contain aged individuals within a classification of the individual's cushions of resources. The welfare ratio is the most comprehensive measure of individual income, since it includes nonmoney income and any help received through living with relatives, as well as the adjustment for need. Persons between fifty-five and sixty-one are shown separately from persons sixty-two and older, since persons can start collecting social security benefits at age sixty-two.

Neither the past earning experience nor the assets of the poor suggest that a large fraction were much better off in the recent past than they were in 1959. Their present level of savings and their rights to health insurance and

TABLE 16-14

FAMILY WELFARE RATIO WITHIN SAVINGS, HEALTH INSURANCE,
AND AGE
(PERCENTAGE DISTRIBUTION OF PERSONS 55 AND OLDER)

Family welfare ratio	Savings, health insurance, and age						All persons 55 and older
	$5,000 or more in savings		Less than $5,000 in savings, health insurance		Less than $5,000 in savings, no health insurance		
	55–61	62 & over	55–61	62 & over	55–61	62 & over	
(Income as a per cent of budget standard)							
0.0–0.44	1	1	3	6	17	12	7
0.45–0.84	2	12	8	15	19	34	18
0.85–1.24	8	11	12	18	25	25	18
1.25–2.04	25	28	35	42	25	22	29
2.05 and over	64	48	42	19	14	7	28
Total	100	100	100	100	100	100	100
Number of persons (in millions)	2.8	3.8	4.7	5.0	3.1	7.9	27.3

pensions suggest that many will be worse off in the future. None of the poor can afford sickness or injury. Some will be unable to retire because they have no pension rights. This substantial long-term poverty suggests the need for an examination of the transmission of poverty from one generation to the next.

Transmission of Poverty between Generations

Many writers have suggested that poor families perpetuate their problems by raising children who cannot support themselves. Others have written about the freedom of opportunity that is the touchstone of success for anyone who chooses to work hard. Neither point of view can be disproved in this statistical study. The evidence is too indirect. Some of the poor have less education and less skilled occupations than their parents. Many of the children of the poor attain substantially better education than their parents. Those children who do not attain more education than their parents may repeat the history of their parents, finding it extremely difficult to earn the income they require to support their families.

Transmission of poverty between generations can be examined from two points of view. How are the characteristics of the poor similar to the characteristics of their parents? And to what extent do the poor transmit their own liabilities to their children?

The median educational attainment of fathers of all heads of spending units was less than eight grades in school. The median attainment of the heads themselves is slightly less than a high school diploma. According to Table 16-15 the heads of poor families had fathers with slightly less education

TABLE 16-15

EDUCATION OF FAMILY HEADS AND THEIR FATHERS, WITHIN LIKELY CAUSES OF POVERTY
(PROPORTIONS FOR POOR FAMILIES)

| Education of family heads and their fathers | Likely causes of poverty — Head of family is: | | | | | | | All poor families | All families |
	1 Aged	2 Disabled (not 1)	3 Single and has children (not 1 or 2)	4 Usually employed, and worked less than 49 weeks during 1959 (not 1-3)	5 Nonwhite (not 1-4)	6 Self-employed businessman or farmer (not 1-5)	7 Not 1-6		
Per cent of fathers with less than 9 grades	57	70	76	66	66	79	63	66	64
Per cent of family heads with less than 9 grades	75	78	60	49	65	55	58	64	32
Per cent of family heads with less than 11 grades	84	93	89	66	80	78	78	81	53
Number of families	137	65	86	65	128	91	183	755	2,800

than did heads of all families, although the differences are not great. However, the education of the heads of poor families is clearly less than the average for all heads of families.

Relative to their fathers, the heads of poor families either failed to go beyond their fathers' educational levels as much as most, or even slipped back. Table 16-16 shows that most failed to rise above their fathers' educational level. More than three-fifths of all spending unit heads whose fathers had less than nine grades of school, went beyond that level themselves. Among the heads of poor families, fewer than two-fifths did so.

Among the groups identified by the sequential classification of likely causes of poverty, family heads who were unusually unemployed during 1959 appear to have significantly more education than the remaining groups. In part this reflects the fact that this group was educated more recently than any other, at a time when standards were high. Similarly the low attainments of the aged and disabled reflect the fact that most were educated at a time when levels of educational achievements were considerably lower. Nevertheless, the unusually unemployed are the only group who attained relatively the same education as their parents; this fact suggests both greater ability and more motivation for the group than is typical of the remaining poor family heads.

TABLE 16-16

EDUCATION OF FAMILY HEADS WITHIN EDUCATION OF THEIR FATHERS
(PERCENTAGE DISTRIBUTION OF POOR FAMILIES)

	Education of fathers		All heads of poor families [a]	All families
Education of heads	0–8 grades	9 grades or more		
0–8 grades	65	23	64	33
9–11 grades	18	23	17	21
12 grades or more	17	54	19	46
Total	100	100	100	100
Number of families	500	72	755	2,800

[a] includes 183 heads for whom education of father was not ascertained

In summary, the low educational attainments of heads of poor families result from a failure to improve educational attainments relative to the previous generation at the same rate as the remaining population. The data offer little support to the hypothesis that a majority of the poor failed to obtain education because of inadequate education on the parts of their fathers. It is quite possible that other children of these same parents may have attained more education and are in good economic positions.

Comparison of the occupations of the two generations, however, shows some correlation between the poor earning power of the present generation and the earning power of their fathers. The fathers of heads of poor families

TABLE 16-17

OCCUPATION OF FAMILY HEADS AND THEIR FATHERS WITHIN LIKELY CAUSES OF POVERTY
(PROPORTIONS FOR POOR FAMILIES)

Occupation of family heads and their fathers	Likely causes of poverty							All poor families	All families
	Head of family is:								
	1 Aged	2 Disabled (not 1)	3 Single and has children (not 1 or 2)	4 Usually employed, and worked less than 49 weeks during 1959 (not 1-3)	5 Nonwhite (not 1-4)	6 Self-employed businessman or farmer (not 1-5)	7 Not 1-6		
Per cent of heads whose fathers were unskilled laborers and farmers	58	64	66	63	75	87	56	64	44
Per cent of family heads who are unskilled laborers and farmers	48	60	58	47	61	80	37	52	31
Number of family heads	137	65	86	65	128	91	183	755	2,800

are more likely to have been farmers or unskilled laborers than are the fathers of all family heads. This lack of skill is also typical of the heads of poor families themselves. Even when heads of poor families are compared to all family heads whose fathers were in the same occupations, the poor family heads show much less upward mobility. Indeed, it appears that a number of the heads of poor families have moved into less skilled jobs than their fathers had.

TABLE 16-18

OCCUPATIONS OF HEADS OF FAMILIES WITHIN OCCUPATIONS
OF THEIR FATHERS
(PERCENTAGE DISTRIBUTION OF POOR FAMILIES)

Occupation of family heads	Occupation of fathers					
	White collar workers	Skilled and semiskilled workers	Unskilled laborers; farmers	Not ascertained; never worked	All poor families	All families
White collar workers	34	9	11	3	13	37
Skilled and semiskilled workers	23	37	21	21	24	35
Unskilled laborers; farmers	28	45	59	51	52	23
Not ascertained; never worked	15	9	9	25	11	5
Total	100	100	100	100	100	100
Number of families	85	112	501	57	755	2,800

Thus the lack of education and skilled occupations among heads of poor families does not result solely from the unskilled and uneducated background of their parents. It also stems from the failure of these persons to improve their skills in the way that typical family heads have improved their skills over the past generation. Skills and education that were adequate for the last generation are marginal in today's labor market. Though no sweeping generalizations can be made on the basis of these few tables, they offer little support for a theory of poverty that rests entirely on intergenerational transmission.

Transmission of Poverty to Children

To what degree do these families transmit their own liabilities to their children? The data offer two pieces of evidence on the extent to which children inherit the inadequate education of their parents.[9] Poor families have substantially lower aspirations for sending their children to college than is true for the national cross section. The usually employed who lost work in 1959

[9] Lenore Epstein summarizes data on the impact of low incomes of children in "Some Effects of Low Incomes on Children and Their Families," *Social Security Bulletin,* 24 (February, 1961), 12–16.

are the most aspiring group. Their expectations that incomes will improve in the near future and their relatively greater educational attainment may be responsible.

TABLE 16-19

EDUCATION EXPECTED FOR BOYS OF FAMILY HEADS
(PERCENTAGE DISTRIBUTION OF HEADS OF POOR FAMILIES,
AND ALL FAMILIES, WITH BOYS 20 OR UNDER)

Education expected for boys of family heads	Poor families with boys aged 20 and under	All families with boys aged 20 and under
Less than 12 grades	4	2
12 grades; 12 grades and nonacademic training	50	24
Some college	31	66
Not ascertained	15	8
Total	100	100
Number of families	343	1,211

For those whose children have finished school, the data offer a similar finding; 45 per cent of the children of poor families completed high school or more. Sixty-five per cent of the children of all families achieved that level of education. A substantial minority of the children of poor families thus obtain enough education to qualify for better jobs than those held by their parents. Unfortunately, more than one-third of the children have less than a grade school education and will probably perpetuate the poverty of their parents. The proportion of children who drop out of school before graduation

TABLE 16-20

EDUCATION ATTAINED BY CHILDREN FINISHED WITH SCHOOL
(PERCENTAGE DISTRIBUTION OF POOR FAMILIES AND ALL FAMILIES
THAT HAVE CHILDREN FINISHED WITH SCHOOL)

Education of children finished with school	All poor families	All families
0–8 grades	34	14
9–11 grades	21	21
High school graduate or more	45	65
Total	100	100
Number of families	755	2,800

is somewhat overstated by Table 16-20 for younger families whose children have not yet reached the last years of high school. Those who remain in school are not counted while those who drop out are included among those finished with school.

Of course, a study such as this gives an incomplete picture of social change, in that only those families who are poor at the present time are analyzed. Some of the present poor came from families which were not poor; likewise, some families that are not poor may produce children who will join the ranks of poverty of the next generation. Also, there are families in the present generation who are not now poor but will become so after retirement or following some catastrophe.

Geographic Distribution of Poor Families

One-half of all the poor families in the sample live in the South. (See Table 16-21.) A sizable majority of poor families live in areas beyond the suburban belts surrounding metropolitan areas, where the variety and number of jobs available are not as great as in the large cities and their environs. (See Table 16-22.) For the most part, however, poor families are not concentrated in economically depressed areas. Seven per cent of all poor families, and 9 per cent of the unusually unemployed group, lived in areas classified as distress areas sometime during 1959. Five per cent of all families live in such areas.

Redistribution of Income to the Poor

The discussion of poor families has focused on the permanence of their economic situation and the transmission of the poverty of these families to their children. Substantial improvement of their economic situation does not appear likely. Some recurrence of poverty among the children seems inevitable. It is unlikely that the economic problems of all poor families will solve themselves. Aid of some kind will be required. In this connection it is of some interest to study the present dependence of the poor on transfers from individuals and government for a portion of their income, and to appraise the degree of additional aid which will be required to eliminate poverty.

The size of transfer income relative to other sources of income is displayed in Table 16-23. These tables classify all *adult units* in the sample according to the ratio of *family* income to *family* budget needs of the family in which the adult unit lives. Thus a dependent adult unit that receives no income whatsoever might be classified in any of the five columns depending on how well the income of other family members serves to cover its needs. Among adult units whose incomes are inadequate more than one-fourth report no earnings during 1959; more than one-half report some transfer income. Such transfers account for more than one-fourth of the gross disposable income of this group of adult units.

The total amount of transfer income shows no inverse relationship to levels of welfare, although transfers are increasingly concentrated in a small number of adult units as the welfare ratio increases. Earnings and capital incomes increase regularly with the welfare ratio. The income tax liability also increases. Thus, transfer of factor income among adult units at different levels of welfare is accomplished by progressive taxation rather than transfer

TABLE 16-21

REGION IN WHICH THE FAMILY IS LIVING, WITHIN LIKELY CAUSES OF POVERTY
(PERCENTAGE DISTRIBUTION OF POOR FAMILIES)

| | Likely causes of poverty | | | | | | | | |
| | Head of family is: | | | | | | | | |
Region	1 Aged	2 Disabled (not 1)	3 Single and has children (not 1 or 2)	4 Usually employed, and worked less than 49 weeks during 1959 (not 1-3)	5 Nonwhite (not 1-4)	6 Self-employed businessman or farmer (not 1-5)	7 Not 1-6	All poor families	All families
Northeast	23	11	13	14	4	5	21	16	23
North Central	27	28	14	28	12	42	20	23	29
South	41	50	64	46	83	45	41	51	33
West	9	11	9	12	1	8	18	10	15
Total	100	100	100	100	100	100	100	100	100
Number of families	137	65	86	65	128	91	183	755	2,800

213

TABLE 16-22

BELT CODE WITHIN LIKELY CAUSES OF POVERTY
(PERCENTAGE DISTRIBUTION OF POOR FAMILIES)

	Likely causes of poverty								
	Head of family is:								
	1	2	3	4	5	6	7		
Belt code	Aged	Disabled (not 1)	Single and has children (not 1 or 2)	Usually employed, and worked less than 49 weeks during 1959 (not 1-3)	Nonwhite (not 1-4)	Self-employed businessman or farmer (not 1-5)	Not 1-6	All poor families	All families
Central cities of 12 largest SMA's	10	15	16	6	17	0	10	11	14
Central cities of other SMA's	14	11	21	30	21	1	12	15	17
Suburban areas of 12 largest SMA's	5	1	6	6	1	1	5	4	13
Suburban areas of other SMA's	7	9	11	15	5	3	10	8	16
Adjacent areas	25	19	12	16	14	31	27	22	19
Outlying areas	39	45	34	27	42	64	36	40	21
Total	100	100	100	100	100	100	100	100	100
Number of families	137	65	86	65	128	91	183	755	2,800

TABLE 16-23

SOURCES OF INCOME WITHIN FAMILY WELFARE RATIO
(MEANS AND PROPORTIONS FOR ALL ADULT UNITS)

Components of adult unit income	Welfare ratio of family in which adult unit lives										All adult units	
	.0–.8		.9–1.2		1.3–1.6		1.7–2.2		2.3 and over			
	Per cent with none	Mean amount	Per cent with none	Mean amount	Per cent with none	Mean amount	Per cent with none	Mean amount	Per cent with none	Mean amount	Per cent with none	Mean amount
Real earnings	25	$ 947	14	$2,917	10	$4,302	7	$5,473	8	$ 9,499	13	$4,560
Gross factor income	17	1,172	8	3,216	7	4,665	5	6,023	4	11,289	9	5,191
Nonfamily transfers	45	419	54	427	63	395	68	344	71	460	60	407
Income tax	83	−17	31	−179	18	−415	15	−659	9	−1868	32	−612
Nonfamily contribution	66	−59	45	−138	33	−187	28	−249	16	−700	38	−261
Nonfamily contributions/gross disposable income		3.7%		4.0%		4.0%		4.4%		7.1%		5.2%
Gross disposable income	0	1,573	0	3,463	0	4,645	0	5,708	0	9,880	0	4,986
Total money income	8	1,347	5	3,314	4	4,618	4	5,779	3	10,720	5	5,078
Disposable money income	8	1,330	5	3,135	4	4,203	4	5,120	3	8,852	5	4,466
Family gross disposable income	0	2,129	0	4,398	0	5,711	0	7,576	0	11,941	0	6,281
Number of adult units	986		606		558		657		589		3,396	

215

benefits whose size is related inversely to income. Contributions show a slight increase at each level of well-being and also contribute to redistribution.

Less than one-fourth of the poor families received public assistance during 1959. The proportions in Table 16-24 reflect the wide range in eligibility for assistance among different groups of poor families, the differences in their asset holdings, and, in all likelihood, differences in the willingness with which these families accept public aid.[10]

TABLE 16-24

PROPORTION OF FAMILIES RECEIVING PUBLIC ASSISTANCE
WITHIN LIKELY CAUSES OF POVERTY
(PROPORTIONS OF POOR FAMILIES)

Likely causes of poverty	Number of families	Per cent receiving public assistance
Head of family is:		
1. Aged	137	29
2. Disabled (not 1)	65	40
3. Single and has children (not 1 or 2)	86	38
4. Usually employed, worked less than 49 weeks in 1959 (not 1–3)	65	17
5. Nonwhite (not 1–4)	128	17
6. Self-employed businessman or farmer (not 1–5)	91	6
7. Not 1–6	183	17
All poor families	755	23

Summary

According to the estimates presented in this chapter, there are some 10.4 million poor families in the United States. Many of the families can be categorized by a classification of likely causes of poverty which stresses situational, involuntary factors that lead to low earning power:

The *aged* have retired and are unable to find work or are limited in their ability to work.

The *disabled* have a severe physical limitation; thus, they are unable to work.

Single family heads with children have the double burden of raising a family and earning a living. Inability to arrange for child care may keep the head from working.

Heads of families who worked less than 49 weeks in 1959 but for whom unemployment is unusual have an obvious explanation for their low incomes in that year.

Nonwhite persons may suffer from severe discrimination so that they are limited in their earning power.

[10] For a more detailed discussion of recipients of public assistance, see Eleanor M. Snyder, *Public Assistance Recipients in New York State, January–February 1957* (State of New York Interdepartmental Committee on Low Incomes, October, 1958).

Farmers and self-employed businessmen suffer from fluctuations in demand and may have low incomes as a consequence.

However, such situational factors do not describe the entire picture of poor families. The heads of poor families, on the average, have never earned as much as it would cost to support their present families at the levels specified by the New York Community Council budgets. This is true in spite of the fact that many of these heads were not always aged, disabled, or without a spouse. Poor education among all but a few heads of poor families is partly responsible; however, a careful analysis of the characteristics of families whose incomes are inadequate reveals that they should earn considerably more than they do on the basis of their education and other characteristics. The multivariate analysis presented in Chapters 4 through 6 indicates that heads of poor families should average $2,204 in earnings. In fact heads of poor families earned an average of only $932 in 1959. The discrepancy may arise from psychological dependency, lack of motivation, lack of intelligence, and a variety of other factors that were not studied.

Comparable census data based on income without regard to a standard of need indicate that in 1958 there were 8.1 million individuals whose own income was less than $2,000 and who, if they lived with others, were in a family whose income was less than $3,000.[11]

The expectation for most poor families is continued dependency or inadequate income. The poor have little protection against the costs of sickness or injury. The majority will receive social security when they reach retirement age, but few will have any other source of income to supplement what is likely to be a minimum payment.

Data on the education and occupations of the parents and children of heads of poor families indicate some transmission of poverty from one generation to the next. They also indicate that the poor include many who have slipped from the level of well-being enjoyed by their parents. The experience of all families implies that heads of poor families should have better education and better occupations than they have actually had. Whether the family environment or personal failures are responsible for the lack of advancement is not clear.

It is clear that rehabilitation, education, training, and substantial increases in financial support will be needed to alleviate the problems of poor families. Despite the many forms of assistance programs and social insurance programs operating in this country, nearly half of the families whose incomes are inadequate received no transfer aid during 1959. Only 23 per cent of all poor families received public assistance, although public assistance is intended to supplement the incomes of those families who do not receive sufficient income.

[11] See U.S. Bureau of the Census, *Current Population Reports, Population Characteristics,* "Family Characteristics of Persons: March, 1959," Series P-20, No. 112 (December 29, 1961), Table H, p. 4.

Chapter 17

THE ECONOMIC POSITION
OF THE DISABLED

Chapters 4, 5, 6, 9, 10, and 11 have already indicated the effects of physical and emotional disabilities on the labor force participation, earning rates, and hours of work of both heads and wives. For a more comprehensive analysis of the impact of disability, it is important to examine the total situation of the disabled.

When a person becomes disabled his income may be curtailed drastically, his social and economic position may be altered, and he may be forced to change his living arrangements. His attitudes toward his abilities, and his goals and plans, may all be affected. The purpose of this chapter is to examine the population of disabled persons, and to compare their sources of income, attitudes and living arrangements with those of nondisabled persons.

Recent concern with disability as a problem for social welfare programs adds another dimension to this study. Analysis of the present economic situation of the disabled and the extent to which they receive aid from current programs of assistance and rehabilitation will provide background for decisions about how more resources might be used most fruitfully in this area.

The disabled were selected by screening questions asked of the head of every spending unit. The first question was: "Have you had an illness, physical condition, or nervous condition which limits the type of work or the amount of work you can do?" A similar question determined whether there were others in the spending unit whose work or schooling was limited. This resulted in a sample of 860 cases, of whom 579 are spending unit heads. The data for heads of spending units are not completely comparable with the data for others. A self-evaluation of limitation is not the same as another person's evaluation of a physical handicap or chronic illness. Nor are either of these judgments comparable to a medical diagnosis; some persons with definite limitations may not report them while others may report minor or imagined maladies.

218

It is not the purpose of this chapter to outline the etiology and pathology of persons with chronic diseases. More accurate materials on the incidence of disability from impairments and chronic diseases are available through the National Health Survey.[1]

This study combines some crude information of disabilities with data on the background and experiences of families containing disabled individuals. The statistics on age, sex, type of disabling condition, and extent of work limitation are best read in relation to other characteristics of the disabled person and his family. Because the basis for selection in this sample was self-perception rather than medical diagnosis, the data provide relatively poor absolute estimates of the fraction of persons in this country who suffer from these conditions. However, they do provide opportunity for analysis of relationships between disabilities and the family's social and economic status.

Data about the disabled are presented for three different units of analysis. The most basic unit of analysis is the disabled individual. The tabulations on this basis describe the population in such a way that it may be compared with other studies of disability. Most of the data based on disabled individuals are presented only for disabled adults; children were excluded from the tabulations because much of the economic analysis was irrelevant for them.

The second unit of analysis is the adult unit, that is: a disabled individual, his or her spouse, and minor children. This nuclear unit was considered to be the most satisfactory in terms of studying living arrangements, earnings, and many sources of transfer income.

The group about which the bulk of information is available consists of disabled spending unit heads, that is: heads of units containing all related persons who live together and pool their incomes. These units include dependent persons who live with relatives because they cannot afford to maintain a separate household or because they are physically unable to live alone. Spending unit heads were interviewed, and it is for this group that type of disability and the extent of work limitation were measured most accurately, and extensive information on attitudes and background collected.

The analysis of disability is divided into five parts. The first part is an analysis of the extent of work limitation reported and its relation to the social and economic circumstances of the disabled. The second section is an evaluation of the rehabilitation potential of the disabled and a brief description of the rehabilitation aid which they now receive. The third part of the analysis examines the living arrangements of the disabled, and the effects of decreased income and increased dependence. The fourth section deals with the income and resources of the disabled. It includes an analysis of income adequacy among the disabled, a description of sources of income, and an

[1] U.S. National Health Survey, *Health Statistics: United States July–September, 1957* (U.S. Department of Health, Education, and Welfare, 1958), B Series.

estimate of the aggregate impact of income loss because of disability. The final section describes the outlook for the disabled in the future.

Characteristics of the Disabled

According to the reports of spending unit heads about 9 per cent of the individuals in the national sample suffer from some limitations on their work. More than half of these are over fifty-five years old. Slightly more than half of the disabled are men and 6 per cent are children under eighteen.

TABLE 17-1

AGE WITHIN SEX
(PERCENTAGE DISTRIBUTION OF DISABLED ADULTS)

| | Sex | | |
Age	Males	Females	All disabled adults
Under 25	5	4	4
25–34	7	6	6
35–44	16	11	14
45–54	18	18	18
55–64	22	26	24
65 and older	32	35	34
Total	100	100	100
Number of disabled persons	446	360	806
Per cent of disabled persons	53	41	94

However, an analysis of the age, sex, and family status of the disabled persons indicates considerable underreporting of disabilities for wives and dependents compared to the reporting for heads of spending units. Table 17-2 suggests that the incidence of disability among wives is roughly half that among female heads of spending units in the same age group. Similarly reporting of disabilities among dependents aged sixty-five and over is roughly half of what might be expected from the reports given by spending unit heads. The pattern is quite consistent and remains when only reports of complete and severely limiting disablements are considered.

The underreporting stems from a number of causes. Disabilities of wives and dependents are not as salient to the head of a spending unit as his own limitation. Also, the screening questions ask specifically for limitations on work or schooling of the dependents. If the wife or dependent does not ordinarily work outside the home, the head of the spending unit may feel that work is not limited. Thus, if an aged dependent retires and becomes disabled, his work is not limited because he would not be working in any case. Similarly, a housewife only has to care for the house and this may not be interpreted as work.

Spending unit heads who reported that they had some work limitation do not in fact correspond to a neatly defined population of persons who have

TABLE 17-2

AGE WITHIN SEX AND RELATION TO SPENDING UNIT HEAD
(PERCENTAGE DISTRIBUTION OF DISABLED ADULTS)
PER CENT DISABLED WITHIN AGE AND RELATION
TO SPENDING UNIT HEAD
(FOR ADULTS)

| | Heads of spending units | | | | Wives of spending unit heads | | Dependent adults | |
| | Disabled | | Per cent of spending unit heads in each class who are disabled | | Disabled | Per cent of spending unit wives in each class who are disabled | Disabled | Per cent of all dependent adults in each class who are disabled |
Age	Males	Females	Males	Females				
18–24	3	2	7	5	3	2	18	9
25–34	6	5	5	12	8	2	11	
35–44	16	10	12	14	15	4	4	25
45–54	18	12	16	16	29	11	5	
55–64	23	27	27	32	24	15	23	25
65 and older	34	44	45	46	21	21	39	17
All adults	100	100	17	24	100	7	100	

221

impairments or diseases which can be diagnosed medically. Nevertheless, the population forms a useful basis for study because it is the group of people whose labor force participation and working habits are most likely to be different from persons in the population with no perceived limit on their work. It is not possible to determine how many of the disabled in this study have no medically diagnosable limits on their activity; nor is it possible to assess the extent to which persons with medically defined limits are not included in the population we have studied. The underreporting of disabilities for dependents suggests that the latter group is probably larger than the former.

The nature and severity of the limitation reported for a disabled individual was assessed from the spending unit head's description of the condition responsible for the disability and the extent of the limit it imposes on work. Work was considered the normal activity at a regular occupation, defined by the age and role of the disabled person to include groups whose normal occupation does not imply labor force participation. In the case of housewives, work referred to their usual housework, while for children the question referred specifically to limitations on their schooling. The descriptions of the conditions causing disablement provided a general classification of the types of conditions. The distribution of the disabled among these general categories is shown in Table 17-3. About 1 per cent were reported to have more than one type of disablement. For these people, Table 17-3 shows the condition which appears first in the listing. Thus a man with both a circulatory ailment and loss of a hand would appear in the classification under *major specific loss.*

TABLE 17-3

TYPE OF DISABILITY
(PERCENTAGE DISTRIBUTION OF DISABLED PERSONS)

Type of disability	*All disabled persons*
Major specific losses (impairments) blindness, deafness, loss of limbs or digits, impairments of extremities	11
Other specific losses (impairments) mental deficiency, speech defects, paralysis	14
Circulatory diseases (ISC^a codes 400–468)	25
Arthritis and rheumatism (ISC codes 720–44 except 726.6, 734, 736–7)	9
Other chronic diseases (ISC codes 470–776 except 533.0, 533.5, 533.7, 751, 752, 755, 758.0, 758.2, 758.4–758.5)	20
Mental and nervous conditions (ISC codes 300–98 except 325, 326.0–326.2, 344, 351, 352, 389, 397–8)	6
Vague disorders and other conditions	10
Not ascertained	5
Total	100
Number of cases	860

^{a} *International Standard Classification of Diseases and Causes of Death*

The Extent of Work Limitation and Its Relation to Other Characteristics of the Disabled

Responses to the question, "How does it (the condition) limit your work?" indicated that more than four-fifths of the disabled persons have some restriction on their work. For about 5 per cent of the disabled individuals the condition placed no limit on their work. Although this appears to be a contradictory response, it generally reflects the fact that the individual has a disabling condition but has adjusted his life and work within the bounds set by the condition. For example, a crippled person may say that no limit is imposed on his work because he has a job tailored to his limitation. For the remaining 12 per cent of disabled individuals the extent of limitation was not reported or the information given was too vague to be coded.

TABLE 17-4

EXTENT OF WORK LIMITATION
(PERCENTAGE DISTRIBUTION OF ALL DISABLED ADULTS
AND DISABLED SPENDING UNIT HEADS)

Extent of Limitation	All disabled adults	Disabled spending unit heads
Complete	19	20
Severe	17	17
Moderate	47	49
None	5	6
Not ascertained	12	8
Total	100	100
Per cent of disabled persons	94	68

The measure of extent of limit is most satisfactory for male heads of spending units under sixty-five. These persons customarily work full time and support their families. Any restriction on this full time contribution can be assessed relatively accurately. Female spending unit heads may be widowed or caring for small children, so they are less likely to appraise their limitation by referring to the demands of a full-time job. For the retired, the limit on activity becomes even more ambiguous because the activities of the retired vary greatly in their physical demands. Where the limitation on activity was reported by the head of the spending unit for a dependent, the measure is less likely to correspond to the nuances of psychological limitation which were expressed by the heads of spending units. Thus, some care must be used in interpreting the reports on extent of work limitation.

In spite of the problems in defining work, the limitation reported is closely related to employment. As Tables 17-5 and 17-6 illustrate, the proportion of disabled persons who were at work at the time of the interview drops dramatically with increasing limitation, as does the proportion who worked a full year during 1959. It is impossible to determine how many of those not employed would be working if they were not disabled.

TABLE 17-5

PER CENT EMPLOYED AT TIME OF INTERVIEW WITHIN
EXTENT OF WORK LIMITATION
(FOR DISABLED ADULTS)

Extent of work limitation	Per cent in each group employed at time of interview
Complete	4
Severe	33
Moderate	58
None	76
Not ascertained	20
All	40
Number of disabled persons	806

TABLE 17-6

WEEKS WORKED DURING 1959 WITHIN EXTENT OF WORK LIMITATION
(PERCENTAGE DISTRIBUTION OF DISABLED SPENDING UNIT HEADS)

Weeks worked during 1959	Extent of work limitation				All disabled spending unit heads [a]
	Complete	Severe	Moderate	None	
None	76	46	18	8	37
1–13	4	5	3	4	4
14–25	4	6	4	3	4
26–49	9	12	21	23	16
50–52	6	22	51	62	35
Not ascertained	1	9	3	0	4
Total	100	100	100	100	100
Per cent of disabled persons	13	11	33	4	68

[a] includes spending unit heads for whom extent of work limitation was not ascertained

Since extent of work limitation was reported, for the most part, by disabled persons themselves and with no explicit standards defined, it was necessary to determine the degree to which the variable represented an independent measure of disability and the extent to which it was related to other characteristics of the disabled persons.

As a number of different characteristics affect work limitation, a multivariate analysis seemed most appropriate. For this purpose, severity of limitation was scaled as follows:

Extent of work limitation	Scale value assigned
Complete	2
Severe	1
Moderate, none, not ascertained	0

Two multivariate analyses were carried out, one for all disabled adults and one for disabled spending unit heads. In both analyses the average extent of limitation reported lies between severe and moderate, at .56. In both analyses the standard deviation was .80.

The variables used in the analysis of spending unit heads can be grouped into three categories: physical characteristics of the disabled person; the abilities and skills of the disabled person and his social and economic situation; and attitudes and motivations of the disabled person. Because most of the attitudes and social characteristics were not available for disabled persons who are not spending unit heads, the analysis of all disabled adults is less extensive.

Classifications by age, sex, and type of disability describe the physical characteristics of disabled persons which affect the extent to which work is limited. The classification by age was used because older persons are likely to have the greatest difficulty finding a job, particularly a less demanding job, and are less likely to receive rehabilitation services. Sex of the disabled person is important because the work activities of males and females are different, so that the same condition may inflict work limitation to differing degrees. A condition which would prohibit a man from holding a regular job might not prevent his wife from doing at least some housekeeping. The type of disability was included because the seriousness and permanence of a physical condition has a decided effect on the extent to which work is limited and the extent to which a disablement can be overcome through rehabilitation. The classification is imperfect, however, since every category includes many degrees of severity.

The abilities and skills of the disabled person are indicated by his education, occupation, and his rank and progress in school. Persons with more education are likely to have greater capacity for adjusting to physical limitations and for being retrained for jobs that are not physically demanding. Also, persons with more education may be able to make more sophisticated assessments of the real effect of their physical condition. Persons with nonmanual occupations are less likely to be limited by physical restrictions than are people with manual jobs, and are less likely to be exposed to disability-creating job hazards. The disabled person's rank and progress in school may affect his work limitation. Persons who were retarded in educational achievement are likely to be more seriously limited by physical disabilities because they have less ability to do nonmanual tasks.

The social setting in which a disabled person finds himself also affects the extent to which his disablement causes work limitation. Persons living in large metropolitan areas have a greater variety of jobs to choose from than do persons living in rural areas, as well as more opportunities for sheltered work and more facilities for rehabilitation. Belonging to a minority race also limits the type and number of jobs available to a person. Occupational discrimination may operate to compound the difficulty facing a nonwhite disabled person, particularly if an employer discriminates racially in the guise of an objection to the disabling condition. Also, the degree to which a disabled person feels secure in his job may affect his perception of his limitation in that people who are most secure may feel less limited than those who feel that they are likely to be laid off or fired.

Because the extent of work limitation being studied is entirely a matter of self-perception, the most important category of characteristics in explaining it may be the disabled person's attitudes and motivations. These are indicated by the need-achievement score and attitude toward hard work, family composition, and race. Persons with high need-achievement scores, and the perception that hard work is effective in getting ahead, may be more likely to attempt to overcome obstacles associated with disability. Also, these persons may be psychologically less able to admit that a limitation cannot be overcome. The composition of the adult unit containing a disabled person is taken as a partial measure of economic motivation to overcome limitation and to work more. Persons with families to support are under greater pressure to earn a living than single persons with no one to support. Race is included in this group because occupational discrimination against nonwhites may make a nonwhite disabled person perceive himself as more severely limited than a white person with the same disabling condition.

The two multivariate analyses of this scale revealed parallel findings. The variables included in both relationships rank quite similarly in order of im-

TABLE 17-7

CHARACTERISTICS USED TO EXPLAIN EXTENT OF WORK LIMITATION
IMPOSED BY DISABILITY
(FOR DISABLED ADULTS AND FOR DISABLED SPENDING UNIT HEADS)

Characteristics of disabled persons	Relative importance (Beta coefficients)		Significance (F ratios)	
	Adults	Spending unit heads	Adults	Spending unit heads
Job security	. . .	.390	. . .	16.01**
Age	.255	.187	9.67**	5.15**
Education	. . .	.180	. . .	3.41**
Occupation	.140	.169	4.37**	5.26**
Attitude toward hard work and need-achievement score	. . .	.141	. . .	2.44*
Sex	.100	.125	8.93**	11.52**
Type of disability	.169	.110	3.64	1.27
Rank and progress in school	. . .	.124	. . .	1.89
Population of city	.087	.092	1.35	1.25
Family composition	.025	.064	0.19	1.01
Race	.034	.004	1.03	0.01

** significant at probability level of .01
* significant at probability level of .05
. . . not used in analysis of adults

portance in explaining the dependent variable. The Spearman coefficient of rank correlation between the beta coefficients of the two analyses is .84. Table 17-7 shows the characteristics used to explain extent of work limitation and their relative importance and significance.

The coefficient of multiple determination of .13 for disabled adults indicates that extent of limitation is largely independent of demographic characteristics of the disabled. A somewhat higher coefficient of .29 was obtained for spending unit heads, mostly as a result of including a variable which distinguishes disabled who work from nonworking disabled.

Although the variable describing each spending unit head's feeling of security in his job was included as a psychological measure, in effect it also discriminates between those who have jobs and those who are not working. Since the question about extent of limitation was related to work, the rela-

TABLE 17-8

EXTENT OF WORK LIMITATION: DEVIATIONS FOR JOB SECURITY
(FOR DISABLED SPENDING UNIT HEADS)

Job security	Number of spending unit heads	Unadjusted deviations [a]	Adjusted deviations [a]
Not working;	296⎫		
Self-employed	89⎭	.22	.22
Work for someone else, would be laid off:			
First	27	−.42	−.42
Near beginning	5	−.56	−.67
In middle	18	−.44	−.35
Near end	41	−.53	−.50
Last	71	−.40	−.45
Do not know	10	−.30	−.34
Not ascertained	22	−.66	−.02

[a] deviations from grand mean of .56

tionship shown in Table 17-8 is not surprising. Among those who are working, the attitude appears to have little effect on the extent of limitation reported. The fact that type of disability has an insignificant effect for disabled spending unit heads is probably a consequence of the inclusion of this variable. (See Table 17-14.)

Both analyses show that the extent of disability reported for the individual increases markedly with age. Young persons are more likely to report that their handicap produces no limit, while older persons, especially those sixty-five and older are likely to report that it imposes a severe limit or completely limits their work.

Spending unit heads with less formal education report greater work limitations from disabilities. The effect of differences in education below the high school level is somewhat uneven, however. The proportion of spending unit heads reporting disabilities decreases as amount of education attained increases. The proportions vary from 52 per cent of spending unit heads with

TABLE 17-9

EXTENT OF WORK LIMITATION: DEVIATIONS FOR AGE
(FOR DISABLED ADULTS AND DISABLED SPENDING UNIT HEADS)

Age	Number of cases		Unadjusted deviations [a]		Adjusted deviations [a]	
	Adults	Spending unit heads	Adults	Spending unit heads	Adults	Spending unit heads
18–24	36	16	−.05	−.29	−.11	.05
25–34	57	37	−.24	−.37	−.23	−.28
35–44	114	87	−.33	−.38	−.33	−.29
45–54	157	107	−.15	−.16	−.12	−.01
55–64	201	148	.00	.01	.02	.09
65 and older	241	184	.27	.31	.24	.10

[a] deviations from grand mean of .56

TABLE 17-10

EXTENT OF WORK LIMITATION: DEVIATIONS FOR EDUCATION
(FOR DISABLED SPENDING UNIT HEADS)

Education	Number of spending unit heads	Unadjusted deviations [a]	Adjusted deviations [a]
None	27	.21	.15
1–8 grades	305	.11	.09
9–11 grades	107	−.15	−.06
12 grades	45	.10	.18
12 grades and nonacademic training	24	−.30	−.28
College, no degree	51	−.24	−.27
College, bachelor's degree	17	−.25	−.23
College, advanced degree	3	−.56	−.24

[a] deviations from grand mean of .56

no education reporting disabilities to 4 per cent of spending unit heads with advanced college degrees doing so. The surprising difference between high school graduates with and without additional vocational training probably indicates that persons with vocational training have sufficiently specialized skills to compensate for their lack of advanced education.

Persons in blue collar occupations are somewhat more likely to report severe disabilities, while those who are self-employed businessmen or farmers are less likely to do so. Differences in severity of limitation reported for disabled adults and heads of spending units are partly accounted for by the fact that deviations for spending unit heads are adjusted for the impact of education. Persons with a professional position are likely to have college education. The additive effects of education and occupaton of spending unit heads parallels the effect shown for all disabled adults in the professional occupations.

TABLE 17-11

EXTENT OF WORK LIMITATION: DEVIATIONS FOR OCCUPATION
(FOR DISABLED ADULTS AND DISABLED SPENDING UNIT HEADS)

Occupation	Number of cases		Unadjusted deviations [a]		Adjusted deviations [a]	
	Adults	Spending unit heads	Adults	Spending unit heads	Adults	Spending unit heads
Professionals and managers	47	38	−.20	−.14	−.23	.09
Clerical and sales workers	93	60	−.20	−.15	−.14	.05
Self-employed businessmen and farmers	119	117	−.01	−.03	−.06	−.27
Blue collar workers	382	313	.02	.03	.02	.08
Never worked; not ascertained	165	51	.15	.20	.17	−.03

[a] deviations from grand mean of .56

Spending unit heads with high need-achievement scores and the perception that hard work is important to success are less likely to report serious limitation in their work than persons who do not show both the motivation and the perception. The effect suggests that disability and work limitation may have some psychosomatic roots. Some persons may be reporting or exaggerating handicaps as an excuse for their failure to get ahead in the world. These same persons should, in theory, score low in the index of need-achievement and should fail to associate success with their own effort. The group for whom need-achievement was not ascertained includes persons for whom the

TABLE 17-12

EXTENT OF WORK LIMITATION: DEVIATIONS FOR ATTITUDE TOWARD
HARD WORK AND NEED-ACHIEVEMENT SCORE
(FOR DISABLED SPENDING UNIT HEADS)

Attitude toward hard work and need-achievement score	Number of spending unit heads	Unadjusted deviations [a]	Adjusted deviations [a]
Hard work is equal to or more important than luck; need-achievement score is in:			
high range	107	−.18	−.08
middle range	193	.00	−.01
low range	90	.10	.04
Hard work is less important than luck; need-achievement score is in:			
high range	27	−.16	−.05
middle range	67	−.14	−.14
low range	55	.06	.12
Need-achievement score not ascertained	40	.56	.33

[a] deviations from grand mean of .56

comparisons on which need-achievement scores were based were so foreign that they were unable to answer the questions. This may be an indication of their lack of need-achievement. Persons to whom need-achievement is salient were able to make the comparisons. Thus it is not surprising to find the not ascertained group reports far more severe limitations than any other group in the classification.

The proportion of spending unit heads reporting disabilities seems to be related more to the attitude toward hard work than to the need-achievement score. The proportion of disabled is lower than average among those who say hard work is more important than luck, higher than average among those who say hard work is less important.

Females report proportionally fewer disabilities, and less severe limitations than males. In part this may have resulted from the form of the question, which asked the extent to which *work* was limited. A disabled retired woman or housewife who felt work referred only to work outside the home might report less limitation because she had no plans to work or expectation of working. The fact that the adjusted deviation for sex shows all disabled adult women to be relatively more disabled than those who are spending unit heads corresponds to the notion that the dependent adults who are disabled are relatively more severely disabled than spending unit heads.

Another difference in the reporting of limitation for disabled adults arose from the fact that all respondents were spending unit heads. Only 26 adult males had their disabilities reported by someone else, while 201 adult females who are not spending unit heads did not report their own limitations.

TABLE 17-13

EXTENT OF WORK LIMITATION: DEVIATIONS FOR SEX
(FOR DISABLED ADULTS AND DISABLED SPENDING UNIT HEADS)

Sex	Number of cases		Unadjusted deviations [a]		Adjusted deviations [a]	
	Adults	Spending unit heads	Adults	Spending unit heads	Adults	Spending unit heads
Males	446	420	.04	.01	.07	.06
Females	360	159	−.05	−.03	−.09	−.17

[a] deviations from grand mean of .56

Persons reporting a mental or nervous condition were most likely to report a severe limit on their work. Those persons may be reporting a handicap as a rationalization for failure in their jobs, but it may be that mental disabilities are more of a handicap than physical ones. Persons with other chronic diseases report consistently less limit on their work than others in the sample, while those with conditions not classified elsewhere report the least limitation. Possibly the two vague categories of conditions not classified elsewhere and conditions which were not ascertained include a large proportion of persons

TABLE 17-14

EXTENT OF WORK LIMITATION: DEVIATIONS FOR TYPE OF DISABILITY
(FOR DISABLED ADULTS AND DISABLED SPENDING UNIT HEADS)

Type of disability	Number of cases		Unadjusted deviations [a]		Adjusted deviations [a]	
	Adults	Spending unit heads	Adults	Spending unit heads	Adults	Spending unit heads
Major specific losses	85	69	−.01	−.07	.03	−.07
Other specific losses	107	74	.11	−.02	.19	.11
Circulatory diseases	206	156	.04	.06	−.01	.02
Arthritis and rheumatism	76	60	.03	.11	−.04	.03
Other chronic diseases	158	122	−.14	−.13	−.13	−.07
Mental and nervous conditions	43	25	.32	.40	.35	.24
All other conditions	86	50	−.12	−.10	−.15	−.14
Not ascertained	45	23	−.15	.03	−.06	−.02

[a] deviations from grand mean of .56

whose disablements are mostly imagined. This variable was not significant for disabled spending unit heads probably because the variable describing the feelings about job security differentiated between working and nonworking disabled.

Several factors included in the multivariate analysis had no significant impact on extent of work limitation. These characteristics are presented in Tables 17-15 through 17-18.

TABLE 17-15

EXTENT OF WORK LIMITATION: DEVIATIONS FOR RANK
AND PROGRESS IN SCHOOL
(FOR DISABLED SPENDING UNIT HEADS)

Rank and progress in school	Number of spending unit heads	Unadjusted deviations [a]	Adjusted deviations [a]
Grades above average	136	−.08	.07
Grades average:			
Not behind age group in school	151	−.01	.01
1–2 years behind age group in school	81	−.08	−.20
Grades below average:			
Not behind age group in school	21	.11	.02
1–2 years behind age group in school	13	−.19	−.21
Grades not above average:			
3 or more years behind age group in school	72	.07	−.04
Position relative to age group cannot be calculated [b]	105	.13	.10

[a] deviations from grand mean of .56
[b] college or nonacademic training or no education

TABLE 17-16

EXTENT OF WORK LIMITATION: DEVIATIONS
FOR POPULATION OF CITIES
(FOR DISABLED ADULTS AND DISABLED SPENDING UNIT HEADS)

	Number of cases		Unadjusted deviations [a]		Adjusted deviations [a]	
Population of cities	Adults	Spending unit heads	Adults	Spending unit heads	Adults	Spending unit heads
Central cities of 12 largest metropolitan areas	101	71	−.11	−.01	−.11	.10
Other cities 50,000 or more	115	83	.15	.11	.13	.12
Urban places:						
10,000–49,999	102	74	−.03	−.07	.00	−.01
Under 10,000	144	112	.00	−.01	.02	−.05
Rural places:						
Near city	73	58	−.02	−.07	−.06	−.10
Not near city	271	181	.00	.01	−.01	−.03

[a] deviations from grand mean of .56

TABLE 17-17

EXTENT OF WORK LIMITATION: DEVIATIONS FOR FAMILY COMPOSITION
(FOR DISABLED ADULTS AND DISABLED SPENDING UNIT HEADS)

	Number of cases		Unadjusted deviations [a]		Adjusted deviations [a]	
Family composition	Adults	Spending unit heads	Adults	Spending unit heads	Adults	Spending unit heads
Two or more adult units in family	266	160	.01	−.07	−.02	−.07
One adult unit in family; adult unit contains:						
single adult, no children	114	114	.11	.10	.03	.00
Married couple, no children	215	143	.12	.19	.02	.00
single adult or married couple with children	211	162	−.21	−.20	−.01	.07

[a] deviations from grand mean of .56

It appears that disabled persons with high levels of education, skilled or professional occupations and physical rather than mental disabilities, are likely to report less severe limitations than other groups. The relationships are not strong, yet they are sufficient to indicate that the need for rehabilitation exists in precisely those groups for whom the potential for retraining is lowest.

TABLE 17-18

EXTENT OF WORK LIMITATION: DEVIATIONS FOR RACE
(FOR DISABLED ADULTS AND DISABLED SPENDING UNIT HEADS)

Race	Number of cases		Unadjusted deviations [a]		Adjusted deviations [a]	
	Adults	Spending unit heads	Adults	Spending unit heads	Adults	Spending unit heads
Whites	674	488	−.01	−.02	−.01	.00
Nonwhites	132	91	.09	.15	.07	−.01

[a] deviations from grand mean of .56

Potential for Rehabilitation of the Disabled

A major concern in past years has been the extent to which additional resources devoted to rehabilitating persons with handicaps might help such persons to be more self-supporting.

In the years since the establishment of a Federal agency for vocational rehabilitation it has become clear that money spent in rehabilitation both provides satisfactions to the recipients and reduces expenditures on public assistance and the burden of dependence on relatives.[2]

Two types of rehabilitation are relevant to this discussion: vocational rehabilitation directed at returning the disabled individual to a job, and nonvocational rehabilitation directed at retraining the individual to enable him to care for himself. The effectiveness of either type of rehabilitation program clearly depends on the skills, education, and intelligence which the individual had prior to the time that he incurred the disability. Success of rehabilitation also depends on the extent to which the impairment or disease places a psychological barrier to self-help. On the following pages the disabled are described in terms of these characteristics so that some judgment about the rehabilitation potential of the disabled may be made.

Persons over sixty-five account for nearly a third of the disabled population. Presumably rehabilitative efforts directed at that group would be concentrated on nonvocational or limited vocational rehabilitation. For persons under sixty-five vocational rehabilitation appears to become germane, given the present resources and capabilities for rehabilitation. For this reason disabled persons sixty-five and older are classified separately from the younger disabled individuals. Characteristics of younger disabled are presented by age to give some perspective on the extent to which vocational rehabilitation

[2] See for example, Paul A. Strachen and Mary Switzer, "Assistance and Rehabilitation of the Physically Handicapped," *Hearings Before a Special Subcommittee of the Committee on Education and Labor,* U.S. House of Representatives, 83rd Cong., 1st Sess. (July, 1953).

See also W. Scott Allan, *Rehabilitation: A Community Challenge* (New York: John Wiley & Sons, Inc., 1958).

efforts can be concentrated in younger age groups with relatively long-term prospects of participation in the labor force.

Many of the disabled have low status or unskilled occupations. Of those under sixty-five nearly half were blue collar workers at the time of the interview or when they last worked. Only 22 per cent were in the white collar, professional, or managerial positions where they might be more able to continue working after some rehabilitation. About 11 per cent of the disabled under sixty-five have never worked. Presumably this group includes those with the most extreme disabilities; also, 9 per cent of those who never worked are housewives.

TABLE 17-19

OCCUPATION WITHIN AGE
(PERCENTAGE DISTRIBUTION OF DISABLED ADULTS)

	Age						
Occupation	Under 25	25–34	35–44	45–54	55–64	All disabled adults under 65	65 and older
Professionals, managers	0	0	2	2	2	6	7
Clerical and sales workers	2	3	3	4	4	16	6
Self-employed	0	1	2	5	5	13	16
Blue collar workers	2	4	11	13	18	48	44
Never worked	1	1	2	2	5	11	16
Not ascertained	1	1	1	1	2	6	11
Total	6	10	21	27	36	100	100
Number of disabled adults	36	57	114	157	201	565	241

Table 17-20 shows that 40 per cent of all disabled adults were employed at the time of the interview. For this group rehabilitation may be needed

TABLE 17-20

PER CENT EMPLOYED AT TIME OF INTERVIEW WITHIN AGE, SEX,
AND RELATION TO ADULT UNIT HEAD
(FOR DISABLED ADULTS AND ALL ADULTS)

Sex and relation to adult unit heads	Age			All disabled adults	All adults
	Under 35	35–54	55 and older		
Males	68	85	35	56	79
Females	28	25	14	19	33
Adult unit heads	20	47	15	22	45
Wives of adult unit heads	32	15	11	16	28
All adults	52	61	25	40	55
Number of disabled adults	93	271	442	806	

if present employment fails to make good use of the talents and latent skills of the employed person. Lack of employment is clearly the greatest problem for the disabled over fifty-five years of age and for women who are heads of adult units. Though the latter group have the same social responsibilities for supporting themselves as do male heads of adult units, less than half as many were employed at the time of the interview.

As a consequence of the method by which data on the disabled were collected, little additional information on disabled members of dependent adult units is available. For spending unit heads and their wives, however, data on education and other measures of skill and motivation were collected. Table 17-21 shows the education of disabled spending unit heads according to their ages. Of those under sixty-five more than two thirds do not have a high school diploma. This proportion is considerably higher than the proportion of all spending unit heads who have no high school diploma. Low levels of education present particular difficulties for vocational rehabilitation.

TABLE 17-21

EDUCATION WITHIN AGE
(PERCENTAGE DISTRIBUTION OF DISABLED SPENDING UNIT HEADS
AND ALL SPENDING UNIT HEADS UNDER 65)

Education	Age					All under 65	All spending unit heads under 65
	Under 25	25–34	35–44	45–54	55–64		
Less than 9 grades	1	2	8	14	24	49	27
9–11 grades	1	3	7	4	7	22	22
12 grades	2	2	5	3	2	14	27
College, no degree	1	2	2	2	3	10	13
College degree	0	0	1	3	1	5	11
Total	5	9	23	26	37	100	100
Number of disabled spending unit heads	16	37	87	107	148	395	

Disabled spending unit heads appear to have approximately the same distribution on the need-achievement index as all spending unit heads. The disabled stress luck as an element in success a little more often than do all spending unit heads. These results suggest somewhat less faith in personal efforts among the disabled than among spending unit heads who are not disabled. The result may reflect, in part, the lower average education of the disabled group.

This general description of characteristics of the disabled which might assist or impede their rehabilitation leads to two conclusions. The past work experience of disabled adults is concentrated largely in blue collar positions which provide a poor base for retraining for less physically demanding occupations. Disabled heads of spending units are also likely to have less education than nondisabled spending unit heads. Considering the level of their formal education, the disabled heads of spending units appear to have about the motivation and work skills which might be expected for them. All in all, they are a somewhat less intellectually able group than the nondisabled.

Assessing Rehabilitation Potential

Table 17-22 summarizes much of the information required to determine priorities and resource allocation for rehabilitation. Vocational rehabilitation concentrated on the 7 per cent of disabled adult unit heads who are now both under forty-five and not employed would appear to have the largest economic payoff. This group has the possibility of working more than twenty years after rehabilitation. However, only a small fraction of this group have high school diplomas and nearly half are dependent on relatives' living with them as dependent adults. Both of these facts would suggest difficulty in making all of these persons employable. Among the disabled adult unit heads between forty-five and sixty-four years old fewer of the group who were not employed at the time of the interview are dependent adult units, suggesting less serious problems for vocational rehabilitation than in the younger age group. However, the average age of the group implies that rehabilitation efforts will require considerable placement skill if workers in this age range are to find successful employment. For the groups that are working now, rehabilitation

TABLE 17-22

AGE AND EDUCATION WITHIN RELATION TO ADULT UNIT HEADS
AND LABOR FORCE STATUS
(PERCENTAGE DISTRIBUTION OF DISABLED ADULTS)

| | Relation to adult unit heads and labor force status | | |
| | Disabled heads of adult units | | Disabled wives of adult unit heads |
Age and education	Employed at time of interview	Not employed at time of interview	
Under 45:	17	7	27
0–11 grades	9	3	15
12 grades or more	7	1	12
Not ascertained	1 [a]	3 [a]	0
45–64:	25	15	50
0–11 grades	18	10	38
12 grades or more	7	2	11
Not ascertained	0 [a]	3 [a]	1
65 and older:	4	32	23
0–11 grades	3	23	19
12 grades or more	1	6	2
Not ascertained	0 [a]	3 [a]	2
Total	46	54	100
		100	
Number of disabled adults	294	344	158

[a] includes only persons who are in dependent adult units, living in relatives' households

may still result in better earnings, job satisfaction, and increased productivity which would more than pay for the initial costs of training and placement.

The disabled wives are shown separately in Table 17-22 because they are less likely to be full-time participants in the labor force. However, this does not imply that their disability involves less income loss to the family. The value of homemaking services has been estimated at about $3,000 a year, when going wages for domestic help and child care are considered.[3] Rehabilitation of disabled wives may enable the breadwinners to dispense with housekeepers who are a heavy cost burden on the family. If this is so, rehabilitation of women to the tasks of homemaking is clearly important even from a pragmatic economic point of view.

Only 3 per cent of disabled adults reported that they received any help in returning to a job after they became disabled. State vocational rehabilitation offices and Veteran's Administration or Workmen's Compensation offices were the most frequently mentioned groups who assisted in the return to work. Typically this help was given to male spending unit heads. A report of aid for wives or dependent adults from either of these agencies appeared only once in the entire sample. Though the number who reported receiving any rehabilitation aid is too small to permit any inferences regarding the type of agencies or the type of disabled persons who receive help, it is clear from these statistics that the vocational rehabilitation field has hardly been tapped.

Those who received some type of vocational rehabilitation aid are not particularly clustered according to age, nor do they appear to be receiving any one particular type of service. About half of the group who received some aid reported that they received vocational training or vocational counseling.

Where disability benefit payments may be affected by rehabilitation, there may exist motives to refuse such rehabilitation services. In one study some claimants gave such reasons explicitly.[4]

Family Status and Living Arrangements of the Disabled

Conservatively estimated, 11 per cent of all disabled persons live in the households of relatives. Eight per cent do not keep finances separate and cannot be classified as separate spending units.

Contrary to what might be expected, less combining of households occurs among the disabled than in the national population at large. Seventeen per

[3] Marie G. Gage, "The Work Load and Its Value for Fifty Homemakers" (unpublished Ph.D. dissertation, Cornell University, 1960).

[4] California State Department of Education, *Vocational Rehabilitation of Industrially Injured Workers,* report to the California Legislature cosponsored by California Vocational Rehabilitation Service and the U.S. Office of Vocational Rehabilitation (Sacramento, California: June, 1961), p. 62.

For additional evidence of the failure of vocational rehabilitation services to reach the worker, see James Morgan and others, *Lump-Sum Redemption Settlements and Rehabilitation* (Ann Arbor: Institute for Social Research, 1959).

cent of all adult units in the national sample live in a relative's household, while 12 per cent of all adult units with disabled members live in a relative's household. Thus it appears that very few of the disabled benefit from the direct support which comes from living with relatives.

The number of disabled who themselves house relatives is about the same as the national sample.

Fifty-seven per cent of the primary adult units containing disabled persons own their homes, compared to 51 per cent of the national sample. Disabled units have about the same number of rooms per person as the national average. The disabled population's housing situation undoubtedly stems from the frequency of aged among the disabled and the greater tendency for the aged to own a home, irrespective of current income.

The 8 per cent of disabled individuals who live in the households of relatives and do not maintain separate finances exhibit markedly different characteristics from the remaining disabled population. For this group complete limitation is reported considerably more often than for disabled who live by themselves or keep separate finances. These dependent adults include a higher proportion of both the very young and the very old than other disabled. These differences are shown in Tables 17-23 and 17-24.

TABLE 17-23

EXTENT OF LIMITATION WITHIN RELATION TO SPENDING UNIT HEAD
(PERCENTAGE DISTRIBUTION OF DISABLED PERSONS)

| Extent of limitation | Relation to spending unit head | | | | | All disabled persons |
	Male spending unit heads	Female spending unit heads	Wives of spending unit heads	Dependent adults	Children under 18	
Complete	21	16	13	31	8	19
Severe	15	21	19	14	22	17
Moderate	51	46	49	17	46	46
None	6	4	4	0	5	5
Not ascertained	7	13	15	38	19	13
Total	100	100	100	100	100	100
Per cent of disabled persons	50	17	19	8	6	100

Little can be said about the differences in type of disability affecting the dependent and nondependent disabled. Dependent disabled would appear to have more impairments falling into the category "other specific losses" than do those who are spending unit heads; however, only vague symptoms were reported for nearly a quarter of the group. It is possible that the spending unit heads who reported the disability were able to describe their own conditions more specifically than the conditions of others in the family.

Both the extent of limitation and age of dependent adults weigh against their successful vocational rehabilitation. One would suspect, however, that many opportunities exist for nonvocational training and guidance among that group. The training might prove an invaluable aid to the relatives in whose households the dependents live.

TABLE 17-24

AGE WITHIN RELATION TO SPENDING UNIT HEAD
(PERCENTAGE DISTRIBUTION OF DISABLED PERSONS)

| Age | Relation to spending unit head | | | | All disabled persons [a] | All dependent adults |
	Male spending unit heads	Female spending unit heads	Wives of spending unit heads	Dependent adults		
Under 18	0	0	0	0	6 ⎫	
18–24	3	2	3	18	4 ⎬	52
25–34	6	5	8	11	6 ⎭	
35–44	16	10	15	4	13 ⎫	
45–54	18	12	29	5	17 ⎬	21
55–64	23	27	24	23	23 ⎭	
65 and older	34	44	21	39	31	27
Total	100	100	100	100	100	100
Per cent of disabled persons	50	17	19	8	100	

[a] includes 6 per cent who are children under 18

The Income Position and Resources of the Disabled

Need for rehabilitation is influenced, in part, by the income position of the disabled. Clearly, those who have managed to earn a relatively good living in spite of their handicap are in less need of further retraining than those who are unable to maintain their standard of living on the basis of income sources available to them after they become disabled. This section will deal with the income and other financial resources of the disabled.

The analysis of income of the disabled falls roughly into three parts: demographic characteristics of the disabled population and their relation to the level of living of the families in which those disabled people live; the sources of income accruing to disabled persons according to the levels of welfare of the family in which they live; and the sources and the amounts of income received by adult units containing disabled persons according to which member is disabled, and a comparison of these amounts with the amounts received by other adult units in the population.

The level of living enjoyed by the unit is measured by the welfare ratio. Low levels of income relative to needs are concentrated in the disabled population to a much greater extent than in the national population. Thirty-six per cent of adult units containing disabled persons have family incomes which cover less than nine-tenths of their budget requirements while only 22 per cent of the national population falls below that level.

Disabled women are less well off than disabled men, and more than one-third of all children who have disabilities live in families whose income falls well below their budget needs. Aged women, who comprise nearly a fourth of the disabled individuals, also have the most extreme financial problems. Nearly half have insufficient income to meet their needs.

TABLE 17-25

FAMILY WELFARE RATIO WITHIN AGE AND SEX
(PERCENTAGE DISTRIBUTION OF DISABLED PERSONS)

	Age and sex							
		Males			Females			All
Family welfare ratio	Children under 18	18–34	35–54	55 and older	18–34	35–54	55 and older	disabled persons
Under 0.9	37	26	31	30	36	30	45	34
0.9–1.2	26	33	21	23	29	24	21	23
1.3–1.6	12	19	16	17	12	20	10	15
1.7–2.2	14	15	16	16	6	14	13	15
2.3 and over	11	7	16	14	17	12	11	13
Total	100	100	100	100	100	100	100	100
Per cent of disabled persons	6	6	18	29	4	12	25	100

The extent of disability is closely associated with the adequacy of income of the family in which the disabled person lives. Nearly one-half of those who report that they are completely limited are in families which have insufficient incomes to cover their basic budget needs. Less than one-fifth of the disabled who report no work limitation are in similar circumstances.

TABLE 17-26
FAMILY WELFARE RATIO WITHIN EXTENT OF LIMITATION
(PERCENTAGE DISTRIBUTION OF DISABLED PERSONS)

Family welfare ratio	Extent of limitation				All disabled persons [a]
	Complete	Severe	Moderate	None	
Under 0.9	43	41	26	17	34
0.9–1.2	21	22	23	32	23
1.3–1.6	14	10	19	11	15
1.7–2.2	14	15	17	9	15
2.3 and over	8	12	15	31	13
Total	100	100	100	100	100
Per cent of disabled persons	19	17	46	5	100

[a] includes 13 per cent of disabled persons for whom extent of limitation was not ascertained

Persons with major impairments appear to be in a better financial situation than any other group of disabled persons. Those with arthritis and vague symptoms appear to be most economically deprived. The relationship between type of disability and economic level can be accounted for in part by the age incidence of these disabilities.

TABLE 17-27

FAMILY WELFARE RATIO WITHIN TYPE OF DISABILITY
(PERCENTAGE DISTRIBUTION OF DISABLED PERSONS)

Family welfare ratio	Type of disability							
	Major specific losses	Other specific losses	Circu-latory diseases	Arthritis and rheuma-tism	Other chronic diseases	Mental and nervous condi-tions	All other condi-tions	All disabled persons [a]
Under 0.9	28	24	34	46	36	30	41	34
0.9–1.2	27	23	19	26	23	29	28	23
1.3–1.6	16	20	16	15	11	10	13	15
1.7–2.2	14	19	15	8	17	15	14	15
2.3 and over	15	14	16	5	13	16	4	13
Total	100	100	100	100	100	100	100	100
Per cent of disabled persons	11	14	25	9	20	6	10	100

[a] includes 5 per cent of disabled persons for whom type of disability was not ascertained

As is true for the population as a whole, disabled nonwhites and disabled farmers and laborers are more likely to display low levels of welfare.

The proportion of disabled farmers who are employed is second among occupation groups only to self-employed businessmen.

Table 17-28 outlines the sources of income of the families in which the disabled persons live. In some cases this income is received by the disabled person. In other cases the income may result from the effort or contributions of other members of the family. Data on income received by the disabled individual, by the adult unit of which he is a part, and by the family in which he belongs permit assessment of the money available to disabled persons whose families enjoy different levels of welfare.

Since Table 17-28 shows the average income for each disabled person, double-counting of some income occurs when there is more than one disabled individual in a family. For example, if both husband and wife in an aged couple report disabilities, then the social security income accruing to that couple would be counted once for the head and once for his wife. The computations serve to indicate the extent to which resources are available to disabled individuals rather than to compare the relative well-being of families with and without disabled individuals.

TABLE 17-28

MEAN INCOME WITHIN FAMILY WELFARE RATIO
(FOR DISABLED PERSONS)

Mean income	Family welfare ratio					All disabled persons
	Under 0.9	0.9–1.2	1.3–1.6	1.7–2.2	2.3 and over	
1. Wages and salaries of disabled persons [a]						
a. aged 18–64	$ 469	$1,470	$2,262	$2,793	$ 4,810	$2,027
b. aged 65 and older	38	129	202	523	1,315	246
2. Real earnings, adult units	648	2,155	3,359	4,712	9,999	3,204
3. Gross factor income, adult units	889	2,619	3,977	5,427	12,756	3,947
4. Transfer income, adult units	609	698	683	657	761	668
a. public contributory transfers	228	436	449	355	357	345
b. social security benefits	(155)	(296)	(278)	(252)	(209)	(227)
c. nonpublic transfers	129	166	188	278	297	190
d. public noncontributory transfers	261	135	85	79	185	169
e. net family transfers	−9	−39	−39	−55	−78	−36
5. Income tax, adult units	13	110	313	541	2,312	452
6. Gross disposable income, adult units	1,506	3,202	4,355	5,524	11,205	4,165
7. Gross disposable income, families	1,808	3,881	5,457	7,091	12,466	4,993
8. Per cent living in relatives' households	11	11	13	12	7	11
Per cent of disabled persons	34	23	15	15	13	100

[a] income from owner-operated business is excluded

Lines 1*a* and 1*b* of Table 17-28 indicate the amount the disabled person is able to contribute to his support through his own earnings. Line 2, the real earnings of the adult unit, shows self-employment income, income from home production, and the income of all other persons in the adult unit, as well as wages and salaries earned by the disabled person. Real earnings increase with the level of welfare of the family, as might be expected.

Line 3 of Table 17-28, gross factor income, shows the combined effect of capital and work effort on income of adult units containing disabled individuals. Clearly, each adult unit at the highest welfare levels is most likely to have the head of the adult unit working, perhaps also his wife, and to have assets from which they receive capital income.

Lines 4*a-e* of Table 17-28 indicate the extent to which disabled individuals benefit from the receipt of various types of transfer income. In view of the way means tests and other devices are designed to promote redistribution of income through public transfer programs, it is surprising that the total transfers show little decline as the adequacy of income rises.

Line 6 of Table 17-28 shows the gross disposable income of the adult unit.

A comparison of these estimates of adult unit incomes with the income of the family in which the disabled person lives, illustrates the contribution to the adult unit's resources which comes from living with relatives. The difference between lines 6 and 7 shows the amount of income which accrued to the family but not to the adult unit containing the disabled individual. A comparison of these two lines indicates that combining households creates substantial additional financial resources for some disabled individuals.

Line 8 indicates that living with relatives is less frequent for disabled families at the highest welfare level.

Because the amount of transfer income appears to be relatively independent of the adequacy of income, it is of some interest to study the components of transfer income and evaluate their impact on disabled individuals in different levels of welfare. Table 17-29 suggests a remarkable similarity in the sources of transfer income received by disabled individuals at each level of welfare. The only components of transfer income which show a marked decline from lower to higher levels of welfare, are those included in public noncontributory transfers. Even here it is surprising to find that about 10 per cent of persons in the top three groups received free medical care. In these groups, however, such transfers are probably in the form of company medical examinations or other job-connected benefits.

TABLE 17-29

PER CENT OF DISABLED PERSONS IN ADULT UNITS WHICH RECEIVED
TRANSFER INCOME FROM INDICATED SOURCES WITHIN
FAMILY WELFARE RATIO

Sources of transfer income	Family welfare ratio					All disabled persons
	Under 0.9	0.9–1.2	1.3–1.6	1.7–2.2	2.3 and over	
Public contributory	31	41	41	28	27	34
social security benefits	23	27	24	19	16	22
veterans' benefits	7	11	15	12	11	10
$500 or more	5	9	12	10	6	8
unemployment compensation	4	5	7	3	6	4
Public noncontributory	30	19	11	15	11	20
welfare income	23	6	3	4	2	11
$500 or more	17	4	1	4	0	7
free medical care	13	13	10	11	8	12
$500 or more	3	4	6	4	3	4
gifts from institutions [a]	3	3	0	0	3	2
Nonpublic	23	23	24	21	26	23
private pensions	7	11	13	12	17	11
$500 or more	6	9	7	11	14	9
regular support payments	3	2	4	2	1	2
gifts from individuals [a]	15	12	12	8	10	12
Per cent of disabled persons	34	23	15	15	13	100

[a] per cent with income of more than $50 from this source

The eligibility requirements of both social security and welfare programs determine the pattern of receipts of transfer income. Table 17-30 illustrates that eligibility for disability benefits under social security may be a substantial source of income in coming years. There may be a few cases in which the wife of the disabled person is receiving social security, so that it is impossible to determine whether the disabled person is receiving disability insurance, survivors' benefits, or old age payments.

TABLE 17-30

MEAN SOCIAL SECURITY BENEFITS RECEIVED BY ADULT UNIT
WITHIN AGE AND SEX OF DISABLED PERSONS
(FOR DISABLED PERSONS)

Age and sex of disabled persons	Per cent in adult units receiving social security	Mean benefits received by disabled persons who received benefits	Mean benefits received by all disabled persons
Males and females under 18	6	$1,196	$ 71
Males			
18–49	0	. . . . .	. . . .
50–64	7	886	62
65 and older	67	1,125	755
Females			
18–49	3	1,802	60
50–61	13	1,106	141
62 and older	43	799	339
All disabled persons	22	$1,017	$227

During 1959, the period covered by this survey, OASDI eligibility was as follows:

Age and sex	Eligible for the following programs
Males and females under 18	Survivors' benefits
Males	
18–49	None
50–64	Disability benefits
65 and older	Old age benefits
Females	
18–49	Survivors' benefits if caring for children under 18
50–61	Survivors' benefits if caring for children under 18 or disability benefits
62 and older	Survivors' or old age benefits

Because eligibility for the separate programs overlaps, coverage of the disability program, as distinguished from other programs can be assessed in Table 17-30 only for males 50–64. Of this group 7 per cent received disability benefits during 1959.

Income Loss from Disablement

The previous section explored the resources available to disabled individuals. To determine income loss, it is necessary to contrast the income available to adult units containing disabled persons with the income available to other adult units in the population. Tabulating incomes of adult units eliminates the double counting in Tables 17-28 through 17-30.

In order that the analysis of adult unit income be more meaningful, adult units containing disabled individuals were classified into five groups. Adult

TABLE 17-31

PER CENT OF ADULT UNITS WHICH RECEIVED INCOME FROM INDICATED SOURCES WITHIN DISABILITIES OF ADULT UNIT MEMBERS

	Disabilities of adult unit members						
	Heads are disabled				Heads are not disabled, wives or		
	18–64			65	children		All
Sources of income	Com- pletely limited	Severely limited	Some- what limited	and older	are disabled	No one disabled	adult units
1. Wages and salaries							
a. heads	24	56	78	18	76	80	74
b. wives	19	24	29	7	21	24	23
2. Gross factor income	64	87	94	81	92	93	91
Transfer income							
3. Public contributory	27	25	22	61	20	17	20
a. social security benefits	16	8	3	56	12	8	11
b. veterans' benefits	12	10	13	11	5	4	6
$500 or more	9	8	8	9	5	2	3
c. unemployment compensation	3	9	6	2	6	6	5
4. Public noncontributory	37	20	12	24	18	9	11
a. welfare income	24	8	5	17	4	2	4
$500 or more	19	4	4	10	2	1	2
b. free medical care	19	15	9	12	12	7	8
$500 or more	9	3	2	3	4	1	2
c. gifts from institutions [a]	3	3	1	1	4	1	2
5. Nonpublic	27	13	18	34	19	17	19
a. private pensions	12	1	5	22	7	4	6
$500 or more	10	1	4	19	5	4	5
b. regular support payments	4	1	4	3	1	2	2
c. gifts from individuals [a]	12	11	11	14	12	12	12
Per cent of adult units	2	2	8	6	4	78	100

[a] per cent with income of more than $50 from this source

units containing disabled heads were classified into four groups according to the age of the head and the severity of his limit without regard to the presence of other disabled individuals in the adult unit. Thus, the averages, shown in Table 17-31 in the columns labeled "head is disabled," include some cases where the wife or a child is also disabled. Cases in which only the wife or a child is disabled are included in the fifth group.

The tabulation reveals a direct and important relationship between sources of income and extent of work limitation. It is to be expected that the proportion of heads who receive wages and salaries falls sharply with increasing limitation. The decline in the proportion of wage-earning wives of disabled persons is more surprising. (See Table 17-31, lines 1a, 1b.) One might have anticipated that as husbands become more disabled wives would go to work to supplement their incomes. That the reverse is true suggests that wives of severely and completely limited men must remain at home to provide nursing care for their husbands.

More than a third of the completely disabled heads under sixty-five and about one-fifth of all the disabled heads who are sixty-five and older have no income from employment or assets. (See Table 17-31, line 2.)

Table 17-31 reveals less correlation between extent of work limitation and the receipt of transfers than might have been expected. Social security, income from welfare, free medical care, and private pensions appear to be the programs which are most likely to aid the disabled according to the extent of limitation. Gifts from relatives and veterans' benefits are surprisingly independent of work limitation.

The impact of disability on *amount* of adult unit income is shown in Table 17-32. Eliminating the double counting of income present in Table 17-28 increases the estimate of the gross disposable income of adult units containing disabled persons from $4,165 to $4,173.

Line 1a of Table 17-32 shows quite clearly the impact of disablement on wages and salaries earned by the head. Line 2a shows the difference between the real earnings of adult units in which no one is disabled and adult units containing disabled individuals. The difference approximates the loss of earnings incurred by the units containing disabled persons. The more severely disabled incur a larger loss of income than those with minor limitations. Loss of earnings for disabled adult unit heads who are sixty-five and older is not particularly relevant because most persons in that age group are retired. Adult units in which the wife or children are disabled do not appear to experience any loss in their earnings relative to the nondisabled. The positive difference shown for units containing disabled wives or children is within sampling error so that it is not clear that this group averages a higher income than the nondisabled.

An alternative and more conservative estimate of the earnings loss suffered by the disabled can be obtained from the results of multivariate analyses of spending unit heads' earnings. (See Chapters 4 through 6.) Table 17-33

TABLE 17-32

MEAN INCOME WITHIN DISABILITIES OF ADULT UNIT MEMBERS (FOR ADULT UNITS)

Income of adult units	Disabilities of adult unit members				Heads are not disabled, wives or children are disabled	No one disabled	All adult units
	Heads are disabled						
	18-64			65 and older			
	Completely limited	Severely limited	Somewhat limited				
1. Wages and salaries [a]							
a. heads	$ 464	$1,433	$3,301	$ 274	$4,174	$3,846	$3,486
b. wives	365	661	599	115	274	501	475
2. Real earnings	1,643	2,697	4,733	617	5,391	4,930	4,560
a. loss of earnings	−3,287	−2,233	−197	−4,313	none	. . . .	. . . .
3. Gross factor income	2,052	3,478	5,378	1,520	6,278	5,526	5,191
4. Transfer income	931	537	306	1,137	442	340	406
a. public contributory transfers	241	216	184	658	189	133	177
b. social security benefits	(159)	(65)	(30)	(559)	(119)	(77)	(108)
c. nonpublic transfers	193	61	147	284	183	157	164
d. public noncontributory transfers	410	123	79	196	138	41	65
e. net family transfers	87	137	−104	−1	−68	9	. . . .
5. Income tax	332	315	666	107	796	652	612
6. Gross disposable income	2,644	3,700	5,018	2,558	5,920	5,215	4,986
a. loss of gross disposable income	−2,571	−1,515	−197	−2,657	none	. . . .	. . . .
Per cent of adult units	2	2	8	6	4	78	100

[a] does not include income from farming or owner-operated businesses

presents work experience of disability groups whose differences in age, education, and other factors are adjusted for by the multivariate analysis. Eighty-eight per cent of the nondisabled spending unit heads worked 2,123 hours during 1959 at an average wage of $2.32. The product of these figures is an estimate that the average nondisabled person earned $4,334 by working 1,868 hours. The disabled who did not work each suffered that loss of income and working time. The disabled who worked lost an amount of income equal to the difference between their estimated average income and $4,334. The fact that these estimates of income loss are smaller than the corresponding

TABLE 17-33

ADJUSTED MEANS FOR 1959 WORK EXPERIENCE WITHIN
EXTENT OF WORK LIMITATION
(FOR SPENDING UNIT HEADS)

Work experience	Extent of work limitation				All spending unit heads
	Completely disabled	Severely disabled	Moderately disabled	Not disabled	
Probability of working	.51	.73	.85	.88	.86
Hours worked by those who worked	1,800	1,588	1,957	2,123	2,092
Hourly earnings of those who worked	$2.16	$2.09	$2.07	$2.32	$2.29
Loss of working time	950	709	205	....	....
Loss of earnings	$−2,351	$−1,911	$−892	....	....

estimates shown in Table 17-32 reflects the fact that part of the lower incomes of disabled persons stems from their lack of education and skilled positions, rather than their physical limitations.

An aggregate estimate of $14.0 billion of income loss because of limitation can be made by multiplying the estimates of loss shown in Table 17-33 by the number of disabled spending unit heads in the United States. These figures are shown in Table 17-34.

TABLE 17-34

AGGREGATE ESTIMATES OF INCOME LOSS IN 1959
WITHIN EXTENT OF LIMITATION
(FOR SPENDING UNIT HEADS)

Extent of limitation	Spending unit heads	
	Number (in millions)	Income loss in 1959 (in billions)
Complete	2.1	$ 5.0
Severe	1.7	3.2
Moderate	6.5	5.8
Total	10.3	$14.0

Another estimate of income loss can be made from the data in Table 17-35. The table shows the difference in hours worked by disabled and non-disabled spending unit heads. The present value of the stream of income lost by disabled persons who are unable to work as many hours as nondisabled persons can be calculated by the appropriate assumptions about rate of discount, mortality of the disabled in each group, and the appropriate wage rate to assign to the different age and education groups.[5] The details of this computation have been left to the reader, since many alternative estimates could be prepared, according to the particular assumptions made about mortality and the degree of rehabilitation which is reasonable to expect for disabled in the different groups. Because the figures shown do not make allowance for other dimensions which affect the hours worked by the disabled and the nondisabled, it is highly likely that factors such as occupation and motivation would continue to produce differences in the hours worked by the two groups even if complete rehabilitation were attempted for everyone.

TABLE 17-35

MEAN HOURS WORKED IN 1959 WITHIN EDUCATION,
DISABILITY, AND AGE
(MEANS FOR SPENDING UNIT HEADS)

| | Education and disability | | | | | |
| | 0–11 grades | | | 12 or more grades | | |
Age	Disabled	Not disabled	Difference	Disabled	Not disabled	Difference
Under 45	1,730	2,093	−363	2,129	2,131	− 2
45–54	1,518	2,158	−609	1,913	2,101	−188
55–64	1,314	1,787	−473	} 78	} 731	} −653
65 and older	361	549	−188			
All	1,051	1,831		1,484	2,044	
Number of spending unit heads	439	1,204		149	1,205	

The transfers received by adult units containing disabled persons appear to increase somewhat irregularly with the severity of the limit of the head, as shown in lines 4a through 4e of Table 17-32. Line 4e indicates some net redistribution of income to the severely disabled arising from living in relatives' households.

Units in which the heads are disabled and sixty-five or older benefit both from relatively more transfer income and from lower Federal income tax liability than any other group. In spite of the transfer of income to the disabled aged, they have smaller gross disposable incomes than any other group,

[5] See, for example, the procedures used by Burton A. Weisbrod, "The Nature and Measurement of the Economic Benefits of Improved Public Health" (unpublished Ph.D. dissertation, Northwestern University, 1958).

Also see Rashi Fein, *Economics of Mental Illness* (New York: Basic Books, Inc., 1958).

TABLE 17-36

FAMILY WELFARE RATIO WITHIN DISABILITIES OF ADULT UNIT MEMBERS
(FOR ADULT UNITS)

	Disabilities of adult unit members						
	Heads are disabled				Heads are not disabled, wives or children are disabled	No one is disabled	All adult units
	18–64			65 and older			
Family welfare ratio	Completely limited	Severely limited	Somewhat limited				
Under 0.9	50	36	28	45	21	18	22
0.9–1.2	21	23	20	23	30	18	19
1.3–1.6	6	13	20	13	13	20	18
1.7–2.2	18	15	15	12	15	24	22
2.3 and over	5	13	17	7	21	20	19
Total	100	100	100	100	100	100	100
Per cent of adult units whose *adult unit* welfare ratio is less than .9	64	49	31	47	22	25	28
Per cent of all adult units	2	2	8	6	4	78	100

including adult units in which the head is completely disabled. The Line 6a of Table 17-32 indicates clearly an increasing loss of income associated with greater disability, even after the impact of tax and transfer programs has been taken into account.

Table 17-36 summarizes the impact of disability on the adequacy of the family income. Including all sources of income, about a third of the adult units containing disabled have substantially less income than they require. Aged and severely disabled are most likely to suffer from such income deficiencies.

The Outlook for the Disabled

The future of the disabled can be assessed in several ways. In view of rehabilitation services presently available it is relatively apparent that all but a very few of those with disabilities at present will either rehabilitate themselves or continue in their present situation. The previous section has made it clear that a high proportion of adult units whose heads are disabled have extremely meager incomes which are entirely inadequate for the needs of their families. Some of these heads will return to work, but the outlook for those who report that they cannot work now appears poor unless substantial rehabilitation is made available.

Furthermore, the assets of the disabled are infinitesimal in relation to their income losses. The disabled in families with the lowest incomes supplement their incomes with only minimal savings and have less than $4,000 net equity in their homes. Table 17-37 shows that the savings of the disabled population fall far short of those held by spending units with no disabled members.

TABLE 17-37

PER CENT WITH SAVINGS OF $1,000 OR MORE WITHIN AGE OF HEADS
AND DISABILITIES OF SPENDING UNIT MEMBERS
(FOR SPENDING UNITS)

Age of spending unit heads	Proportion in each group with savings of $1,000 or more	
	Someone is disabled	No one is disabled
Under 25	7 (18)	24 (246)
25–34	28 (55)	38 (531)
35–44	35 (136)	53 (536)
45–54	38 (152)	55 (441)
55–64	49 (180)	63 (305)
65–74	41 (133)	72 (136)
75 and older	50 (73)	70 (55)
All spending units	40 (747)	50 (2,250)
Per cent of spending units	24	76

( ) number of cases

Table 17-38 indicates that less than half of spending units containing disabled are covered by hospitalization insurance. For the younger disabled the problem is somewhat less serious; nevertheless, in every age group spending units which do not have disabled members are more likely to have insurance. Persons aged sixty-five and older are substantially underprotected against long illnesses. Moreover, they are more likely to need hospitalization, and are less well insured than the nondisabled aged.

TABLE 17-38

PER CENT OF SPENDING UNITS IN WHICH EVERYONE IS COVERED
BY HOSPITALIZATION INSURANCE WITHIN AGE OF HEADS
AND DISABILITIES OF SPENDING UNIT MEMBERS
(FOR SPENDING UNITS)

Age of spending unit heads	Proportion in which everyone in the spending unit is covered by hospitalization insurance	
	Someone is disabled	No one is disabled
Under 25	63 (18)	65 (246)
25–34	46 (55)	71 (531)
35–44	65 (136)	73 (536)
45–54	52 (152)	68 (441)
55–64	56 (180)	68 (305)
65–74	36 (133)	55 (136)
75 and older	23 (73)	37 (55)
All spending units	49 (747)	68 (2,250)
Per cent of spending units	24	76

( ) number of cases

The future of the disabled can be seen through their eyes by examining their attitudes and plans. Many of their attitudes reflect pessimism about planning ahead and future improvements in their income situation. More than half say they are unable to plan ahead. In part, this is associated with the high median age of disabled people. It is interesting to note, however, that 26 per cent blame their inability to plan on their present life situation, while only 10 per cent of the national sample do so.

Generally the disabled do not expect better incomes in the future. Only a third report that their financial situation will improve, while more than half of the nondisabled express this opinion.

The disabled most often say that hard work is more important than luck for getting ahead in the world. Sixty-one per cent say that hard work is most important. In this respect their opinions are very close to the opinions of the nondisabled. Their willingness to say that hard work is more important than luck, even after what they may consider a series of unlucky breaks as far as their health is concerned, gives hope that there is some untapped incentive for rehabilitation and self-help among the disabled.

Summary

An examination of the economic situation of the disabled presents a dreary picture. Approximately 9 per cent of the individuals in the national sample reported some work limitation from a disablement. Many of these persons are over fifty-five. Nineteen per cent of all disabled adults suffer complete work limitation, 17 per cent suffer severe limitation, and 46 per cent are moderately limited. The extent of work limitation appears to be relatively independent of the demographic characteristics and other attitudes of the disabled.

The problem of assessing the rehabilitation potential of disabled persons is a thorny one. The effectiveness of rehabilitation programs clearly depends to a great extent on the degree to which disablement imposes psychological barriers, and on the skills, education, and intelligence which the person had before becoming disabled. Of the disabled under sixty-five, nearly half were blue collar workers and more than two-thirds did not have high school diplomas.

Disabilities serve to compound the problems of low levels of education, advanced age, and unskilled occupations, so that for most of the disabled incomes are inadequate and resources are scarce. Earnings of the disabled and the level of welfare enjoyed by families containing disabled are closely related to the extent of work limitation. Increasing limitation is associated with decreasing labor force participation, decreasing wages, and decreasing number of hours worked, even when other factors such as age, education, and race are taken into account. Private and public transfers do surprisingly little to improve the economic level of living of units containing disabled persons. For completely disabled adult unit heads, transfers comprise about one-third of their gross disposable incomes; however, their incomes are still well below those of the nondisabled. The contributory aspects of major public programs, and the tendency for the disabled to maintain separate households rather than move in with relatives, leave many disabled in a vulnerable economic position.

Neither is the outlook for the disabled particularly encouraging. The assets of the disabled are inadequate to compensate for their income losses. The savings of the disabled fall far short of those held by units with no disabled members. Less than half the spending units containing disabled persons are covered by hospitalization insurance. In consequence, many of the disabled express attitudes which reflect pessimism about planning ahead and future improvements in their income situation.

In view of rehabilitation services presently available, it is apparent that all but a very few of the disabled will have to rehabilitate themselves or continue in their present situation. It is clear that additional rehabilitation aid is sorely needed, but the problem of optimal distribution remains perplexing

PART IV

Distribution and Redistribution of Income and Welfare

Chapter 18

VOLUNTARISM AND PHILANTHROPY

The distribution of income has now been studied, including the income redistributed in the form of transfer incomes. An assessment of the distribution of welfare requires more. Some income is given away to others, or taken away in taxes. The benefits of the expenditure of tax funds benefit some more than others. And finally, the enjoyment of leisure is part of a man's standard of living, yet some people spend more hours earning their income than others. The next four chapters attempt to provide some basis for assessing the most important of these adjustments and qualifications.

Contributions made to others, as well as people's attitudes toward their responsibility to others, are studied in Chapter 18.

The redistributive effects of property taxes, and of the current benefits from having children in public schools, are analyzed in Chapter 19. While property taxes are not the largest source of tax revenue, nor public schools the largest type of expenditure, their distributions have been of great interest because of their supposed unequal impact and their relation to one another.

Chapter 20 assesses the effect of income taxes on the over-all inequality of income, and also shows how the definition of income and the size of the analysis unit affect estimates of inequality.

Finally, Chapter 21 examines the amount of time used in securing the family's income. Without attempting to measure job satisfaction, it is still possible to observe differences in the amount of time spent earning a living and to see whether those with higher money incomes devote more or less time to earning them.

As governments take over more and more responsibility for those who would otherwise be dependent on friends or relatives or private charity, it is important to know what people feel about their private responsibilities and what they are doing to help others.[1]

---

[1] No other country provides so many tax advantages to givers. See a forthcoming National Bureau of Economic Research report on a Conference on Philanthropy held at the Merrill Center, and a forthcoming National Bureau study on trends in private philanthropy by Frank Dickinson and others.

With the increase in government responsibility has come a tendency for families to separate into nuclear units so that people are much less likely to be living in the same household with relatives. (See Chapter 14.) However, there are still enough people living with relatives to complicate an examination of the relative importance of transfers by governments, by private philanthropic organizations, or by individuals. One such complication is the choice of a relevant unit of analysis. No estimate of private transfers would be complete without taking account of the free rent and food provided by those who house relatives. Consequently, most of this analysis uses the concept of the adult unit or nuclear family.

On the other hand, in a discussion of the family's ability to absorb extra adult units, or of other contributions made outside the dwelling, it is the whole family and family income that are relevant for the analysis. Therefore, the unit of analysis will change depending on the particular behavior or attitude being analyzed.

Contributions

People help one another in several ways: through taxes and government expenditures such as income maintenance programs, schools, and to some extent through all government expenditures; through insurance, where the lucky help the unlucky, while all benefit from the elimination of risk; through contributions to churches and organized private charities or foundations; through contributions made directly to relatives and friends outside the dwelling unit; through unequal sharing of expenses within a household containing more than one adult unit.

The first of these is involuntary, the second involuntary in its details, but the rest are mostly voluntary, except where relative responsibility requirements in state laws or alimony requirements in divorce decrees are involved. About 62 per cent of all adult units reported that they made some kind of voluntary contribution.

To provide some over-all perspective, Table 18-1 shows for all families, and for six different levels of income, the average amounts of earned income, transfer income, and out-transfers in the form of taxes and contributions. Both the transfer income and the contributions in this table contain private transfers not generally included in the national accounts because of the difficulties in estimating them. The figures exclude insurance premiums and benefits. Clearly, the Federal income tax is far more redistributive between income groups than either transfer income, contributions, or their net combined effect.

Information on contributions was elicited by four questions: "Did you pay out any money to help support anyone in 1959; that is, friends, parents, children, or relatives, or did you pay alimony or anything like that?" "Did you give your friends or relatives more than $50 of food, clothing, or large gifts?

TABLE 18-1

MEAN GROSS FACTOR INCOME, TRANSFER INCOME, INCOME TAX,
AND CONTRIBUTIONS WITHIN GROSS DISPOSABLE INCOME
(FOR FAMILIES)

Family gross disposable income	Number of families	Gross factor income	+ Transfer income	− Federal income tax	− Nonfamily contri- butions	= Net real income
Under $1,000	148	$ 121	$368	$ 1	$ 68	$ 420
$1,000–1,999	357	830	675	23	65	1,417
$2,000–2,999	320	1,839	744	81	147	2,355
$3,000–4,999	601	3,753	555	275	162	3,871
$5,000–7,499	677	6,429	350	600	253	5,926
$7,500 and over	697	12,623	449	1,865	689	10,518
All families	2,800	$ 6,282	$493	$ 741	$315	$ 5,719

How much would you say this was worth?" "Now, what about the church or religious organizations, would you say that in the course of the year you contributed more than $25 altogether to the church or religious organizations? About how much did you contribute?" "How about donations to other organizations, did you give more than $25 altogether to things like community chest, schools, cancer or heart associations, and so forth? About how much did you contribute to such organizations?"

The $50 minimum on gifts was intended to exclude minor gifts. Of all adults units only 12 per cent reported receiving irregular gifts of $50 or more; another 2 per cent reported alimony or regular contributions. On the other hand, 23 per cent reported giving gifts or regular contributions, while another 3 per cent reported contributing to children who were away at college.

The amounts reported were also larger for gifts than for receipts. It is possible that people exaggerated their giving, and likely that some recipients forgot the gifts they had received. Unpublished studies at the Survey Research Center have shown that more people remember money owed to them than report that they owe money to someone.

The $25 minimum on contributions to church and to charity was intended to avoid embarrassment to those who gave little or nothing. Nearly everyone professes some religious preference, but 40 per cent say they do not give as much as $25 to a church. Therefore, any attempt to estimate aggregate church contributions might understate the amount substantially. It is likely that at least some of these units contribute something, though less than $25. Likewise, of the two-thirds who do not give $25 or more to charity, some may have given small amounts.

Crude expansions of the data indicate that 53.4 million families in the United States gave more than $6 billion to churches, more than $2 billion to charity, and more than $7 billion to other individuals in 1959, for a total of nearly $17 billion. Unless people exaggerate a great deal the expansions are probably underestimates because of the exclusion below lower limits.

This does not include help given to individuals who live with relatives, in the form of free housing and food and perhaps other necessities and amenities. The estimates of the value of food and free housing alone amount to roughly $4.5 billion given to the 11 million extra adult units who live with relatives. Here again, the amounts probably are underestimates because they do not include estimates of support in the form of free transportation, clothing, and other items given to dependents within the household.

Previous survey data on contributions are nearly ten years old or older and mostly include only city families.[2]

The Bureau of Labor Statistics study also found that people in smaller towns and rural areas, people in the South, and older people gave more money to churches, in spite of lower incomes. People with larger families gave about the same fraction of their income to churches, but much smaller fractions to charity.

The contributions made outside the household, as shown in Table 18-1, consisted of four parts: contributions to individuals, contributions to churches and religious organizations, contributions to nonreligious organizations, and contributions to children away at college. The last of these is so infrequent in a cross section that it is not analyzed in detail here.[3]

In Tables 18-2 through 18-7, family contributions to individuals, churches, and charitable organizations are related to explanatory characteristics of the givers. In view of the exclusion of small gifts, only the proportions of families who give $50 or more a year and the proportions who give $250 or more a year are shown.

Table 18-2 shows that the Jews give substantially more to each of the recipient groups than any other religious group, including the Episcopalians who have somewhat higher incomes than the Jews. There are several explanations for this. The Jewish population has a cultural tradition with a high sense of community among its members, a well-developed organization for the extraction of money and the exertion of pressures, a long history of persecu-

---

[2] Helen H. Lamale and Joseph Clorety, Jr., "City Families as Givers," *Monthly Labor Review* (December, 1950), 1303–1311. See also *Giving U. S. A.,* American Association of Fund-Raising Counsel, New York, 1961.

For a summary table of previous survey data, as well as tables from *Statistics of Income* showing deducted contributions for each income group, see C. Harry Kahn, *Personal Deductions in the Federal Income Tax* (Princeton: Princeton University Press, 1960), pp. 73–83.

The Surveys and the Income Statistics both show a relatively stable proportion of income given to philanthropy except at the extremes of the income scale. Those with very low incomes give a slightly higher proportion of their income, and those with the highest incomes also give a higher proportion of their income.

[3] For detail combining data from several cross-section samples, see John B. Lansing and others, *How People Pay for College* (Ann Arbor: Survey Research Center, Institute for Social Research, University of Michigan, 1960).

TABLE 18-2

PROPORTION CONTRIBUTING MORE THAN STATED AMOUNTS WITHIN RELIGIOUS PREFERENCE OF HEADS
(FOR PRIMARY SPENDING UNITS)

Per cent who gave $50 or more to:	Baptists	Other Funda-mentalist Protestants	Roman Catholics	Lutherans	Other non-Funda-mentalist Protestants	Presby-terians	Jews	Episco-palians	All [a]
				Religious preference of heads					
Individuals	23	20	24	31	38	26	45	28	25
Church	41	52	65	67	46	59	55	63	52
Charity	10	8	20	25	19	28	51	43	19
Per cent who gave $250 or more to:									
Individuals	11	6	11	14	13	16	25	15	12
Church	11	18	10	10	10	14	18	9	11
Charity	1	0	1	3	2	1	17	8	2
Number of spending units	672	308	562	171	675	166	70	78	2,800

[a] includes 13 family heads whose religious preferences were non-Christian, non-Jewish, and 85 whose preferences were not ascertained

tion and hostile environment providing a constant pressure to maintain a sense of community, and innovation in techniques of collection.[4] It is useful in looking at Table 18-2 to remember that there are substantial differences in the incomes of the different religious groups. They are listed in order according to their average incomes.

Table 18-3 indicates that more frequent church attendance leads to greater giving to the church, and also somewhat more to other individuals and to charities.

TABLE 18-3

PROPORTION CONTRIBUTING MORE THAN STATED
AMOUNTS WITHIN FREQUENCY OF CHURCH ATTENDANCE OF HEAD
(FOR PRIMARY SPENDING UNITS)

	Frequency of church attendance of head						
Per cent who gave $50 or more to:	More than once a week	Once a week	Two or three times a month	Once a month	A few times a year	Never	All primary spending units [a]
Individuals	31	24	27	24	24	26	25
Church	81	72	51	42	33	11	52
Charity	17	22	20	19	18	14	19
Per cent who gave $250 or more to:							
Individuals	10	11	13	12	13	14	12
Church	31	18	6	4	3	0	11
Charity	2	1	1	2	3	2	2
Number of spending unit heads	335	862	342	200	767	249	2,800

[a] includes 45 primary spending unit heads for whom church attendance was not ascertained

Table 18-4, which arrays groups according to the earning potential of the spending unit head, indicates that both age and earning potential affect giving.

Table 18-5 shows that those who think the government should have primary responsibility for the aged are less likely to be contributing, not only to other individuals but also to church and charity.

Table 18-6 shows that people with children are more likely to contribute to the church, but that older couples are more likely to contribute to charity and to other individuals, often to their children who have left home.

Table 18-7 shows the powerful relationship between income and philanthropy. The mean amounts contributed by each income group range between

[4] See Merle Curti, "American Philanthropy and the National Character," *American Quarterly*, 10 (Winter, 1958), 420–437;

Eli Ginzberg, *Agenda for American Jews* (New York: Columbia University Press, 1950).

TABLE 18-4

PROPORTION CONTRIBUTING MORE THAN STATED AMOUNT WITHIN EARNING POTENTIAL OF HEAD
(FOR PRIMARY SPENDING UNITS)

| | | | | Earning potential of head | | | | | | |
| | | | | White, nonfarm, nonretired | | | | | | |
Per cent who gave $50 or more to:	Retired or disabled and not working	Nonretired, nonwhite	White, nonretired farmer	18–34 years old, 0–11 grades	18–34 years old, 12 grades	18–34 years old, some college	35 and older, 0–11 grades	35 and older, 12 grades	35 and older, some college	All primary spending units [a]
Individuals	20	28	22	15	23	23	24	28	42	25
Church	41	35	59	33	50	63	48	63	74	52
Charity	10	8	8	9	9	20	15	27	49	19
Per cent who gave $250 or more to:										
Individuals	8	14	8	8	6	7	11	14	25	12
Church	5	4	12	8	8	14	9	18	25	11
Charity	2	0	0	1	1	1	1	4	7	2
Number of primary spending units	299	360	165	208	161	186	743	353	308	2,800

[a] includes 17 family heads for whom earning potential was not ascertained

4 and 6 per cent of gross disposable income, except for the lowest income group where a few negative incomes make the proportion inordinately high. There are some units even in the highest income groups who give nothing at all.[5]

All types of contributions to church, to charities, or to individuals, and food and housing provided for relatives in the household are the greatest for units in which the head is between forty-five and sixty-four years old. These are also the years of greatest income. Figure 18-1 shows the proportion in

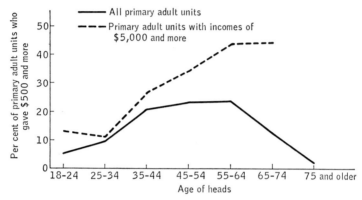

Figure 18-1. Contributions outside the dwellings within age, for all and for high-income units.

TABLE 18-5

PROPORTION CONTRIBUTING MORE THAN STATED AMOUNTS WITHIN ATTITUDE OF HEAD TOWARD RESPONSIBILITY FOR THE AGED (FOR PRIMARY SPENDING UNITS)

| | Attitude of head toward responsibility for the aged | | | | | |
| Per cent who gave $50 or more to: | Relatives should have | | Relatives and government should share responsibility | Government should have | | All primary spending units [a] |
	Sole responsibility	Primary responsibility		Primary responsibility	Sole responsibility	
Individuals	28	25	31	26	22	25
Church	62	54	53	42	40	52
Charity	24	20	21	12	13	19
Per cent who gave $250 or more to:						
Individuals	13	12	17	11	11	12
Church	16	11	14	7	7	11
Charity	3	3	1	1	1	2
Number of primary spending units	773	827	247	161	648	2,800

[a] includes 144 family heads whose attitude was not ascertained

[5] Kahn, *Personal Deductions in the Federal Income Tax*, pp. 73–83.

TABLE 18-6

PROPORTION OF SPENDING UNITS CONTRIBUTING MORE THAN STATED AMOUNTS WITHIN STAGE OF ADULT UNIT LIFE CYCLE (FOR ALL SPENDING UNITS) [a]

		Stage of adult unit life cycle								
	Unmarried, head under 45, no children	Married, wife under 45			Married, wife 45 or older		Unmarried		All Spending units
		No children	Children		Children	No children	Head 45 or older, no children	Children	
Per cent who gave $50 or more to:			Some under 6	All 6 or older					
Individuals	26	31	21	23	27	33	22	12	25
Church	29	50	56	66	59	56	37	32	50
Charity	8	20	15	28	21	28	10	4	18
Per cent who gave $250 or more to:									
Individuals	14	14	8	11	12	17	11	5	12
Church	2	14	12	17	17	14	5	4	11
Charity	1	2	1	5	2	3	2	0	2
Number of spending units	285	211	729	352	225	542	468	185	2,997

[a] This table and Table 18-7 include 197 related secondary spending units, who were excluded from previous tables. A comparison of the "all" columns will indicate that it makes little difference whether the related secondaries are included or not.

each age group who gave $500 or more outside the immediate family, for all income groups, and separately for those with income of $5,000 or more. It is clear from the differences between the lines that the decline in contributions among older units is almost entirely the result of declining income, and disappears if only the high income units are examined.

On the other hand, the lower contributions of younger people are low even for high income units, with the possible exception of the very young where the importance of an income of $5,000 or more may be greater. These very young high income units are as likely as any age group to contribute to the church, but not to other individuals or charities.

TABLE 18-7

PROPORTION CONTRIBUTING MORE THAN STATED
AMOUNTS WITHIN GROSS DISPOSABLE INCOME
(FOR SPENDING UNITS)

	Gross disposable income of spending unit						
Per cent who gave $50 or more to:	Less than $1,000	$1,000– 1,999	$2,000– 2,999	$3,000– 4,999	$5,000– 7,499	$7,500 or more	All spending units
Individuals	10	11	20	22	26	40	25
Church	12	20	32	44	61	77	51
Charity	0	2	2	9	17	48	18
Per cent who gave $250 or more to:							
Individuals	3	3	8	9	12	22	12
Church	0	1	2	7	12	26	11
Charity	0	0	0	0	1	7	2
Number of spending units	173	410	395	688	687	644	2,997

Multivariate Analysis of Total Contributions Outside of the Household

Nonfamily contributions to church, charity, and individuals outside the immediate household are about the same proportion of the family income at all levels. In order to discover what other characteristics of the family determine the level of its contributions, a multivariate analysis of nonfamily contributions was done, using eleven predicting characteristics. This analysis does not include contributions to others in the family. The mean for the nonfamily contributions was $315, with a standard deviation of $725. The analysis accounted for 22 per cent of the variance in these contributions. The relative importance and significance of the predictors is given in Table 18-8.

Income, of course, is the most important predictor of family contributions. Earning potential of the family head and a combination of religious preference and church attendance were also important predictors.

TABLE 18-8

CHARACTERISTICS USED TO EXPLAIN AMOUNT
OF NONFAMILY CONTRIBUTIONS
(FOR FAMILIES)

Characteristics of families	Relative importance (Beta coefficients)	Significance (F ratios)
Gross disposable income	.416	69.00**
Earning potential of heads	.125	6.23**
Religious preference and church attendance of heads	.109	7.11**
Number of living children of heads	.066	1.74
Political preference of heads	.064	1.84
Age of heads at birth of eldest living child	.049	1.44
Number of siblings of heads	.042	.70
Background of heads	.035	.88
Attitude of heads toward responsibility for the aged	.034	.69
Sex	.008	.23
Family housing of relatives	.001	.00

** significant at probability level of .01

Contributions vary with income. Of course, the proportion who file itemized income tax returns increases as one moves up the income scale, and the marginal tax savings per dollar of charity-giving deducted also increases. Hence, it seems clear that the giving of lower income families represents a larger net cost to them than the costs of giving by high income families, in terms of the net costs after taxes.

TABLE 18-9

NONFAMILY CONTRIBUTIONS: DEVIATIONS
FOR GROSS DISPOSABLE INCOME
(FOR FAMILIES)

Gross disposable income	Number of cases	Per cent of families	Unadjusted deviations [a]	Adjusted deviations [a]
None	5	0.1	$-166	$-134
$1–499; negative	47	1.3	-160	-134
$500–999	110	2.9	-279	-219
$1,000–1,999	353	9.5	-251	-212
$2,000–2,999	318	9.7	-168	-141
$3,000–4,999	598	22.3	-153	-143
$5,000–7,499	679	27.4	- 61	- 53
$7,500–9,999	365	14.4	126	98
$10,000–14,999	238	9.1	362	303
$15,000 and over	87	3.3	1,527	1,433

[a] deviations from grand mean of $315

Even when considered jointly with the family's gross disposable income, the longer-run measure of the family head's earning potential has an effect on the family's contributions. It is a strange effect, not entirely representing potential earnings. The old contribute more than one would otherwise expect, and the young contribute less. When the head is thirty-five or older, more education and earning power lead to more contributions, but among younger heads, more education seems to lead to smaller contributions to others.

TABLE 18-10

NONFAMILY CONTRIBUTIONS: DEVIATIONS
FOR EARNING POTENTIAL OF HEADS
(FOR FAMILIES)

Earning potential of heads	Number of cases	Per cent of families	Unadjusted deviations [a]	Adjusted deviations [a]
Retired or disabled and not working	299	11.2	$ 96	$ 18
Nonretired nonwhite	360	9.4	−137	− 20
Nonretired white farmers	165	4.9	− 38	11
Nonretired white nonfarmers:				
18–34 years old;				
0–11 grades	208	7.7	−128	− 73
12 grades	161	6.2	−160	−154
some college	186	7.2	− 88	−145
35 years old and older;				
0–11 grades	743	27.5	− 67	− 12
12 grades	353	13.6	159	61
some college	308	11.7	416	183
Not ascertained	17	0.6	− 72	−235

[a] deviations from grand mean of $315

The religious preference of the family head and the frequency of his church attendance have a significant impact on the level of the family's contributions outside the household. The non-Christians, mostly Jews, contribute the most

TABLE 18-11

NONFAMILY CONTRIBUTIONS: DEVIATIONS FOR RELIGIOUS
PREFERENCE AND CHURCH ATTENDANCE OF HEADS
(FOR FAMILIES)

Religious preference and church attendance of heads	Number of cases	Per cent of families	Unadjusted deviations [a]	Adjusted deviations [a]
Catholics				
attend more than once a month	444	16.9	$− 14	$− 25
attend once a month or less	118	4.5	− 93	− 68
Fundamentalist Protestants				
attend more than once a month	564	18.2	− 14	66
attend once a month or less	416	14.0	−161	− 64
Non-Fundamentalist Protestants				
attend more than once a month	522	19.0	166	93
attend once a month or less	568	21.1	− 74	− 98
Non-Christians; not ascertained	168	6.3	253	120

[a] deviations from grand mean of $315

even after adjustments for their other characteristics, such as higher income. Merle Curti comments: "American philanthropy owes much to the ancient Jewish doctrine which taught rules about the duty of giving and the right of those in need to receive. It is hardly too much to say that Jewish, Catholic, and Protestant doctrines and practices have been central in the development of philanthropy in America." [6] Among the Christian groups, the most persistent effect is that of frequency of attendance at services; the more frequently the head attends church, the larger are the contributions. A very large difference between the Fundamentalist and the non-Fundamentalist Protestants is almost entirely eliminated by the adjustments for other characteristics like income and education. The Catholics who attend regularly remain low in spite of the adjustments.

The rest of the classifications did not add much to the explanation, and did not appear significant with a crude F test. Some deviations have patterns that would be significant with a more discriminating test, and for some the lack of effect is important.

A test for pattern probably would show a significant tendency for families with more living children to make smaller contributions, despite the fact that the heads of such families are older and have higher incomes.

TABLE 18-12

NONFAMILY CONTRIBUTIONS: DEVIATIONS FOR NUMBER
OF LIVING CHILDREN OF HEADS
(FOR FAMILIES)

Number of living children of heads	Number of cases	Per cent of families	Unadjusted deviations [a]	Adjusted deviations [a]
None	573	20.9	$− 42	$ 52
One	509	19.1	19	6
Two	638	23.3	93	40
Three	459	16.6	12	− 48
Four	269	9.2	− 44	− 47
Five	142	4.7	−101	− 87
Six	74	2.2	−180	− 93
Seven	45	1.4	− 89	− 60
Eight or more	89	2.6	−161	− 79
Not ascertained	2	0.0	−315	5

[a] deviations from grand mean of $315

Republicans contribute more, but adjustments for their higher incomes and ages leave them nearly equal to the Democrats. Only the independents contribute more than the mean amount.

Where the father was very young when his first child arrived, the family not only had less income and less savings, but even after taking account of

[6] Curti, *American Quarterly,* 10, p. 424. Used with permission of the *American Quarterly.*

TABLE 18-13

NONFAMILY CONTRIBUTIONS: DEVIATIONS FOR
POLITICAL PREFERENCE OF HEADS
(FOR FAMILIES)

Political preference of heads	Number of cases	Per cent of families	Unadjusted deviations [a]	Adjusted deviations [a]
Strong Democrats	627	22.7	$— 60	$— 32
Not very strong Democrats	649	23.0	— 8	— 3
Independents closer to Democrat	171	6.5	141	95
Independents closer to neither	304	10.8	— 1	35
Independents closer to Republican	130	4.9	107	58
Not very strong Republicans	446	16.1	40	32
Strong Republicans	272	10.2	68	— 27
Other	11	0.3	—253	— 49
Not ascertained	190	5.5	—204	—120

[a] deviations from grand mean of $315

income also contributed less to others. Without making too much of such small differences, the possibility remains that lack of planning may account for the differences both in income and in contributions. It is difficult to account for the failure of those who marry late or do not have children to contribute as much as the average. The former may find their family financial needs pressing at a time when their income is not rising.

TABLE 18-14

NONFAMILY CONTRIBUTIONS: DEVIATIONS FOR AGE OF HEADS
AT BIRTH OF ELDEST LIVING CHILD
(FOR FAMILIES)

Age of heads at birth of eldest living child	Number of cases	Per cent of families	Unadjusted deviations [a]	Adjusted deviations [a]
No children	604	21.9	$— 39	$— 58
Under 18	66	1.8	—250	— 22
18–19	133	4.3	—142	27
20–24, not ascertained	796	28.1	— 34	35
25–29	653	24.0	38	17
30–39	480	17.4	117	— 5
40 and older	68	2.5	— 37	— 47

[a] deviations from grand mean of $315

Apparently the number of brothers and sisters the head had does not, through any increase in his family obligations or feelings of familism, lead to greater contributions to others. (Table 18-15.)

The place where the head grew up has no apparent effect on the extent of the family's voluntarism. (Table 18-16.)

Any systematic tendency for larger contributions from those who felt relatives should be responsible for aged people was largely a spurious relation.

TABLE 18-15

NONFAMILY CONTRIBUTIONS: DEVIATIONS FOR NUMBER
OF SIBLINGS OF HEADS
(FOR FAMILIES)

Number of siblings of heads	Number of cases	Per cent of families	Unadjusted deviations [a]	Adjusted deviations [a]
None	197	7.1	$— 50	$— 86
One	305	11.2	65	— 4
Two	381	13.9	59	22
Three	340	12.4	25	— 18
Four	317	11.1	— 13	4
Five	294	10.8	— 1	1
Six	241	8.6	— 61	— 11
Seven	166	5.9	0	47
Eight or more	450	15.0	— 54	5
Not ascertained	109	4.0	— 4	64

[a] deviations from grand mean of $315

TABLE 18-16

NONFAMILY CONTRIBUTIONS: DEVIATIONS FOR BACKGROUND
OF HEADS
(FOR FAMILIES)

Background of heads	Number of cases	Per cent of families	Unadjusted deviations [a]	Adjusted deviations [a]
Grew up in the Deep South:				
on a farm or in a small town	572	18.1	$—69	$ 31
in a large city, or in several places	100	3.4	—61	— 3
Grew up in the United States outside the Deep South:				
on a farm or in a small town	1,170	41.9	—31	—18
in a large city, or in several places	688	26.5	111	20
Grew up in foreign country	153	5.9	—21	— 2
Not ascertained	117	4.2	—13	—74

[a] deviations from grand mean of $315

Adjustments for income, age, and education leave only a slight effect in that direction. (Table 18-17.)

Neither sex of the family head nor the presence of extra units in the household had any effect on the amount of contributions.

As indicated in Table 18-10, the younger adult units contribute less than middle-aged and older units. Since many adult units whose heads are under thirty-five are young families just getting started, it has been hypothesized that the demands on their income for household goods or for the support of small children offset the effects of their generally higher educations. Also, since among the younger heads those with higher educations contribute least, it is possible that their higher educations give them a target living standard above that provided by their incomes, so that they have little money left to con-

TABLE 18-17

NONFAMILY CONTRIBUTIONS: DEVIATIONS FOR ATTITUDE OF HEADS
TOWARD RESPONSIBILITY FOR THE AGED
(FOR FAMILIES)

Attitude of heads toward responsibility for the aged	Number of cases	Per cent of families	Unadjusted deviations [a]	Adjusted deviations [a]
Relatives should have sole responsibility	773	28.9	$ 77	$ 5
Relatives should have primary responsibility	827	29.7	17	14
Relatives and government should share responsibility	247	9.0	68	36
Government should have primary responsibility	161	5.6	− 78	12
Government should have sole responsibility	648	21.8	−107	−34
Other sources of responsibility	23	0.9	−112	38
Not ascertained	121	4.1	−106	−58

[a] deviations from grand mean of $315

TABLE 18-18

NONFAMILY CONTRIBUTIONS: DEVIATIONS FOR SEX
OF HEAD OF THE FAMILY
(FOR FAMILIES)

Sex of heads	Number of cases	Per cent of families	Unadjusted deviations [a]	Adjusted deviations [a]
Male	2,265	82.4	$ 31	$ 3
Female	535	17.6	−144	−13

[a] deviations from grand mean of $315

TABLE 18-19

NONFAMILY CONTRIBUTIONS: DEVIATIONS FOR HOUSING
OF RELATIVES
(FOR FAMILIES)

Housing of relatives	Number of cases	Per cent of families	Unadjusted deviations [a]	Adjusted deviations [a]
No extra adult unit in family	2,311	82.6	$−10	$ 0
Extra adult unit in family	489	17.4	46	−1

[a] deviations from grand mean of $315

tribute to others. Table 18-20 shows mean contributions within age groups according to the family welfare ratio and the per cent in each group which made some contribution. There is very little over-all pattern to the per cent who gave, but at every welfare level the mean contribution of the youngest group is substantially less than that of any other group except those seventy-five and older, and considerably less than the mean contributions for all units

TABLE 18-20

MEAN CONTRIBUTIONS WITHIN AGE OF FAMILY HEAD AND FAMILY WELFARE RATIO
(MEANS FOR FAMILIES)

Age of family heads

Family welfare ratio	18–24 Per cent who gave and mean amount		25–34 Per cent who gave and mean amount		35–44 Per cent who gave and mean amount		45–54 Per cent who gave and mean amount		55–64 Per cent who gave and mean amount		65–74 Per cent who gave and mean amount		75 and older Per cent who gave and mean amount		All Per cent who gave and mean amount	
Less than .9	25	$ 24	38	$ 57	51	$ 99	42	$119	46	$ 54	42	$ 65	30	$ 41	41	$ 73
	(54)		(123)		(153)		(164)		(143)		(86)		(64)		(787)	
1.0–1.2	70	105	57	113	68	166	76	278	55	160	64	149	57	87	64	166
	(39)		(118)		(115)		(88)		(67)		(52)		(28)		(507)	
1.3–1.6	70	137	71	175	80	250	80	298	76	236	85	205	62	55	76	222
	(38)		(101)		(143)		(88)		(56)		(27)		(16)		(469)	
1.7–2.2	71	203	78	258	87	369	90	320	86	356	85	209	76	321	84	306
	(24)		(133)		(126)		(113)		(85)		(46)		(8)		(535)	
2.3 and over	92	296	86	372	97	653	95	1066	93	996	82	950	100	469	92	822
	(12)		(66)		(115)		(128)		(124)		(50)		(7)		(502)	

( ) number of families

273

at the respective welfare levels. The same is true to a lesser extent for adult units whose heads are twenty-five to thirty-four. Because the welfare ratio takes account of the differing needs of different age groups, it may be that philanthrophy is less important to younger persons than it was to their parents, and that the absolute levels of voluntarism and philanthropy will decline in the future.

As frequently happens in studies of economic behavior, a few important economic or quasi-economic variables account for some of the variance, and other factors, even considered simultaneously, add little. Only religious preference and church attendance made a significant addition to the explanation provided by income and earning potential. The powerful effects of age, combined with the original question of whether increased public programs would lead to the demise of private voluntarism, present the possibility that the younger generations feel less concern for others.

Individual Contributions and Transfer Incomes

The multivariate analysis of family contributions dealt only with family contributions outside the household, including those which pass through intermediaries like the church or charitable organizations. By including data on income from such transfers, as well as contributions within the dwelling, it is possible to determine the individual effects of voluntarism.

Table 18-21 shows contributions given to and received by adult units within age groups. This indicates the extent to which individual voluntarism is going from an older generation to a younger one, or from children to their parents. These data include contributions given and received by adult units within a family, since this is an important form of interindividual and inter-

TABLE 18-21

TRANSFERS AMONG INDIVIDUAL ADULT UNITS WITHIN AGE OF HEAD
(FOR ADULT UNITS)

Per cent who gave $500 or more to:	Age of head						75 and older	All adult units
	18–24	25–34	35–44	45–54	55–64	65–74		
Individuals outside the dwelling	2	4	8	10	8	5	1	6
Others in the dwelling (net)	2	3	9	15	13	7	7	8
Per cent who received $500 or more from:								
Others in the dwelling	32	5	2	3	5	8	19	8
Individuals outside the dwelling [a]	4	5	3	2	1	0	5	5
Number of adult units	434	631	694	624	517	317	179	3,396

[a] excludes alimony and regular support, which are received by only 2 per cent of adult units

generational aid. The table presents data for adult units rather than for family units, since contributions and receipts within a family which contains more than one adult unit balance and cancel each other out.

Table 18-21 shows that middle-aged units at the peak of their earning power are supporting others both younger and older than themselves, mostly their parents and children. This redistribution is in addition to that produced by the social security system, by organized charity, and by private pension plans and retirement savings.

Attitudes toward Voluntarism and Relatives' Responsibility

It is important to know not only the extent to which people are supporting their relatives but also how they feel about such income transfers. Indeed, it would be good to be able to go back and find out how people felt twenty or thirty years ago, before the advent of an extensive system of income maintenance programs. Perhaps the development of these programs has reduced to some extent the need for individuals to take care of their own relatives and the social compulsion to do so. Even without such past data, however, it is interesting to look at people's present feelings as an indication of the extent to which voluntarism will continue in the future, as a supplement to data on the actual amount of transfers, and as a benchmark to measure changes if the same questions are asked again in ten or twenty years.

Chapter 14 showed that people who can afford to live by themselves prefer to do so. However, people may still feel financially responsible for their relatives. One can take care of one's aged parents without having two families in one household. People's feelings about their responsibilities in this area were ascertained by the following question: "If the older people don't have enough money, do you think their relatives should support them, or should the government take care of them, or what? Why do you say so?"

In the United States a substantial number of older people have some income from private savings, pensions, or the social security system, and the question must have implied to many people: "If, in spite of these income maintenance programs and pensions, an aged person did not have enough money, who then should be responsible?" Two-thirds of the spending unit heads who expressed an opinion felt that relatives should be primarily responsible for older people who are in need. This implies that although people do not want their aged parents living with them, they still feel a sense of responsibility in case other sources of support are insufficient.

A majority of heads who felt that relatives should be responsible for older people gave moral or normative reasons for their attitude. One who felt that relatives should be solely responsible said: "It's their duty, just like it was the parents' duty to take care of the kids." Many who gave moral reasons reiterated this idea of a debt to the parents.

Some felt that relatives should be responsible because the government

TABLE 18-22

REASONS FOR ATTITUDE TOWARD RESPONSIBILITY FOR THE AGED WITHIN ATTITUDE (PERCENTAGE DISTRIBUTION OF SPENDING UNIT HEADS)

Reasons for attitude toward responsibility for the aged [a]	Relatives should have: Sole responsibility	Relatives should have: Primary responsibility	Relatives and government should share responsibility	Government should have: Primary responsibility	Government should have: Sole responsibility	All spending unit heads [b]
Relatives should have responsibility because:						
Government pensions are too low	1	1	6	5	0	1
Government expenses are too high	11	9	3	1	0	6
Families should care for their own	75	44	29	14	0	38
Older people prefer help from relatives	6	5	2	2	0	3
Other reasons	4	2	6	1	0	2
Who should have responsibility depends:						
On finances	11	44	27	23	0	20
On other things	2	4	4	10	0	3
Government should have responsibility because:						
Government pensions are adequate	0	2	8	11	13	5
Relatives cannot afford to support them	0	6	16	15	33	11
This is the government's job	0	11	33	45	49	19
Older people prefer government help	0	0	1	4	5	2
Other reasons	0	4	6	6	8	4
Number of spending unit heads	836	881	266	182	681	2,997

[a] Does not add to 100 per cent because some spending unit heads gave more than one reason and some gave no reasons. Note that people can give contrary reasons.

[b] Includes 151 spending unit heads whose feeling about responsibility for aged was not ascertained.

already has too many responsibilities or too many expenses: "There is too much feeling nowadays that the government is responsible for all of an individual's problems, rather than the individual himself." "The government can't afford to support everybody," said one, and some thought that "taxes are too high as it is."

Some persons believed that older people themselves would prefer help from their own families rather than from the government: "The old folks have their dignity, they don't want to panhandle from the government;" and "It's bad enough to be getting from their children, but that's better than being on the government."

About one-fifth of the spending unit heads felt that responsibility depended upon whether the old people had children, or whether the children were financially able to help them.

Those who believed that the primary responsibility belonged to the government spoke mostly of the responsibility in terms of the government's role and its obligations. Many people felt that "old folks have been paying taxes all of their lives, they should get some of it back." Some mentioned that "the government should start using taxes for our problems instead of for foreign problems." The idea that old people should get some kind of payment in return for their taxes was the most prominent reason given by those who felt the government should be responsible for older people.

The next most important reason for government responsibility was that relatives could not afford to support anyone outside their immediate families. "Most people can barely take care of themselves," said several; "most folks around here do all they can just to make ends meet." A few heads believed that "social security is for that—the government should give them pensions if they got it coming."

The extent to which people definitely expect to care for their own parents in the future seems to be related only slightly to their attitude toward general responsibility for the aged. A somewhat smaller proportion of those who say the government should be solely responsible expect to take care of parents in the future. To complete this comparison, however, information is necessary about whether any of the family's parents are still living and likely to be in need of help.

It seems clear that the feeling of family responsibility for indigent relatives is still strong. It is doubtful that people would prefer to provide for their parents the support that social security and private pensions are now providing, however.[7]

[7] There are no comparable data for representative samples from earlier periods to which these could be compared. For small studies see: Robert M. Dinkel, "Attitudes of Children toward Supporting Aged Parents," *American Sociological Review,* 9 (August, 1944), 370–379;

Robert J. Havighurst and Ruth Albrecht, *Older People* (New York: Longmans, Green & Co., Inc., 1953).

TABLE 18-23

EXPECTATIONS ABOUT CARING FOR PARENTS WITHIN ATTITUDE
TOWARD RESPONSIBILITY FOR THE AGED
(PERCENTAGE DISTRIBUTION OF SPENDING UNIT HEADS
WHO ARE NOT RETIRED)

Expectations about caring for parents	Attitude toward responsibility for the aged					All nonretired spending unit heads [a]
	Relatives should have:		Relatives and government should share responsibility	Government should have:		
	Sole responsibility	Primary responsibility		Primary responsibility	Sole responsibility	
Will give them general financial help	13	11	16	14	8	11
Will pay specific expenses	1	2	1	0	2	1
Will house them	7	4	5	5	5	6
Will give them general care	10	11	14	15	8	11
Caring for them now	4	5	2	5	3	4
Will not care for them	60	62	54	56	68	61
Do not know; depends	3	3	6	4	5	4
Not ascertained	2	2	2	1	1	2
Total	100	100	100	100	100	100
Number of spending unit heads	771	803	249	170	586	2,694

[a] Includes 115 spending unit heads whose attitude toward responsibility for the aged was not ascertained.

Multivariate Analysis of Attitudes toward Responsibility for the Aged

Some differences of opinion exist among spending unit heads about financial responsibility for the aged. In order to determine whether these differences are solely the result of differences in income, age, and family composition, or if cultural and personality measures also affect this attitude, a multivariate analysis was done, using the attitude as the dependent variable. Responses to the question about responsibility for the aged were converted into a numerical scale. Thus, the dependent variable became an index of the extent to which spending unit heads favored government responsibility for the aged. The scale was:

Attitude	Scale value assigned
Relatives should have sole responsibility for older people	1
Relatives should have primary responsibility, government should help	2
Relatives and government should share responsibility equally	3
Government should have primary responsibility, relatives should help	4
Government should have sole responsibility for older people	5

The grand mean of the index of attitudes was 2.59; on the average heads were somewhat more in favor of relatives' responsibility than of government responsibility. The standard deviation was 1.53.

Twelve explanatory characteristics with a total of eighty-one subclasses were used in the analysis. These explained only one-tenth of the total variance. Table 18-24 shows the explanatory characteristics in order of their relative importance.

TABLE 18-24

CHARACTERISTICS USED TO EXPLAIN ATTITUDE TOWARD
RESPONSIBILITY FOR THE AGED
(FOR SPENDING UNIT HEADS)

Characteristics of spending unit heads	Relative importance (Beta coefficients)	Significance (F ratios)
Earning potential	.144	7.21**
Gross disposable income of spending unit	.136	6.43*
Adult unit composition	.100	4.47**
Political preference	.077	3.71**
Attitude toward hard work	.068	2.07*
Feeling of ability to plan	.067	2.81*
Per cent of aged in state who receive Old Age Assistance or social security benefits	.065	4.41**
Number of siblings	.064	2.56*
Urban-rural migration	.062	2.41*
Movement out of the Deep South	.061	2.25*
Religious preference and church attendance	.051	1.36
Self-employment	.025	.65

** significant at probability level of .01
* significant at probability level of .05

The two most important predictors are the indicators of economic or financial status: earning potential and spending unit gross disposable income. The next most important predictor, adult unit composition, is an index of demands on income and housing space.

Those with low earning potential, namely the retired and the nonwhites, are more in favor of government responsibility; the rest of the population tends to be more in favor of individual responsibility. The proportion of white non-retired who favor individual responsibility increases as ages and potential incomes rise. The adjusted coefficients for earning potential were, of course, somewhat smaller than the unadjusted coefficients because other character-istics like spending unit income, which are correlated with earning potential, took over some of the credit.

The next most important predictor is gross disposable income. It is inter-esting to note that it remains an important predictor even after the adjust-ments for earning potential. Again the direction of the relationship is the same: low income people are more likely to feel that the government should be

TABLE 18-25

ATTITUDE TOWARD RESPONSIBILITY FOR THE AGED: DEVIATIONS
FOR EARNING POTENTIAL
(FOR SPENDING UNIT HEADS)

Earning potential	Number of cases	Unadjusted deviations [a]	Adjusted deviations [a]
Retired or disabled and not working	273	.42	.15
Nonretired nonwhite	358	.63	.47
Nonretired white farmers	162	.15	−.04
Nonretired white nonfarmers:			
18–34 years old;			
0–11 grades	240	.15	.11
12 grades	215	−.14	−.03
some college	205	−.46	−.24
35 years old and older;			
0–11 grades	721	.17	.08
12 grades	354	−.39	−.26
some college	303	−.57	−.29
Not ascertained	15	−.05	−.09

[a] deviations from grand mean of 2.59

TABLE 18-26

ATTITUDE TOWARD RESPONSIBILITY FOR THE AGED: DEVIATIONS
FOR GROSS DISPOSABLE INCOME OF SPENDING UNITS
(FOR SPENDING UNIT HEADS)

Gross disposable income of spending units	Number of cases	Unadjusted deviations [a]	Adjusted deviations [a]
None	4	.32	.31
$1–499; negative	46	.62	.42
$500–999	119	.78	.63
$1,000–1,999	372	.50	.38
$2,000–2,999	372	.18	.10
$3,000–4,999	646	.01	−.03
$5,000–7,499	667	−.10	−.08
$7,500–9,999	342	−.23	−.12
$10,000–14,999	205	−.44	−.25
$15,000 or more	73	−.62	−.38

[a] deviations from grand mean of 2.59

responsible for aged relatives even though they are somewhat less opposed to living with relatives. (See Chapter 14.)

The third most important predictor is a measure of adult unit composition. Married couples with no children are most likely to assign responsibility to the government. Among the married couples, those with children are more likely to assign responsibility to the individual. Thus the factors that would make it most difficult to live with aged parents seem to be associated with a greater feeling of responsibility toward relatives. This dramatizes the fact that

TABLE 18-27

ATTITUDE TOWARD RESPONSIBILITY FOR THE AGED:
DEVIATIONS FOR ADULT UNIT COMPOSITION
(FOR SPENDING UNIT HEADS)

Adult unit composition	Number of cases	Unadjusted deviations [a]	Adjusted deviations [a]
Single male			
No children	309	.09	−.13
Children	17	.16	−.10
Single female			
No children	406	−.03	−.20
Children	156	.00	−.21
Married			
No children	696	.20	.23
One child	367	−.15	−.01
Two children	392	−.18	−.02
Three or more children	503	−.08	−.02

[a] deviations from grand mean of 2.59

people can be opposed to living with aged parents and still be in favor of being financially responsible for them.

The next most important factor in explaining attitudes toward responsibilities for the aged is political affiliation. As one might expect, the strong Democrats were somewhat more in favor of government responsibility. There is no marked difference in the attitudes among those who do not feel strongly about their political affiliation.

TABLE 18-28

ATTITUDE TOWARD RESPONSIBILITY FOR THE AGED:
DEVIATIONS FOR POLITICAL PREFERENCE
(FOR SPENDING UNIT HEADS)

Political preference	Number of cases	Unadjusted deviations [a]	Adjusted deviations [a]
Strong Democrats	645	.24	.18
Not very strong Democrats	671	.03	.03
Independents	622	−.12	−.05
Not very strong Republicans	453	−.10	−.07
Strong Republicans	274	−.30	−.21
Not ascertained	181	.25	−.07

[a] deviations from grand mean of 2.59

The head's attitude toward hard work was included on the assumption that those who stressed self-reliance and independence would also feel that people should be independent of the government and take care of their own relatives. As expected, those who spoke in terms of hard work were more likely to say that people should be responsible for their relatives; those who talked

TABLE 18-29

ATTITUDE TOWARD RESPONSIBILITY FOR THE AGED:
DEVIATIONS FOR ATTITUDE TOWARD HARD WORK
(FOR SPENDING UNIT HEADS)

Attitude toward hard work	Number of cases	Unadjusted deviations [a]	Adjusted deviations [a]
Hard work is more important than luck	1,312	−.07	−.09
Hard work is more important, qualified	565	−.11	.00
Hard work and luck are equally important	407	−.07	.06
Luck is more important, qualified	109	.08	.02
Luck is more important than work	320	.46	.22
Normative responses	11	.36	.34
Other responses	39	.07	.12
Not ascertained	83	.46	.17

[a] deviations from grand mean of 2.59

The question was: "Some people say that people get ahead by their own hard work; others say that lucky breaks and help from other people are more important. What do you think about this?"

about luck and help from friends were more likely to say that the government should be responsible for the care of older people who cannot take care of themselves. The differences are small, however.

Those who said they felt able to plan ahead were more likely to feel that people should be responsible for their own aged relatives. These patterns persist even after the adjustments for age, education, income, and a number of other variables; however, differences among adjusted deviations are small. A substantial portion of the unadjusted differences associated with this attitude were apparently attributable to other factors.

A variable describing the per cent of aged in the state who receive OASDI or OAA was included on the assumption that the community or area in which

TABLE 18-30

ATTITUDE TOWARD RESPONSIBILITY FOR THE AGED:
DEVIATIONS FOR FEELING OF ABILITY TO PLAN
(FOR SPENDING UNIT HEADS)

Feeling of ability to plan	Number of cases	Unadjusted deviations [a]	Adjusted deviations [a]
Feel able to plan	1,193	−.21	−.09
Feel able to plan, qualified	315	−.02	.05
Feel unable to plan, qualified	177	−.08	−.18
Feel unable to plan	1,056	.25	.11
Do not know	42	.21	.11
Not ascertained	63	.17	.12

[a] deviations from grand mean of 2.59

The question was: "Some people feel that they can make pretty definite plans for their lives for the next few years. Others feel that they aren't in a position to plan ahead. How about you? Do you feel able to plan ahead or not?"

one lived might influence his attitudes. If a substantial fraction of the aged people in a state are getting OASDI and OAA, then people in that state might be more likely to see the government as responsible for older people. It is difficult to determine the direction of the causation, since the administration of social programs in a state may themselves be the result of public attitudes. In any case, the proportion of the aged getting some kind of government aid does seem to be correlated with people's attitudes. Where less than 70 per cent of the old people are geting OAA or OASDI, people are more likely to talk in terms of the relatives' responsibilities. Among a very small group of 100 cases, less than 3 per cent of the sample, who were living in states where more than 80 per cent of the old people were getting some kind of assistance, there is substantially more feeling that the government should be responsible for aged people. These states are Mississippi, Louisiana, and Alabama. Again this is true even after taking account of income, earning potential, and the other factors.

TABLE 18-31

ATTITUDE TOWARD RESPONSIBILITY FOR THE AGED: DEVIATIONS
FOR PER CENT OF AGED IN STATE WHO RECEIVE OLD AGE
ASSISTANCE OR SOCIAL SECURITY BENEFITS
(FOR SPENDING UNIT HEADS)

Per cent of aged in state who receive Old Age Assistance or social security benefits	Number of cases	Unadjusted deviations [a]	Adjusted deviations [a]
Less than 70.0 per cent	464	−.08	−.10
70.0–74.9 per cent	1,121	−.06	−.05
75.0–79.9 per cent	1,161	.04	.05
80.0 per cent and over	100	.72	.48

[a] deviations from grand mean of 2.59

Another measure of cultural influence not included in the multivariate analysis displayed a similar relationship to the head's attitude toward responsibility for the aged. This was the amount of OAA per inhabitant of the state. In states where OAA programs pay larger than average amounts per inhabitant, people are slightly more likely to feel that the aged are the responsibility of the government. Only a very small group who live in states with the largest amount per inhabitant differ significantly from the rest of the population.

If people from large families are more likely to exhibit familism and to feel a sense of responsibility for their extended families, one might think that the more siblings a man had, the more he would believe in relatives' responsibility. However, the reverse was true. The more siblings a person has, the more likely he is to feel that the government should be responsible for the care of aged people and those with no siblings at all are most likely to feel that relatives should take care of the aged, in spite of the fact that indigent parents would be more of a burden for those with no siblings to share the responsibility. It is possible that people from large families, who are more likely to have indigent relatives, are more willing to have the government take responsibility for them, whereas those who are unlikely to have any substantial call on their funds can say the socially acceptable thing without much concern.

TABLE 18-32

ATTITUDE TOWARD RESPONSIBILITY FOR THE AGED:
DEVIATIONS FOR NUMBER OF SIBLINGS
(FOR SPENDING UNIT HEADS)

Number of siblings	Number of cases	Unadjusted deviations [a]	Adjusted deviations [a]
None	202	−.33	−.21
One	326	−.18	−.02
Two	390	−.28	−.15
Three	365	−.06	−.02
Four or more	1,462	.18	.08
Not ascertained	101	−.03	.04

[a] deviations from grand mean of 2.59

It would appear that those who either moved from farm to city or from city to rural area are more likely to say the children should be responsible for their parents. These upwardly mobile persons generally have higher incomes and earning potentials, and the adjustments for these factors substantially reduced the importance of this predictor from its unadjusted form.

TABLE 18-33

ATTITUDE TOWARD RESPONSIBILITY FOR THE AGED:
DEVIATIONS FOR URBAN-RURAL MIGRATION
(FOR SPENDING UNIT HEADS)

Urban-rural migration of heads	Number of cases	Unadjusted deviations [a]	Adjusted deviations [a]
Grew up on farms, now live:			
in rural areas	555	.32	.16
in towns of 2,500–49,999	251	.27	.11
in cities of 50,000 or more	166	.05	−.12
Grew up in towns or cities, now live:			
in rural areas	493	−.27	−.12
in towns or cities of 2,500 or more	1,333	−.07	−.02
Other; not ascertained	48	−.04	.00

[a] deviations from grand mean of 2.59

The variables which measured movement out of the Deep South contribute little to the explanation of attitudes toward relatives' responsibility for the aged.

A combination of the head's religious preference and frequency of church attendance is not very powerful and the coefficients change rather dramatically

TABLE 18-34

ATTITUDE TOWARD RESPONSIBILITY FOR THE AGED:
DEVIATIONS FOR MOVEMENT OUT OF DEEP SOUTH
(FOR SPENDING UNIT HEADS)

Spending unit heads' movement out of the Deep South	Number of cases	Unadjusted deviations [a]	Adjusted deviations [a]
Grew up in the United States outside the Deep South; now live:			
in the South	389	−.19	−.18
in the non-South	119	.32	.04
Grew up in the Deep South; now live:			
in the South	568	.22	−.08
in the non-South	1,587	−.06	.07
Grew up outside the United States	153	.14	.01
All others [b]	30	−.16	−.17

[a] deviations from grand mean of 2.59
[b] includes persons who grew up in more than one region and those for whom region was not ascertained

when other factors in this analysis are taken into account. The unadjusted coefficients are largely the result of income and other differences among the religious groups. After adjustments for other factors, the Catholics and the non-Christian sects are more likely to believe that the government should be responsible, whereas the non-Fundamentalist Protestants who attend church more frequently are more likely to speak of the responsibility of relatives for their aged parents.[8] Within each religious group, however, those who attend

TABLE 18-35

ATTITUDE TOWARD RESPONSIBILITY FOR THE AGED:
DEVIATIONS FOR RELIGIOUS PREFERENCE
AND CHURCH ATTENDANCE
(FOR SPENDING UNIT HEADS)

Religious preference and church attendance	Number of cases	Unadjusted deviations [a]	Adjusted deviations [a]
Catholics			
attend more than once a month	463	.02	.07
attend once a month or less	120	.20	.11
Fundamentalist Protestants			
attend more than once a month	558	.11	−.04
attend once a month or less	429	.26	.07
Non-Fundamentalist Protestants			
attend more than once a month	532	−.26	−.13
attend once a month or less	588	−.07	.00
Other religions	156	−.08	.09

[a] deviations from grand mean of 2.59

[8] This is the reverse of what was found with a small, nonrepresentative sample of high school and college students. See Dinkel, *American Sociological Review,* 9, 370–379.

church more frequently are more likely to express the values their religion teaches by talking in terms of the responsibility of people for their own relatives.

The deviations for self-employment of the head were the least important. The differences between the self-employed and the employed were well within sampling error. Only those who were not working were significantly more in favor of government responsibility. This difference is a small residual remaining after adjustments for the other factors removed a much larger difference.

TABLE 18-36

ATTITUDE TOWARD RESPONSIBILITY FOR THE AGED:
DEVIATIONS FOR SELF-EMPLOYMENT
(FOR SPENDING UNIT HEADS)

Self-employment	Number of cases	Unadjusted deviations [a]	Adjusted deviations [a]
Self-employed	427	−.06	−.04
Not self-employed	1,781	−.10	−.01
Not working	638	.33	.06

[a] deviations from grand mean of 2.59

People who are most able to afford it are more likely to feel responsibility for the aged belongs to their relatives. This is indicated by the importance of the head's earning potential and the spending unit's gross disposable income in explaining attitudes toward responsibility for the aged. Other characteristics, such as adult composition, political preference, and frequency of church attendance were of lesser importance. Needless to say, not too much reliance should be placed on a few relatively simple questions in assessing attitudes toward voluntarism. It is also important to look at people's attitudes about the relative acceptance of other kinds of governmental aid and to study their actual contributions. It is possible, however, to note that there are differences of opinion about who should be responsible for old people and that there is a large and perhaps growing body of people who feel that this is the government's responsibility. It would be most interesting to examine the attitudinal differences between the United States and other countries like India where extended family responsibilities are extreme and some in Europe where the government's responsibility is almost complete.[9]

Summary

While the forms which voluntarism takes have been changing, in the United States today contributions to church, charities, and relatives are substantial.

[9] For some evidence of the variety of emphasis on relatives' responsibility which can be elicited by various questions, and some evidence that older people are more reluctant to receive help than younger people to believe they should ask for it, see Ethel Shanas, *Family Relationships of Older People*, Health Information Foundation Research Series #20 (New York: Health Information Foundation, 1961).

The most rapidly disappearing form of aid to others is through providing them with food and lodging in one's own home. Moving in with relatives in times of need is disappearing, and people are overwhelmingly opposed to it. At the same time, a sense of responsibility for one's own parents remains strong among many people.

Total contributions outside the household to church, charities, and other individuals are determined largely by income, with roughly the same proportion of income being contributed at all income levels. In terms of redistribution then, contributions are neutral, while transfer incomes are only mildly redistributive. The Federal income tax remains the most powerful redistributive factor today.

The Jewish people contribute more to others, even after adjustments for income; among the Protestants, frequency of attendance has as much to do with giving as the denomination to which the individual belongs. More complex analyses, both of contributions and of attitudes about the responsibilities of relatives, indicate that other factors besides mere ability to afford philanthropy are important. Whether changing attitudes affect philanthropy, or the changing needs for philanthropy change attitudes, the fact remains that attitudes and behavior are related.

Attitudes toward direct responsibility for relatives were studied here, though they proved to be related to the amounts people gave to church and charity as well. As public programs do a better and better job of taking care of people, it is interesting to speculate what will happen to the attitudes toward, and contributions to, organized charities and churches, part of whose help goes abroad.

Perhaps the most dramatic unexplained finding is the tendency for more education to be associated with less philanthropic giving among the young, white, nonfarm population, but to be associated with more giving among the older, white, nonfarm people. Only an elaborate convariance analysis would tell whether this results from different income effects for different subgroups. Perhaps the young, highly educated have lower incomes relative to longer term expectations, hence spend more for their own living, leaving less for charity. Perhaps the young, highly educated have parents who are also well off and need no help.

Finally, there is an interesting question in dynamics of change and the way in which changing economic situation and changing public programs may affect attitudes, which may then affect future legislation. It will be important to measure both the attitudes toward and practice of voluntarism again at intervals, in order to understand this process of social change.

Chapter 19

PROPERTY TAXES AND THE
BENEFITS OF PUBLIC EDUCATION

At any point in time, an economic system which paid people only for the value of their current contribution to the national product would leave some with no income and some with far more than they could use. The distribution of factor incomes thus can be considered a starting point from which various forms of redistribution have their effects. The most important redistributional mechanisms are the Federal income tax and the public and private transfer systems. Income from transfers was examined in Chapter 13, and the redistributive effects of philanthropy and family aid in Chapter 18. The over-all impact of income taxes and of transfers on the inequality of income distributions will be shown in Chapter 20.

Any tax or any government expenditure will, of course, have some redistributional aspects. Some people will pay more tax than others, or receive greater benefit from the government expenditures. It is generally hoped that the total impact is reasonably fair. To focus on individual parts of the system is likely to be misleading. Indeed, for many individual taxes and forms of government expenditure it is even difficult to determine the ultimate burden or benefit.

This chapter focuses on one tax and one benefit: the residential property tax and the public schools, both because they seem more specialized in their impact than other taxes or government expenditures and because they are generally related. Much of the property tax revenue is used for public schools, and much of the public school support comes from property tax funds.

Before beginning, however, it is important to understand the limitations of such an analysis. In an interdependent economic system, the incidence of a tax in the fullest sense would mean the redistributional effects of the tax and of the expenditure of the money, after all the repercussions had worked themselves out. In other words, one would have to compare an economic system in equilibrium before the tax, with the system after the tax and expenditure had been imposed and a new equilibrium had established itself.

No one has ever succeeded in such an ambitious analysis. The solving of

288

general equilibrium systems has been restricted to rather simple structures and not enough is known about the speed and extent of reactions of people and markets. On the other hand, simply to look at the characteristics of those who pay a tax without asking whether they are shifting its burden immediately to someone else is deceptive. The cigarette manufacturer may pay a cigarette tax directly, but it is generally assumed that the amount of the tax is added to the price of the cigarettes and paid by the customer, at least in the long run. Some attempts have been made to allow for the major first-stage shifting of taxes, and to assess the over-all incidence of the major forms of taxes.[1] In a few cases, some attempt has been made to take account also of the incidence of the government expenditure of tax money.[2]

Assumptions and Limitations

The analysis of property taxes and public school benefits in this chapter must make some operating assumptions about the incidence of these taxes and benefits. It will be assumed that the benefits of public education accrue to parents who have children in school, as though they would be compelled to provide the same education for their children in any case. The benefits to society of an informed electorate and a productive labor force in the future will not be considered, though they are, of course, an important element. The property tax will be analyzed as though it is paid by the occupant of the dwelling, that is, the owner-occupier or the renter. In other words, it is assumed that property taxes on rental property are shifted to the renters in the form of higher rents. In the short run, particularly where there is rent control, this may not happen, but the generally low profit level and free competition in rental housing would justify the assumption that in the long run rents must cover all costs including taxes. These are only rough shifting assumptions and do not pretend to assess the ultimate incidence of property taxes or public school benefits in a general equilibrium system.

Previous studies have allocated a portion of the tax on rental real estate to the owner of the property, on the grounds that some portion of the tax was tax on the site value which would exist in the absence of any improvements.[3]

---

[1] See Richard A. Musgrave, "Incidence of the Tax Structure and Its Effect on Consumption," *Federal Tax Policy for Economic Growth and Stability,* U.S. Census, Joint Economic Committee, 84th Cong., 1st Sess. (November 2, 1955), pp. 96, 113. For a study of a single state see Richard A. Musgrave and Darwin W. Daicoff, "Who Pays the Michigan Taxes?," *Michigan Tax Study Staff Papers,* Chapter 4 (Lansing, Michigan: House of Representatives Legislative Committee and Citizens Advisory Committee, Michigan Tax Study, 1958).

[2] See Alfred H. Conrad, "Redistribution through Government Budgets in the United States, 1950," *An Income Redistribution and Social Policy,* Alan T. Peacock, ed. (London: Jonathan Cape, Ltd., 1954), pp. 178–267.

[3] See Richard A. Musgrave and others, "Distribution of Tax Payments by Income Group," *National Tax Journal,* 4 (March, 1951), pp. 1–53.

This would require a relatively small adjustment, based on rather tenuous estimates of site values. For rental properties, such adjustments would have to be made to estimates of property taxes which are already rough estimates, so it has not been attempted. Later in this chapter separate tabulations for renters are provided from which the reader can easily calculate the effect of such an adjustment.

It has also been suggested that the stream of future property taxes to be paid represents a reduction in the net benefit, and hence in the present capital value of a house, and that a new purchaser will take this into account in buying the house and thus avoid the tax. In practice, however, increased property taxes also involve increased local expenditure for schools and other services, which increase the value of the property. Hence, the available empirical evidence shows no effect of changing property taxes on house values.[4]

There remains, however, some truth in the notion of capitalization. A replacement of property taxes by income taxes would provide unearned capital gains to the present owners of houses and rental properties in the form of an increased stream of net benefits, which they could sell. And an attempt, *a la* Henry George, to rely more heavily on the property tax and less on other taxes, would have the opposite result. Both types of results would appear inequitable to some people.

A final warning is in order before turning to the analysis. The incidence of a tax or public benefit in any one year must be examined in the context of a longer time span. There is a system of social compacts, written and unwritten, by which redistributions at a point in time are repaid by other redistributions earlier or later. Everyone pays for public education; those with children currently in public schools benefit a great deal. Younger families expect to benefit later when their children go to school. Older families whose children are finished with school have already benefited. Hence, the distribution of the benefits of public education in a single year vastly exaggerate the long-run concentration of those benefits. The same considerations apply to transfer incomes and transfer payments.

On the other hand, the use of data for a single year is meaningful in an analysis of the short-run concentration of benefits. In the case of property taxes, the short-run analysis may even be preferable. The value of a man's house may depend on his lifetime income, and the large house of an older person may represent a successful lifetime. But this does not help him pay his property taxes now.

Characteristics of the Property Tax

The property tax lends itself to inclusion in this study for several reasons. It is the major source of revenue for public school expenditures in most local-

---

[4] See Darwin W. Daicoff, "Capitalization of the Property Tax" (unpublished Ph.D. dissertation, University of Michigan, 1961).

ities, and public school expenditures are of interest because investment in human capital affects the nation's progress in general, and individual advancement in particular. The property tax is also a large, infrequent, and conspicuous expenditure for the individual, so that survey data on amounts of property tax are reasonably reliable. Finally, the property tax is a very significant source of revenue for state and local governments in general, so that it would warrant study even apart from its link with public education.

Among taxes levied in the United States the property tax ranks third in terms of total yields produced; its yield of $15 billion in 1959 was exceeded only by those of the personal and corporate income taxes ($43 billion and $22 billion respectively). Approximately 60 per cent of the families in the United States own their homes; for most of them the property tax is second in size only to the income tax among taxes paid. While renters usually occupy less expensive housing relative to their incomes, they too pay property taxes indirectly.

The property tax is the mainstay of local government finances, accounting for 87 per cent of local tax receipts and 49 per cent of local general revenue from all sources. School districts rely especially heavily on the property tax; it provides 98 per cent of their tax collections ($5.4 billion in 1959) and 85 per cent of their total revenues other than state and Federal aid.[5] However, property taxes are small in comparison with some $27 billion in transfer incomes, and some $148 billion in total Federal, state, and local government expenditures in 1959.

The residential property tax differs from the Federal income tax and the transfers already discussed. It is a tax on the housing consumed by the family and will vary from family to family according to their preferences for simple or more elaborate housing even among families with the same level of income. This contrasts with the income tax which takes relatively similar levels of tax among all families with the same level of income. Differences in tax can occur, of course, because of differences in the form of the income, the deductions allowed to the family, and the number of their exemptions.

Variation in families' preferences for spending their income on housing is also associated with whether the family owns or rents its housing. Typically families that own are larger and have higher levels of income than renters. Owners therefore tend to spend more money on housing than renters. However, even where owners and renters in the same income group and with similar family structures are compared, the owner typically spends more on his housing than the renter. These differences in consumption of housing are also reflected in the level of property taxes paid by owners and renters. Differences between the two groups will be analyzed later in the chapter.

[5] Data from the U.S. Department of Commerce, Bureau of the Census, *Government Finances in 1959* (Washington, D.C., 1960), pp. 16, 23.

Coverage of the Analysis in Relation to Property Taxes in 1959

This analysis of property taxes is limited to study of taxes paid on residential nonfarm properties. Property taxes paid by farmers and self-employed businessmen are excluded. Most persons in both these groups would find it difficult to distinguish adequately between taxes paid on their residences and taxes paid on farm and business land, structures, machinery, equipment, and inventories.

In 1956 residential nonfarm property represented 40.2 per cent of the assessed value of all property subject to tax.[6] Assuming that the average effective tax rate is the same for all classes of property, and that the 1956 ratio of the locally assessed value to total assessed value is applicable to 1959, residential nonfarm property taxes amount to approximately $6 billion.

Procedures used to Estimate Property Taxes

For home owners the amount of property taxes paid was ascertained from the response to the question: "How much do you pay in property taxes on this house every year, including city, county, and school taxes?" Heads of families who neither own nor rent were asked whether or not they paid property taxes on the house, and if so, how much. The reliability of the response could not be checked for this sample, but the results of a similar survey, which were subjected to checking in the offices of local assessors, suggest a high level of reliability.[7]

In the case of renters who are assumed to bear the tax paid in the first instance by landlords, it would have been impossible to obtain reasonably accurate reports of the property tax paid on the dwelling occupied, so a procedure for estimating the amounts was devised.

First, the values of rental dwellings were estimated by asking home owners the value of their homes and how much it would cost them to rent a dwelling similar to the one they occupied, and then using the relationship between rental value and house value to impute house value to dwellings occupied by renters.

Effective tax rates for owner-occupied housing were estimated from property tax and house value information collected from the home owners in the sample. The effective tax rate was defined as the ratio of mean tax reported

[6] Derived from U.S. Department of Commerce, Bureau of the Census, *Property Tax Assessments in the United States: 1957 Census of Governments Advance Releases, Number 5* (Washington, 1957), pp. 13, 15.

Locally assessed real property accounted for 74.4 per cent of the total assessed value of taxable property; of that amount, 54.1 per cent was nonfarm residential.

[7] In the Detroit Area Study of 1958–1959 the home owner's estimate of his property tax was matched with the actual liability as found in the records of the local assessor for a probability sample of 487 home owners. The correlation was .78.

to mean house value reported, within a classification of sample points by urbanization and geographic area.

Estimates of the taxes paid on rental dwellings are then calculated by multiplying estimated house value by the effective tax rate for the area.[8]

The Results

Money income has been most commonly used as the basis for estimating tax incidence or distribution among income groups, largely because it has been the most readily available measure of income. Money income is used in the first set of tables presented here to provide comparability with data on the impact of other taxes. Later in the analysis gross disposable income and the ratio of income to budget needs are used because they are more meaningful concepts for the analysis of the impact of the tax and the effects of benefits.

An estimate of the incidence of the tax on residential property is presented in Table 19-1. This table suggests a rather steeply regressive distribution of the tax for family money incomes up to $5,000. A regressive tax is one which

TABLE 19-1

MEAN PROPERTY TAX, RATIO OF PROPERTY TAX TO MONEY INCOME
WITHIN MONEY INCOME
(FOR FAMILIES WHOSE HEADS ARE NEITHER FARMERS
NOR SELF-EMPLOYED BUSINESSMEN)

Money income	Number of families	Mean property tax [a]	Ratio of mean tax to mean money income
Under $1,000	208	$ 30	.057
$1,000–1,999	299	60	.040
$2,000–2,999	240	89	.036
$3,000–4,999	446	93	.023
$5,000–7,499	594	112	.018
$7,500–9,999	312	173	.020
$10,000 and over	287	253	.018
All	2,386	$123	.021

[a] actual payment for owners and families who neither own nor rent; estimated payment for renters

takes a larger proportion of income at lower income levels. Within this range, the proportion of income paid in property taxes by all families in the sample, including renters and owners, but excluding families whose heads are farmers and self-employed businessmen, drops from almost 6 per cent to 2.3 per cent.

Regression in the property tax frequently has been attributed in part to the alleged tendency to assess residences at a decreasing proportion of market

[8] See Appendix C for a detailed explanation of the estimating procedure.

TABLE 19-2

MEAN PROPERTY TAX, RATIO OF PROPERTY TAX TO HOUSE VALUE
WITHIN HOUSE VALUE
(FOR FAMILIES WHO OWN THEIR HOMES AND WHOSE HEADS
ARE NEITHER FARMERS NOR SELF-EMPLOYED BUSINESSMEN)

House value	Number of families	Mean property tax	Ratio of mean tax to mean house value
Under $3,000	81	$ 26	.015
$3,000–5,999	149	92	.021
$6,000–8,999	242	97	.013
$9,000–11,999	233	141	.014
$12,000–14,999	217	188	.015
$15,000–17,999	189	236	.015
$18,000–20,000	109	271	.014
$21,000 and over	131	385	.013
All	1,351	$177	.014

value as the latter increases.[9] However, the data presented in Table 19-2 offer little or no support for this position.[10]

Table 19-3 illustrates the impact of the property tax on different age and income groups. There appears to be a clear-cut tendency for the ratio of property tax to income to rise with advancing age. This is because people acquire bigger houses as they grow older, even relative to their income. Except for the small group with incomes under $1,000, the tax is roughly proportionate for both the under thirty-five and the thirty-five to fifty-four age groups. Some of those in the lowest income group are there only temporarily, in any case. Regression emerges again for families with heads aged fifty-five to sixty-four and less clearly for the sixty-five and older group.

The principal objective of this study of tax incidence is to determine the extent to which property taxes bring about a change in the distribution of income. For this purpose the income definition chosen is crucial. It may be argued, for example, that money income is inadequate as a measure of the family's ability to pay. It does not include such elements of income as imputed rental income of home owners, the value of goods and services produced and consumed in the home, and transfers received in goods rather than money. Nor does it make allowance for the fact that income is involuntarily reduced by the Federal income tax. The gross disposable income measure includes all of these factors and the relationship of tax to income changes appreciably when this measure of income is substituted for money income.

[9] See, for example, Harold M. Groves, *Financing Government,* 5th ed. (New York: Henry Holt and Company, Inc., 1958), pp. 57–58; and Kenyon E. Poole, *Public Finance and Economic Welfare* (New York: Rinehart & Company, Inc., 1956), p. 292.

[10] Nor do data from Surveys of Consumer Finances; see E. Scott Maynes and James Morgan, "The Effective Rate of Real Estate Taxation," *Review of Economics and Statistics,* XXXIX (February, 1957), 14–22.

TABLE 19-3

MEAN PROPERTY TAX, RATIO OF PROPERTY TAX TO MONEY INCOME
WITHIN AGE OF HEAD AND MONEY INCOME
(FOR FAMILIES WHOSE HEADS ARE NEITHER FARMERS
NOR SELF-EMPLOYED BUSINESSMEN)

Age of head and money income	Number of families	Mean property tax [a]	Ratio of mean tax to mean money income
Under 35			
Under $1,000	34	$ 16	.060
$1,000–1,999	64	24	.015
$2,000–2,999	69	44	.018
$3,000–4,999	145	67	.017
$5,000–7,499	206	100	.016
$7,500–9,999	88	127	.015
$10,000 and over	48	154	.011
All	654	$ 89	.015
35–54			
Under $1,000	47	$ 35	.081
$1,000–1,999	76	37	.024
$2,000–2,999	81	94	.039
$3,000–4,999	205	95	.024
$5,000–7,499	275	110	.018
$7,500–9,999	173	190	.022
$10,000 and over	157	292	.020
All	1,014	$145	.021
55–64			
Under $1,000	57	$ 39	.069
$1,000–1,999	64	67	.044
$2,000–2,999	36	89	.035
$3,000–4,999	57	117	.030
$5,000–7,499	84	139	.022
$7,500–9,999	37	233	.027
$10,000 and over	63	242	.017
All	398	$143	.023
65 and older			
Under $1,000	70	$ 29	.045
$1,000–1,999	95	79	.053
$2,000–2,999	54	125	.025
$3,000–4,999	39	143	.037
$5,000–7,499	29	150	.025
$7,500–9,999	14	108	.012
$10,000 and over	19	229	.014
All	320	$101	.030

[a] actual payment for owners and families who neither own nor rent; estimated payment for renters

When the imputations for gross disposable income are made, the over-all pattern of the income distribution remains the same, but substantial shifts take place in the position of individual families. The imputation for rental income from owner-occupied housing increases the gross disposable incomes of low income families by a greater proportion than it does the income of higher income families. This is mainly the result of the large net equity in a

TABLE-19-4

MEAN PROPERTY TAX, RATIO OF PROPERTY TAX TO GROSS
DISPOSABLE INCOME WITHIN GROSS DISPOSABLE INCOME
(FOR FAMILIES WHOSE HEADS ARE NEITHER FARMERS
NOR SELF-EMPLOYED BUSINESSMEN)

Gross disposable income	Number of families	Mean property tax [a]	Ratio of mean tax to mean gross disposable income
Under $1,000	127	$ 29	.048
$1,000–1,999	281	36	.024
$2,000–2,999	271	68	.027
$3,000–4,999	522	93	.023
$5,000–7,499	610	116	.019
$7,500–9,999	330	187	.022
$10,000 and over	245	270	.020
All	2,386	$123	.021

[a] actual payment for owners and families who neither own nor rent; estimated payment for renters

home and the low cash incomes of retired people. On the other hand, the
Federal income taxes deducted are greatest for those with the highest incomes.
The shift to a more adequate measure of ability to pay makes the retired with
low cash income look better off, and the high income middle-aged look less
well off after taxes.

As a consequence of these shifts, in the income range beyond $1,000 the
tax on residential property no longer appears regressive. Rather, it is roughly
proportionate.

The amount paid in property taxes is, in part, a function of the size of the
house and this, in turn, depends on the number of persons in the family.
Furthermore, the ratio of family income to budget needs is a far more appro-

TABLE 19-5

MEAN PROPERTY TAX, RATIO OF PROPERTY TAX TO GROSS
DISPOSABLE INCOME WITHIN FAMILY WELFARE RATIO
(FOR FAMILIES WHOSE HEADS ARE NEITHER FARMERS
NOR SELF-EMPLOYED BUSINESSMEN)

Family welfare ratio	Number of families	Mean property tax [a]	Ratio of mean tax to mean gross disposable income
Under 0.9	627	$ 46	.023
0.9–1.2	442	82	.020
1.3–1.6	428	118	.021
1.7–2.2	485	154	.022
2.3 and over	404	218	.020
All	2,386	$123	.020

[a] actual payment for owners and families who neither own nor rent; estimated payments for renters

priate measure of the family's economic well-being or ability to pay taxes than is income alone. The relationship between average property tax as a proportion of gross disposable income and a measure of family welfare is presented in Table 19-5. The ratio of tax to gross disposable income is virtually invariant between families grouped by the welfare ratio—the ratio of gross disposable income to budget needs. Relative to the family's level of economic well-being, the property tax is almost precisely proportionate.

The adjustment for different family sizes in the estimates of budget needs took account of the fact that within each income level the largest families tend to have the largest houses and the largest property taxes, but also the lowest income per capita or ability to pay.

Comparisons of Owner and Renters

Most survey data on property taxes have focused on nonfarm home owners, omitting the renters because of difficulties in estimating the amount of property taxes in their rent. But renters also tend to have less housing than owners. Hence it is important to look separately at the two groups.

The estimates shown in Table 19-6 suggest that renters at each income

TABLE 19-6

MEAN PROPERTY TAX, RATIO OF PROPERTY TAX TO MONEY INCOME
WITHIN HOUSING STATUS AND MONEY INCOME
(FOR FAMILIES WHOSE HEADS ARE NEITHER FARMERS
NOR SELF-EMPLOYED BUSINESSMEN)

Housing status, money income	Number of families [a]	Mean property tax [b]	Ratio of mean tax to mean money income
Owners			
Under $1,000	76	$ 53	.097
$1,000–1,999	108	99	.064
$2,000–2,999	106	149	.059
$3,000–4,999	228	137	.034
$5,000–7,499	366	151	.024
$7,500–9,999	234	216	.025
$10,000 and over	233	291	.020
All owners	1,351	$177	.026
Renters			
Under $1,000	95	$ 22	.042
$1,000–1,999	161	32	.021
$2,000–2,999	116	39	.016
$3,000–4,999	203	50	.013
$5,000–7,499	217	57	.009
$7,500–9,999	72	59	.007
$10,000 and over	52	106	.017
All renters	916	$ 51	.010

[a] 119 families who neither own nor rent are excluded
[b] actual payments for owners; estimated payments for renters

level pay less in property taxes than home owners at the same income level. Since the estimates are based on the assumption that effective property tax rates are the same on owner-occupied properties as they are on rented properties, this means that renters generally are consuming less housing than owners in each income group.

The renters, however, tend to have lower incomes than owners. Therefore, when the two groups are combined, the mixture of low income renters with lower property taxes and less housing, and higher income owners with higher property taxes and more housing, provides the impression given in Table 19-1 of considerably less regression than appears in either part of Table 19-6.

Hence, analyzing only home owners has tended to exaggerate the impression of regressivity of the property tax, particularly when imputed rental income is not included. Low income home owners are largely retired people. Other low income families are largely renters, paying lower property taxes. Hence, it is valid in assessing the incidence of the property tax, to take account of the tendency for people at higher incomes to become home owners and pay more property taxes because they have more housing.

Changing to gross disposable income makes very little difference in the

TABLE 19-7

MEAN PROPERTY TAX, RATIO OF PROPERTY TAX TO GROSS DISPOSABLE
INCOME WITHIN HOUSING STATUS AND GROSS DISPOSABLE INCOME
(FOR FAMILIES WHOSE HEADS ARE NEITHER FARMERS
NOR SELF-EMPLOYED BUSINESSMEN)

Housing status, gross disposable income	Number of families [b]	Mean property tax [a]	Ratio of mean tax to mean gross disposable income
Own			
Under $1,000	37	$ 54	.080
$1,000–1,999	77	51	.035
$2,000–2,999	115	105	.042
3,000–4,999	247	142	.035
$5,000–7,499	376	155	.025
$7,500–9,999	256	218	.025
$10,000 and over	208	292	.021
All owners	1,316	$177	.026
Rent			
Under $1,000	68	$ 21	.038
$1,000–1,999	162	30	.020
$2,000–2,999	129	41	.017
$3,000–4,999	232	49	.012
$5,000–7,499	213	58	.010
$7,500–9,999	53	71	.008
$10,000 and over	27	129	.009
All renters	884	$ 51	.011

[a] estimated payment for renters; actual payment for owners
[b] 119 families who neither own nor rent are excluded

pattern of property taxes for renters, but reduces the apparent regressivity within the home-owner group because of the imputed rental income.

Even with this improved measure of income, however, combining owners and renters into a single group as was done in Table 19-4 eliminates the spurious impression of regressivity which appears when the two groups are considered separately.

Race and Property Taxes

In view of prevailing patterns of segregation in residential housing, it is interesting to compare the incidence of the property tax between white and nonwhite families. Table 19-8 shows that the nonwhite families pay somewhat lower property taxes at each level of the welfare ratio except one. It is possible that nonwhites live in areas where fewer services are provided.

TABLE 19-8

MEAN PROPERTY TAX, RATIO OF PROPERTY TAX TO GROSS DISPOSABLE
INCOME WITHIN RACE AND FAMILY WELFARE RATIO
(FOR FAMILIES WHOSE HEADS ARE NEITHER FARMERS
NOR SELF-EMPLOYED BUSINESSMEN)

Race, family welfare ratio	Number of families	Mean property tax [a]	Ratio of mean tax to mean gross disposable income
White			
Under 0.9	397	$ 50	.026
0.9–1.2	378	83	.020
1.3–1.6	396	121	.022
1.7–2.2	458	153	.022
2.3 and over	394	219	.020
All whites	2,023	$130	.021
Nonwhite			
Under 0.9	230	$ 36	.018
0.9–1.2	64	75	.018
1.3–1.6	32	75	.013
1.7–2.2	27	164	.024
2.3 and over	10	151	.014
All nonwhites	363	$ 67	.018

[a] actual payment for owners and families who neither own nor rent; estimated payment for renters

Although more of the nonwhite families are renters, Table 19-9 shows that this is not the sole explanation for the differences. Nonwhite home owners pay lower property taxes relative to their incomes than white owners, at all welfare levels, whereas nonwhite renters pay greater property taxes relative to their incomes. If housing discrimination forces nonwhites to pay higher rents and higher house prices for equivalent housing, this would produce such a pattern of differences. Since actual rents paid were used to estimate property taxes of renters, nonwhite renters would appear to be paying more taxes. In fact, the owners of these buildings may not be paying higher taxes, if buildings are assessed according to their physical characteristics rather than the income they produce.

For owners, their reports of the property taxes they paid were used. If nonwhites, by being excluded from many areas, pay higher prices for equivalent houses, and assessors do not revise assessments upwards because of this, then nonwhites will be buying smaller homes than whites at the same income level, and will end up paying lower property taxes relative to their incomes. The tax may be just as high relative to the housing they occupy.

This hypothesis is corroborated by the fact that nonwhite owners tend to pay lower property taxes relative to what they report as house value. In the house value range of $6,000 to $12,000, white owners report taxes at about 1.35 per cent of house value, nonwhites at 1.1 per cent. The distribution of

TABLE 19-9

MEAN PROPERTY TAX, RATIO OF PROPERTY TAX TO GROSS DISPOSABLE
INCOME WITHIN HOUSING STATUS, RACE, AND FAMILY WELFARE RATIO
(FOR FAMILIES WHOSE HEADS ARE NEITHER FARMERS
NOR SELF-EMPLOYED BUSINESSMEN)

Housing status, race, family welfare ratio	Number of families [b]	Mean property tax [a]	Ratio of mean tax to mean gross disposable income
White owners			
Under 0.9	156	$ 78	.036
0.9–1.2	198	123	.028
1.3–1.6	230	170	.029
1.7–2.2	338	190	.026
2.3 and over	309	264	.023
All white owners	1,231	$183	.026
Nonwhite owners			
Under 0.9	56	$ 49	.020
0.9–1.6	38	113	.022
1.7 and over	26	177	.021
All nonwhite owners	120	$106	.021
White renters			
Under 0.9	200	$ 36	.020
0.9–1.2	161	42	.011
1.3–1.6	158	56	.011
1.7–2.2	113	63	.010
2.3 and over	78	76	.008
All white renters	710	$ 52	.011
Nonwhite renters			
Under 0.9	141	$ 30	.016
0.9–1.2	41	60	.016
1.3 and over	24	73	.012
All nonwhite renters	206	$ 45	.014

[a] actual payment for owners; estimated payment for renters
[b] 119 families who neither own nor rent are excluded

white and nonwhite owners and renters between urban and rural areas and North and South does not account for these differences. Indeed rural owners are more likely to be white than urban owners. It is possible that concentration of nonwhite renters in the high-tax central city areas would explain the high property taxes attributed to them. It must be kept in mind that the effective tax rates assumed in this analysis were estimated separately for different regions and city sizes.

Table 19-9 also shows that even within the owner and renter groups separately, there is little regression left in the impact of the property tax, except for the white owners and renters with the lowest levels of welfare. The lack of regression in the over-all tables cannot, then, be a spurious result of any underestimate of the property taxes of renters combined with varying proportions of renters. The differences in taxes between owners and renters reflect, at least in part, a tendency for owners to have more housing than renters, even within the same income groups.[11] The question of whether or not they also reflect differences in assessments between apartments and single family homes, the former largely rented and the latter largely owned, is beyond the scope of this study.

Public School Benefits

The distribution of benefits from public expenditure is difficult to measure.[12] In order to arrive at some reasonable estimate of the incidence of direct current benefits from public school expenditures, data on per capita expenditures in each sampling area were combined with information on the number of school children in each family in the sample. In the metropolitan areas, expenditures per pupil were calculated separately for the central city, and for its suburbs, arranged in a series of concentric rings or belts defined according to their distance from the central city. When there were several school districts within a belt the estimate used was an average of the expenditures for each school district. Outside the metropolitan areas expenditures were calculated by counties within each primary sampling unit.[13]

[11] See Martin David, *Family Composition and Consumption* (Amsterdam: North-Holland Publishing Co., 1961), pp. 53–81.

[12] See, for example, Musgrave and Daicoff, *Michigan Tax Study Staff Papers*.

Also, John H. Adler, "The Fiscal System, the Distribution of Income, and Public Welfare," in Kenyon E. Poole (ed.), *Fiscal Policies and the American Economy* (Englewood Cliffs, N.J., Prentice-Hall, Inc., 1951), pp. 359–409.

[13] Per capita expenditures for the school districts within each belt or county varied, of course, with an average difference within groups of about one-fifth of the over-all average, and a relative variance between one-fourth and one-fifth. Some of the differences are spurious results of differing accounting procedures, combinations of state aid, or varying transportation costs for transporting high school pupils from one district to another. A district providing high school education for neighboring districts would increase its expenditures by more than its enrollment because high school costs per pupil are greater than elementary school costs.

When there were no reporting school districts within a sampling point, the average expenditure of all reporting school districts in the county were used. This was largely a problem in rural areas.

Average public school expenditures per pupil were estimated for 133 separate areas. (See Appendix C.) The benefits from public education received by each family in the sample were determined by multiplying the per capita expenditure in its area by the number of children in the family who attend public school.

It is obviously incorrect to allocate all the benefits of public school education to the pupils' families. The parents do benefit to the extent that they would have paid for the education if it were not free. The children's increased earnings from the added education will far exceed its cost at almost any reasonable rate of discount to present values. However, society at large enjoys some benefit as well, since education assures more productive workers, a more informed electorate, and a more socially responsible community.

Furthermore, even the direct benefits are more widely spread. Some families with preschool children or children yet to come will benefit later. Other fam-

TABLE 19-10

MEAN PUBLIC SCHOOL BENEFITS, MEAN PROPERTY TAX, RATIO OF PROPERTY TAX, PUBLIC SCHOOL BENEFITS TO GROSS DISPOSABLE INCOME WITHIN HEADS' STAGE IN ADULT UNIT LIFE CYCLE (FOR FAMILIES WHOSE HEADS ARE NEITHER FARMERS NOR SELF-EMPLOYED BUSINESSMEN)

Family heads' stage in adult unit life cycle	Number of families	Mean public school benefits	Mean property tax [a]	Ratio of mean tax to mean gross disposable income	Ratio of public school benefits to gross disposable income
Unmarried, no children head under 45	146	$ 12 [b]	$ 53	.013	.003
Married, wife under 45					
No children	175	12 [b]	102	.015	.001
Children under 6	631	295	127	.020	.046
Children 6–17	271	574	167	.022	.077
Married, wife 45 or older					
Children	167	521	139	.019	.073
No children	418	8 [b]	163	.023	.001
Unmarried, head 45 or older					
No children	410	9 [b]	85	.028	.003
Unmarried					
Children	168	480	74	.019	.125
All	2,386	$212	$123	.021	.036

[a] actual payment for owners and families who neither own nor rent; estimated payment for renters

[b] school benefits for children in the family who are not members of the head's adult unit

ilies whose children have grown, benefited in the past. And the children who have grown up and formed their own families are now benefiting from their own past education. This is only one of a number of such social arrangements which must be looked at from a long-range viewpoint.

There are undoubtedly substantial differences among schools in the return for their expenditures for education. Some have higher costs, bus routes to maintain, or more activities in addition to primary and secondary education, such as adult education, recreation, or the public library. Nevertheless, the main purpose is education, and in a rough sense dollars spent represent real activities.

Table 19-10 shows the differences in importance of both public school benefits and property taxes, for families at different stages in the life cycle. Married people, particularly those who have school age children or whose children have left home, pay more property taxes because they have larger homes. Families with children of school age receive most of the current direct benefits of public schools, of course. It is this discrepancy between property taxes which are spread over time, and school benefits which appear to be concentrated, which makes the connection between the two in the voters' minds unfortunate.

Tables 19-11, 19-12, and 19-13 show differences in the impact of the benefits of free public education, when families are ranked according to three

TABLE 19-11

MEAN PUBLIC SCHOOL BENEFITS RECEIVED AND RATIO TO
MEAN MONEY INCOME WITHIN MONEY INCOME
(FOR FAMILIES WHOSE HEADS ARE NEITHER FARMERS
NOR SELF-EMPLOYED BUSINESSMEN)

Money income	Number of families	Mean public school benefits received	Ratio of mean benefits to mean income
Under $1,000	208	$ 54	.101
$1,000–1,999	299	101	.067
$2,000–2,999	240	175	.070
$3,000–4,999	446	203	.051
$5,000–7,499	594	277	.045
$7,500–9,999	312	261	.031
$10,000 and over	287	220	.015
All	2,386	$212	.035

different income measures: money income, gross disposable income, and the welfare ratio. The progressivity, or extent to which the benefits per dollar of income go to low income families, appears a little smaller when families are ranked by gross disposable income rather than by money income. When families are grouped according to their welfare ratio the progressivity appears much greater. Even the average dollar amounts of benefits per family are greater for those with the lower levels of economic welfare. These are large

TABLE 19-12

MEAN PUBLIC SCHOOL BENEFITS RECEIVED AND RATIO TO MEAN
GROSS DISPOSABLE INCOME WITHIN GROSS DISPOSABLE INCOME
(FOR FAMILIES WHOSE HEADS ARE NEITHER FARMERS
NOR SELF-EMPLOYED BUSINESSMEN)

Gross disposable income	Number of families	Mean public school benefits	Ratio of mean benefits to mean gross disposable income
Under $1,000	127	$ 54	.087
$1,000–1,999	281	79	.053
$2,000–2,999	271	145	.057
$3,000–4,999	522	185	.044
$5,000–7,499	610	259	.041
$7,500–9,999	330	309	.034
$10,000 and over	245	239	.017
All	2,386	$212	.035

TABLE 19-13

MEAN PUBLIC SCHOOL BENEFITS AND RATIO TO GROSS DISPOSABLE
INCOME WITHIN FAMILY WELFARE RATIO
(FOR FAMILIES WHOSE HEADS ARE NEITHER FARMERS
NOR SELF-EMPLOYED BUSINESSMEN)

Family welfare ratio	Number of families	Mean public school benefits	Ratio of mean benefits to mean gross disposable income
Under 0.9	627	$251	.128
0.9–1.2	442	289	.069
1.3–1.6	428	225	.041
1.7–2.2	485	184	.026
2.3 and over	404	108	.010
All	2,386	$212	0.35

families with more children in school. The benefits of free public education appear to go largely to those who would find it hardest to pay for them.

The tendency for the benefits of free education to be concentrated among families with the greatest need persists even when white and nonwhite home owners and renters are considered separately. Nonwhite families benefit disproportionately, both absolutely and relative to their income levels, from the provision of free public education (Table 19-14). They have more children in the public schools, and the average nonwhite family lives in a community where the expenditure per pupil is only 3 per cent less than it is for whites. In the South, the inability to separate white and nonwhite school expenditures within school districts or counties may cause some underestimation of real differences that exist in segregated systems. However, insistence on separate but equal facilities may be narrowing the gap.

TABLE 19-14

MEAN PUBLIC SCHOOL BENEFITS AND RATIO OF BENEFITS TO GROSS
DISPOSABLE INCOME WITHIN HOUSING STATUS, RACE, AND
FAMILY WELFARE RATIO
(FOR FAMILIES WHOSE HEADS ARE NEITHER FARMERS
NOR SELF-EMPLOYED BUSINESSMEN)

Housing status, race, family welfare ratio	Number of families [a]	Mean public school benefits	Ratio of mean school benefits to mean gross disposable income
White owners			
Under 0.9	156	$239	.108
0.9–1.2	198	339	.076
1.3–1.6	230	286	.048
1.7–2.2	338	223	.030
2.3 and over	309	122	.010
All white owners	1,231	$231	.029
Nonwhite owners			
Under 0.9	56	$348	.136
0.9–1.6	38	528	.101
1.7 and over	26	155	.019
All nonwhite owners	120	$362	.072
White renters			
Under 0.9	200	$219	.119
0.9–1.2	161	202	.049
1.3–1.6	158	131	.025
1.7–2.2	113	89	.014
2.3 and over	78	46	.005
All white renters	710	$150	.030
Nonwhite renters			
Under 0.9	141	$329	.167
0.9–1.2	41	261	.062
1.3 and over	24	148	.022
All nonwhite renters	206	$283	.085

[a] 119 families who neither own nor rent are excluded

These data on public school expenditures per pupil indicate some limitation in the degree to which education facilitates mobility and opportunity. Differences in the costs of living between different communities in this country are relatively small. To the extent that differences in teachers' salaries represent differences in real salary levels, they also may indicate differences in the quality of the teaching. Because salary levels largely determine the level of public school expenditures, a part of the difference in expenditure per pupil represents differences in the quality of the education being received by the children. Table 19-15 shows that the spending units with lower incomes generally live in areas where the public school expenditures per pupil are also lower. Hence, the degree to which education equalizes opportunity is something less than it might be. The children of high income families not only receive more stimulation and help at home, but they tend to go to public

TABLE 19-15

MEAN PUBLIC SCHOOL EXPENDITURE PER PUPIL WITHIN
SPENDING UNIT'S GROSS DISPOSABLE INCOME
(FOR SPENDING UNITS)

Spending unit gross disposable income	Number of spending units	Mean public school expenditure per pupil	Proportion of spending units in each group with children in public school
Under $1,000	173	$276	13
$1,000–1,999	410	293	18
$2,000–2,999	395	307	24
$3,000–4,999	688	315	31
$5,000–7,499	687	328	42
$7,500–9,999	357	339	52
$10,000–14,999	208	333	48
$15,000 and over	79	337	33
All	2,997	$318	35

schools which offer a somewhat better quality of education.[14] However, the differences are relatively small.

Over-all, the estimates of public school expenditures may conceal some variation within an area or within school districts, but any substantial differences between large and small cities, suburbs and open country, North and South, should appear in the data. The relatively small differences result partly from the fact that differences in family incomes within the subareas are much greater than is popularly supposed. Some low income people live in high income school districts and vice versa. Also, in many areas state aid equalizes school expenditures through more aid to poorer school districts.

It is still possible that expenditures per pupil differ from one school to another within a school district, particularly where segregation still exists, but the inefficiencies of rural schools and of "separate but equal" facilities may even lead to larger but inefficient expenditures per pupil where family incomes are low.

In addition, the quality of education per dollar may be affected by the cultural and educational level of the community, so that schools containing largely uneducated or low income families may find it difficult to produce as much real education per dollar spent.

The fact that children of the highest income families attend schools where expenditures per child are 6 per cent above average, and children in the lowest income families go to schools where the expenditure per child is 13 per cent below average, must therefore be interpreted cautiously. Yet, it seems clear that some difference in educational opportunity probably exists and perpetuates differences from one generation to the next.

[14] For a variety of data on inequality of opportunity in public schools, see Patricia C. Sexton, *Education and Income* (New York: The Viking Press, Inc., 1961).

Table 19-16 shows a similarly slight but evident tendency for the highly educated to live where the public schools spend more per child. Except for the spending unit heads with no education the differences in expenditures range from 5 per cent below average to 5 per cent above average.

TABLE 19-16

MEAN PUBLIC SCHOOL EXPENDITURE PER PUPIL
WITHIN EDUCATION OF HEAD
(FOR SPENDING UNITS)

Education of head	Number of spending units	Mean public school expenditure per pupil
None	56	$286
1–8 grades	972	302
9–11 grades	615	321
12 grades	451	331
12 grades and nonacademic training	263	330
Some college	340	327
College, bachelor's degree	225	324
College, advanced degree	75	332
All	2,997	$318

Summary

The regressive nature of the property tax, so long accepted as fact, is not upheld by an analysis which includes renters and takes account of the imputed rental income resulting from the owner's equity in his own home, of Federal income tax liability, and of family size and structure, in assessing ability to pay. The property tax is not particularly inequitable between high and low value residential properties. Nor does it represent a higher proportion of incomes of lower income than higher income families.

The importance of selecting the most meaningful income measure is illustrated by the fact that the regressivity which appeared when money income was used was reduced substantially when nonmoney components of family income were taken into consideration and all but eliminated when the unit's welfare ratio was used.

The data do not show the relative equity of taxes paid on residential property compared to other forms of property, nor possible inequities resulting from erratic local assessments. Whether these two inequities exist or not will require further study and investigation, but the findings of this study indicate that the existence of such inequities should not be assumed without further evidence.

The current direct benefits of free public education go largely to families with high absolute incomes but lower welfare ratios. The current situation is not irrelevant if one is considering whether families could finance for themselves the education of their children. It is somewhat less relevant for comparing benefits with property taxes, since parents benefit currently, in this sense, only when their children are in school, but pay taxes all their lives. The average results of this process are difficult to unravel, but are probably more equitable than most people realize.

It is clear that the nonwhites benefit more both absolutely and relatively from free public education. Free public education is a powerful redistributive force, both in the short run for the parents and later through its effect on the future earnings of the pupils. The data herein produce evidence of only a mild tendency for the disadvantaged to receive education of slightly lower cost per child.

Comparisons of property taxes and school benefits of the same individuals have been neglected for a number of reasons. Not all property taxes are used for schools, and not all school expenditures are financed from property taxes. Also some property taxes paid on nonresidential property support the schools. Families pay taxes every year, but the direct benefits of public education can be measured and assessed only during the years when the family's children are actually in school. Since most people have children, and they tend to have more housing and pay more property taxes if they have more children, it seems unlikely that any substantial inequity exists from this system.

Chapter 20

INCOME INEQUALITY—THE EFFECT OF UNIT OF ANALYSIS AND MEASURE OF INCOME

Inequality in the distribution of the fruits of an economic system among its people needs to be properly measured because it is an important phenomenon. It is important for a number of reasons.

First, any economy which relies upon market prices and demands to indicate what producers should produce, must justify such a system of allocation on the grounds that market demands backed by money represent valid indicators of social need. It is therefore necessary though not entirely adequate to assume that people have incomes sufficient to cover their basic needs, and extra income to reward them for special services to society. Extreme inequality would cast doubt on the validity of this assumption.

Secondly, since the market mechanism rewards productive effort and contributions of individuals, and of their accumulated capital assets, the distribution of factor incomes currently earned is never adequately distributed relative to needs. A complex system of transfers of income—public and private, voluntary and compulsory, contributory and noncontributory—exists. It is important not only to assess the resulting inequality after these transfers, but also to know just how much effect transfers have on the distribution of purchasing power among families. The redistribution of income so effected will alter the kinds of commodities demanded in the markets of the country, and may also affect the aggregate consumption and investment demands and the rate of economic growth.

Finally, proper measures of inequality, independent of institutions or units of measurement, are important in determining differences between countries, or between different periods of time in the same country. A measure should be relatively independent of differences in family living arrangements, or of differences in the relative importance of money as against nonmoney income.

The Definition of Inequality

Previous work on the development of a measure of inequality was referred to in Chapter 2. The search for the best single measure of the extent to which income is concentrated in the receipts of a few high income families led to the Lorenz curve, and to the Lorenz coefficient or Gini index. The Lorenz curve shows the cumulated fraction of aggregate income plotted against the cumulated proportion of families, when families are arranged in ascending order by income. It is a straight line bisecting a square area if all incomes are equal, or the bottom and right side of a square if one unit receives all the income and the others receive nothing. In practice, it is a sagging curve, which has more sag, the more inequality exists. (See Figure 20-1.)

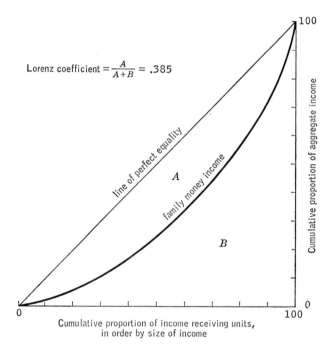

Figure 20-1. Lorenz curve and coefficient of inequality for family money income.

Use of the whole curve has the advantage of showing changes that concentrate at one end of the distribution. During the Depression of the thirties, smaller profits reduced inequality at the top, but unemployment increased it at the bottom. However, the Lorenz curves associated with different income measures are difficult to distinguish graphically and a single numerical measure is desirable. The Lorenz coefficient or Gini index is defined as the proportion of the triangular area which is between the curve and the diagonal line.

In Figure 20-1 it would be the ratio of area A to area A plus B. A simple method of approximating these areas was given by Woytinsky and a still simpler method by one of the authors.[1] The straightforward mathematical properties of the Lorenz coefficient and its simple geometric interpretation, combined with the intuitive meaningfulness of the definition even for extreme cases, assured the measure's acceptance. Some have felt the measure is too insensitive, but others point out that by the nature of the problem it is affected markedly by a few very high incomes. The second is an important problem because survey data do not provide precise estimates about high income families.

In practice, the Lorenz coefficient has proved remarkably stable when estimated from surveys by different agencies and at different points in time. It has also been shown to be little affected by changing distributions of age or occupation within the population.[2]

Clearly the measurement of inequality will depend upon the income receiving unit used, and the definition of income. This chapter will show that the use of families rather than more nuclear units tends to understate inequality, and that failure to take account of nonmoney income tends to exaggerate inequality.

Inequality Depends on the Unit of Analysis

The proper unit of analysis depends upon the purpose for which an inequality measure is desired. Family units are the conventional base for many income statistics and represent the unit which shares decisions concerning living arrangements and means of support. It is easier to measure family income than to allocate capital income or imputed rent among smaller units. Decisions made about living with relatives represent an adjustment to economic circumstances, the result of which is represented in the family income distribution.

However, families consisting of more than one adult unit are continually being formed as children reach their eighteenth birthdays and continue to live at home, or as people move in to live with their relatives. At the same time other families are dividing into separate families as children leave home, or other changes occur.

Perhaps the least stable family unit is one containing more than one

[1] W. S. Woytinsky, *Earnings and Social Security in the United States* (Washington: Social Science Research Council, 1943), Appendix;

James N. Morgan, "The Anatomy of Income Distribution," *Review of Economics and Statistics*, XLIV (August, 1962), Appendix;

For a mathematical definition of the measure, see Morris G. Kendall, *Advanced Theory of Statistics*, Vol. 1 (New York: Hafner Publishing Company, 1943), pp. 42–44.

[2] James N. Morgan, *Review of Economics and Statistics* (August, 1962);

Also see Lee Soltow, "The Distribution of Income Related to Changes in the Distribution of Education, Age, and Occupation," *Review of Economics and Statistics*, XLII (November, 1960). 450–453.

spending unit. A secondary spending unit by definition has separate finances and some income. Many are children about to marry and establish a household of their own.

Spending units are the natural units for decisions about major expenditures on cars and durables, saving, and so forth. Hence, they are the units most commonly used in the Surveys of Consumer Finances of the Survey Research Center for the past fifteen years. During this time, the proportion of families with related secondary spending units has been cut in half as the housing shortage eased and prosperity continued.[3]

Any adult or adult couple is a potentially distinct household. The adult unit or nuclear family is therefore a basic unit, and measures of inequality using adult units indicate what the distribution of income might be if no one lived with relatives. Not only has prosperity and more housing brought a great reduction in the proportion of adults living with relatives, but most people are opposed to the ideas of having parents live with their children. (See Chapter 14.)

Liabilities and benefits of public tax and transfer programs are also generally computed on an adult unit basis. Indeed, once one leaves the family unit, there are persuasive reasons to move all the way to the adult unit, since dependent adult units which are not spending units are the most likely to be unwillingly living with relatives under the pressure of economic circumstances—being unable to afford a separate household.[4]

Because of changes over time in the number of secondary spending units and dependent adult units, Lorenz coefficients calculated from family units would not be comparable for different points in time. And because family patterns differ between countries and between subareas, such comparisons of family Lorenz curves would also be distorted.

Any attempt to disaggregate further from adult units to individual adults appears nearly impossible because of the pooling of resources in the nuclear family and the joint obligation to provide for children.

It is true, of course, that the number of adult units is not completely independent of economic conditions. Marriage and divorce rates are somewhat affected by the level of the unit's income. Thus the combination of two adult units into one husband-wife couple, and the dissolution of couples by divorce and separation may depend on the distribution of income.[5] However, marriages are concentrated among younger people, and separations are relatively infrequent, and dissolution of marriages through death is determined primarily

[3] Survey Research Center, *1960 Survey of Consumer Finances* (Ann Arbor: University of Michigan, 1961), p. 259.

[4] Census statistics on the number of adults living with relatives show that increased separation into component adult units has taken place over the last ten years. See *U.S. Census of the Population: 1960,* "General Population Characteristics, U.S. Summary, Final Report" (U.S. Bureau of the Census, 1961), p. xvi.

[5] Guy Orcutt and others, *Microanalysis of Socioeconomic Systems* (New York: Harper & Brothers, Inc., 1961), pp. 99–102.

by noneconomic factors. Hence, the adult unit is more stable than the family which may absorb or discharge adult units at any time without legal process.

The effect of dividing one family income into two or more spending unit or adult unit incomes would not lead inevitably to increased inequality estimates. In practice, however, the units which are split off, particularly dependent adults, have so little income that the use of a finer unit produces larger inequality estimates, even if one assumes that when living separately they would still receive the same amount of help from their relatives.

Since this effect is confounded with the effects of different measures of income, the next section deals with measures of income and the following section with the actual results of varying the unit, the measure, or both.

Inequality Depends on the Measure of Income Used

Most survey data on income are restricted to money income, including some but not all transfer incomes. Regular payments from retirement pensions, annuities, social security, alimony, or even welfare are included, but not irregular gifts or free housing. Since the purpose of most inequality measures is not to assess the distribution of rewards from productive effort, it is not a matter for concern that the earnings of more than one person are involved, or that income from capital and transfer incomes are included.

But if one is interested in the distribution of control over the goods and services available for consumption, the use of money income understates the real resources available to units which own their own home, or have other nonmoney income from home production, free medical care, or food and housing by living with relatives. For dependent adult units, the free food and housing provided by their relatives are frequently the major or only source of income.

Gross factor income can be thought of as income earned by the unit's labor and capital. In addition to earned money income it includes the real income earned by savings resulting from home grown food or home repairs. But it does not include transfer incomes.

Table 20-1 shows for each level of gross factor income the amounts of transfer income from outside the dwelling and from other units of the family within the dwelling. The latter consists mostly of estimated free food and housing given to or received from the relatives with whom people live. The table also shows the estimated mean income tax paid by adult units at each gross factor income level. The income tax was estimated using tax tables and applying the gross taxable income and number of dependents for each case. Estimated deductions were assumed to be the same fraction of gross taxable income as the average reported for that taxable income level.[6]

6 U.S. Treasury Department, "Individual Income Tax Returns," *Statistics of Income* (1959). See Appendix C.

TABLE 20-1

MEAN GROSS FACTOR INCOME, NONFAMILY TRANSFER INCOME, NET
INTRAFAMILY TRANSFERS, INCOME TAX, GROSS DISPOSABLE INCOME
WITHIN GROSS FACTOR INCOME
(FOR ADULT UNITS)

Gross factor income	Number of adult units	Gross factor income	Nonfamily transfer income	Net intra-family transfers	Income tax	Gross disposable income
None	311	$ 0	$669	$ 440	$ 0	$ 1,109
$1–499; negative	291	143	749	188	0	1,079
$500–999	252	714	870	87	5	1,666
$1,000–1,999	359	1,456	823	12	43	2,248
$2,000–2,999	287	2,460	406	− 2	131	2,734
$3,000–4,999	531	3,984	314	− 59	312	3,927
$5,000–7,499	617	6,110	230	− 76	576	5,688
$7,500–9,999	354	8,584	115	−121	950	7,628
$10,000–14,999	273	11,768	164	−128	1,507	10,297
$15,000 and over	121	23,004	295	−179	4,922	18,198
All adult units	3,396	$ 5,191	$407	$ 0	$ 612	$ 4,986

Gross disposable income results from adding transfer income to gross factor income and deducting income tax. It is the most complete estimate of the unit's control over goods and services it may want to consume. One might deduct nonfamily contributions to derive net real income, but since these contributions are assumed to be completely voluntary, they can be considered a disposition of income rather than deduction from it. They are also so well distributed that their deduction has practically no effect on the Lorenz coefficient.

It is clear that income taxes and transfers tend to make the distribution of income more nearly equal. The effects of nonmoney incomes are not derivable from the table but tend in the same direction.

The Unit, the Measure and Inequality—the Findings

The actual Lorenz coefficients for each of the three units of analysis and for the most important income concepts are given in Table 20-2. Inequality estimates are somewhat larger on a spending unit basis than on a family basis, and a great deal larger on an adult unit basis than on a spending unit basis. This results from the lower incomes of the secondary units, particularly the dependent adult units. It is true even when the income measure includes all the transfers. Free food and housing is included in gross disposable income. This is equivalent to assuming that family help would continue even if the units were separated.

Adult units tend to live with related adult units when the income of one or both units is low. Combining their incomes thus tends to hide the fact that

TABLE 20-2

LORENZ COEFFICIENTS OF INEQUALITY FOR VARIOUS UNITS
OF ANALYSIS AND MEASURES OF INCOME

	Adult units	Spending units	Families
Gross factor income	.485	.431	.419
Less: imputed rent of home owners			
Less: home production			
Plus: regular money transfers			
= Money income	.448	.393	.385
Less: Federal income taxes			
= Disposable money income	.422	.363	.355
Plus: imputed rent of home owners			
Plus: home production			
Plus: nonmoney and irregular transfers including food and housing provided by relatives			
= Gross disposable income	.402	.353	.346
Divided by budget standard			
= Welfare ratio	.346	...	.309

such low incomes exist, as well as to reduce the difficulty they cause. Even at the adult unit level, the inequality of gross factor income reflects more than the distribution of productive skills and income-earning capital, because the earnings of working wives are included.

The differences between inequality measures in the first two rows—gross factor income versus money income—result from the fact that the equalizing effects of regular money transfer income which is added are more powerful than those of nonmoney earnings (home production and imputed rent) which are deducted to arrive at money income.

The differences between the inequality measures when one goes from money income to disposable money income show the equalizing effect of Federal income taxation.

The further reduction in inequality when imputed rent, and home production are reintroduced and nonmoney and irregular transfers added to form gross disposable income is much greater for adult units than for family units. The reason is that most of the effect is from intrafamily transfers which cancel out for all the adult units in each family, but still make a difference on an adult unit basis. This demonstrates the fact that the separation of families into adult units requires dealing with transfers made within the family.

The estimates of intrafamily transfers are probably underestimates, since they include only the value of food and housing provided, minus any return payments. A more thorough analysis of the help provided to relatives living in the same household would provide gross disposable income estimates for adult units with somewhat less inequality, and hence somewhat closer to the measures for gross disposable income of families.

However, the estimate of .402 for the inequality in the distribution of gross disposable income among adult units remains the most fundamental and stable measure. Offsetting adjustments make it close in size to the inequality of family money income, but this might not be true in other countries or other periods of history. Figure 20-2 compares the three most extreme measures.

Comparison with Data from Tax Returns

All these coefficients are based on estimates of shares of income which are particularly sensitive to a few very high incomes, and hence have substantial sampling errors. Therefore, it is interesting to examine the Lorenz coefficient for Federal income statistics based on all income tax returns filed, although comparability with the coefficient shown in Table 20-2 is limited by the exclusion from the Federal data of the units which file no returns. The Federal statistics of adjusted gross income exclude transfer and nonmoney income and are on a tax return basis, rather than a family basis, closer to the gross factor income concept on an adult unit basis. The preliminary data for 1959 individual income tax returns give a coefficient of .424.[7]

Inequality of Income or of Welfare?

If the purpose of inequality measures is to assess the justice or the mercy with which the good things of society are distributed, then there are two shortcoming of any measure of command over real goods and services. First, the needs of adult units differ, depending on the number, ages, and sexes of the unit's members. Secondly, different units will devote different amounts of time and energy to earning their incomes. While it is true that some people enjoy their jobs more than others, and that leisure may be an unwanted and unappreciated commodity to the unemployed, it is not a matter of indifference how many hours of work were devoted to earning the family income.

An analysis of work and leisure is presented in Chapter 21. The inequality of income relative to needs, however, can be treated by treating the welfare ratio—the ratio of gross disposable income to a budget standard of needs—as a quantity and assessing the inequality in its distribution. The last line in Table 20-2 provides estimated Lorenz coeffiicents for the welfare ratio.

The adjustment for needs, largely for different family sizes, produces an estimate of inequality far smaller even than the estimates based on gross disposable income. One can think of the welfare ratio as a measure of supernumerary income, and a measure of the inequality of the welfare ratio as measuring the egalitarianism in the distribution of satisfaction, if satisfaction depends on one's income relative to his needs.

[7] Data from *Individual Income Tax Returns for 1959,* Publication #198, Internal Revenue Service (U.S. Treasury Department, 1961), Table 1, p. 12.

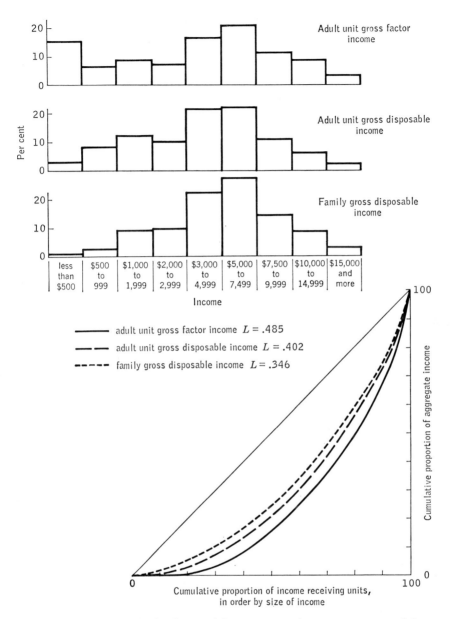

Figure 20-2. Percentage distributions and Lorenz curves for some measures of income (for adult units and families).

One Year versus Lifetime Income

The distribution of one year's income for a cross section of the population reflects the inequality in current new command over goods and services, but does not indicate the distribution or inequality in lifetime incomes. Entirely apart from short run fluctuations resulting from illness, unemployment, or more fortunate temporary events, a more important problem is that a cross section includes the low incomes of the young and the very old, and the higher incomes of the middle-aged.

One way to approach this problem is to look at the inequality within age groups. Since there are differential rates of promotion and advancement between individuals, and since some people accumulate assets which also earn income, it is reasonable to expect that incomes will become increasingly unequal from one age group to the next. This tendency has been shown to exist in the data. More detailed examination by one of the authors of this book has shown, moreover, that much of the increase in inequality is the result of the impact of extra earners, and of less than full year work, the latter much more common among those with less formal education.[8]

Since education affects both the level of earnings and the extent to which individuals may be affected by unemployment, it is instructive to look at measures of inequality for different age-education groups separately, as in Table 20-3.

TABLE 20-3

LORENZ MEASURES OF INEQUALITY IN THE DISTRIBUTION OF GROSS FACTOR INCOME WITHIN AGE AND EDUCATION OF HEADS (FOR ADULT UNITS)

Age of heads	Education of heads		
	0–11 grades	12 grades	Some college
Under 45	.446	.362	.367
45–64	.441	.432	.370
65 and older		.716	

The inequality of the distribution of gross factor income within each of seven groups according to age and education is shown by the Lorenz coefficients. There is no necessary connection between the value of these Lorenz coefficients and the coefficient shown for the entire population in Table 20-2. Because of differences in mean *amounts* of income, two groups which have perfectly equally distributed incomes separately may have a Lorenz coefficient anywhere from zero to one when combined. Conversely, two groups each with perfectly unequally distributed incomes, when combined may have a Lorenz coefficient of substantially less than one.

[8] See Morgan, *Review of Economics and Statistics* (August, 1962).

The extreme inequality among adult units headed by someone sixty-five or older is the expected result of the cumulated lifetime differences in accumulation of capital, and the fact that some are still working. Among the rest, inequality appears much more strongly a function of education level than of age. The increased differentials by age are thus seen to be largely associated with differences between those with different amounts of education.

It should not be inferred that age differences in inequality do not exist. Those associated with education differences have been removed from Table 20-3 by separating educational levels. The broad age ranges used may hide the remaining differences. The large inequality measures for those under forty-five result from the large differences between the earnings of those aged twenty-five and those aged forty. In the range from forty-five to sixty-four years of age, the mean differences between individuals of different ages are smaller and the inequality measure is more dominated by differences between individuals.

Not only is some of the inequality in gross factor income the result of differences according to education level, but within educational groups, it is those with low education which show the most internal inequality. This results from the unequal incidence of unemployment, disability, and sickness, which affect the uneducated and unskilled the most.

The transfer system and the Federal income tax system alter these distributions. Because it is the intent of these tax and transfer systems to reduce the inequality of well-being of families with incomes above and below average, it is instructive to examine the Lorenz coefficients for those same groups calculated for gross disposable income, which includes the effects of these transfers and the income tax. Table 20-4 shows the effect.

TABLE 20-4

LORENZ MEASURES OF INEQUALITY IN DISTRIBUTION OF GROSS DISPOSABLE INCOME WITHIN AGE AND EDUCATION OF HEADS (FOR ADULT UNITS)

	Education of heads		
Age of heads	0–11 grades	12 grades	Some college
Under 45	.378	.302	.316
45–64	.380	.386	.338
65 and older		.469	

The greatest reduction in inequality is, of course, among those sixty-five and older. Retirement pensions and imputed rent on net equity in an owned home are most important for this group.

Among the remaining groups, the extent to which inequality estimates are reduced by taking account of transfers and Federal income taxes is greater for the less educated and the younger. The reduction is not simply proportional to the original extent of inequality. The young high school graduates had the most nearly equal distribution of gross factor income, and a further substantial reduction in inequality from taxes and transfers.

These young high school graduates are somewhat more likely than those with less education to have jobs which qualify them for unemployment compensation, and somewhat more likely than those with more education to be unemployed so that they actually receive compensation. They also attain a normal stable earning level sooner than those with less education and are less likely to be farmers.

On the other hand, older high school graduates are more likely to report declining earnings. These declines, which result from layoffs, sickness, and lower employability affect some but not all individuals, and may account for the greater inequality of their incomes and the smaller impact of transfers in reducing it.

The units headed by highly educated older people start with less inequality than most, but their inequality is least affected by taxes and transfers. Differential impacts of other income, particularly the earnings of the wife, are also involved, since these are adult unit incomes.

Summary

The use of family units rather than some smaller more basic unit tends to understate the degree of inequality in the distribution of income, regardless of the measure of income used.

On the other hand, failure to include estimates of nonmoney income leads to exaggeration of the degree of inequality, whatever the unit of analysis used.

Even though these two effects largely offset each other in the present-day United States, they may well be important sources of distortion in intertemporal or international comparisons of income distribution. Increasing home ownership, and decreasing amounts of home production have real effects which would not be recorded in money incomes. More important, there may be greater combining of households because of recession or wartime housing shortage, or the separation of complex households into nuclear units because of increased transfer programs. These changes would produce apparent but largely spurious differences in the distribution of family income. Using real income of adult units mitigates these difficulties.

Second, the comparison of levels of income in different countries can be done most accurately by measuring income for adult units. This would avoid spurious differences in income inequality resulting from differences in living arrangements and housing conditions.

In addition, all the measures tend to exaggerate the inequality in the distribution of welfare by failing to take account of differences in needs. Families with the lowest incomes are also generally smaller, so that the distribution of the walfare ratio is less unequal than that of gross disposable income.

The final assessment of the distribution of current welfare must take account of the amount of work devoted to earning the unit's income. The analysis of total hours spent earning income appears in Chapter 21.

While one-year incomes are a measure of current new control over consumption goods and services, and relevant for many welfare considerations, lifetime incomes are also of interest. Cross section data allow only rough indications of inequality in lifetime incomes through examination of levels and inequality for different age groups. The differential effects of education on earnings and on the impact of unemployment appear to account for much of the difference in lifetime earnings.

Finally, evaluation of the unit's ability to pay for socially desirable goods, such as higher education or adequate medical care, can best be determined by relating the unit's income to some estimate of its budget requirement.

Chapter 21

TIME: THE THIRD DIMENSION OF WELFARE

The level of welfare enjoyed by a family cannot be measured without taking account of the time spent by the family in earning its income. That is, a given amount of time is an essential part of the family's resources and the total real income of a family includes its leisure time.

Leisure is difficult to define precisely. It is even more difficult to attach a value to it. Some people enjoy work; some are bored by leisure. Some people's hobbies are both productive and enjoyable. It is possible to work and relax simultaneously, for example, by reading while watching children, or by ironing while looking at television.

Without attempting to solve these numerous problems one can still relate a minimal estimate of working time to families' levels of welfare as measured in the previous chapters. Table 21-1 shows a distribution of total hours that adult units spent earning real income in 1959. The distributions are shown separately for married and single adult units, since married adult units have twice as much time to spend. Units with and without children are also shown separately, since the time demands of housekeeping differ for the two groups.

The hours include the time spent by the head and wife in paid employment and in growing food or repairing the home. The estimate of hours of home production is conservative, based on the assumption of one hour per dollar saved. Many do-it-yourself projects are inefficient in terms of yield per hour, but additional time used was assumed to be recreational rather than productive.

The fact that people enjoy their work or home production is not a relevant objection to studying their work hours. Work hours are a measure of productive effort, without which the real goods and services available to the unit would be less.

In previous studies, far more attention has been given to the wife's work involving participation in the employed labor force than to time spent in household tasks or home production.

Even the hours in Table 21-1 take no account of the time spent in housework and child care. Yet such time is economically productive in the same sense that growing food or repairing the house is. In order to devote less time to housework and child care, a wife would have to pay someone else to do it, a maid or the producers of TV dinners, or suffer a decrease in the family's real income through less careful housekeeping. The amount of time required for housework and child care depends, of course, upon whether there are preschool or school children in the home. Economically speaking, the com-

TABLE 21-1

HOURS WORKED WITHIN MARITAL STATUS AND AGE OF CHILDREN

| | Marital status and age of children | | | | | |
| | Single | | Married | | | |
Hours worked in 1959 [a]	No children	Children	No children	Children under 6	Children all over 6	All adult units
None	33	20	7	0	0	14
1–949	21	24	11	1	3	11
950–1,949	15	24	12	10	8	13
1,950–2,949	29	28	35	53	41	36
2,950–3,949	2	3	13	21	23	12
3,950–5,949	0	0	20	12	20	11
5,950 and over	0	0	1	2	4	2
Not ascertained	0	1	1	1	1	1
Total	100	100	100	100	100	100
Number of adult units	1,118	210	758	759	551	3,396

[a] total hours of head and wife, including home production but not housekeeping

parison of families with and without children requires both treating the time spent in child care as productive activity, and including in real income the satisfaction of seeing one's children grow and develop. Because there is no way to value such satisfaction, it has been ignored in this analysis and only the total time that might reasonably be required for housework and child care has been included. One justification for this is that the satisfactions from having children are spread over time, while the investment of time in their care is concentrated during a few years, so that the apparently worse over-all position of those with children which results from this procedure may be true in the short run.

Little is known about how people spend their time. Hence there is little information on which to base estimates of the time required for housework, particularly for units with preschool children at home. Small children require supervision twenty-four hours a day but not to the exclusion of other activities.

Many studies of the use of time by homemakers have been made, largely from the point of view of efficiency and time budgeting. Some of them examine the effect of a wife's labor force participation on the time she devotes to household tasks, and the extent to which her husband helps.[1] There is little evidence that working wives use shortcuts in their housework more extensively than nonworking wives. Historical studies of changing patterns of labor force participation of wives have discussed the growing ease of housework and the fewer hours required for it.[2]

In order to improve estimates of the total time spent in some productive activity, it was necessary to take account of differences in the time required for housekeeping and child care. The following crude estimates were made about the minimal time required for housekeeping and child care:

Single person with no children	500 hours a year
Married couple, no children	1,000 hours a year
Married couple with school children all 6 or older, or single adult with children	1,500 hours a year
Married couple with preschool children	2,000 hours a year

These estimates are quite conservative since only an irreducible minimum of necessary time was desired here.

Tables 21-2 and 21-3 show the effect of adding these estimates to the estimates of time spent earning money or producing food or home repairs.

It seems clear from Tables 21-2 and 21-3 that some people achieve high levels of welfare, in terms of real income relative to needs, by devoting more

[1] Francena L. Nolan and Dawn H. Tuttle, *Certain Practices, Satisfactions, and Difficulties in Families with Employed Homemakers,* Pennsylvania State College of Agriculture, Experimental Station Bulletin #655 (August, 1959);

Alva Myrdal and Viola Klein, *Women's Two Roles* (London: Routledge and Kegan Paul, Ltd., 1956).

[2] Stanley Lebergott, "Population and Labor Force Relationships," *Demographic and Economic Change in Developed Countries* (Princeton: Princeton University Press, 1960).

TABLE 21-2

TOTAL ADULT UNIT WORK HOURS INCLUDING HOUSEKEEPING,
WITHIN ADULT UNIT WELFARE RATIO
(PERCENTAGE DISTRIBUTION OF ADULT UNITS WHOSE HEADS
ARE SINGLE)

Total work hours including housekeeping	Adult unit welfare ratio					All adult units whose heads are single
	Less than .9	.9–1.2	1.3–1.5	1.6–2.0	2.1 and over	
949 or less	58	33	20	14	15	40
950–1,849	20	17	10	11	4	15
1,850–2,149	4	9	8	7	5	6
2,150–2,949	11	26	42	54	49	27
2,950–3,949	5	12	18	11	19	10
3,950–5,949	2	2	2	2	5	2
5,950 and more	0	0	0	0	2	0
Not ascertained	0	1	0	1	1	0
Total	100	100	100	100	100	100
Number of adult units	737	208	116	132	135	1,328

hours to productive efforts, and that others with relatively low real income relative to needs, are working less than average. It is not possible to distinguish here between voluntary and involuntary substitutions of free time for income.

TABLE 21-3

TOTAL ADULT UNIT WORK HOURS INCLUDING HOUSEKEEPING,
WITHIN ADULT UNIT WELFARE RATIO
(PERCENTAGE DISTRIBUTION OF ADULT UNITS WHOSE HEADS
ARE MARRIED)

Total work hours including housekeeping	Adult unit welfare ratio					All adult units whose heads are married
	Less than .9	.9–1.2	1.3–1.5	1.6–2.0	2.1 and over	
Married adult units with no children:						
Less than 1,850	51	27	18	10	6	19
1,850–2,149	3	3	3	3	1	2
2,150–2,949	13	15	7	14	6	10
2,950–3,949	19	30	35	43	37	34
3,950–5,949	11	18	33	27	40	29
5,950 and more	2	5	3	2	9	5
Not ascertained	1	2	1	1	1	1
Total	100	100	100	100	100	100
Number of adult units	144	116	70	151	278	759
Married adult units with children:						
Less than 1,850	3	1	0	0	0	1
1,850–2,149	3	0	0	0	0	1
2,150–2,949	5	2	1	1	1	2
2,950–3,949	27	20	18	18	11	18
3,950–5,949	54	63	72	62	63	63
5,950 and more	5	13	8	17	25	14
Not ascertained	3	1	1	2	0	1
Total	100	100	100	100	100	100
Number of adult units	321	272	204	259	253	1,309

When the retired and the disabled are excluded, the resulting distributions include fewer people who worked very little, but the same positive relationship between the adult unit's welfare level and the number of hours of leisure it has given up to achieve that level remains.

The analysis of hours worked by spending unit heads showed a negative relationship between the head's wage rate and the number of hours he worked. (See Chapter 6.) One implication drawn from this relationship was that heads with high wage rates take some of the benefits of higher earning potential in the form of more leisure. Similarly, wives tend to work less when the other family income is higher. (See Table 9-6.) But Tables 21-2 and 21-3 show the opposite relationship for all adult units; high levels of welfare, ignoring leisure, frequently are associated with more than full time work and with working wives; low levels of welfare frequently accompany less than full year's work. The relationship is clearer for single adult units, partly because of the narrower range of possible work hours, and because of the varied impact of family size on both hours worked and the welfare level index among the adult units with a wife and children. The arbitrary assumptions about the time required for housekeeping and child care would not account for these patterns.

These apparently contradictory findings emphasize the importance of distinguishing between the net effect of rewards on work time and the over-all relationship between work hours and levels of welfare. Many outside forces influence both wages and hours in the same direction. Yet once these circumstances are taken into account the individual does tend to value his leisure and take some of his gains in the form of leisure rather than more money.

The over-all relationship between work hours and levels of welfare is important, then, not as a description of causal influences in individual decisions, but as a picture of the entire distribution of welfare. Those with more income relative to their needs tend to be those who spend more time working.

Put another way, those with more income in the form of goods and services tend to have less real income in the form of leisure. Therefore, if leisure is valuable, this over-all negative correlation between gross disposable income and leisure means that estimates of inequality of welfare based on gross disposable income will exaggerate the true inequality in welfare.

If people were merely choosing between more leisure and more command over physical goods and services, free from the forces which push their wages and hours in the same direction, then an over-all positive relationship between leisure and gross disposable income would be likely. Individuals would take the gains from higher wage rates partly in the form of leisure. In this case, measures of inequality based only on gross disposable income would understate the true inequality of the distribution of total satisfaction or welfare. Those with higher gross disposable income would also be working less and enjoying more leisure.

This implies that there are biases in measures of inequality which ignore the value of leisure. These biases depend on the extent to which those with higher incomes also have more leisure. Individuals voluntarily tend to treat income and leisure as substitutes, while forces like unemployment, illness, disabilities, and educational differences make for the reverse relationship. Thus, the extent to which these measures of inequality exaggerate or understate the true inequality of welfare distribution depends upon the relative importance of free individual choice versus outside constraints, in the amount of time spent working.

If involuntary unemployment or unwanted retirement accounted for most of the difference in work hours, and people had no choice about the amount of leisure time they consumed, then the inequality of income would not be exaggerated. The "leisure" of the low-income unemployed or the disabled provides no offset to their low money incomes. Thus, it is necessary to know two things in order to include the use of time in a measure of income: the relationship between income from goods and services, and leisure; and the extent to which leisure is a desired and appreciated commodity or an involuntary and unwanted necessity.

Summary and Implications

Forces outside the unit affect both the unit's income and its work hours in the same direction, and these forces tend to offset the tendency to value leisure and to take some income in the form of leisure time. Because of this, units with higher incomes relative to their budget needs tend to spend more hours working. Even when work hours are adjusted to include time spent in housework and child care, which tends to reduce the welfare ratio and increase the work hours of units which include children, units with the highest welfare ratios still tend to have the least leisure. Therefore, measures of inequality based on any income or welfare measures which do not attempt to value leisure exaggerate the inequality in the distribution of welfare to the extent that leisure is desired and appreciated.

A great deal is now known about the amounts of money people earn and how they spend it, but little is known about how they use time. It appears that there are great differences in the amount of time people spend in economically productive activities even within the United States. A promising area for future research both here and abroad is in the use of time.

Studies of the use of time will throw light on what determines the man-hours available for productive work in the labor market, and on the amounts of previously unmeasured productive activity that never go through the market place. This does not imply that evaluative studies of the creative use of leisure, or the extent to which people enjoy work or dislike free time are necessary. What is proposed is the study of proportions of time devoted to broad categories of uses, such as working for money, doing necessary household tasks, sleeping, and engaging in directly satisfaction-creating activities. Whether the individual initiated the activity may also be used to classify it.

Economic growth and economic welfare depend on how time is used. It is in these dimensions that one can compare different groups within a culture and average patterns of behavior between cultures. Such data will describe the extent to which the economy is a market place economy as well as the extent to which satisfactions, real income, are created and consumed simultaneously.

This has implications for studies over time and between countries, not only as to levels of income but as to inequality. The usual measures would underestimate inequality in countries where there was much freedom as to the amount of work or lesiure one chose, as compared with countries where work patterns were more fixed. Similarly, if opportunities for second jobs, or jobs for women increase, then the number of voluntary substitutions of leisure for income may increase, and the extent to which income measures understate inequality would also increase.

PART V

The Dynamics of Social and Economic Change

Chapter 22

PATTERNS OF CHANGE AND THEIR INTERRELATIONSHIPS

Part of the mechanism through which family incomes and levels of welfare are determined is reflected in the over-all social and economic changes which take place from one generation to the next. This section is concerned with the dynamics of such change and the way this change is reflected in relative levels of income and welfare in succeeding generations.

A discussion of such change rightly begins with an over-all view of the dramatic shifts which have taken place in the population of the United States during the last half century. Some of these changes are depicted in Tables 22-1 and 22-2. The proportion of white collar workers has more than doubled, while farm workers have declined to a small proportion of the labor force. The proportion of foreign born has decreased by half.

TABLE 22-1

CHARACTERISTICS OF THE UNITED STATES POPULATION
IN SELECTED YEARS

Per cent of total population who were	1900	1910	1920	1930	1940	1950
Foreign born [a]	14	15	13	12	9	7
Over 65 [b]	4	4	5	5	7	8
Married [c]	53	54	58	59	60	68
White collar workers [d]	18	21	25	29	31	37
Skilled and semiskilled workers	23	26	29	29	31	35
Laborers and service workers	39	36	31	30	28	21
Farmers	20	17	15	12	10	7

[a] U.S. Bureau of the Census, *Statistical Abstract of the United States: 1956* (Washington, D. C., 1956), Table 27, p. 33.

[b] U.S. Congress, Senate Subcommittee on Problems of the Aged and Aging, *The Aged and Aging in the United States: A National Problem* (86th Cong., 1st Sess., Feb., 1960), Table 1, p. A2.

[c] *Statistical Abstracts of the United States: 1956,* Table 42, p. 44.

[d] Bureau of the Census, Working Paper No. 5, *Occupational Trends in the United States 1900 to 1950* (Washington, D.C., 1958), Table 2, p. 7.

The increase in the amount of formal education received by the average American has been striking. Less than half of the spending unit heads born before 1905 went beyond grade school, while 85 per cent of those born after 1925 went to high school or beyond.

TABLE 22-2

EDUCATION WITHIN AGE
(PERCENTAGE DISTRIBUTION OF SPENDING UNIT HEADS)

	Age and year of birth		
Education	Born prior to 1905 55 and older	Born 1905–1925 35–54	Born 1925–1942 18–34
None	4	1	0
1–8 grades	49	26	15
9–11 grades	17	23	23
12 grades	8	18	21
12 grades and nonacademic training	5	11	11
College, no degree	9	10	18
College, bachelor's degree	6	8	10
College, advanced degree	2	3	2
Total	100	100	100
Number of spending units heads	883	1,265	849

These over-all trends reflect the complex process of social change through which the character of a society evolves from one generation to the next. The dynamics of these social and economic changes are illustrated in the relationships between the characteristics of succeeding generations in a particular family.

Along with the over-all changes in society, individual families are steadily changing their positions relative to society as a whole. The characteristics of some families change in the direction of increased incomes and status; the characteristics of others change in directions which imply stable or decreasing status and attainments.

Some of this movement occurs by chance. However, this section will examine the hypothesis that the characteristics of parents exert a strong influence on the social and economic positions of their children. If this hypothesis is true, some important insights into the nature of social and economic change and growth can be gained by studying the dynamic relationships between characteristics of one generation in a family and those of the next.

One approach to the study of social and economic change is to follow the history of cohorts. Each cohort is affected by some particular historical influence, such as the Depression or World War II. The social and economic characteristics of each cohort will reflect these events. Because spending unit heads in a cross section sample are of varying ages, intergenerational change affecting those heads represents changes in families that span a long period of time. Where it is most crucial to determine an historically changing relationship, particular age groups (cohorts) are examined separately. Most of the analysis in this section assumes that some important forces which determine social and economic change transcend the particular historical events affecting the cohorts studied, so that valid data on dynamic relationships can be obtained by studying the whole sample.

The first part of this chapter explores the extent to which characteristics are transmitted from one generation to the next, by comparing characteristics of the spending unit head with those of his father. This process shows the over-all pattern of change over time in the proportions who have moved up from the absolute levels of their fathers, and examines change relative to concomitant changes in society as a whole.

In the latter part of this chapter these indexes of change are related to other measures of mobility to test the hypothesis that different kinds of movement are interrelated to a mobility syndrome.[1]

The amount of education which an individual attains is most influenced by the social and economic position of his parents. His education, in turn, affects his own career patterns and those career patterns describe his social and economic position. Chapter 23 examines these relationships between education and career patterns.

Chapter 24 describes the extent to which education is transmitted to the spending unit head from his father, and the characteristics of both the head and the father which influence the absolute level of the head's educational attainment.

Chapter 25 completes the picture of transmission of education by relating characteristics of the spending unit head to the education attained by his grown children.

The process examined here is not a precise description of individual mobility through the social class structure. Rather it illustrates in microcosm the over-all social and economic changes which occur from one generation to the next. Also, it analyzes the characteristics of a family that cause changes in the family's relative well-being from one generation to the next. Some characteristics of each generation in a family are transmitted to it from the generation before; some are a function of belonging to that particular generation. The persistence of a family's relative position on the economic scale, regardless of changes in absolute levels, may be transmitted from father to son. Upward changes in the relative social and economic level which a family occupies may result from exogenous factors, or from a combination of inherited characteristics, or both. These changes are examined in Chapters 24 and 25.

[1] Leo F. Schnore, "Social Mobility in Demographic Perspective," *American Sociological Review,* 26 (June, 1961), 407–423.

TABLE 22-3

EDUCATION OF SPENDING UNIT HEADS WITHIN THEIR AGE AND THE EDUCATION OF THEIR FATHERS
(PERCENTAGE DISTRIBUTION OF SPENDING UNIT HEADS)

Education of spending unit heads	Education of heads' fathers													All spending unit heads			
	0–8 grades			9–11 grades			12 grades			Some college				Heads under 35	Heads 35–54	Heads 55 and older	All
	Heads under 35	Heads 35–54	Heads 55 and older	Heads under 35	Heads 35–54	Heads 55 and older	Heads under 35	Heads 35–54	Heads 55 and older	Heads under 35	Heads 35–54	Heads 55 and older					
0–8 grades	21	32	60	6	9	18	2	11	16	1	7	14		15	27	53	32
9–11 grades	29	25	17	14	23	16	16	10	21	8	8	16		23	23	17	21
12 grades	31	29	11	46	20	31	32	36	27	22	19	17		32	29	13	25
Some college	19	14	12	34	48	35	50	43	36	69	66	53		30	21	17	22
Total	100	100	100	100	100	100	100	100	100	100	100	100		100	100	100	100
Number of spending unit heads	561	1,031	752	96	67	20	118	96	64	75	71	46		850	1,265	882	2,997

Patterns of Change

In Table 22-3 and succeeding tables in this section each father is represented in proportion to the number of his children who are spending unit heads. Therefore, members of the last generation who had no children are not represented, and members of the last generation who had nine children who are now spending unit heads are given nine times as much importance as those who had one. As a consequence, the analysis illustrates both the dynamics of transmission of characteristics from one generation in a family to the next and the size of the population to which a characteristic is transmitted.

Most spending unit heads have acquired more education than their fathers. Most heads whose fathers had only grade school education have gone to high school; most heads whose fathers graduated from high school have gone to college. Moreover there has been a marked shift in the educational attainments of spending unit heads of differing ages in relation to the attainments of their fathers, indicating an acceleration of the process of change. Of the spending unit heads whose fathers had only grade school educations or less, only 40 per cent of those fifty-five and older went to high school or beyond, while almost 80 per cent of those under thirty-five attained at least some high school.

Differences in occupation are another indicator of change in socioeconomic status. However, while education is irreversible, occupation is not. People are continually moving up and down the occupational scale. In the following tables fathers of spending unit heads are shown according to their occupation at the time the head was growing up. Spending unit heads are shown according

TABLE 22-4

OCCUPATION OF SPENDING UNIT HEADS WITHIN OCCUPATION
OF THEIR FATHERS
(PERCENTAGE DISTRIBUTION OF SPENDING UNIT HEADS
WHOSE OCCUPATION IS KNOWN)

Occupation of spending unit heads	Occupation of fathers				All spending unit heads whose occupation is known [a]
	White collar workers	Skilled and semiskilled workers	Unskilled workers	Farmers	
White collar workers	65	35	26	27	39
Skilled and semiskilled workers	25	48	39	35	37
Unskilled workers	9	16	30	19	18
Farmers	1	1	5	19	6
Total	100	100	100	100	100
Number of cases	670	706	469	851	2,873

[a] includes 177 cases for whom occupation of the father was not ascertained

to their occupation at the time of interview. Thus, the younger heads are in their first jobs while others are at the peak of their careers or beyond. Former occupations are used for persons who were not working at the time of the interview.

Children of skilled workers are most likely to move into white collar work; children of laborers and farmers are most likely to move into skilled work. The pattern suggests that unskilled workers and farm laborers move into professional occupations over the course of two generations with the intermediate generation occupying a skilled or semiskilled job.

An examination of occupational mobility for different age groups provides some idea of changes in occupational mobility over time. This approach has its shortcomings because different age groups are shown at different stages in their careers. The upward mobility of spending unit heads under thirty-five is understated since some of them will probably move into higher status occupations when they are older. Despite these shortcomings, Table 22-5 shows that movement into skilled and white collar positions on the part of heads whose fathers were unskilled workers was greater among younger heads.

If actual proportion in each cell of Table 22-5 is divided by the corresponding proportion in the summary columns, the resulting ratio may be interpreted as a measure of the mobility between occupational groups which adjusts for the differing demand for workers in various occupations. Rogoff defines this ratio as social distance mobility.[2] Unlike indexes of absolute change from one generation to the next, the measure of social distance mobility describes individual change relative to the over-all changes in society as a whole. An index greater than one indicates more movement from one occupation to another than one would expect if people randomly went into occupations in proportion to the total numbers in that occupation, regardless of their fathers' occupations.

Table 22-6 presents the social distance mobility for the age and occupation groups shown in Table 22-5. Along the diagonal, numbers greater than one thus indicate a tendency to stay in the same occupation as the father, in the upper right a tendency to move to a higher ranking and more skilled occupation than the father's, and in the lower left a tendency to move to a lower ranking occupation. There is a pattern of increasing upward mobility of younger children of unskilled workers even when allowing for the general upward movement in the occupational distribution. There is also increasing tendency, relative to demand for farmers, for younger heads whose fathers were farmers to become farmers.

Transmission of characteristics of the father to the next generation includes the propensity to be self-employed. Table 22-7 shows that spending unit heads whose fathers were self-employed report self-employment almost three times as often as heads whose fathers were not self-employed. The correlation

[2] See Natalie Rogoff, *Recent Trends in Occupational Mobility* (Glencoe: Free Press, 1953), p. 32.

TABLE 22-5

OCCUPATION OF SPENDING UNIT HEADS WITHIN THEIR AGE AND THE OCCUPATION OF THEIR FATHERS
(PERCENTAGE DISTRIBUTION OF SPENDING UNIT HEADS WHOSE OCCUPATION IS KNOWN)

Occupation of spending unit heads	Occupation of heads' fathers												All spending unit heads whose ocupation is known [a]			
	White collar workers			Skilled and semiskilled workers			Unskilled workers			Farmers						
	Heads under 35	Heads 35–54	Heads 55 or older	Heads under 35	Heads 35–54	Heads 55 or older	Heads under 35	Heads 35–54	Heads 55 or older	Heads under 35	Heads 35–54	Heads 55 or older	Heads under 35	Heads 35–54	Heads 55 or older	All
White collar workers	66	67	60	36	34	36	31	25	19	27	28	26	40	40	36	39
Skilled and semiskilled workers	25	25	26	48	52	43	46	39	30	38	39	29	40	38	31	37
Unskilled workers	8	7	12	16	14	19	21	31	44	22	14	24	17	15	23	18
Farmers	1	1	2	0	0	2	2	5	7	13	19	21	3	7	10	6
Total	100	100	100	100	100	100	100	100	100	100	100	100	100	100	100	100
Number of spending unit heads	177	301	192	241	312	153	163	205	101	160	365	326	741	1,183	772	2,873

[a] includes 177 cases for whom occupation of father is not known

TABLE 22-6

SOCIAL DISTANCE MOBILITY WITHIN OCCUPATIONS OF SPENDING UNIT HEADS AND FATHERS AND AGE OF HEADS

Occupation of spending unit heads	White collar workers			Skilled and semiskilled workers			Unskilled workers			Farmers		
	Heads under 35	Heads 35–54	Heads 55 or older	Heads under 35	Heads 35–54	Heads 55 or older	Heads under 35	Heads 35–54	Heads 55 or older	Heads under 35	Heads 35–54	Heads 55 or older
White collar workers	1.65	1.68	1.67	0.90	0.85	1.00	0.78	0.62	0.58	0.68	0.70	0.72
Skilled and semiskilled workers	0.62	0.66	0.84	1.20	1.37	1.39	1.15	1.05	0.97	0.95	1.03	0.94
Unskilled workers	0.47	0.47	0.52	0.94	0.93	0.83	1.24	2.07	1.91	1.29	0.93	1.04
Farmers	0.33	0.14	0.20	0.00	0.00	0.20	0.67	0.71	0.70	4.33	2.71	2.10

Occupation of heads' fathers

between self-employment in two generations may stem from the fact that family businesses and farms are handed down from father to son.

Another aspect of mobility may be seen in differences between the socio-economic status of the religious group for which the spending unit head expresses preference and the group he reports for his father. Religious mobility between generations was measured by comparing the socioeconomic status of the spending unit head's religious preference with that of his father. This status was determined for each religious group by the average income and

TABLE 22-7

SELF-EMPLOYMENT OF SPENDING UNIT HEADS WITHIN
SELF-EMPLOYMENT OF THEIR FATHERS
(PERCENTAGE DISTRIBUTION OF SPENDING UNIT HEADS
WHO ARE WORKING)

| Self-employment of spending unit heads | Self-employment of fathers | | All spending unit heads who are working |
	Worked for someone else [a]	Self-employed	
Works for someone else	90	72	82
Self-employed; farmer	10	28	18
Total	100	100	100
Number of spending unit heads	1,350	945	2,295

[a] This category also includes fathers whose self-employment was not ascertained, and who never worked.

education of its members. Religions are listed in Table 22-8 in order of increasing socioeconomic status. (See Appendix D.)

Table 22-8 shows that two-thirds of the spending unit heads have religious preferences in the same general category as the preferences of their fathers. About 15 per cent have religions with higher socioeconomic status, and 13 per cent with lower. Religious preference, unlike previous characteristics examined, does not show any particular trend from generation to generation. Furthermore, religious preferences appear much less subject to change than occupation or education.

It is possible that religious mobility is a slower process than other forms of mobility, requiring two generations to complete the transition from one group to another. The middle generation may remain in the group to which their fathers belonged, but attend church only infrequently. Their children, in turn, may receive less religious training and be more likely to change religion if they find a different religious group that is more appropriate to their situation. This hypothesis is suggested by the fact that the proportion who move from their father's religion is much higher for spending unit heads whose fathers did not go to church regularly. Indeed it is three times as high for Catholics whose fathers did not attend regularly, and one and one-half times as high for the two major Protestant groups. Movements between different denominations

TABLE 22-8

RELIGIOUS PREFERENCE OF SPENDING UNIT HEADS WITHIN RELIGIOUS PREFERENCE OF THEIR FATHERS
(PERCENTAGE DISTRIBUTION OF SPENDING UNIT HEADS)

Religious preference of spending unit heads	Baptist	Other Fundamentalist Protestant	Roman Catholic	Lutheran	Other non-Fundamentalist Protestant	Presbyterian	Jewish	Episcopalian	Not ascertained	All [a]
Baptist	68	16	2	3	12	7	0	6	20	21
Fundamentalist Protestant other than Baptist	7	59	2	5	7	6	0	1	12	11
Roman Catholic	2	1	86	5	5	5	0	9	10	22
Lutheran	2	2	2	63	3	1	0	8	2	7
Non-Fundamentalist Protestant other than Lutheran, Presbyterian, Episcopalian	14	17	4	15	65	15	0	11	21	24
Presbyterian	4	3	1	5	5	60	0	8	3	6
Jewish	0	0	0	0	0	0	95	0	1	3
Episcopalian	2	0	0	2	2	3	0	57	3	3
Other; not ascertained	1	2	3	2	1	3	5	0	28	3
Total	100	100	100	100	100	100	100	100	100	100
Number of spending unit heads	718	291	609	213	724	124	82	71	143	2,997

Religious preference of fathers

[a] includes 22 fathers whose religious preference was non-Christian, non-Jewish

within the major groups probably would be higher also where the head's father attended church only infrequently. There is some slight tendency for spending unit heads in the lower status denominations who have incomes above the average for that denomination to attend church less frequently. However, for the most part church attendance of those with incomes above or below the average for their denomination does not differ extensively or systematically from the average attendance for the denomination.

Intergenerational change appears to be most marked for education and occupation. Change in both of these characteristics is strongly related to the lifetime earnings of the individual. High school graduates accumulate approximately $40,000 more in lifetime earnings than do persons with one to three years of high school, and college graduates accumulate approximately $151,000 more in lifetime earnings than high school graduates.[3] High educational attainments are associated with longer working lives and with steadier employment as well as with higher hourly wage rates. Employment in professional, managerial, or self-employed occupations is related to higher than average wage rates and longer hours of work.

Clearly these findings are not independent. Employment in many skilled positions requires substantial education. Thus there is likely to be a strong relationship between educational and occupational change from one generation to the next. This relationship is examined in Chapters 23 and 24.

Relationships among Mobility Measures

Writers have suggested that many different kinds of mobility are interrelated to form a mobility syndrome. "A person who moves up in the social hierarchy will tend to change his friends, join new organizations, move to a new neighborhood; perhaps he will even change his religious affiliation; in some cases he will change his name; often he will alter his political attitudes."[4] This hypothesis can be tested by a set of mobility measures which include social and economic changes within the working life of an individual, as well as longer range changes from one generation to the next. In this section indexes of the educational and occupational changes examined earlier are compared with other measures of mobility to determine whether evidence for such a syndrome exists.

The intragenerational change of occupation between the head's first full-time job and his present job is unrelated to amount of geographic mobility measured by the number of states in which the head has lived. It is also

---

[3] Herman P. Miller, "Annual and Lifetime Income in Relation to Education, 1939–1959," *American Economic Review,* 50 (December, 1960), 962–986.

[4] Seymour Lipset and Reinhard Bendix, *Social Mobility in Industrial Society* (Berkeley: University of California Press, 1959), p. 6. Used with permission of the Regents of the University of California. This work also includes references to the literature on social mobility.

unrelated to educational mobility. Those who attained more education than their fathers started out with higher status occupations, but they did not move up more than any other group. Of course, this reflects in part the fact that they were already near the top.

Intergenerational mobility was measured by comparing the occupation of each head with that of his father, and comparing the proportions who had clearly moved up the scale of occupations. The following rank order was used to measure change: (1) professionals, (2) managers and self-employed businessmen, (3) clerical and sales workers, (4) skilled workers, (5) semiskilled workers, and (6) unskilled laborers. Movement to a higher-ranked category was considered upward mobility; movement to a lower-ranked category was considered downward mobility. People whose occupation or whose fathers' occupation was farmer, government protective worker, or member of the armed services were not included in either movement group because each of these groups is so heterogeneous that it was impossible to rank them. People whose occupation, or whose fathers' occupation, was not ascertained were also excluded.

Table 22-9 presents a summary of the relationships between intergenerational occupational mobility and other mobility measures.

Geographic mobility in one generation was measured by three types of migration: movement between urban places and rural places, movement out of the Deep South and the number of states in which the spending unit head has lived since he entered the labor force. The first two measures indicate differences in the place where the head grew up and where he lives now, while the last one is a continuous indicator of all his adult movement.

The South is composed of some relatively prosperous, rapidly developing states like Florida and Texas on the one hand, and the less progressive "Deep" South on the other hand. The Deep South was defined to include Georgia, North Carolina, South Carolina, Virginia, Alabama, Kentucky, Mississippi, Tennessee, and Louisiana. In order to provide the best chance for a significant finding, persons who grew up in the Deep South and moved out, not just to other southern states, but to the Northeast, North Central, or West were isolated from those who made less significant moves or did not move at all. Since this group does not differ appreciably in terms of other types of mobility, it is doubtful that a larger group including those who made less drastic moves would be significantly different.

Except for educational mobility between generations, the occupational mobility concept has little relation to other mobility measures. There is some relationship between educational change and occupational change between generations, but it is surprising that there is not more since formal education is practically a prerequisite for certain occupations. Finally, people who change religion are not significantly more likely to change occupation in the same status direction, or to change occupation at all.

Difference in the amount of education attained by the spending unit head

TABLE 22-9

PROPORTION WHOSE OCCUPATIONS ARE CLEARLY HIGHER, LOWER THAN
THOSE OF THEIR FATHERS, WITHIN VARIOUS MOBILITY MEASURES
(FOR SPENDING UNIT HEADS)

Movement out of the Deep South	Per cent in each mobility group whose occupations are clearly higher than those of their fathers	Per cent clearly lower	Number of spending unit heads
Heads grew up in the Deep South, moved into the North or West	20	22	125
Amount of geographic mobility			
Since entering the labor force, heads have lived in:			
one state:			
within 100 miles of present location	26	18	1,575
more than 100 miles from present location	23	18	330
two states	23	20	598
three or more states	25	18	418
Urban-rural migration [a]			
Heads grew up in urban areas, now live in rural areas	31	22	510
Heads grew up in rural areas, now live in urban areas	11 [b]	8 [b]	443
Educational mobility			
Heads have same level of education as their fathers or less	19	20	1,954
Heads have one level more education than their fathers	33	17	721
Heads have two levels more education than their fathers	36	12	322
Religious mobility			
Heads' religious preference scaled lower than fathers'	25	17	422
Heads' religious preference scaled the same as fathers'	24	20	2,037
Heads' religious preference scaled higher than fathers'	27	14	538
All spending unit heads	24	19	2,997

[a] Three per cent who grew up in foreign countries or for whom movement was not ascertained are excluded.

[b] Few clear movements because most had fathers who were farmers.

and his father, used to measure educational mobility, has almost no relationship to any other measure of mobility. Table 22-10 shows almost complete absence of any correlation between educational and geographic mobility, in any of its forms. The table includes only white male spending unit heads thirty-five and older who are in the labor force. White male spending unit heads were selected in order to eliminate groups handicapped by barriers to mobility, such as occupational discrimination against nonwhite persons and

TABLE 22-10

SOME MEASURES OF GEOGRAPHIC MOBILITY WITHIN DIFFERENCE IN EDUCATION OF SPENDING UNIT HEADS AND THEIR FATHERS

(PROPORTIONS OF WHITE MALE NONFARMER SPENDING UNIT HEADS 35 AND OLDER IN THE LABOR FORCE)

Geographic mobility	Difference in education of heads and fathers [a]				All white male nonfarmer spending unit heads 35 and older in the labor force
	Heads have fewer levels than fathers	Heads have same level as fathers	Heads have 1 level more than fathers	Heads have 2 levels more than fathers	
Amount of geographic mobility					
Since entering labor force, heads have lived in: one state:					
within 100 miles of present location	42	46	51	44	47
more than 100 miles from present location	11	13	12	12	12
in two states	24	22	20	23	22
in three or more states	20	18	16	19	18
Movement out of the Deep South					
Heads grew up in the Deep South, moved into the North or West	2	2	2	1	2
Urban-rural migration					
Heads grew up in urban areas, now live in rural areas	27	17	24	22	26
Heads grew up in rural areas, now live in urban areas	4	17	8	13	12
Number of spending unit heads	71	590	290	134	1,085

[a] levels of education: for fathers—0–8 grades, 9–12 grades, college; for heads—0–11 grades, 12 grades, college

344

women. Heads thirty-five and older were selected to confine the analysis to persons with similar degrees of exposure to the possibility of movement. For the most part, distributions of comparable heads under thirty-five show patterns very similar to those presented.

Amount of geographic mobility is seemingly unaffected by educational mobility; indeed, even the absolute level of the spending unit head's education is not correlated with the amount of his geographic mobility. Likewise, those who move up or down the educational ladder are no more likely to have moved out of the Deep South or between urban and rural places, than are those whose educational attainments are at the same level as those of their fathers. There is a slight tendency for those who grew up in rural areas and stayed there to have the same level of education as their fathers and because these persons are largely farmers, it is a low level.

Since members of different religious groups have widely differing average incomes and educational levels, it is important to determine whether a son who gets more education than his father may also change his religion to join a group whose members are more like him in income and education. Table 22-11 shows that this is only rarely the case. It is interesting to note that there is also no relation between the need-achievement score and any change in religious preference, either in direction or frequency of attendance.

TABLE 22-11

CHANGES IN RELIGION WITHIN DIFFERENCES IN EDUCATION
BETWEEN HEADS AND FATHERS
(PERCENTAGE DISTRIBUTION OF SPENDING UNIT HEADS)

Differences in religion between heads and fathers [a]	Difference in education of heads and fathers [b]			
	Heads have one level less education than their fathers	Heads have same level of education as their fathers	Heads have one level more education than their fathers	Heads have two levels more education than their fathers
Heads' religion two or more levels lower than fathers'	11	13	9	11
Heads' religion one level lower than fathers'	3	3	3	4
Heads' religion same level as fathers'	72	68	68	66
Heads' religion one level higher than fathers'	2	5	4	5
Heads' religion two or more levels higher than fathers'	12	11	16	14
Total	100	100	100	100
Number of spending unit heads	182	1,772	721	322

[a] according to average socioeconomic levels of religious groups
[b] levels of education: for fathers—0–8 grades, 9–12 grades, college; for heads—0–11 grades, 12 grades, college

The various forms of change or mobility measured here are surprisingly uncorrelated with one another. There are apparently many forces in addition to the ambition and upward aspirations of the individual which produce these changes, and the forces must be different for different types of movement. Perhaps mobility is too broad a concept, and all geographic movement is not part of a carefully thought-out plan for personal economic advancement. Some people may move merely to leave an impossibly bad situation. Others may move to areas where friends or relatives have moved, without much thought of the alternative opportunities. Religious change may result from marriage, or purely local forces like attractions of the minister or church location, or from philosophical or theological considerations. It remains possible that some planned geographic moves are related to upward economic mobility. What is called for in the future is clearer and more detailed discrimination among various kinds of changes. The planned, purposeful moves toward places of greater opportunity should be distinguished from moves that result from shiftlessness or instability or untenable situations.

Summary

Dramatic social and economic changes have taken place in the population of the United States during the last half century. The dynamics of these changes are illustrated in the relationship between characteristics of succeeding generations of a family. In order to study the over-all changes by an examination of changes which have taken place in the social and economic status of a particular family over two generations, it is necessary to determine which of the characteristics transmitted from father to son are related to the process of social mobility. Then, these characteristics and their transmission can be studied in order to understand something about the process of social change, and to describe the economic effects of this process from one generation to the next.

In order to measure intergenerational change within a family, characteristics of spending unit heads were compared with characteristics of their fathers. Most spending unit heads have more education than their fathers. Moreover, the process shows some acceleration over time, since the youngest unit heads went further beyond the attainments of their fathers than did the older spending unit heads.

A comparison of occupation of heads and fathers shows consistent movement upward. As with education, the upward movement has increased among younger spending unit heads.

The movement between generations of a family *relative to the over-all movement* repeats the pattern of increasing upward mobility of younger children of unskilled workers, even allowing for the general upward movement in the occupational distribution.

A comparison of the socioeconomic status of the spending unit head's religious preference with that of his father shows little movement from one generation to the next.

Intergenerational change appears to be most evident in education and occupation. Further, these characteristics are strongly related to lifetime earning patterns. In order to examine the hypothesis that upward movement of one kind was related to other kinds of mobility, indexes of occupational and educational change were made. These indexes were related to other mobility measures to determine whether a mobility syndrome does indeed exist.

Three measures of geographic mobility and an index of religious change were examined in relation to educational and occupational change, and almost no relationship was found. The effect of increased exposure of older persons to the possibility of movement should have produced some spurious correlation among mobility measures, but even this relationship did not appear.

Educational and occupational change appear to be the most appropriate measures of social and economic change from one generation to the next. Because so little correlation appeared between educational mobility and any other forms, the remainder of this section will concentrate on the effects of education as it is transmitted from one generation to the next, and on the accompanying changes in social and economic position.

Chapter 23

THE IMPACT OF EDUCATION ON CAREERS

In this chapter, level of education is related to several aspects of the careers of spending unit heads.[1] This analysis supplements the findings in Chapters 5 and 6, where it appeared that less educated persons tend to work for lower wages and to work shorter hours.

It is difficult to determine whether the relationships between education and employment are the result of differences in the ability, motivation, training, or family backgrounds of spending unit heads with different levels of education. Education is a measured classification which represents a mixture of these more fundamental attributes in unknown proportions. The process of education presumably sharpens an individual's natural abilities, and gives him a range of information and acquired skills which he might not otherwise have. It may also give him certain attitudes and values which affect his behavior. These acquired skills may explain only a part of the differences in the careers of persons with different levels of education. The remaining differences in the careers of persons with different levels of education may be because of the somewhat arbitrary process of selection by which some talented persons receive little education while others receive a great deal.

Some persons drop out of school because of low interest or motivation, and others drop out because they do not have sufficient intellectual ability. Of course, differing financial resources make it easier for some persons to continue in school. Consequently, the level of completed education is a measure of what the individual has learned or the values he may have acquired; and also a rough measure of his motivation, his native abilities; also an indication of his parent's finances and standards.

[1] The literature on careers and social mobility has been explored and annotated in Seymour Lipset and Reinhard Bendix, *Social Mobility in Industrial Society* (Berkeley: University of California Press, 1959);

Harold L. Wilensky offers a brief bibliography of major work in the field of "Work, Careers, and Social Integration," *International Social Science Journal,* 12 (Fall, 1960), 553.

Clearly, ability, motivation, and skills of individuals with different levels of education influence their careers. However, it is difficult to generalize from the patterns observed in this study to the probable impact of specific levels of education on the careers of individuals in future generations. Changing quality of education and changing emphasis on remedial training for those who now drop out of school because of lack of interest or ability may produce a situation in future years in which the level of education, as measured here, will be related to career patterns in a different way.

C. Arnold Anderson points out that education is not the only determinant of vertical mobility and that observed patterns of intergenerational mobility conform more closely to patterns determined by random processes than to patterns determined mechanically by educational achievement alone. He suggests that quality of education may be partly responsible for the lack of correlation and notes that education will account for less of the variance in upward mobility between generations, as the population becomes more highly trained. However, none of these points destroys the assertion that education is a necessary prerequisite to advancement into the highest occupational and income levels. The argument underlines the fact that the number of grades completed is not the only aspect of education which affects vertical mobility and suggests that other factors may also be of some consequence.[2]

Education and Entry into the Labor Force

Education first influences the career of an individual at the time he enters the labor force. Very few spending unit heads without a college degree entered the labor force in professional and technical work. Few without a high school diploma entered in clerical and sales work. More than 70 per cent of all spending unit heads with less than high school educations entered in semi-skilled and unskilled occupations.

The first regular job held by the head of the spending unit is closely related to his present occupation. Thirty-eight per cent of persons in the labor force are in the same occupational group in which they began work. A somewhat smaller proportion remain in the same occupation for their entire working lives. For young persons present occupation and first regular job are one and the same. Because Table 23-2 does not distinguish young and old, it understates mobility or lifetime change.

Changes in occupation show surprisingly definite patterns. The most frequent transitions (underlined in Table 23-2) divide white collar and blue collar occupations into two almost completely different strata. Persons who enter semiskilled occupations are likely to move into skilled positions, but are unlikely to enter any other occupational group except self-employed businessmen. Conversely, of all the white collar occupations only the clerical and

[2] C. Arnold Anderson, "A Skeptical Note on the Relation of Vertical Mobility to Education," *American Journal of Sociology,* LXVI (May, 1961), 560–570.

TABLE 23-1

FIRST OCCUPATION WITHIN EDUCATION
(PERCENTAGE DISTRIBUTION OF SPENDING UNIT HEADS
WHO HAVE WORKED)

	Education					All spending unit heads who have worked
First occupation	0–8 grades	9–11 grades	12 grades	12 grades and non-academic training	College, no degree	College degree	
Professionals	0	2	2	8	18	57	10
Managers	0	0	1	1	4	8	1
Self-employed businessmen	0	0	1	1	2	0	0
Clerical and sales workers	6	12	29	33	33	16	18
Skilled workers	5	8	11	14	9	4	8
Semiskilled workers	21	30	22	17	11	3	20
Unskilled workers	62	40	26	22	14	3	36
Farmers	1	1	1	1	2	1	1
Government protective workers	0	1	1	0	1	1	1
Not ascertained	5	6	6	3	6	7	5
Total	100	100	100	100	100	100	100
Number of spending unit heads	976	601	444	261	319	296	2,897

sales workers are likely to take up a manual occupation. Taken together Tables 23-1 and 23-2 indicate the profound effect of education on career patterns. Education not only influences the first regular job a person obtains; it also determines his subsequent career.

Job Stability and Prospects

Education and occupation jointly determine the stability of the spending unit head's employment and his future prospects. Different occupations have different patterns of layoffs and working hours. Once the earner is laid off and looking for a job, however, it is a combination of education, occupational skills, age, race, and sex that determines the length of his unemployment.

Tables 23-3 through 23-5 present three measures of job stability for spending unit heads with different levels of education. Since job stability is affected by age, and since age composition varies with education levels, the data are presented within age as well. Many other factors are relevant here, of course. These tabulations provide an over-all view of the impact of education on the careers of spending unit heads, but they do not describe the many intermediate relationships which produce these results.

Over a third of those who work for others and do not have high school diplomas report that they were unemployed at some time during the last five

TABLE 23-2

PRESENT OCCUPATION WITHIN FIRST OCCUPATION

(PERCENTAGE DISTRIBUTION OF SPENDING UNIT HEADS IN THE LABOR FORCE)

Present occupation	First occupation						All spending unit heads in the labor force [a]
	Professionals	Managers	Clerical and sales workers	Skilled workers	Semiskilled workers	Unskilled workers	
Professionals	74 [b]	11	10	3	5	2	12
Managers	9	43	9	5	2	3	6
Self-employed businessmen	4	13	8	16	6	7	8
Clerical and sales workers	6	19	44	7	8	7	15
Skilled workers	2	2	9	44	26	17	18
Semiskilled workers	1	3	10	17	40	22	20
Unskilled workers	1	3	7	5	9	27	13
Farmers	1	4	1	1	2	14	6
Government protective workers	1	2	2	1	2	1	2
Not ascertained	1	0	0	1	0	0	0
Total	100	100	100	100	100	100	100
Number of spending unit heads	194	34	335	159	388	729	2,053

[a] includes persons whose first occupation was not ascertained and who were self-employed businessmen, farmers, and government protective workers. The latter groups are not shown separately as there are too few persons reporting self-employment, farming, or protective service as first occupations.

[b] In each column the two most frequent transitions are underlined.

351

years. Only 7 per cent of those with college degrees were similarly affected. This pattern appears in all age groups. Because of their unemployment, the group without high school diplomas are more likely to report that their income varies from year to year than are high school and college graduates.

Despite high unemployment among spending unit heads without high school diplomas, only a small proportion have less than two years of seniority on their present job. Those with less than two years of seniority are most subject to layoffs. Thirty per cent of those with less than two years of seniority reported that they would be among the first to be laid off; only 5 per cent of those with two years of seniority or more said the same thing.

TABLE 23-3

PER CENT UNEMPLOYED DURING PAST FIVE YEARS
WITHIN EDUCATION AND AGE
(FOR SPENDING UNIT HEADS WHO WORK FOR OTHERS
OR ARE UNEMPLOYED)

Age	Education		
	0–11 grades	12 grades; 12 grades and some college	College degree
Under 25	57 (70)	24 (136)	4 (12)
25–34	39 (224)	23 (207)	12 (71)
35–44	27 (233)	24 (213)	2 (65)
45–54	32 (255)	9 (129)	6 (44)
55–64	33 (191)	22 (67)	0 (28)
65 and older	26 (36)	0 (4)	0 (7)
All	34 (1,009)	21 (756)	7 (227)

( ) number of spending unit heads

Seventy-two per cent of those with training beyond high school report that they would have a good chance of finding another job that pays about the same if they should lose their present job. Only 48 per cent of those with less than high school education report equal confidence in their employability.

Slightly more than one out of ten who report that it would be difficult to find a job give their lack of training and experience as reasons; nearly half of those who think it would be easy to find a job refer to their training and experience.

For some high school drop-outs, layoffs resulting from lack of seniority on the next job create serious and continuing instability of employment and income. The disadvantageous position of the high school drop-out makes it easy to understand the difficulty that earners in nonretired, nondisabled, poor families have in finding steady employment. (See Chapter 16.)

Spending unit heads with less than high school educations also report that chances for promotion are slim. In every age group a higher proportion with high school and college training report that they are likely to have a good chance for a promotion. Skills and training were not mentioned as reasons

TABLE 23-4

CHANCES OF FINDING ANOTHER JOB WITHIN EDUCATION
(PERCENTAGE DISTRIBUTION OF SPENDING UNIT HEADS WHO WORK FOR OTHERS)

Chances of finding another job [a]	Education						All spending unit heads who work for others
	0–8 grades	9–11 grades	12 grades	12 grades and nonacademic training	College, no degree	College degree	
Good	28	34	47	52	48	67	43
Good, qualified	15	19	17	14	18	10	16
Neither good nor bad	2	4	4	6	4	2	3
Bad, qualified	20	18	15	14	13	7	16
Bad	25	18	12	9	10	7	15
Do not know	7	2	2	2	3	2	3
Not ascertained	3	5	3	3	4	5	4
Total	100	100	100	100	100	100	100
Number of spending unit heads	481	423	327	180	215	224	1,850

[a] The question was: "If you should lose your present job, what would you say were your chances of finding another job that paid about the same? Why is that?"

TABLE 23-5

PER CENT WITH GOOD CHANCE FOR PROMOTION
WITHIN EDUCATION AND AGE
(FOR SPENDING UNIT HEADS WHO WORK FOR OTHERS)

Age	Education		
	0–11 grades	12 grades; 12 grades and some college	College degree
Under 25	24 (60)	47 (131)	87 (12)
25–34	27 (203)	59 (198)	81 (71)
35–44	28 (209)	40 (203)	48 (63)
45–54	18 (225)	33 (119)	45 (43)
55–64	11 (169)	22 (67)	29 (28)
65 and older	7 (31)	24 (4)	0 (7)
All	21 (897)	43 (722)	56 (224)

( ) number of spending unit heads
The question was: "What would you say are your chances for promotion or getting ahead? Why is that?"

for good or bad chances for promotion as frequently as were local conditions and age.

Lifetime Income and Asset Patterns

As a consequence of more frequent unemployment, and comparatively poor chances for promotion, spending unit heads with less than high school educations have lower levels of income and less optimistic income expectations than more educated spending unit heads. Heads with high school diplomas or college training report maximum earnings substantially higher than those reported by spending unit heads with less education. Peak earnings are the largest amount that each spending unit head has ever earned in one year.

High school graduates over twenty-five report higher average peak earnings than the high school drop-outs in any age group. Moreover, the average peak earnings of high school graduates continue to rise until the head reaches retirement.

TABLE 23-6

MEAN PEAK EARNINGS WITHIN EDUCATION AND AGE
(FOR SPENDING UNIT HEADS WHO WORKED)

Age	Education		
	0–11 grades	12 grades; 12 grades and some college	College degree
Under 25	$3,060	$ 3,203	$ 2,977
25–34	5,097	6,028	6,850
35–44	5,202	7,111	9,982
45–54	5,263	8,259	10,692
55–64	5,240	10,664	10,734
65 and older	4,147	7,172	13,509
All	$4,929	$ 6,774	$ 9,125

In addition to relatively low peak earnings the high school drop-out is more likely to have experienced an extended period of declining income. While only 14 per cent of those with college degrees report their highest income was earned five or more years prior to the time of interview, 24 per cent of the high school drop-outs report such a decline in income. As one might expect, declining income is more likely to affect older spending unit heads than younger ones. However, the high school drop-outs appear to be more vulnerable to declining income during the time that they are thirty-five to fifty-four than other spending unit heads in those age groups.

TABLE 23-7

PER CENT WHOSE PEAK EARNINGS WERE RECEIVED IN 1955 OR BEFORE
WITHIN EDUCATION AND AGE
(FOR SPENDING UNIT HEADS UNDER 65 WHO WORKED)

Age	Education		
	0–11 grades	12 grades; 12 grades and some college	College degree
Under 25	5 (79)	1 (159)	7 (17)
25–34	11 (254)	11 (244)	13 (81)
35–44	25 (300)	21 (277)	10 (82)
45–54	28 (349)	20 (182)	8 (54)
55–64	38 (313)	31 (104)	32 (44)
All	24 (1,295)	16 (966)	14 (278)

( ) number of spending unit heads

The level of peak earnings and the likelihood of declining earnings are reflected also in the amounts of liquid assets which spending units are able to accumulate.

The general pattern of earnings received by persons with different levels

TABLE 23-8

PER CENT OF SPENDING UNITS WITH SAVINGS OF $5,000 OR MORE
WITHIN EDUCATION AND AGE OF SPENDING UNIT HEADS
(FOR SPENDING UNITS)

Age	Education		
	0–11 grades	12 grades; 12 grades and some college	College degree
Under 25	0 (82)	0 (165)	0 (17)
25–34	1 (260)	4 (245)	10 (81)
35–44	5 (313)	14 (277)	25 (82)
45–54	11 (356)	21 (183)	38 (54)
55–64	13 (334)	32 (106)	56 (45)
65 and older	19 (298)	28 (78)	53 (21)
All	10 (1,643)	14 (1,054)	28 (300)

( ) number of spending units

of education is also mirrored in their expectations about their future financial situation. Persons with less than high school education are unlikely to report that their financial situation will be better after they reach the age of thirty-five; persons with college degrees continue to have predominately optimistic expectations about their financial situation until they reach fifty-five.

TABLE 23-9

PER CENT EXPECTING BETTER FINANCIAL SITUATION IN FUTURE
WITHIN EDUCATION AND AGE
(FOR NONRETIRED SPENDING UNIT HEADS)

| Age | Education | | |
	0–11 grades	12 grades; 12 grades and some college	College degree
Under 25	68 (82)	85 (165)	83 (17)
25–34	61 (260)	77 (245)	92 (81)
35–44	48 (312)	63 (276)	78 (82)
45–54	31 (349)	48 (183)	61 (54)
55–64	17 (296)	26 (96)	42 (37)
65 and older	2 (123)	0 (25)	0 (10)
All	37 (1,422)	62 (990)	72 (281)

( ) number of spending unit heads
The question was: "A few years from now, would you think you or your family will have a better income than you have now, or will you be in the same situation, or in a less satisfactory situation? Why do you say so?"

Reports of higher expected wages and salaries dominate the reasons given for a better financial situation. Reports of fewer earners in the family are given almost as often as decreasing wages and salaries as reasons why the financial situation will be worse in years to come.

People are generally aware of the fact that the amount of education a person receives has an important effect on his career, his job security, and his chances for advancement. When asked how much education everybody should be getting these days, over 50 per cent of spending unit heads replied that some college education was necessary, at least for some parts of the population. Some spending units differentiated between boys and girls, or between students with and without ability to learn. Most of those who thought some college is necessary indicated that everyone should have a college degree.

Table 23-10 gives the reasons why everyone should have a given level of education. These reasons are overwhelmingly in terms of the economic impact of education on incomes and careers.

Persons who spoke in terms of economic reasons were most concerned with finding and keeping a job: "A boy needs college if he wants any kind of money when he gets out," and "All you can do without college is manual work." Even persons who felt that high school was the optimal level spoke in financial terms: "An employer won't even talk to you unless you finish high school."

For many who spoke in financial terms, education appeared to be the touchstone to financial success: "If you have a good education, you can surely get good money," and "If I'd finished high school, I'd be making a lot more money now."

Persons who gave social reasons for education said such things as: "College broadens your outlook," and "Education is necessary for a full life." One man, with only eight grades of school replied: "Kids should learn all there is to learn—then they're better equipped to face the problems of our world." The proportion who gave social and personal reasons for education increased with the education of the head.

Indefinite positive answers were those such as: "Education is necessary nowadays," while negative answers were like: "College is a waste of money" and "There is no point educating girls more than high school."

Some persons differentiated in the amount of education everybody should have, saying that it depended on whether the child was able to learn or was interested in learning, whether the family could afford it, or whether the child was a boy or a girl.

TABLE 23-10

REASONS FOR THE AMOUNT OF EDUCATION EVERYONE SHOULD HAVE
WITHIN EDUCATION OF HEADS
(PERCENTAGE DISTRIBUTION OF SPENDING UNIT HEADS)

Reasons for the amount of education everyone should have [a]	Education			All spending unit heads [b]
	0–11 grades	12 grades	Some college	
Economic reasons	66	61	51	61
Social reasons	7	12	19	11
Indefinite positive answers	18	19	20	19
Negative answers	2	1	1	1
Depends:				
on ability	3	6	14	6
on finances	4	4	2	4
on sex	4	6	7	5
on interest; other qualifications	6	9	9	7
Number of spending unit heads	1,643	714	640	2,997

[a] The question was: "How much education do you think children ought to get these days? Why is that?"

[b] Columns do not add to 100 per cent because some spending unit heads gave more than one reason.

Summary

Education affects every phase of a man's career from the time he enters the labor force: his occupation, his income, and his expectations concerning future promotions and his ability to find equally good positions with other employers. Clearly, education is an important determinant of the socioeco-nomic level of the head of the spending unit and his family. Spending unit heads with little education have less income and fewer assets at every stage of their careers than spending unit heads with college training. They are also unlikely to obtain steady employment or jobs requiring managerial or tech-nical skills.

Chapter 24

THE TRANSMISSION OF EDUCATION FROM FATHERS TO SPENDING UNIT HEADS

The persistence of change in levels of education from one generation to the next can be studied by analyzing the educational attainments of succeeding generations. In this chapter factors determining the level of education of the spending unit head were studied through a multivariate analysis. Such an analysis is a means of determining how much of the level of education achieved by the head is transmitted through family characteristics and how much results from exogenous factors.

Since this is an analysis of spending unit heads, the relationships apply only to males and unmarried females who are financially independent, rather than to the entire adult population.

Education was scaled to emphasize the completion of different levels of schooling. High school graduates are distinguished by one point from non-graduates, and those who achieve a college degree are differentiated by one point from those who started college but did not receive a degree. The effect of the scaling is to give persons who have not completed the formal requirements for a degree or diploma somewhat less credit than would be indicated by the number of years of schooling they have completed. The scale is as follows:

0. None
1. 1–8 grades
2. 9–11 grades
3. 12 grades
4. 12 grades and nonacademic training
5. College, no degree
6. College, bachelor's degree
7. College, advanced degree

The variables used in the multivariate analysis of spending unit heads' education may be grouped roughly into three categories: those which reflect underlying motivation on the part of the head or his parents to achieve a high level of education for the head; those which indicate the availability of facilities for education; and those which serve as an index of the economic difficulty or ease with which the family could afford to educate its children. Educating children involves both the direct expenses of schooling and the indirect loss of earnings which the child could contribute to the family if he were not in school.

The motivation of the parents is measured by the education of the head's father, his religious preference, where he grew up, and his occupation. These variables are only crude indicators of motivation, but represent the information about the head's father that is most probably related to motivation. The father's education reflects a motivating force to the extent that each parent desires as much or more education for his children than he achieved. The religion of the head's father might indicate cultural values stressing educational achievements. Thus preference for a religious group high on the socioeconomic scale would be associated with high educational achievements by the children.

Parents who grew up in foreign countries are the more mobile persons in their own country. They may have broader horizons and higher aspirations for educating their children than nonimmigrants. Moreover some regions may stress educational attainments more than others do. Parents raised in the South may feel that education is less important than parents raised in the North. These hypotheses will be tested in the analysis of spending unit heads' aspirations for their children. (See Chapter 26.)

It is probable that parents with high status occupations demonstrate to their children the need for education to obtain remunerative and rewarding jobs. Presumably these same persons would encourage their children to get as much education as possible in order to be able to obtain similar types of work. Occupation is also an approximate indicator of income and the family's ability to finance its children's educations.

Self-employment of the head's father was taken as an indicator of the father's ambition and attitude toward self-help. Because this is a sample of spending unit heads and is not a representative sample of fathers of spending unit heads, the relationships shown are implicitly weighted by the number of living children of the father who are spending unit heads. Unless the number of living children who are spending unit heads interacts with other characteristics in its effect on the head's education, the effects of the weighting are negligible, however.

Several characteristics of the head were also included in the analysis. The head's need for achievement and his attitude toward hard work as a means to success were included as another measure of the motivation for high educational attainments. McClelland and others suggest that the need for achievement is formed very early in childhood by parental independence training.[1] Therefore, a high level of need-achievement should be a strong incentive to excel and to complete a maximum of formal education.

The measure of need-achievement was obtained after the head had completed his education so that it is possible that amount of education influenced his ability to score well on the measure. This analysis relies on the assumption that need-achievement affects education rather than the reverse. To the extent that high levels of need-achievement are transmitted early to the children, such an assumption seems reasonable.

The place where the head grew up was used to indicate the availability of education to the head. If the head grew up in the South or in a rural area or small town, it is likely that fewer and inferior schools were available to him. In rural areas the pressures to skip school and help on the farm might also affect educational attainments.

Race was also used as a measure of availability of education. Public schools attended solely or primarily by nonwhites may be inferior to schools for whites and colleges may have discriminatory admissions policies. Hence education may be less accessible to nonwhites. Belief that prejudice limits the advancement of nonwhites beyond unskilled occupations might reduce the nonwhites' incentives to acquire educations.

Age of the head is used as another measure of the availability of schools. For persons over sixty-five, far fewer high schools were available in proportion to the population than there were available to younger persons. In addition, increasing emphasis on education over the past half century has resulted in increases in standards of education in this country. Therefore, a negative correlation should exist between age and education.

Number of siblings of the head should indicate the ease or difficulty with which the family could afford to educate all its children.

Sex of the spending unit head may be thought of as a variable related to economic pressures on the parental family. If there was little income to be spent on educating the children, the family may have educated its boys and let the girls drop out of school. If so, girls attain less education than boys whose families have similar characteristics.

Table 24-1 shows the results of the multivariate analysis. The factors included in the analysis explain 35 per cent of the population variance. The average education of all spending unit heads is slightly less than a high school diploma as indicated by a grand mean of 2.82. The standard deviation is 1.79.

Education of the head's father was by far the most important of the factors determining the spending unit head's education. The average education of heads whose fathers were college graduates is 3½ points higher than the education of the heads whose fathers had no education. Since the education of

[1] David C. McClelland and others, *The Achievement Motive* (New York: Appleton-Century-Crofts, Inc., 1953).

TABLE 24-1

CHARACTERISTICS USED TO EXPLAIN EDUCATION
(FOR SPENDING UNIT HEADS)

Characteristics of spending unit heads	Relative importance (Beta coefficients)	Significance (F ratios)
Education of fathers	.246	46.23**
Age	.180	24.75**
Occupation of fathers	.175	15.60**
Number of siblings	.163	24.36**
Attitude toward hard work and need-achievement score	.145	16.06**
Background	.139	17.71**
Religious preference of fathers	.119	7.21**
Regions where fathers grew up	.054	1.91
Race	.034	5.30*
Self-employment of fathers	.019	1.65
Sex	.013	0.77

** significant at probability level of .01
 * significant at probability level of .05

the head's father is highly correlated with the age of the head and with the father's occupation, these effects are attenuated by the multivariate adjustment. However, even after adjustments for the other variables, education of the father remains the most powerful predictor.

The pattern of adjusted deviations in Table 24-2 shows two interesting results. First, it lends support to the hypothesis that motivation for people to continue in school is directly related to the educational attainment of their parents. Children of more educated parents attain more education than the average. Second, the results indicate some regression of children to the average educational attainment. Even the unadjusted means indicate that children of parents with no education enter high school, while children of college grad-

TABLE 24-2

EDUCATION: DEVIATIONS FOR EDUCATION OF FATHERS
(FOR SPENDING UNIT HEADS)

Education of fathers	Number of spending unit heads	Unadjusted deviations [a]	Adjusted deviations [a]
None	151	−1.40	− .61
1–8 grades	1,760	− .20	− .15
9–11 grades	183	1.01	.60
12 grades	278	1.18	.70
College, no degree	99	1.48	.87
College degree	93	2.17	1.13
Not ascertained	433	− .91	− .44

[a] deviations from grand mean of 2.82

uates average slightly less than "college, no degree." For parents with college training this result was to be expected. Not all children have the ability to complete a college course successfully. The superior accomplishment of the children whose education exceeds that of their parents suggests that community influences motivate children to complete a minimum education no matter what their parents' background. (For a bivariate analysis of heads' and fathers' educations, see Table 22-3.)

As was anticipated, older persons attained substantially less education than younger persons. The differences may be interpreted as a trend toward increasing educational standards and increasing availability of school facilities. This trend may decline over time; in the future differences in the education achieved by different age cohorts in the population very likely will diminish.

The reduction in the estimated size of the effect when the coefficients are adjusted for the other variables comes largely from the correlation between age and education of the head's father: younger heads are likely to have fathers with more education.

TABLE 24-3

EDUCATION: DEVIATIONS FOR AGE
(FOR SPENDING UNIT HEADS)

Age	Number of spending unit heads	Unadjusted deviations [a]	Adjusted deviations [a]
18–24	263	.60	.29
25–34	586	.48	.33
35–44	673	.28	.25
45–54	593	− .15	−.12
55–64	485	− .36	−.26
65–74	269	− .80	−.53
75 and older	128	−1.01	−.65

[a] deviations from grand mean of 2.82

Several interpretations of the relationship between occupation of fathers and educational attainment of spending unit heads can be developed. One possibility is that the link between education and particular career lines is demonstrated to the children through the occupation and success of the parent. Children may relate the ability of the parent to do professional work to the parent's educational achievements. This would provide incentive for the children of professionals and managers to obtain more education.

An alternative interpretation is that occupation serves as an indirect measure of the earnings of the family. Professionals and managers are better able to afford college educations for their children than semiskilled or unskilled workers. Some support for the latter interpretation comes from the fact that the occupation of the spending unit head bears little relationship to his aspira-

TABLE 24-4

EDUCATION: DEVIATIONS FOR OCCUPATION OF FATHERS
(FOR SPENDING UNIT HEADS)

Occupation of fathers	Number of spending unit heads	Unadjusted deviations [a]	Adjusted deviations [a]
Professionals	140	1.75	.71
Managers	73	1.32	.62
Self-employed businessmen	328	.59	.37
Clerical and sales workers	168	1.08	.42
Skilled workers	402	.27	.12
Semiskilled workers	329	− .21	−.20
Unskilled workers	461	− .72	−.33
Farmers	892	− .55	−.22
Government protective workers	27	.63	.32
Not ascertained; never worked	177	− .23	−.12

[a] deviations from grand mean of 2.82

tions for educating his sons in a relationship in which his income is also taken into account. (See Chapter 26.)

A somewhat unexpected finding is that semiskilled workers show a negative deviation from the grand mean nearly as large as unskilled workers, although their mean income is considerably higher.

The differences between the adjusted and unadjusted deviations shown in Table 24-4 exhibit the advantages of the multivariate technique used to obtain the adjusted results. A simple set of averages attributes to occupation differences which a multivariate technique assigns to education and other dimensions. As a result the adjusted effect of occupation is substantially smaller than the unadjusted effect.

The larger the family is, the greater are the demands made upon its income for current needs; the less it can afford the double cost of sending children to college and foregoing the income that they could earn. Therefore the

TABLE 24-5

EDUCATION: DEVIATIONS FOR NUMBER OF SIBLINGS
(FOR SPENDING UNIT HEADS)

Number of siblings	Number of spending unit heads	Unadjusted deviations [a]	Adjusted deviations [a]
None	210	.77	.43
One	338	.88	.41
Two	410	.57	.27
Three	378	.19	.11
Four or more	1,539	−.52	−.20
Not ascertained	122	.07	−.72

[a] deviations from grand mean of 2.82

number of children in a family should be associated closely and inversely with the average amount of schooling achieved by children. Table 24-5 shows this effect very clearly.

The reduction in the impact when the coefficients are adjusted follows from the correlation between parents' education, age of head, and family size: more recent generations and more educated parents had smaller families and educated them more.

The head's need-achievement score and perception that hard work gets one ahead in the world are strongly related to his level of education. Heads with high levels of need-achievement also have better than average educations. In part this correlation may be an artifact of the process by which need-achievement was measured. (See Appendix C.) Educated persons may be better able to evaluate differences between occupations and the relative difficulty of occupations than are uneducated persons who may have much more limited experience. However, correlation between the underlying ranking of each occupation and education is not particularly high; also, both a high achievement score and a perception that hard work is necessary to get ahead are needed to cause a substantial positive deviation from the grand mean. These facts taken together indicate that an important dimension of motivation probably has been tapped.

TABLE 24-6

EDUCATION: DEVIATIONS FOR ATTITUDE TOWARD HARD WORK
AND NEED-ACHIEVEMENT SCORE
(FOR SPENDING UNIT HEADS)

Attitude toward hard work and need-achievement score	Number of spending unit heads	Unadjusted deviations [a]	Adjusted deviations [a]
Hard work is equal to or more important than luck; need-achievement score is in:			
high range	714	.52	.28
middle range	1,071	.09	.05
low range	511	−.36	−.23
Hard work is less important than luck; need-achievement score is in:			
high range	132	.08	.08
middle range	270	−.70	−.49
low range	177	−.96	−.48
Not ascertained	122	.04	.34

[a] deviations from grand mean of 2.82

Heads who grew up in the South or on a farm average less education than heads who grew up in Northern cities. Poorer educational facilities and lower incomes in the South, and the frequent need for farm children to stay home and help run the farm may produce these differences. The table shows that the foreign born also attain somewhat less education than the average, even after allowing for the education, occupation, background of their fathers, and their generally advanced age.

TABLE 24-7

EDUCATION: DEVIATIONS FOR BACKGROUND
(FOR SPENDING UNIT HEADS)

Background	Number of spending unit heads	Unadjusted deviations [a]	Adjusted deviations [a]
Grew up in the Deep South:			
on a farm or in a small town	597	−.73	−.27
in a large city or several places	106	.10	−.07
Grew up in the United States, outside the Deep South:			
on a farm or in a small town	1,254	−.05	−.08
in a large city or several places	748	.61	.19
Grew up in foreign countries	163	−.53	−.13
Not ascertained	129	.32	.91

[a] deviations from grand mean of 2.82

When religious groups are grouped according to the average income level of their memberships and the proportion of the membership who are college graduates, a significant relationship appears between the affiliation of the parent and the educational attainment of the children. In Table 24-8 groups are shown approximately in order of the average income and education received by the members.

Jewish, Presbyterian, and Episcopalian parents appear to provide more education for their children than would be expected on the basis of other characteristics, while Roman Catholics provide less.[2]

This finding may be interpreted in a number of ways. The scale of religious preference may provide an indication of the ability of the parents to afford an education for their children not accounted for by other factors. The scale may also measure the degree to which a particular reference group provides a standard of educational attainment which guides the parent in educating his children. Alternatively the effect attributed to religious preference may stem from the value structure implied by membership in a particular denomination. Without further evidence, which is not available in this body of survey

[2] Lenski reports that Jews are less likely to drop out of school or college than members of other religious groups. However, he does not control for the background and economic level of families with different religious preferences. Hence, the finding is comparable to the unadjusted deviations shown in Table 24-8.

See Gerhard Lenski, *The Religious Factor* (New York: Doubleday & Company, Inc., 1961), p. 60.

See also Neil J. Weller, "Religion and Social Mobility in Industrial Society" (unpublished Ph.D. dissertation, The University of Michigan, 1961).

TABLE 24-8

EDUCATION: DEVIATIONS FOR RELIGIOUS PREFERENCE OF FATHERS
(FOR SPENDING UNIT HEADS)

Religious preference of fathers	Number of spending unit heads	Unadjusted deviations [a]	Adjusted deviations [a]
Baptist	718	− .36	.00
Fundamentalist Protestant other than Baptist	291	.00	.08
Roman Catholic	608	− .21	−.30
Lutheran	213	.10	.00
Non-Christian, non-Jewish	22	1.16	.65
Non-Fundamentalist Protestant other than Lutheran, Presbyterian, Episcopalian	725	.10	.02
Presbyterian	124	.90	.48
Jewish	82	1.28	.58
Episcopalian	71	.80	.26
Not ascertained	143	− .33	.07

[a] deviations from grand mean of 2.82

data, no more definite statement can be made about the validity of these interpretations.

Nonwhite spending unit heads average slightly less education than white spending unit heads. Though the unadjusted difference in the education of the two groups is large, the father's education, occupation, and other characteristics included in the analysis appear to account for most of the difference as indicated by the adjusted deviations.

TABLE 24-9

EDUCATION: DEVIATIONS FOR RACE
(FOR SPENDING UNIT HEADS)

Race	Number of spending unit heads	Unadjusted deviations [a]	Adjusted deviations [a]
Whites	2,580	.09	.02
Nonwhites	417	−.75	−.18

[a] deviations from grand mean of 2.82

The effects shown in Tables 24-10, 24-11, and 24-12 are not particularly important. However, such impact as the deviations do suggest generally is in the expected direction.

Children whose fathers grew up in the North Central region and the West have slightly more education; those whose fathers grew up in the South have slightly less education than the average.

Though female heads of spending units average slightly less education than

TABLE 24-10

EDUCATION: DEVIATIONS FOR REGION WHERE FATHERS GREW UP
(FOR SPENDING UNIT HEADS)

Regions where fathers grew up	Number of spending unit heads	Unadjusted deviations [a]	Adjusted deviations [a]
Northeast	428	.32	−.07
North Central	661	.35	.14
South	1,118	−.33	−.05
West	116	.37	.18
Foreign countries	579	−.08	−.02
Several regions	27	.04	.00
Not ascertained	68	−.70	−.31

[a] deviations from grand mean of 2.82

male heads, the difference is not statistically significant. Because a large proportion of the female heads are elderly widows, they belong to a cohort whose experience includes little education for both males and females. The difference is not surprising, and the adjusted deviations are not significant.

TABLE 24-11

EDUCATION: DEVIATIONS FOR SEX
(FOR SPENDING UNIT HEADS)

Sex	Number of spending unit heads	Unadjusted deviations [a]	Adjusted deviations [a]
Male	2,386	.03	.01
Female	611	−.13	−.05

[a] deviations from grand mean of 2.82

This investigation does not provide a good test for the effects of sex since it includes only females who are heads of spending units; these comprise only one-fifth of the country's women.

TABLE 24-12

EDUCATION: DEVIATIONS FOR SELF-EMPLOYMENT OF FATHERS
(FOR SPENDING UNIT HEADS)

Self-employment of fathers	Number of spending unit heads	Unadjusted deviations [a]	Adjusted deviations [a]
Self-employed	1,286	−.09	.04
Not self-employed	1,711	.07	−.03

[a] deviations from grand mean of 2.82

The differences for self-employment of fathers are not significant or important.

Stability of the Relationship

Because the level of educational attainments has changed so remarkably within the time in which the spending unit heads in this sample were educated, it seemed quite possible that the relationships shown in the analysis have also changed. To ascertain whether the relationships shown are independent of the time when the head of the spending unit was educated, the analysis was repeated for spending unit heads under thirty-five years of age. Characteristics shown to be insignificant in the analysis of the entire cross section were omitted from the subsequent analysis.

Spending unit heads under thirty-five comprise less than one-third of the sample. This age group is most likely to have benefited from education received in the armed services or under the GI Bill. Thus one might expect the parental influence on the head's education to differ from the parental influence on earlier generations.

The average attainment for the young spending unit heads was 3.34. This average is half a level higher than the mean for the entire cross section. Table 24-3 shows that roughly .30 of this difference can be attributed to the difference in age or factors related to the time when these young people were educated. The remaining difference in average educational level of the cross section and the young spending unit heads results from the difference in their characteristics. The parents of young spending unit heads averaged considerably more education, included fewer farmers, and had smaller families than is typical for the cross section as a whole. The change in each of these distributions implies greater educational attainments.

However, the relationships obtained were very similar to those already presented. Even the prominent differences between the Jewish; non-Christian, non-Jewish; and Roman Catholic groups were about as important. Thus it seems that the change in educational attainments which has occurred over the last fifty years results from a process which has not altered fundamentally during the period. Parents' education, occupation, and background appear to produce the same differences in educational attainments among young spending unit heads as was true for previous generations.

Summary

The analysis of the amount of education achieved by spending unit heads supports the hypothesis of transmission of characteristics from one generation to the next and reveals a powerful impact of background factors on educational achievement.

The education of the head's father was by far the most important determinant of the level of education received by the head. Likewise, the father's occupation and religious preference had important effects.

Many characteristics of the spending unit head himself were important as well. Younger heads tend to receive considerably more education than do older ones, even with an adjustment for the fact that younger heads tend to have more highly educated fathers. The head's need-achievement score and his attitude toward hard work also had an important impact on his educational achievement.

The level of educational attainment has changed so dramatically over the period of time in which the heads in this sample were educated. In order to test the stability of the relationships shown in the analysis, and determine whether they are independent of the time in which the head was educated, the analysis was repeated for spending unit heads under thirty-five. The average attainment for the younger group was half a level higher than that of all spending unit heads. Approximately .30 of this can be attributed to differences in the time at which the younger group was educated. The remaining differences result from differences in characteristics of the younger group and the total sample.

Chapter 25

THE TRANSMISSION OF EDUCATION FROM SPENDING UNIT HEADS TO THEIR CHILDREN

The analysis of the average educational achievements of children of spending unit heads differs conceptually from the findings of the previous chapter in several ways. More data about the head of the spending unit and his wife are available to relate to educational attainment of their children than were available for explaining the educational attainments of the heads. This advantage is partially offset by the fact that the analysis is limited to those families who have children finished with school, about a third of all spending units.

The dependent variable in this analysis differs in several respects from the index of educational attainments used previously. Educational achievements of children are measured by the number of grades completed, without giving added weight to the attainments of those who completed a degree program.

Cases where the education of children was not ascertained are excluded. Grades completed refers only to academic schooling, with some college considered 13 years; bachelor's degree, 16 years; master's degree, 17 years; and Ph.D. or M.D., 20 years.

Secondly, the measure used is an average of the number of grades completed by all the living children of the spending unit head who are finished with school. Thus all children are represented, regardless of whether they are the heads of spending units. The average is a convenient summary measure of the attainments of the children, but it must be multiplied by the number of children in the family in any discussion of the distribution of actual attainments. Studying the average attainment has the disadvantage that it makes it impossible to consider the impact of characteristics of the individual child on his educational attainment. So long as the characteristics of individual children have an effect which is in addition to the effect of family characteristics rather than interacting with them, the results are not biased.

The average somewhat understates educational attainments. Teen-agers who have already dropped out of school are included in the average while those who are still in school and will show above average attainments are not included. In all likelihood, the downward bias has a negligible effect on relationships in the analysis.

The variables used to explain educational attainments of the children of spending unit heads parallel those used in the previous analysis wherever possible.

In both analyses, parental motivation was represented by education, occupation, religious preference, and region. Since more information was available concerning spending unit heads, several new variables were included to make the measurements more precise. Education of the wife and of the head's father were used to describe the educational standards of the family more completely. Religious preference of the spending unit head was classified in less detail to permit simultaneous analysis of the effect of the frequency of his church attendance on his children's educational attainments. Age of the head was included on the assumption that younger parents would have higher standards for educating their children. Two variables which indicate the geographical mobility of the head were used to test the hypothesis that mobile parents have children with more education. The two mobility variables are movement out of the Deep South and urban-rural migration of the spending unit head. Self-employment of the head was omitted from the analysis because it appeared to be relatively unimportant in the analysis of the head's education.

Need-achievement of the spending unit heads was included in the analysis in place of the need-achievement level of the children. Theoretically the parents' level of need-achievement is transmitted to the children. Thus parents with high levels of need-achievement should have children who desire to excel in school and who desire a high level of education. The parents should also put more pressure on their children to progress in school.

The availability of educational facilities again was indicated by race. The background of the children is approximated by the two mobility variables, although the children were not necessarily educated in the same type of place as that in which the head now lives. The ages and sexes of the children could not be used in this analysis of average education.

The financial ability of the family to educate its children was again indicated by number of children, although in this analysis only living children were included. The highest income the head ever earned replaces his occupation as a more precise indicator of the income of the family at the time its children were in school. Age of the head at the birth of his first child indicates the timing of the financial burden of raising a family.

Table 25-1 shows the relative importance and significance of each of the indicators used to explain educational achievements of children. The charactistics appear in roughly the same order as in the analysis of spending unit heads' educations. (See Table 24-1.)

TABLE 25-1

CHARACTERISTICS USED TO EXPLAIN AVERAGE COMPLETED
EDUCATION OF CHILDREN
(FOR SPENDING UNIT HEADS WHO HAVE CHILDREN
FINISHED WITH SCHOOL)

Characteristics of spending unit heads	Relative importance (Beta coefficients)	Significance (F ratios)
Education	.374	32.00**
Difference in education of heads and wives	.187	9.33**
Occupation	.153	4.16**
Number of living children	.122	7.94**
Movement out of the Deep South	.114	4.16**
Attitude toward hard work and need-achievement score	.104	2.89**
Highest income ever earned	.098	1.71
Religious preference and church attendance	.096	2.46*
Age at birth of eldest living child	.091	2.21*
Difference in education of heads and fathers	.087	4.04**
Race	.069	7.62**
Urban-rural migration	.045	0.65
Age	.037	0.73

** significant at probability level of .01
 * significant at probability level of .05

The explanatory variables account for two-fifths of the variance in children's completed education, as indicated by a coefficient of multiple determination of .41. On the average, children who are finished with school received slightly less than twelve grades of schooling. The standard deviation is 2.56 grades.

Education of the spending unit head proved to be the most important factor influencing the education of children. The pattern of adjusted deviations in Table 25-2 is much the same as the pattern shown in Table 24-2. Children of parents with no education attain some high school in both cases; children of college graduates attain slightly less than a college degree, while the earlier analysis indicated a somewhat lower attainment for spending unit heads. Part of the difference in the two results may be attributed to the fact that the data here describe a younger generation. The differences may also result from differences in the dependent variables and differences in the population studied. The earlier analysis gave added weight to completion of high school or college, where the present analysis treats education as a linear scale.

Average education attained by children is also influenced by the educational achievements of the mother. The more education the wife has relative to her husband, the more education the children attain. Thus the attainments of both parents appear to stimulate education of children. The adjusted deviations in Table 25-3 suggest an asymmetry in the effect of differences in the parents' educations. Where the wife has less education than the head, achieve-

TABLE 25 2

AVERAGE COMPLETED EDUCATION OF CHILDREN:
DEVIATIONS FOR EDUCATION
(FOR SPENDING UNIT HEADS WHO HAVE CHILDREN
FINISHED WITH SCHOOL)

Education of spending unit heads	Number of spending unit heads	Unadjusted deviations [a]	Adjusted deviations [a]
None	26	−2.68	−1.60
1–8 grades	478	− .96	− .68
9–11 grades	177	.19	− .12
12 grades	92	.99	.98
12 grades and nonacademic training	50	.94	.65
College, no degree	65	2.08	1.65
College, bachelor's degree	35	2.88	1.89
College, advanced degree	16	3.90	3.06

[a] deviations from grand mean of 11.82 grades

ments of the children are impeded but not so much as they are advanced when the wife has more education than the head.

By definition, certain combinations of the head's education and differences in education of head and wife cannot exist. For example, it is impossible for the head to have an advanced college degree and his wife to have more education than he. Also, the two extreme groups on the scale typically include wives or heads with a high school education or more.

TABLE 25-3

AVERAGE COMPLETED EDUCATION OF CHILDREN: DEVIATIONS
FOR DIFFERENCE IN THE EDUCATION OF HEADS AND WIVES
(FOR SPENDING UNIT HEADS WHO HAVE CHILDREN
FINISHED WITH SCHOOL)

Difference in education of spending unit heads and wives [a]	Number of spending unit heads	Unadjusted deviations [b]	Adjusted deviations [b]
Wives have two or more levels more than heads	61	1.34	1.37
Wives have one level more than heads	103	− .01	.46
Wives and heads have the same level	310	− .48	− .10
Wives have one level less than heads	79	1.07	− .06
Wives have two or more levels less than heads	67	1.30	− .94
Not ascertained	9	.16	.09
Heads are unmarried	310	− .42	− .11

[a] levels of education are defined as:

none	12 grades and nonacademic training
1–8 grades	college, no degree
9–11 grades	college, bachelor's degree
12 grades	college, advanced degree

[b] deviations from grand mean of 11.82 grades

The effect of occupation shown in Table 25-4 is slightly different from the effect observed in the earlier analysis. The attainments of children of semi-skilled workers are more nearly the same as the attainments of children of skilled workers, while the previous analysis showed a rather large difference between the two groups. The differences between this table and the effects shown in Table 24-4 may stem from the fact that the income level of the parents is partly accounted for simultaneously in this analysis.

TABLE 25-4

AVERAGE COMPLETED EDUCATION OF CHILDREN:
DEVIATIONS FOR OCCUPATION
(FOR SPENDING UNIT HEADS WHO HAVE CHILDREN
FINISHED WITH SCHOOL)

Occupation of spending unit heads	Number of spending unit heads	Unadjusted deviations [a]	Adjusted deviations [a]
Professionals	59	2.60	.32
Managers	39	2.17	.75
Self-employed businessmen	62	1.04	.54
Clerical and sales workers	100	1.11	.49
Skilled workers	124	.05	−.05
Semiskilled workers	164	− .48	−.14
Unskilled workers	219	−1.37	−.56
Farmers	103	− .75	−.13
Government protective workers	10	1.33	.06
Occupation not ascertained; never worked	59	− .96	.13

[a] deviations from grand mean of 11.82 grades

As hypothesized, family size is negatively correlated with average education received by children. The effects of this difference are indicated by the proportion of children represented, which is, of course, larger for the larger families.

TABLE 25-5

AVERAGE COMPLETED EDUCATION OF CHILDREN:
DEVIATIONS FOR NUMBER OF LIVING CHILDREN
(FOR SPENDING UNIT HEADS WHO HAVE CHILDREN
FINISHED WITH SCHOOL)

Number of living children of spending unit heads	Per cent of children	Number of spending unit heads	Unadjusted deviations [a]	Adjusted deviations [a]
One	7	208	.76	.32
Two	16	231	.45	.23
Three or four	34	292	.03	−.07
Five or more	43	208	−1.47	−.54

[a] deviations from grand mean of 11.82 grades

It was postulated that children of mobile families have somewhat more education than other children because mobile families have broader horizons and are probably more motivated to take advantage of economic opportunities. Children whose parents grew up in the Deep South and remained in the South received less education than those whose parents moved to the North or West. Nearly half of those who moved out of the Deep South are Negroes. For children whose parents grew up outside the Deep South geographic mobility does not affect education.

Children of foreign-born parents achieve more education than would be expected on the basis of other characteristics of their parents. These findings are not completely consistent with the earlier analysis. Spending unit heads whose fathers grew up in foreign countries did not achieve more than average education. Perhaps the difference results from the different immigration restrictions and differences in national origins of immigrants to the United States since the 1920s.

TABLE 25-6

AVERAGE COMPLETED EDUCATION OF CHILDREN: DEVIATIONS
FOR MOVEMENT OUT OF DEEP SOUTH
(FOR SPENDING UNIT HEADS WHO HAVE CHILDREN
FINISHED WITH SCHOOL)

Spending unit heads' movement out of the Deep South	Number of spending unit heads	Unadjusted deviations [a]	Adjusted deviations [a]
Grew up in the United States outside the Deep South; now live:			
in the South	121	.24	.07
in the non-South	484	.42	.07
Grew up in the Deep South; now live:			
in the South	201	−1.34	−.54
in the non-South	38	−1.02	.06
Grew up outside the United States	78	.35	.54
All others [b]	17	− .08	.16

[a] deviations from grand mean of 11.82 grades
[b] includes persons who grew up in more than one region of the country and cases in which region was not ascertained

The need-achievement score appears to make an independent contribution to the explanation of the number of grades completed by the children of the spending unit heads. Though the finding appears parallel to the relationship shown in Chapter 24, conceptually it is quite different. In this analysis the level of need-achievement of the spending unit head is related to the attainments of his children. Need-achievement of the parent is clearly a personality attribute that was formed prior to the children's educations. Therefore, it is much safer to interpret the relationship as a causal one in this analysis than it was in the previous analysis, which related the level of need-achievement of the head to his own education.

Children of parents who score high on the need-achievement score obtain more schooling than children of parents who do not. The head's attitude toward hard work as a means of getting ahead in the world does not have as strong an effect as before. In spite of the perception that hard work is less important than luck in getting ahead in the world, a small group of persons who score high on the need-achievement index have children who perform well above the expectation based on the other characteristics. The children of this group attain more education than children of the group who feel that hard work is important. This reversal in the expected direction of the effect of believing in hard work may be associated with a tendency for minority groups with high need-achievement scores to perceive that for them luck and help from others may be more important than hard work. For the remaining group it cannot be said that attitude toward work makes any difference in the educational achievement of children. This attitude may, of course, have changed since the time when decisions were being made about children's educations.

TABLE 25-7

AVERAGE COMPLETED EDUCATION OF CHILDREN: DEVIATIONS FOR
ATTITUDE TOWARD HARD WORK AND NEED-ACHIEVEMENT SCORE
(FOR SPENDING UNIT HEADS WHO HAVE CHILDREN
FINISHED WITH SCHOOL)

Heads' attitude toward hard work and need-achievement score	Number of spending unit heads	Unadjusted deviations [a]	Adjusted deviations [a]
Hard work is equal to or more important than luck; need-achievement score is in:			
high range	190	.96	.32
middle range	334	.08	.03
low range	169	− .51	−.25
Hard work is less important than luck; need-achievement score is in:			
high range	34	1.29	.75
middle range	100	− .96	−.32
low range	72	−1.20	−.26
Need-achievement score not ascertained	40	− .28	−.26

[a] deviations from grand mean of 11.82 grades

Because need-achievement is a dimension of personality which is formed very early in the life of an individual and affects his income and occupational success, the unadjusted deviations in Table 25-7 are meaningful. Both the immediate effect of the head's level of need-achievement on the child's early independence training and the indirect impact of need-achievement on the head's occupation and education produce the striking unadjusted deviations shown.

Alternate interpretations are equally valid. The need-achievement index may measure the extent to which parents place high values on jobs which require substantial education and little value on those jobs which do not. It may also measure the intelligence of the spending unit heads. In either case the same relationship to educational attainments would be expected.

The maximum annual earnings received by the head of the spending unit were included in the analysis to measure the family's financial ability to educate its children. Though the relationship between level of highest earnings and childrens' education is somewhat irregular, the deviations are in the expected direction; high incomes are associated with more than the average educational attainment.

A number of conceptual and empirical factors weakened the effect of this variable. Highest earned income was thought to present the most favorable earning measure for retired persons and others whose incomes have declined since the period when their children were in school. However, the reported level indicated by maximum earnings may be distorted by memory errors; the level may reflect atypical earnings during a very brief period; or, because of changing living costs, the level may correspond to disparate relative income positions for different age cohorts in the sample. As a consequence, peak earnings do not necessarily reflect lifetime earning patterns and the ability of the family to support children in school. Education and occupation may be more closely associated with real relative lifetime earning patterns.

TABLE 25-8

AVERAGE COMPLETED EDUCATION OF CHILDREN: DEVIATIONS
FOR HIGHEST INCOME EVER EARNED
(FOR SPENDING UNIT HEADS WHO HAVE CHILDREN
FINISHED WITH SCHOOL)

Highest income ever earned by spending unit heads	Number of spending unit heads	Unadjusted deviations [a]	Adjusted deviations [a]
$1–449	21	−1.10	.01
$450–949	30	−1.74	−.38
$950–1,949	66	−1.61	−.28
$1,950–2,949	87	−1.03	−.32
$2,950–4,949	178	− .24	.12
$4,950–7,449	224	.34	−.01
$7,450–9,949	52	1.03	.08
$9,950 and over	97	1.87	.37
Not ascertained	119	− .05	.19
Never worked	65	−1.25	−.60

[a] deviations from grand mean of 11.82 grades

Average education received by children is related to the socioeconomic status of the head's religious preference. The effect of irregular church atten-

TABLE 25-9

AVERAGE COMPLETED EDUCATION OF CHILDREN: DEVIATIONS FOR
RELIGIOUS PREFERENCE AND CHURCH ATTENDANCE
(FOR SPENDING UNIT HEADS WHO HAVE CHILDREN FINISHED
WITH SCHOOL)

Religious preference and church attendance of spending unit heads	Number of spending unit heads	Unadjusted deviations [a]	Adjusted deviations [a]
Catholics; attend church:			
twice a month or more	122	.23	.08
once a month or less	30	− .38	−.13
Fundamentalist Protestants; attend church:			
twice a month or more	211	− .55	.07
once a month or less	150	−1.31	−.55
Non-Fundamentalist Protestants; attend church:			
twice a month or more	165	.95	.24
once a month or less	213	.33	.09
Non-Christians; no preference	48	.65	−.06

[a] deviations from grand mean of 11.82 grades

dance has no easy explanation, except perhaps as indication of strongly held values such as family responsibility.

Age of the head at the birth of his eldest living child was assumed to measure the extent to which the family exercised some foresight and planning for financial demands of a family. Families who had children late, whether by plan or accident, also would have more savings and greater opportunity to earn income by having both the husband and the wife in the labor force.

TABLE 25-10

AVERAGE COMPLETED EDUCATION OF CHILDREN: DEVIATIONS FOR
AGE OF HEAD AT BIRTH OF ELDEST LIVING CHILD
(FOR SPENDING UNIT HEADS WHO HAVE CHILDREN FINISHED
WITH SCHOOL)

Age of spending unit heads at birth of eldest living child	Number of spending unit heads	Unadjusted deviations [a]	Adjusted deviations [a]
Under 18	42	−2.35	−.92
18–19	62	−1.12	−.41
20–24	344	− .36	−.01
25–29	259	.45	.13
30–39	188	.76	.15
40 or older	25	.14	.00
No children [b]	19	− .39	−.51

[a] deviations from grand mean of 11.82 grades
[b] includes inconsistent responses and heads with adopted children

The birth of a child shortly after an early marriage limits the wife's ability to work and imposes a burden on the husband's income. Thus the variable provides an index of both the planning horizons of the family and its ability to accumulate assets. While the deviations shown in the table are not highly significant, they are sufficiently systematic to support the hypothesis that the younger couples are when they first have children, the less likely it is that their children will have much education even relative to the education of their parents.

Children learn from and are motivated by the experiences of their parents. Presumably they also recognize the educational achievements of their grand-parents and use the experiences of that generation to judge the value of an education. In cases where the grandfather has more education than either parent, the children will achieve more than would be expected on the basis of other factors in the family's background. Where the grandfather has less education than the parents, the educational achievements of the children should not be affected, although some regression to the accomplishments of the grandfather would not be surprising.

The multivariate analysis confirms part of this hypothesis. Children of heads with less education than their fathers are likely to attain half a grade more schooling than the average. Where heads have achieved more education than the grandfather, however, both a positive and a negative deviation from the mean are shown. The negative effect could be interpreted as a regression of all children to an average level of education; the positive effect could be interpreted as the transfer of the parents' extremely high mobility to their children.

TABLE 25-11

AVERAGE COMPLETED EDUCATION OF CHILDREN: DEVIATIONS FOR
DIFFERENCES IN EDUCATION OF HEADS AND FATHERS
(FOR SPENDING UNIT HEADS WHO HAVE CHILDREN FINISHED
WITH SCHOOL)

Difference in education of heads and their fathers [a]	Number of spending unit heads	Unadjusted deviations [b]	Adjusted deviations [b]
Heads have fewer levels than fathers	56	.43	.50
Heads have the same level as fathers	674	−.59	−.02
Heads have one level more than fathers	129	1.09	−.37
Heads have two levels more than fathers	80	2.51	.39

[a] Levels of education: for fathers—0–8 grades, 9–12 grades, college; for heads—0–11 grades, 12 grades, college
[b] deviations from grand mean of 11.82 grades

The difference between the unadjusted and adjusted deviations for the nonwhites implies that parents of nonwhite children are more likely to

TABLE 25-12

AVERAGE COMPLETED EDUCATION OF CHILDREN: DEVIATIONS
FOR RACE
(FOR SPENDING UNIT HEADS WHO HAVE CHILDREN FINISHED
WITH SCHOOL)

Race	Number of spending unit heads	Unadjusted deviations [a]	Adjusted deviations [a]
White	805	.21	.06
Nonwhite	134	−1.82	−.52

[a] deviations from grand mean of 11.82 grades

exhibit other characteristics associated with low educational attainment: the parents are poorly educated and have low paying occupations requiring little education. The difference in educational attainments of white and nonwhite children should not be underrated. The adjusted deviations suggest racial differences in cultural values and the availability of facilities which account for more than half a grade of difference in educational attainments. The unadjusted deviations point out that the cumulative impact of race is to produce an average difference of two years between white and nonwhite groups.

The difference between the effects of race for spending unit heads and their children is somewhat unexpected. However, many heads grew up at a time when few people went very far in school, particularly in the South. Their children have grown up during a period when most people go to high school. As a consequence, differences in the educational facilities available to whites

TABLE 25-13

AVERAGE COMPLETED EDUCATION OF CHILDREN: DEVIATIONS
FOR URBAN-RURAL MIGRATION
(FOR SPENDING UNIT HEADS WHO HAVE CHILDREN FINISHED
WITH SCHOOL)

Urban-rural migration of spending unit heads	Number of spending unit heads	Unadjusted deviations [a]	Adjusted deviations [a]
Grew up on farms, now live:			
in rural areas	235	−.97	−.06
in towns 2,500–49,999	111	−.77	−.13
in cities 50,000 or more	65	.33	.37
Grew up in small towns, large cities, now live:			
in rural areas	131	.26	−.04
in towns or cities	369	.56	.02
All others [b]	28	.04	.03

[a] deviations from grand mean of 11.82 grades
[b] includes persons who grew up in several places and persons for whom locality was not ascertained

and nonwhites produced more noticeable differences in the educational attainments of spending unit heads' children.[1]

Though the effects shown in Table 25-13 parallel the effects shown for movement out of the Deep South, they are so small that they are relatively unimportant.

Age of the spending unit head was included in the analysis on the assumption that older persons, who were educated in a period when educational standards were lower than at present, might have less motivation for educating their children than younger parents. This notion is refuted by Table 25-14. Attainments do not vary inversely with the age of the parent.

The small negative deviations for the younger age groups result from the fact that the only young parents included here are those whose children have finished school and therefore have very little education. Other parents of the same age whose children will have college educations are excluded from the analysis because their children are still in school.

TABLE 25-14

AVERAGE COMPLETED EDUCATION OF CHILDREN: DEVIATIONS FOR AGE
(FOR SPENDING UNIT HEADS WHO HAVE CHILDREN FINISHED
WITH SCHOOL)

Age of spending unit heads	Number of spending unit heads	Unadjusted deviations [a]	Adjusted deviations [a]
30–39	30	−1.57	−.11
40–49	186	− .51	−.19
50–64	457	.32	.05
65 or older	266	− .03	.05

[a] deviations from grand mean of 11.82 grades

Though the age of the spending unit head was also included in the multivariate analysis of his own education, the role of this variable in the analysis of children's education is conceptually different from its role in the earlier analysis. In the previous analysis, age indicated the period when the head of the spending unit was in school; no variable was included in the analysis which related the head's education to the age of his father. In the present analysis the ages of the children are not included. There is no direct measure of the period when the children were educated. Families vary sufficiently in the age at which they have children and in the spacing of their children that the age of the head bears little relationship to the time when his children were

[1] For a further description of racial inequalities in schooling, see C. Arnold Anderson, "Inequalities in Schooling in the South," *The American Journal of Sociology,* LX (May, 1955), 547–561.

See also Patricia C. Sexton, *Education and Income* (New York: The Viking Press, Inc., 1961).

educated. Thus the lack of a relationship between age and children's attainments is a totally different finding from the effect seen in Table 24-3.

Summary

Analysis of the average number of grades completed by children of spending unit heads is almost completely consistent with the analysis of the education achieved by the heads themselves. Because the data relate to different generations and to different populations, the consistency between the two sets of findings indicates the general validity of the model which was used to explain educational attainments.

Characteristics of parents have a substantial effect on the amount of education their children complete. The education of the father and mother and the father's occupation and the number of children to be educated are primary determinants. The father's need-achievement score and attitude toward hard work, and religious preference and church attendance also affect the educational attainments of children. The analysis here does not permit any conjectures about whether these influences are strong enough to keep untalented children in school and prevent talented children from continuing their educations, but they certainly could work in that direction to the extent to which basic intelligence is not inherited directly.

Wthin this persistence from generation to generation, there remains, of course, a great deal of diversity. The 59 per cent of the variance which was not explained leaves a great deal of latitude for the effects of basic intelligence and motivation to determine the amount of education each person completes.

PART VI

Educational Expectations and Attitudes

Chapter 26

PARENTS' ASPIRATIONS FOR EDUCATING THEIR CHILDREN

As demonstrated in Part V, education is an important part of the process that brings about change from one generation to the next and determines the social and economic position of each succeeding generation. Because parents are interested in the well-being of their children, they must be concerned with the amount of education the children can acquire.

This section examines the aspirations of parents for the education of children still in school. In Chapter 26, characteristics of the parents are related to aspirations for the education of children, and the process of transmission and change is projected to future generations. Chapter 27 presents some implications of the demand for education, comparing present levels of attainment and present facilities with those implied by parental aspirations for education. Chapter 28 describes parents' plans for implementing their aspirations to send children to college, and Chapter 29 examines the part which people feel the government should take in financing higher education.

Parents' aspirations for educating their children were measured by answers to two questions: "How much education do you expect your boys to have before they stop going to school?" and "How much education do you expect your girls to have before they stop going to school?" The questions were asked of all heads of spending units with children of the appropriate sex aged twenty and under. The answers were coded according to the highest level of education mentioned. The few spending unit heads who report, for example, that one boy will go to college but the others will not, are included with those who report that all boys will go to college.

The responses suggest that parents are extremely optimistic in their expectations for educating their children. Table 26-1 shows that two-thirds of the parents of boys and more than half of the parents of girls expect their children to attain some education beyond high school.

These findings are roughly consistent with other studies of parents' aspirations for their children. Roper estimates that 69 per cent of the children

TABLE 26-1

EXPECTED EDUCATION
(PERCENTAGE DISTRIBUTION OF SPENDING UNITS WITH CHILDREN
20 OR UNDER)

Education levels expected by spending unit heads	Index values	For boys	For girls
0–8 grades	1	1	0
9–11 grades	2	1	1
12 grades	3	23	31
12 grades and nonacademic training	4	1	4
Some college	5	4	6
College, bachelor's degree	6	58	49
College, advanced degree	7	4	1
Do not know; general responses	–	5	5
Not ascertained	–	3	3
Total		100	100
Mean value of index		5.15	4.77
Number of spending units		1,128	1,069

– excluded from the analysis of expected education

presently below eighteen years of age are expected by their parents to go to college.[1] Data for Lansing and others report a similar figure.[2] In the Roper and Lansing studies parents were asked a specific question pertaining to the education of each child. This somewhat greater emphasis on the education of individual children may have elicited proportionately more responses of college expectations.

The data from the Roper and Lansing studies are presented for individual children, thereby giving more weight to the larger families. The percentages shown in Table 26-1 do not show the proportion of children for whom each level of education is expected; they present the proportion of spending units which have children who are expected to complete each level. Weighting the data by the number of children produces little difference in the proportion of children for whom each level is expected, as is shown below.

The Lansing study estimates that 20 to 40 per cent of the children for whom college is planned will not attend; the mortality in plans depends upon the income and social class of the parents.[3] This suggests that parents' plans for sending their children to college are quite optimistic, especially when the present capacity of colleges is also considered. It does not imply, however, that parents' aspirations do not represent a real demand for college education. In Chapter 27 some data are presented which indicate surprising consistency between parents' aspirations for educating children who are not yet through

[1] Elmo Roper and others, "Parents' College Plans Study," prepared for the Education Program of the Ford Foundation, 1959, p. 1.

[2] John B. Lansing and others, *How People Pay for College* (Ann Arbor: The Survey Research Center, University of Michigan, 1960), pp. 100–101.

[3] Lansing and others, *How People Pay for College*, pp. 104–111.

TABLE 26-2

EXPECTED EDUCATION
(PERCENTAGE DISTRIBUTION OF CHILDREN 20 OR UNDER)

Education expected for children	Per cent of all children
0–8 grades	1
9–11 grades	1
12 grades	32
12 grades and nonacademic training	3
Some college	5
College, bachelor's degree	56
College, advanced degree	2
Total	100
Mean value of index	4.86

school and projections obtained by extrapolating the analysis of completed education to the educational attainments of the next generation.

If, as seems reasonable, there is a close association between education attained by children who are finished with school and the educational aspirations of parents for their younger children, the factors which accounted for two-fifths of the variance in educational attainment should also account for much of the variance in parents' aspirations for children who have yet to complete their schooling. (See Chapter 25.) To these factors two other independent variables have been added: the ratio of college enrollment to population within each area comprising a primary sampling unit, and the age of the oldest boy or girl twenty or under.

The ratio of college enrollment to population is designed as a measure of the availability of facilities for higher education close to home. This variable may influence both the cost and accessibility of higher education. In addition, the availability of colleges and universities may create a greater awareness of the importance of education beyond high school. This factor was not used to explain the achieved education of children who had finished school because many of the children were educated when the parents were living in different communities.

The age of the oldest boy or girl under twenty indicates how close the family is to a time of decision about college. The level of education which parents expect their children to achieve in many instances may be quite unrealistic. It is likely that as children approach the age at which they would go to college, their parents' plans become more realistic. Hence, the older the children, the lower the expected level of schooling should be.

In place of the peak earnings, which were used in the analysis of completed education, as a measure of lifetime earning patterns, current gross disposable income was used in the analysis of educational aspirations. Current income describes the family's present financial situation, which probably influences aspirations for children who are not yet finished with their schooling.

Age of the spending unit head was not included in the analysis of expectations because it showed no relationship to actual attainments. Moreover, spending unit heads whose children are still in school are much more homogeneous as to age than those whose children are finished with school.

Fourteen characteristics were used to explain parents' aspirations. These characteristics account for about one-third of the variance in level of education expected by heads of spending units for their children aged twenty or under. The coefficient of multiple determination obtained for boys was .31, while for girls it was somewhat lower, .28. The mean expected level for boys is 5.15, some college; for girls the mean expected level is 4.77, between high school plus nonacademic training, and some college. The standard deviations are 1.41 for boys and 1.45 for girls.

TABLE 26-3

CHARACTERISTICS USED TO EXPLAIN EXPECTED LEVEL OF EDUCATION
(FOR SPENDING UNIT HEADS WITH CHILDREN 20 OR UNDER)

Characteristics of spending unit heads	Relative importance				Significance	
	Rank		Beta coefficients		F ratios	
	Boys	Girls	Boys	Girls	Boys	Girls
Education	1	1	.374	.407	32.50**	35.10**
Gross disposable income of spending unit	2	4	.190	.130	6.52**	3.13**
Difference in education of heads and wives	3	3	.143	.145	5.54**	5.20**
Attitude toward hard work and need-achievement score	4	5	.118	.116	3.77**	3.33**
Number of living children	5	2	.129	.155	6.77**	8.91**
Difference in education of heads and fathers	6	11	.104	.086	5.86**	3.66*
Age at birth of eldest living child	7	10	.099	.086	2.66*	1.83
Occupation	8	6	.088	.116	1.40	2.22*
Ratio of college enrollment to population	9	12	.076	.078	1.34	1.29
Urban-rural migration	10	7	.073	.096	1.73	2.73*
Movement out of Deep South	11	13	.063	.074	1.29	1.62
Age of eldest boy or girl 20 or under	12	14	.047	.036	0.90	0.48
Religious preference and church attendance	13	8	.047	.090	0.60	2.00
Race	14	9	.005	.088	0.04	11.49**

** significant at probability level of .01
* significant at probability level of .05

The relative importance and significance of each of the predictive characteristics are indicated in Table 26-3.

The education of the spending unit head is far more important than any of the other variables in predicting educational aspirations. Education expected for both boys and girls is a consistently increasing function of the head's education. Even after the influence of the other variables is removed, where the spending unit head holds a college degree he expects his boys to complete more than one full level of schooling beyond that expected for sons by heads with less than 12 grades.

The influence of the college experience of the head appears to be somewhat greater with respect to educational expectations for girls than for boys. At others levels of education of the head, the difference in expectations between boys and girls is insubstantial. This may suggest that the college experience

TABLE 26-4

EXPECTED EDUCATION: DEVIATIONS FOR EDUCATION OF HEADS
(FOR SPENDING UNIT HEADS WITH CHILDREN 20 OR UNDER)

Education of spending unit heads	Number of spending unit heads		Unadjusted deviations [a]		Adjusted deviations [a]	
	Boys	Girls	Boys	Girls	Boys	Girls
None	10	5	−.93	.00	−.13	−.39
1–8 grades	309	313	−.91	−.82	−.66	−.70
9–11 grades	269	253	−.24	−.33	−.36	−.40
12 grades	191	162	.24	.27	.21	.30
12 grades and nonacademic training	105	113	.51	.36	.53	.38
College, no degree	130	110	.71	.73	.66	.83
College, bachelor's degree	87	85	.87	1.07	.68	.81
College, advanced degree	27	28	1.08	1.12	.75	.86

[a] deviations from grand mean: 5.15 for boys, 4.77 for girls

of parents tends to give them a greater appreciation of the nonvocational benefits of higher education. At any rate the fact that the spending unit head has attended college appears to bring about more nearly equal expectations for the education of girls and boys.

The current gross disposable income of the spending unit is the second most important determinant of the level of education expected for boys. Its importance, however, is considerably smaller with respect to girls. Once the other variables have been taken into account, the level of education expected for boys in spending units with incomes between $1,000 and $1,999 is almost one and one-half levels below that expected by heads of spending units with incomes of $15,000 and over. The spread for girls is only half as wide.

The importance and consistency of the effect of income on aspirations contrasts with the irregular relationship between peak earnings of the head and the average completed education of his children. (See Table 25-8.) The fact that income affects aspirations lends support to the earlier argument that the lack of relationship of peak earnings with completed education is probably a result of the fact that peak earnings are a relatively crude measure of real earnings at the time decisions were being made about children's education.

The education expected for children appears to be a function of the wife's

TABLE 26-5

EXPECTED EDUCATION: DEVIATIONS FOR GROSS DISPOSABLE INCOME
(FOR SPENDING UNIT HEADS WITH CHILDREN 20 OR UNDER)

Gross disposable income of spending units	Number of spending unit heads		Unadjusted deviations [a]		Adjusted deviations [a]	
	Boys	Girls	Boys	Girls	Boys	Girls
Less than $500; negative	11	11	− .07	− .17	−.01	−.10
$500–999	14	10	−1.10	− .68	−.48	−.05
$1,000–1,999	82	87	−1.50	−1.07	−.83	−.58
$2,000–2,999	118	121	−1.00	− .69	−.46	−.29
$3,000–4,999	234	249	− .32	− .23	−.12	−.08
$5,000–7,499	344	304	.11	.05	.06	.07
$7,500–9,999	199	156	.44	.36	.19	.18
$10,000–14,999	101	103	.62	.59	.29	.15
$15,000 and over	25	28	1.13	.99	.49	.20

[a] deviations from grand mean: 5.15 for boys, 4.77 for girls

education as well as the spending unit head's education. In those cases in which the wife has had substantially more education than the head, more education is expected for the children than might be indicated on the basis of the head's education. The converse is true when the head has substantially more education than his wife.

TABLE 26-6

EXPECTED EDUCATION: DEVIATIONS FOR DIFFERENCES IN EDUCATION
OF HEADS AND WIVES
(FOR SPENDING UNIT HEADS WITH CHILDREN 20 OR UNDER)

Difference in education of spending unit heads and wives [b]	Number of spending unit heads		Unadjusted deviations [a]		Adjusted deviations [a]	
	Boys	Girls	Boys	Girls	Boys	Girls
Wives have two or more levels more than heads	112	99	−.02	−.07	.34	.30
Wives have one level more than heads	185	173	−.05	.05	.19	.34
Wives have same level as heads	372	345	−.14	−.27	.01	−.05
Wives have one less level than heads	170	157	.28	.32	−.15	−.09
Wives have two or more levels less than heads	137	143	.51	.57	−.37	−.31
Education of wives not ascertained	4	3	−.97	.68	−.69	−.57
Heads are single, widowed, or divorced	148	149	−.51	−.38	.05	−.05

[a] deviations from grand mean: 5.15 for boys, 4.77 for girls
[b] levels of education are defined as:

none	12 grades and nonacademic training
1–8 grades	college, no degree
9–11 grades	college, bachelor's degree
12 grades	college, advanced degree

The adjusted deviations of Table 26-7 indicate that the need-achievement score reflects an important determinant of educational aspirations. However, expectations for boys of parents who feel that luck is more important do not appear to vary systematically with the need-achievement score; parents with low need-achievement scores and the perception that luck is an important factor in getting ahead have somewhat higher aspirations than might be expected after the multivariate adjustments are completed.

TABLE 26-7

EXPECTED EDUCATION: DEVIATIONS FOR ATTITUDE TOWARD
HARD WORK AND NEED-ACHIEVEMENT SCORE
(FOR SPENDING UNIT HEADS WITH CHILDREN 20 OR UNDER)

Heads' attitude toward hard work and need-achievement score	Number of spending unit heads		Unadjusted deviations [a]		Adjusted deviations [a]	
	Boys	Girls	Boys	Girls	Boys	Girls
Hard work is equal to or more important than luck; need-achievement score is in:						
high range	282	261	.45	.42	.22	.20
middle range	401	389	.09	.06	.00	.03
low range	198	183	−.32	−.29	−.13	−.15
Hard work is less important than luck; need-achievement score is in:						
high range	53	44	−.04	.20	−.06	.17
middle range	93	97	−.56	−.43	−.37	−.27
low range	70	63	−.76	−.88	−.01	−.35
Need-achievement score not ascertained	31	32	−.42	−.20	−.17	.00

[a] deviations from grand mean: 5.15 for boys, 4.77 for girls

The number of children of the head is a major factor influencing the level of education expected for children. This factor operates as a constraint, particularly with respect to aspirations for the schooling of girls. In the case of girls it is second in importance only to the education of the head of the spending unit. Other things being equal, girls and boys in families with one or two children are expected to obtain a substantially higher level of education than those who are members of families having five or more children.[4]

The only other characteristic of spending unit heads with a statistically significant relationship to expected education for both boys and girls is the difference in education of the head and his father.

Spending unit heads who had less education than their fathers appear to base their aspirations for their children in part on the experience of their

---

[4] Though number of children affects aspirations, aspirations to send children to college do not appear to affect planning and family size according to Charles F. Westoff, *Family Planning in Metropolitan America*, V (Princeton, New Jersey: Princeton University Press, 1961), p. 256.

TABLE 26-8

EXPECTED EDUCATION: DEVIATIONS FOR NUMBER OF LIVING CHILDREN
(FOR SPENDING UNIT HEADS WITH CHILDREN 20 OR UNDER)

Number of living children of spending unit heads	Number of spending unit heads		Unadjusted deviations [a]		Adjusted deviations [a]	
	Boys	Girls	Boys	Girls	Boys	Girls
One	145	147	.45	.43	.25	.31
Two	324	297	.25	.30	.10	.15
Three or four	440	408	.00	−.03	−.02	−.04
Five or more	219	217	−.83	−.78	−.35	−.40

[a] deviations from grand mean: 5.15 for boys, 4.77 for girls

fathers. Similarly, if the heads achieved more education than their fathers this fact lessens parents' aspirations for their children.

Table 26-9 clearly suggests a pattern of regression that was not evident in the analysis of completed education attained by children. (See Table 25-11.) The adjusted deviations indicate that once the family has had experience with education beyond grade school, aspirations for educating children are substantially increased, even though the head does not attain as much education as his father. The persistence of mobility reported in the previous chapter does not appear here, probably because in this younger generation those with two levels more than their fathers have so much education that it is difficult for their children to have more.

TABLE 26-9

EXPECTED EDUCATION: DEVIATIONS FOR DIFFERENCE IN EDUCATION
OF HEADS AND FATHERS
(FOR SPENDING UNIT HEADS WITH CHILDREN 20 OR UNDER)

Difference in education of spending unit heads and fathers [a]	Number of spending unit heads		Unadjusted deviations [b]		Adjusted deviations [b]	
	Boys	Girls	Boys	Girls	Boys	Girls
Heads have fewer levels than fathers	67	70	.14	−.04	.49	.26
Heads have same level as fathers	639	615	−.37	−.35	.03	.07
Heads have one level more than fathers	298	272	.38	.41	−.15	−.14
Heads have two levels more than fathers	124	112	.73	.76	−.04	−.16

[a] levels of education:
  for fathers—0–8 grades, 9–12 grades, college;
  for heads—0–11 grades, 12 grades, college
[b] deviations from grand mean: 5.15 for boys, 4.77 for girls

Parents' aspirations for the education of their boys are associated with the age of the spending unit head at the time his eldest living child was born.

As was suggested earlier, birth of the first child when the spending unit head is under twenty may indicate an inability to plan adequately for the future. Such spending unit heads may frequently find themselves under heavy financial pressure at the outset of their marriages, pressure which appears to lead to less ambitious plans for the education of their children than their other characteristics would suggest. The findings in Table 26-10 reiterate the findings about educational levels attained by children whose schooling has been completed. (See Table 25-10.)

TABLE 26-10

EXPECTED EDUCATION: DEVIATIONS FOR AGE OF HEAD AT BIRTH
OF ELDEST LIVING CHILD
(FOR SPENDING UNIT HEADS WITH CHILDREN 20 OR UNDER)

Age of spending unit heads at birth of eldest living child	Number of spending unit heads		Unadjusted deviations [a]		Adjusted deviations [a]	
	Boys	Girls	Boys	Girls	Boys	Girls
Under 18	26	25	−1.16	−.83	−.22	−.14
18–19	68	80	− .76	−.63	−.30	−.37
20–24	429	371	− .01	−.11	.03	.00
25–29	343	334	.14	.11	.08	.05
30–39	223	214	.26	.35	.02	.06
40 or older	27	35	−1.04	−.15	−.64	−.15
No children [b]	12	10	− .67	−.75	−.43	−.62

[a] deviations from grand mean: 5.15 for boys, 4.77 for girls
[b] includes heads with adopted children and inconsistent responses

Relationships between education expected for boys and occupation, urban-rural migration, movement out of the Deep South, religious preference and church attendance, age of the eldest boy under twenty, race, and availability of educational faciilties were not statistically significant. However, the hypotheses relating education expected for girls to occupation, urban-rural migration, and race were supported. Tables 26-11 through 26-17 present, for the reader's information, effects of these seven characteristics, whether or not the F-ratios are statistically significant. Most of the other differences are in the expected direction. One-tailed tests or pattern tests might have shown significance, but it is the direction and level of importance that are most relevant.

Sizable difference between unadjusted and adjusted deviations appear in the relationship between occupation of the spending unit head and education expected for his sons. The average level of education expected for the sons of professionals is about the level of a college degree (5.15 plus unadjusted deviation of .78), compared with the average of college, no degree expected for all boys. But the adjusted deviation of .09 for this group shows that the fact that the head is a professional contributes little to the level of education expected for boys, once the education of the head, gross disposable income of the spending unit, and the other determinants of aspirations are also taken into account; much the same is true for all other occuptaional groups.

However, the net association between the occupation of the head of the spending unit and educational aspirations for his daughters is statistically significant, indicating some contrast in expectations held for girls and expectations held for boys. Farmers appear to expect about the same level of education for both girls and boys. This level is greater than the average for all girls,

TABLE 26-11

EXPECTED EDUCATION: DEVIATIONS FOR OCCUPATION OF HEAD
(FOR SPENDING UNIT HEADS WITH CHILDREN 20 OR UNDER)

Occupation of spending unit heads	Number of spending unit heads		Unadjusted deviations [a]		Adjusted deviations [a]	
	Boys	Girls	Boys	Girls	Boys	Girls
Professionals	111	106	.78	.90	.09	.08
Managers	59	51	.69	.91	.07	.48
Self-employed businessmen	76	67	.31	.32	.11	.14
Clerical and sales workers	120	123	.52	.44	.23	.11
Skilled workers	206	186	.06	−.18	−.04	−.15
Semiskilled workers	236	217	−.31	−.36	−.05	−.08
Unskilled workers	173	172	−.85	−.72	−.19	−.15
Farmers	95	92	−.68	−.29	−.12	.20
Government protective workers	27	34	.17	.23	−.08	−.20
Not ascertained; never worked	25	21	−.33	−.38	.20	.08

[a] deviations from grand mean: 5.15 for boys, 4.77 for girls

less than the average for all boys. Perhaps farmers regard their sons as being likely to continue in farming where educational requirements may be less than they are off the farm, while they expect their daughters to leave the farm and require more education. Alternatively, or as a complementary influence, it may be that opportunities for working on the farm are greater for boys than for girls, so that the opportunity costs of keeping girls in school are less than they are for boys. However, no readily apparent parallel explanation accounts for the substantially greater expectations shown for girls whose fathers are managers.

Though some differences in aspirations are associated with the availability of college facilities, nearly all the variation can be accounted for by differences in the other characteristics of families living in these areas.

This is an example of the advantages of multivariate analyses, and an illustration of the difficulties in dealing with community or group influences. If people in a group or an area behave alike, it is difficult to tell whether they are subject to the same exogenous influences, or they joined the group because they agreed with its members, or the group really influences its members. In the present case it was possible to identify influences which accounted for

TABLE 26-12

EXPECTED EDUCATION: DEVIATIONS FOR THE RATIO
OF COLLEGE ENROLLMENT TO POPULATION
(FOR SPENDING UNIT HEADS WITH CHILDREN 20 OR UNDER)

Ratio of college enrollment to local population	Number of spending unit heads		Unadjusted deviations [a]		Adjusted deviations [a]	
	Boys	Girls	Boys	Girls	Boys	Girls
No college in the area	267	262	−.41	−.38	−.13	−.05
Under 1.0 per cent	103	95	.09	−.10	.04	−.01
1.0–1.4 per cent	154	164	−.01	−.03	.05	.00
1.5–1.9 per cent	217	201	.26	.13	.12	−.07
2.0–2.9 per cent	121	122	.13	.26	−.10	.06
3.0–3.9 per cent	90	74	.18	.13	−.14	−.18
4.0–4.9 per cent	84	72	.28	.44	.09	.18
5.0 per cent and over	92	79	−.38	.05	.13	.33

[a] deviations from grand mean: 5.15 for boys, 4.77 for girls

most of the group differences, but even if the adjusted deviations had remained significant, the problem of whether people influence each other's aspirations, or move to communities where others share theirs would have persisted.

Spending unit heads who grew up on farms and still live in rural areas expect their daughters to acquire significantly less education than do heads who grew on farms and now live in large cities. Where the parent lives now makes little difference if he did not grow up on a farm.

It is somewhat surprising that urban-rural migration affects aspirations for girls when its impact on attainments is insignificant. (See Table 25-13.)

TABLE 26-13

EXPECTED EDUCATION: DEVIATIONS FOR URBAN-RURAL MIGRATION
(FOR SPENDING UNIT HEADS WITH CHILDREN 20 OR UNDER)

Urban-rural migration of spending unit heads	Number of spending unit heads		Unadjusted deviations [a]		Adjusted deviations [a]	
	Boys	Girls	Boys	Girls	Boys	Girls
Grew up on farms, now live:						
in rural areas	244	225	−.65	−.53	−.18	−.24
in towns 2,500–49,999	88	89	−.22	−.06	.24	.09
in cities 50,000 or more	47	43	−.28	−.07	.04	.26
Grew up in small towns, large cities, now live:						
in rural areas	228	205	.24	.06	.02	−.09
in towns or cities	498	486	.21	.18	.02	.09
All others [b]	23	21	−.05	.07	−.04	.05

[a] deviations from grand mean: 5.15 for boys, 4.77 for girls
[b] includes persons who grew up in several places and persons for whom locality was not ascertained

TABLE 26-14

EXPECTED EDUCATION: DEVIATIONS FOR MOVEMENT OUT
OF THE DEEP SOUTH
(FOR SPENDING UNIT HEADS WITH CHILDREN 20 OR UNDER)

Movement out of Deep South by spending unit heads	Number of spending unit heads		Unadjusted deviations [a]		Adjusted deviations [a]	
	Boys	Girls	Boys	Girls	Boys	Girls
Grew up in the United States outside the Deep South, now live:						
in South	157	151	.17	.27	.02	.08
in non-South	625	583	.11	.07	−.05	−.03
Grew up in the Deep South, now live:						
in South	241	229	−.31	−.23	.12	.03
in non-South	61	54	−.53	−.59	−.11	−.27
Grew up in foreign countries	37	39	−.04	.15	.18	.25
All others [b]	7	13	.63	.70	.57	.57

[a] deviations from grand mean: 5.15 for boys, 4.77 for girls
[b] includes persons who grew up in several regions of the country and cases in which region was not ascertained

Similarly, it is curious that movement out of the Deep South is significantly related to attainments but does not affect aspirations. (See Table 25-6.) The difference may again reflect the difference in average age of the spending unit heads with children finished with school and those with children still in school. Children who are now finished with school may have been educated at a time when educational facilities in Southern parts of the United States were less adequate than they are today.

Though the unadjusted deviations support the hypothesis that expectations decline with increasing age of the eldest child, the adjusted deviations are in the expected pattern but not significantly different.

TABLE 26-15

EXPECTED EDUCATION: DEVIATIONS FOR AGE OF ELDEST BOY
OR GIRL 20 OR UNDER
(FOR SPENDING UNIT HEADS WITH CHILDREN 20 OR UNDER)

Age of eldest boy or girl of the spending unit head	Number of spending unit heads		Unadjusted deviations [a]		Adjusted deviations [a]	
	Boys	Girls	Boys	Girls	Boys	Girls
Under 10	539	518	.18	.13	.04	.02
10–12	204	187	−.07	.02	.04	.05
13–15	179	165	−.18	−.07	−.04	.00
16–17	121	123	−.05	−.30	−.02	−.10
18–20	85	76	−.51	−.33	−.21	−.11

[a] deviations from grand mean: 5.15 for boys, 4.77 for girls

While the set of deviations by religious preference and church attendance is not statistically significant, it is interesting that more frequent attenders expect to provide more education for their children. (See Table 25-9.) The expectations of Catholics are lowest, particularly with respect to their daughters.

TABLE 26-16

EXPECTED EDUCATION: DEVIATIONS FOR RELIGIOUS PREFERENCE AND CHURCH ATTENDANCE OF HEADS
(FOR SPENDING UNIT HEADS WITH CHILDREN 20 OR UNDER)

Religious preference and church attendance of spending unit heads	Number of spending unit heads		Unadjusted deviations [a]		Adjusted deviations [a]	
	Boys	Girls	Boys	Girls	Boys	Girls
Catholics, attend church:						
twice a month or more	196	183	.06	−.02	−.05	−.13
once a month or less	46	48	−.13	−.59	−.02	−.39
Fundamentalist Protestants, attend church:						
twice a month or more	252	246	−.21	−.08	.00	.10
once a month or less	181	168	−.51	−.49	−.11	−.07
Non-Fundamentalist Protestants, attend church:						
twice a month or more	198	183	.35	.37	.05	.08
once a month or less	206	191	.14	.13	.03	.03
Non-Christians; no preference	49	50	.55	.57	.18	.25

[a] deviations from grand mean: 5.15 for boys, 4.77 for girls

Table 26-17 demonstrates clearly the importance of disentangling the influences which affect educational expectations. Unadjusted deviations show that whites and nonwhites have substantially different expectations for educating their boys. However, the difference appears to be associated with differences in the education, income, and other characteristics of the two groups, because the adjusted deviations contribute nothing to an explanation of parents' aspirations.

However, the two groups agree more closely in their expectations for educating girls. When expectations are adjusted for education, income, and other differences, it becomes clear that nonwhites have higher aspirations for girls than would otherwise be expected.

The large positive deviation for nonwhite girls results from the assumption that parents expect similar differences in levels of education for their girls and boys at all levels. Table 26-17 shows that whites, who are probably referring to differences in education at the college level, make some distinction between girls and boys; nonwhites, who anticipate high school educations for their children, do not make such distinctions. The positive deviation for nonwhite

TABLE 26-17

EXPECTED EDUCATION: DEVIATIONS FOR RACE
(FOR SPENDING UNIT HEADS WITH CHILDREN 20 OR UNDER)

Race	Number of spending unit heads		Unadjusted deviations [a]		Adjusted deviations [a]	
	Boys	Girls	Boys	Girls	Boys	Girls
Whites	952	897	.09	.03	.00	−.05
Nonwhites	176	172	−.67	−.23	−.02	.34

[a] deviations from grand mean: 5.15 for boys, 4.77 for girls

girls brings their expected level of education up from the girls lower grand mean to within .02 of the expected level for nonwhite boys.

Using the unadjusted deviations shown in Table 26-17, the absolute expected levels are:

	Boys	Girls
Whites	5.24	4.80
Nonwhites	4.48	4.54

These data do not settle the question of whether the lower aspirations of nonwhite families result from their lower incomes and educations. However, the extent to which these changeable factors influence aspirations leaves room for hope that progress is possible in increasing education of nonwhite persons.

Summary

The forces which influence parents' aspirations for the education of their children are consistent with those which have influenced the education of children already finished, and the education of the heads themselves. Education of the parents and current gross disposable income are the most important determinants. A substantial amount of transmission of educational status from one generation to the next exists, but there are enough departures to indicate that some selection on other bases, hopefully ability and motivation, may exist.

Chapter 27

SOME IMPLICATIONS FOR THE DEMAND FOR EDUCATION

Predictions of future education levels can be developed by projecting relationships shown in the various multivariate analyses, in particular the analysis of completed education of children. The model on which the multivariate analysis is based allows one to estimate for any individual the amount of education he will get, according to a series of adjustments for each characteristic used in the analysis. Some of the classifications used in the analysis are things for which the population distribution will change in the future. For instance, the distribution of the income level of parents or of the education level of the parents can be forecast by making trend extrapolations. By applying the coefficients of the multivariate analysis one can determine what effect these shifts will have on the average level of completed education of children.

The analysis of completed education of children of the head includes all living children, but is based on spending unit heads who may have differing numbers of children. Hence, even with the population distributions of all the independent variables in the analysis from Chapter 25, a biased estimate of the average level of completed education of children would result. It is necessary to estimate the average number of children for each group of families as well as the average level of completed education. For a description of educational aspirations weighted by family size see Table 26-2.

An alternative method of projection arises from the fact that one of the major determinants of the level of education of any individual is the education of his father. Thus, the probability of an individual going to college is, in part, a function of whether or not his father went to college. The transmission of education from one generation to the next can be regarded as a series of conditional probabilities. One can take the distributions of education of an older and a younger generation and apply the shifts in such a matrix to predict the educational distribution of the third generation. Then, it is possible to take this distribution of the third generation, and apply the same matrix to determine the educational distribution of the following generation. This can be done separately for each age group. Here again one must be careful because families are of different sizes. Furthermore, there are several relationships between the education of one generation and the education of the next that can be used for this purpose: the relationship of the education of the spending unit head to that of his father, the relationship of the head's education to the completed education of his children, or the relationship between the head's education and the education he expects for his children who have not finished school.

Table 27-1 shows a relationship between the education of spending unit heads under thirty-five years of age and the education of their fathers. By substituting the educational distribution of heads for the educational distribution of *fathers* the heads can be thought of as a new set of fathers. Then it is possible to estimate the distribution of education among their children.

TABLE 27-1

EDUCATION OF SPENDING UNIT HEADS WITHIN EDUCATION
OF THEIR FATHERS
(PERCENTAGE DISTRIBUTION OF SPENDING UNIT HEADS UNDER 35)

Education of spending unit heads	Education of heads' fathers					Estimated education received by children of spending unit heads under 35 [a]
	0–8 grades	9–11 grades	12 grades	Some college	Total	
0–8 grades	21	6	2	1	15	6
9–11 grades	29	14	16	8	23	15
12 grades	31	46	32	22	32	32
Some college	19	34	50	69	30	47
Total	100	100	100	100	100	100

[a] The estimated distribution of education is obtained by multiplying the proportion of the subgroup in Table 27-1 by the proportions in the total column and adding the products. In other words $(19 \times 15) + (34 \times 23) + (50 \times 32) + (69 \times 30) = 47$ per cent, which is an estimate of the number of college graduates among the next generation. Estimates of the proportions who will be high school graduates and so forth are obtained in the same fashion.

The last column of Table 27-1 is quite consistent with the Office of Education's projection that roughly 44 per cent of all persons between the ages of eighteen and twenty-one will be in college by 1970.[1]

The problem of differing family sizes does not enter into the analysis of

[1] Dexter M. Keezer, ed., *Financing Higher Education* (New York: McGraw-Hill Book Co. Inc., 1960), p. 15.

See also "School Enrollment and Education of Young Adults and Their Fathers: October, 1960," *Current Population Reports Series P-20,* #110 (U.S. Bureau of the Census, July 24, 1961), Table A, p. 1.

spending unit heads because the analysis started with the heads and related their educations to that of their fathers. However, to the extent that spending unit heads differ from the rest of the population any projections for the entire population are biased if they are based solely on spending unit heads.

A crucial problem for any projections into the future, however, is not just unbiased mechanical extrapolation of either the past trends or of past transition probabilities. It is the extent to which people's attitudes, plans, and aspirations are likely to change in the future. The motivations, values, and educational attainments of parents clearly imply increasing educational attainment and more widely held aspirations for college education for the next generation.

There are therefore three ways in which educational achievement will be increased in the future. First, as the educational attainments of each generation increase, that generation tends to see to it that its children get still more education. This is the process previously described as a set of conditional probabilities. Second, factors other than the parents' education affect the education provided and these factors for children, may also change. Third, and most difficult to project, the general level of people's concern with education and realization of its importance may grow so that parents in all situations will tend to be more concerned with their children's education. People are generally aware of the personal economic advantage of more education. Some are becoming aware of the national needs for trained personnel, and perhaps the noneconomic and nonmilitary advantages of education may ultimately be more widely appreciated.

To what extent this is a limited process is an interesting question. Educational levels will not continue to increase indefinitely because there is little need for training beyond a college degree for any but those who intend to go into certain professions.

TABLE 27-2

PROJECTED EDUCATION OF DESCENDENTS
OF SPENDING UNIT HEADS UNDER 35

Education	Great-grandchildren of spending unit heads under 35	Great-great grand-children of spending unit heads under 35
0–8 grades	3	2
9–11 grades	12	12
12 grades	28	28
Some college	57	58
Total	100	100

It is also clear that from the close relationship between the education of one generation and the education of the next in the same family that there is some perpetuation of poverty through low relative educational levels and there is perpetuation of high status through continuation of high levels of education. However, as more and more people finish high school and go to college, these differences become narrowed and their importance decreases. Using the conditional probabilities described in Table 27-1, a state of equilibrium is resolved within a few generations, illustrated in Table 27-2. Although the educational distribution stabilizes, the shifting of various families between groups continues.

Chapter 28

PLANS FOR SENDING CHILDREN TO COLLEGE

Since the decisions to attend a public rather than a private college, and to live at home or at the college play so large a role in determining how much a college education costs, it is interesting to discover as much as possible about factors that may influence these decisions. A related set of findings involves the extent to which parents expect their children to support themselves in college. An analysis of these factors should cast further light on the realism of parents' aspirations for the college education of their children, and provide some insights into the problems which will be encountered in implementing these aspirations.

Realism of expectations can be assessed by comparing families' education plans with their financial resources. Families with low incomes and low savings are less likely to realize plans for children's college educations than are more prosperous families. Degrees of realism are also apparent in the proportion of parents who expect their children to go to college but have no specific plans for implementing these expectations.

The Choice of Public or Private Colleges

Spending unit heads' expectations about whether their children will attend public or private colleges are related to income, religious preference, and other factors. Table 28-1 shows that the proportion of parents who indicated that their children will attend private colleges is approximately twice as large for those with incomes over $10,000 as for those with incomes under $3,000. This is not surprising since attendance at private colleges is more costly. The high proportion of indefinite answers in the low income group is significant as an indication of lack of planning.

A second factor that is clearly related to the choice between private and public colleges is religious preference, as is indicated in Table 28-2. Little difference exists among Fundamentalist and non-Fundamentalist Protestants, but a larger proportion of Catholics who attend church regularly expect their children to go to private colleges.

TABLE 28-1

PLANS TO SEND CHILDREN TO PUBLIC COLLEGES
WITHIN GROSS DISPOSABLE INCOME OF SPENDING UNITS
(PERCENTAGE DISTRIBUTION OF SPENDING UNIT HEADS
WHO EXPECT CHILDREN TO ATTEND COLLEGE)

Plans to send children to public colleges	Gross disposable income					All spending unit heads who expect children to attend college
	Under $3,000	$3,000– 4,999	$5,000– 7,499	$7,500– 9,999	$10,000 and over	
Some or all will attend public colleges	87	83	78	75	70	78
All will attend private colleges	13	17	22	25	30	22
Total	100	100	100	100	100	100
Per cent with no plans	32	24	24	20	23	24
Number of spending unit heads in group	138	229	355	217	169	1,108

The sixty-six primary sampling areas were classified into four groups, according to whether they contained private colleges, public colleges, both, or neither, indicating the availability of the two types of institutions. In those areas which contain only public colleges, more than nine-tenths of the parents expect their children to attend public rather than private colleges. Similarly, when there is no college of either kind in the area the choice lies to a clearly disproportionate extent with the public college. Where there is only a private college, and where both private and public colleges exist, the choice still lies with the public college but to a lesser extent. The similarity in the proportions shown in the second and fourth columns of Table 28-3, relating to these two types of areas, is somewhat puzzling and not readily explainable.

Other characteristics did not seem to affect plans to send children to public or private schools. There is no discernible pattern related to the extent to which the children are expected to support themselves in college or the expected sources of money for colleges expenses.

The preceding tables have dealt with proportions of spending unit heads. Seventy per cent of the children whose parents have definite plans for their going to college are expected to attend a public college. This compares with the fact that in the fall of 1959 public colleges and universities accommodated 60 per cent of the American college enrollment.[1] These data do not permit precise comparisons with present enrollment ratios, but they show that, along with an increase in the number of children attending college in the future,

[1] United States Department of Health, Education, and Welfare, Office of Education, *Opening (Fall) Enrollment in Higher Education, 1959: Analytic Report* (1960), p. 17.

TABLE 28-2

PLANS TO SEND CHILDREN TO PUBLIC COLLEGES WITHIN RELIGIOUS PREFERENCE AND CHURCH ATTENDANCE

(PERCENTAGE DISTRIBUTION OF SPENDING UNIT HEADS WHO EXPECT CHILDREN TO ATTEND COLLEGE)

Plans to send children to public colleges	Religious preference and church attendance							All spending unit heads who expect children to attend college
	Catholics; attend:		Fundamentalist Protestants; attend:		Non-Fundamentalist Protestants; attend:		Non-Christians; no preference	
	Twice a month or more	Once a month or less	Twice a month or more	Once a month or less	Twice a month or more	Once a month or less		
Some or all will attend public colleges	64	30	79	87	79	83	71	78
All will attend private colleges	36	20	21	13	21	17	29	22
Total	100	100	100	100	100	100	100	100
Per cent with no plans	23	31	25	28	22	22	28	24
Number of spending unit heads in group	191	46	235	133	216	226	61	1,108

407

TABLE 28-3

PLANS TO SEND CHILDREN TO PUBLIC COLLEGES
WITHIN AVAILABILITY OF COLLEGES IN AREA
(PERCENTAGE DISTRIBUTION OF SPENDING UNIT HEADS
WHO EXPECT CHILDREN TO ATTEND COLLEGE)

Plans to send children to public colleges	Availability of colleges in area [a]				All spending unit heads who expect children to attend college
	No college in area	Only private college in area	Only public college in area	Public and private colleges in the area	
Some or all will attend public colleges	85	74	94	73	78
All will attend private colleges	15	26	6	27	22
Total	100	100	100	100	100
Per cent with no plans	21	25	13	28	24
Number of spending unit heads in group	220	201	125	562	1,108

[a] area is a primary sampling unit (see Appendix D)

public colleges will be expected to accommodate a larger proportion of the larger total enrollment.

The Choice of Living at Home or at College

Another factor influencing the cost of going to college is whether or not the student lives away from home. Sixty-one per cent of children whose parents have definite plans for their going to college will live away from home while attending college. Lansing's data about college students revealed that approximately two-thirds of the students were living away from home.[2] Thus the expectations of parents with respect to where their children will live while attending college do not differ appreciably from the actual experience of students in 1960.

Whether the children are expected to live at home or go away to college depends in large part upon the income of the spending unit of which they are members. Forty per cent of heads of spending units with gross disposable incomes under $5,000 expect that all of their children who will go to college will live at home, whereas for the group with $10,000 and over the proportion is only 17 per cent. The proportion who have made no plans decreases as income rises.

The availability of a public or private college in the area also exerts a major influence on expectations about where children will live while in college. The substantial difference between areas with only public and only private colleges in the proportion who expect children to live at home is undoubtedly due in

[2] John B. Lansing and others, *How People Pay for College* (Ann Arbor: The Survey Research Center, University of Michigan, 1960), p. 19.

TABLE 28-4

PLANS FOR CHILDREN TO LIVE AT HOME WHILE IN COLLEGE
WITHIN GROSS DISPOSABLE INCOME OF SPENDING UNITS
(PERCENTAGE DISTRIBUTION OF SPENDING UNIT HEADS
WHO EXPECT CHILDREN TO ATTEND COLLEGE)

Plans for children to live at home while in college	Gross disposable income of spending units					All spending unit heads who expect children to attend college
	Under $3,000	$3,000–4,999	$5,000–7,499	$7,500–9,999	$10,000 and over	
All will live at home	44	39	37	30	17	33
Some will live at home; some away	4	4	9	11	14	9
All will live away from home	52	57	54	59	69	58
Total	100	100	100	100	100	100
Per cent with no plans	32	32	29	22	17	27
Number of spending unit heads in group	138	229	355	217	169	1,108

part to differences in cost. A local public college offers the combined attraction of low tuition and saving through the opportunity to live at home, whereas the higher tuition of a private institution near home will offset at least a part of the costs of living away from home in order to attend a public college or university.

TABLE 28-5

PLANS FOR CHILDREN TO LIVE AT HOME WHILE IN COLLEGE
WITHIN AVAILABILITY OF COLLEGES IN AREA
(PERCENTAGE DISTRIBUTION OF SPENDING UNIT HEADS
WHO EXPECT CHILDREN TO ATTEND COLLEGE)

Plans for children to live at home while in college	Availability of colleges in area				All spending unit heads who expect children to attend college
	No college in area	Only private college in area	Only public college in area	Public and private colleges in the area	
All will live at home	9	16	51	46	33
Some will live at home; some away	4	13	16	8	9
All will live away from home	87	71	33	46	58
Total	100	100	100	100	100
Per cent with no plans	16	24	27	32	27
Number of spending unit heads in group	220	201	125	562	1,108

Table 28-6 further emphasizes the importance of the availability factor by showing the proportion of the local population which is attending college. It adds to the evidence suggesting that the fulfillment of parents' aspirations for the higher education of their children will depend for many of them on

TABLE 28-6

PLANS FOR CHILDREN TO LIVE AT HOME WHILE IN COLLEGE WITHIN RATIO OF COLLEGE ENROLLMENT TO LOCAL POPULATION
(PERCENTAGE DISTRIBUTION OF SPENDING UNIT HEADS WHO EXPECT CHILDREN TO ATTEND COLLEGE)

Plans for children to live at home while in college	Ratio of college enrollment to local population [a]						All spending unit heads who expect children to attend college
	No college in area	0.1–0.9%	1.0–1.9%	2.0–2.9%	3.0–3.9%	4.0% and over	
All will live at home	9	29	35	33	60	49	33
Some will live at home; some away	4	13	9	14	7	12	9
All will live away from home	87	58	56	53	33	39	58
Total	100	100	100	100	100	100	100
Per cent with no plans	16	26	29	39	21	30	27
Number of spending unit heads in group	220	102	387	140	91	168	1,108

[a] within primary sampling units

410

the extent to which colleges are available within easy reach of the potential student's home, enabling him to avoid the extra costs of room and board away from home.

As in the choice between the public and private college, the age of the eldest child in the family appears to exert little influence on the expectations that the potential student will live at home or at college. Even the incidence of indefinite responses is not reduced appreciably as the eldest boy or girl in the family approaches college age.

It appears that the extent to which parents' aspirations for the college education of their children will be fulfilled in the next ten to twenty years will depend in part upon the availability of low-tuition public institutions serving the local community. Aspirations for the higher education of children are found at income levels which may not, realistically, permit financing higher education either if the student must live away from home or if he must pay the tuition charges required by private institutions. Present indications are, however, that public facilities serving primarily a commuter population do not now exist to an extent adequate to meet the expressed desires of parents. Alternatively, of course, the need may be met, at least in part, by an expanded program of public and private aid to students. However, the over-all costs of such an approach would appear to be very much greater than the costs of bringing the institution to the student.

Sharing of College Expenses by Parents and Children

Only 3 per cent of parents who plan college for their children expect the children to finance their college educations entirely. Almost 60 per cent of the parents expect the children to contribute something to their own support. Fifteen per cent of the parents indicated that they would expect their children to contribute nothing, while the remaining quarter could not answer the question.

Income, savings, and number of children in the family are clearly associated with the extent to which parents expect children to support themselves in college. The higher the gross disposable income of the spending unit, the less the head expects his children to contribute for their college education. More than half of those with incomes over $10,000 expect the children to contribute little or nothing to their own college expenses. Surprisingly, 22 per cent of heads of spending units with incomes of less than $3,000 expressed the same expectation. This may be attributable to the fact that the incomes of some people in the latter group were temporarily low in 1959, because of illness, unemployment, business losses, and so forth; or it may represent less realistic aspirations. Parents with incomes under $3,000 are less likely to have plans about any of the details of their children's college educations, a poor omen for the realization of their expectations.

On the other hand, the tremendous variety of behavior in the use of money and the generally high level of real incomes in this country would indicate that parents determined to send their children to college might do it without much advance planning and without savings or very high income. It is possible to postpone other expenditures for a few years, if necessary. The financial pressure would be severe for some families, however, and a clamor for public aid may well result.

TABLE 28-7

EXTENT TO WHICH CHILDREN WILL SUPPORT THEMSELVES IN COLLEGE
WITHIN GROSS DISPOSABLE INCOME OF SPENDING UNITS
(PERCENTAGE DISTRIBUTION OF SPENDING UNIT HEADS
WHO EXPECT CHILDREN TO ATTEND COLLEGE)

Extent to which children will support themselves in college	Gross disposable income of spending units					All spending unit heads who expect children to attend college
	Under $3,000	$3,000– 4,999	$5,000– 7,499	$7,500– 9,999	$10,000 and over	
Completely or mostly	38	19	14	16	9	16
Partially	40	49	42	38	34	41
A little or not at all	22	32	44	46	57	43
Total	100	100	100	100	100	100
Per cent with no plans	39	31	26	15	17	24
Number of spending unit heads in group	138	229	355	217	169	1,108

Ability to support children in college is a function of both income and number of children. This finding is clearly illustrated in Table 28-8. Within each broad income group the extent of expected contributions from children increases for larger families. The number of children is important for groups having incomes of less than $10,000. For those with incomes of $10,000 and over it does not appear to make a substantial difference.

The better the education of the head, suggesting increasing ability to finance higher education, the less parents expect that their children will contribute toward college expenses. Except for spending unit heads with no education or with grade school educations, having a child close to college age does not lead to a less optimistic view of the prospects of contributing toward the costs of sending children to college.

The savings of the spending unit also are related to children's expected contributions to their college expenses. Table 28-9 suggests that heads of spending units with current savings over $5,000 less frequently anticipate their children supporting themselves in college than do those with less savings.

The presence of a working wife or one who has work experience shows no particular relationship to the extent to which the head expects his children to meet their college expenses. However, unmarried spending unit heads expect, to a disproportionately large extent, that the children will meet their own college expenses. The frequency with which they expect children to sup-

TABLE 28-8

EXTENT TO WHICH CHILDREN WILL SUPPORT SELVES IN COLLEGE

WITHIN GROSS DISPOSABLE INCOME OF SPENDING UNITS AND NUMBER OF MINOR CHILDREN

(PERCENTAGE DISTRIBUTION OF SPENDING UNIT HEADS WHO EXPECT CHILDREN TO ATTEND COLLEGE)

Extent to which children will support selves in college	Gross disposable income and number of minor children											All spending unit heads who expect children to attend college [a]
	Less than $5,000				$5,000–9,999				$10,000 and over			
	One	Two	Three	Four or more	One	Two	Three	Four or more	One	Two	Three or more	
Completely or mostly	18	22	23	33	12	11	13	26	11	13	6	16
Somewhat	45	48	48	51	34	46	44	42	30	33	41	41
A little or not at all	37	30	29	16	54	43	43	32	59	54	53	43
Total	100	100	100	100	100	100	100	100	100	100	100	100
Per cent with no plans	33	37	32	20	17	24	20	25	18	15	14	24
Number of spending unit heads in each group	116	98	53	74	155	182	116	91	45	54	57	1,108

[a] includes 67 cases for whom number of children was not ascertained because all children live away from home

413

TABLE 28-9

EXTENT TO WHICH CHILDREN WILL SUPPORT SELVES IN COLLEGE
WITHIN SAVINGS OF SPENDING UNITS
(PERCENTAGE DISTRIBUTION OF SPENDING UNIT HEADS
WHO EXPECT CHILDREN TO ATTEND COLLEGE)

| | Savings of spending units | | | | | |
| | Less than $500 | | | | | All spending |
Extent to which children will support selves in college	Never $500 in past 5 years	$500 or more in past 5 years	$500–999	$1,000–4,999	$5,000 and over	unit heads who expect children to attend college [a]
Completely or mostly	18	17	12	15	11	16
Somewhat	44	43	35	43	26	41
A little or not at all	38	40	53	42	63	43
Total	100	100	100	100	100	100
Per cent with no plans	26	26	25	19	19	24
Number of spending unit heads in group	247	194	158	249	124	1,108

[a] includes 136 spending unit heads whose savings were not ascertained

port themselves, either completely or with only small help from the family, is double the average for all spending unit heads.

Although spending unit heads were not asked specifically about sources of the funds to finance their children's college educations, about half of those who plan to support their children in college volunteered this information. Savings and other assets were the most frequently mentioned sources, with insurance and current income also accounting for a substantial number of responses.[3]

Summary

The realism of expressed plans to send children to college can be assessed by comparing families' education plans with their financial resources. Because the decisions to attend a public or private college, and to live at home or at the college, play so important a role in determining college costs, these plans were examined in the light of the families' present and potential resources.

The extent to which children are expected to support themselves in college varies with income, amount of savings, and the number of children in the family. Almost 60 per cent of parents who plan college for their children expect the children to contribute something to their own support.

The availability of public college facilities appears to be the most important factor in determining the realism of college plans. Aspirations for higher education are found at income levels which may not, realistically, permit financing higher education if the student must live away from home or pay high tuition charges.

[3] More complete data on plans for financing college educations are available in Lansing and others, *How People Pay for College*, pp. 73–97.

Chapter 29

ATTITUDES TOWARD PUBLIC SUPPORT OF HIGHER EDUCATION

A large proportion of spending unit heads expect their children to go to college and three-fourths of this group look to the publicly supported colleges and universities to educate their children. It is obvious that current levels of tax support for higher education will not permit the education of all of these children in public colleges. Pertinent questions, in the light of these circumstances, are: (1) do people in this country generally favor an increase in the extent to which higher education costs are financed out of tax receipts? and (2) if students, rather than or in addition to institutions, are to be supported with public money, what criteria are favored for distributing such support?

Tax Support for Institutions of Higher Education

The views of spending unit heads on whether or not tax support for colleges should be increased were elicited by the following question: "Part of the costs of college are now paid for out of tax funds, and part by college students and their families. Do you think that tax funds should cover more of the costs than they do now, or less, or what?"

One-fourth of all spending unit heads could not answer this question. This probably reflects failure to understand the question or lack of forethought; it does not imply any lack of realistic thinking as was the case in Chapter 28. Of those for whom answers were obtained, 52 per cent expressed the view that a larger part of the costs of higher education should come out of tax funds, 30 per cent prefer things as they are, and the remainder, 18 per cent, suggested that taxes should cover a smaller proportion of the costs than they now do. Surprisingly, self-interest does not appear to affect the responses of spending unit heads who expect their children to go to college; they are less in favor of increased tax support to colleges than are other spending unit heads. However, parents who expect their children to attend private colleges are more inclined to believe that tax support should be reduced than are parents who expect their children to go to public colleges.

As income increases the proportion of spending unit heads who favor more tax support declines and the proportion who favor existing levels of support increases. Rising levels of education and occupation of the spending unit heads are associated with similar attitudes toward tax support for colleges.

TABLE 29-1

TAXES FOR COLLEGES WITHIN GROSS DISPOSABLE INCOME
(PERCENTAGE DISTRIBUTION OF SPENDING UNIT HEADS)

Taxes for colleges	Gross disposable income					All spending unit heads
	Under $3,000	$3,000– 4,999	$5,000– 7,499	$7,500– 9,999	$10,000 and over	
Tax support for colleges should be:						
higher	56	53	55	45	41	52
same	25	29	30	36	37	30
lower	19	18	15	19	22	18
Total	100	100	100	100	100	100
Per cent with no opinion	35	27	24	19	21	27
Number of spending unit heads in group	978	688	687	357	287	2,997

Catholics and Fundamentalist Protestants are more frequently in favor of higher tax support for colleges than are non-Fundamentalist Protestants. This would appear to be related to income differences in the case of Catholics; lower incomes seem to outweigh the preference for private colleges. (See Table 28-2.)

Spending unit heads' views on the level of tax support for college appear to be clearly associated with the number of children in the unit. As Table 29-2 indicates, those who have no children differ markedly in their response from those who have three or more children.

Differences between white and nonwhite spending unit heads are undoubtedly due, at least in part, to differences in income and education between the two groups. Nonwhites may favor a larger role for publicly supported colleges because of the belief that opportunities for admission will be less subject to discrimination in the public college than in the private college, as well as because of cost considerations.

The common image of Republicans as less inclined than Democrats to favor higher taxes and more public spending is supported in Table 29-4. Along the political spectrum from "strong Democrat" to "strong Republican" the proportion favoring higher tax support for college declines. It is interesting to note that those who label themselves "independent" respond precisely like the sample as a whole.

TABLE 29-2

TAXES FOR COLLEGES WITHIN NUMBER OF CHILDREN UNDER 18
IN SPENDING UNIT
(PERCENTAGE DISTRIBUTION OF SPENDING UNIT HEADS)

Taxes for colleges	Number of children under 18 in spending unit				All spending unit heads
	None	One or two	Three or four	Five or more	
Tax support for colleges should be:					
higher	48	55	59	59	52
same	31	31	26	33	30
lower	21	14	15	8	18
Total	100	100	100	100	100
Per cent with no opinion	27	26	25	31	27
Number of spending unit heads in group	1,505	900	445	147	2,997

TABLE 29-3

TAXES FOR COLLEGES WITHIN RACE
(PERCENTAGE DISTRIBUTION OF SPENDING UNIT HEADS)

Taxes for colleges	Race		All spending unit heads
	White	Nonwhite	
Tax support for colleges should be:			
higher	49	75	52
same	32	14	30
lower	19	11	18
Total	100	100	100
Per cent with no opinion	27	29	27
Number of spending unit heads in group	2,580	417	2,997

The data provided in Table 29-5 permit a test of the consistency of people's views with respect to the role of government on two widely different issues—care of the aged and higher education. Those who think that government should assume sole or primary responsibility for care of the aged also tend to favor a larger role for government through tax support in higher education than do people who believe that the aged should be cared for by the family. This consistency was to be expected, since both sets of preferences are associated with similar characteristics, including political and religious preferences, and income.

There is a wide range among states in the current level of tax support for higher education. In 1956, the latest year for which comparable data are available, the amounts ranged from $1 to $11 per capita. In Table 29-6 spending unit heads are grouped according to the per capita levels of tax support for higher education in the states in which they live. There is some tendency for people to favor increased tax support where existing support is comparatively low.

TABLE 29-4

TAXES FOR COLLEGES WITHIN POLITICAL PREFERENCE
(PERCENTAGE DISTRIBUTION OF SPENDING UNIT HEADS)

Taxes for colleges	Political preference					All spending unit heads[a]
	Strong Democrat	Not very strong Democrat	Independent	Not very strong Republican	Strong Republican	
Tax support for colleges should be:						
higher	56	56	52	45	40	52
same	28	31	30	32	36	30
lower	16	13	18	23	24	18
Total	100	100	100	100	100	100
Percent with no opinion	24	27	24	27	25	27
Number of spending unit heads in group	668	696	648	469	291	2,997

[a] includes 225 spending unit heads whose political preference was not ascertained

418

TABLE 29-5

TAXES FOR COLLEGES WITHIN ATTITUDE TOWARD RESPONSIBILITY FOR THE AGED
(PERCENTAGE DISTRIBUTION OF SPENDING UNIT HEADS)

Taxes for colleges	Attitude toward responsibility for the aged					All spending unit heads [a]
	Relatives should have:		Relatives and government should share responsibility	Government should have:		
	Sole responsibility	Primary responsibility		Primary responsibility	Sole responsibility	
Tax support for colleges should be:						
higher	43	53	61	59	57	52
same	35	31	23	28	27	30
lower	22	16	16	13	16	18
Total	100	100	100	100	100	100
Per cent with no opinion	23	28	19	35	25	27
Number of spending unit heads in group	836	881	266	182	681	2,997

[a] includes 151 spending unit heads for whom attitude toward government responsibility for the aged was not ascertained

TABLE 29-6

TAXES FOR COLLEGES WITHIN PER CAPITA SUPPORT FOR
HIGHER EDUCATION IN STATE OF RESIDENCE
(PERCENTAGE DISTRIBUTION OF SPENDING UNIT HEADS)

Taxes for colleges	Per capita tax support for higher education in state of residence		All spending unit heads
	Less than $5	$5 or more	
Tax support for colleges should be:			
higher	57	48	52
same	26	33	30
lower	17	19	18
Total	100	100	100
Per cent with no opinion	28	26	27
Number of spending unit heads in group	1,305	1,692	2,997

Differences among geographic regions in the extent to which state and local taxes finance higher education reflect similar tendencies. The role of the publicly controlled institution is, in general, much larger in the North Central region and in the West than in the Northeast and South. These differences are reflected in the data presented in Table 29-7. Where tax support is comparatively low, in the South and the Northeast, almost 60 per cent of heads of spending units express the view that it should be higher, compared with only 46 per cent for the North Central states and the West.

TABLE 29-7

TAXES FOR COLLEGES WITHIN REGION
(PERCENTAGE DISTRIBUTION OF SPENDING UNIT HEADS)

Taxes for colleges	Region				All spending unit heads
	Northeast	North Central	South	West	
Tax support for colleges should be:					
higher	58	46	56	46	52
same	26	32	28	39	30
lower	16	22	16	15	18
Total	100	100	100	100	100
Per cent with no opinion	27	25	30	23	27
Number of spending unit heads in group	645	855	1,044	453	2,997

Public Aid for College Students

All spending unit heads were asked: "Should tax money be used to support only those with ability, only those who have financial need, or should everyone be supported?" Almost half of the spending unit heads favored the use of tax funds to support all college students, without selection based on either need or ability. Roughly equal proportions indicated that they preferred granting assistance on the basis of need or ability, or both combined. Only 3 per cent said that taxes should not be used to support college students; however, this was not one of the alternatives offered by the question, so the proportion is understated.

Spending unit heads with children aged twenty and under are somewhat more likely to favor aiding all students or needy students than are other spending unit heads. Parents who plan to send children to college are more likely to focus on ability, alone or combined with need, as a criterion for support from tax funds; those who do not expect to send their children to college are more likely to focus on need as the criterion for aid. Both groups,

TABLE 29-8

TAXES FOR COLLEGE STUDENTS WITHIN EDUCATION EXPECTED
FOR CHILDREN
(PERCENTAGE DISTRIBUTION OF SPENDING UNIT HEADS
WITH CHILDREN 20 OR UNDER)

Taxes for college students	Education expected for children				All spending unit heads with children 20 or under [a]
	12 grades or less	College, no degree	College, bachelor's degree	College, advanced degree	
Tax support should go to:					
students with ability	7	6	16	23	13
students with need	22	29	11	13	15
students with both ability and need	9	11	17	24	15
everyone	49	51	50	28	48
no one	2	0	1	4	2
do not know; other responses; not ascertained	11	3	5	8	7
Total	100	100	100	100	100
Number of spending unit heads	472	68 [b]	897 [b]	49 [b]	1,598

[a] includes 112 spending unit heads whose expectations for children's education were not ascertained

[b] The sum of the columns showing expectations for college is less than the number shown in Chapter 28 because 94 spending unit heads have no definite expectations of college attendance for their children, but indicate a possibility of some children attending college.

however, are predominately in favor of aid to everyone. The group that discriminates most highly is the very small one that expects its children to have advanced college degrees. Almost half of these people mention the ability criterion, either alone or in combination with need. Parents who plan to send their children to private colleges do not differ in their feelings about tax support for students from parents who plan to send their children to public colleges.

As income rises ability is mentioned more often, need less often. Only in

TABLE 29-9

TAXES FOR COLLEGE STUDENTS WITHIN GROSS DISPOSABLE INCOME
(PERCENTAGE DISTRIBUTION OF SPENDING UNIT HEADS)

	Gross disposable income					All spending unit heads
Taxes for college students	Under $3,000	$3,000– 4,999	$5,000– 7,499	$7,500– 9,999	$10,000 and over	
Tax support should go to:						
students with ability	6	12	16	19	19	13
students with need	26	18	14	13	11	18
students with need and ability	12	15	14	18	20	15
everyone	39	46	47	43	38	43
no one	3	2	2	2	7	3
do not know; other responses; not ascertained	14	7	7	5	5	8
Total	100	100	100	100	100	100
Number of spending unit heads	978	688	687	357	287	2,997

the $10,000 and over group is there an appreciable fraction who would prefer to assist no one.

Table 29-10 relates the number of minor children of the spending unit head to his attitudes about tax support for college students. The frequency with which heads favor support for everyone increases as the number of children increases, although ability is mentioned by about the same proportion in all groups but the one containing those with five or more children.

Unlike its relation to attitudes about higher or lower levels of tax support for education, political preference has little effect on attitudes toward tax

TABLE 29-10

TAXES FOR COLLEGE STUDENTS WITHIN NUMBER OF MINOR CHILDREN
(PERCENTAGE DISTRIBUTION OF SPENDING UNIT HEADS)

	Number of minor children of spending unit heads				All spending unit heads
Taxes for college students	None	One or two	Three or four	Five or more	
Tax support should go to:					
students with ability	13	12	16	7	13
students with need	20	16	13	16	18
students with ability and need	15	17	12	11	15
everyone	39	46	50	54	43
no one	4	2	1	0	3
other responses; do not know; not ascertained	9	7	8	12	8
Total	100	100	100	100	100
Number of spending unit heads	1,505	900	445	147	2,997

support for students. Democrats are somewhat more likely to mention need than are Republicans.

Finally some interesting contrasts appear when spending unit heads are grouped by broad geographic regions. As the data in Table 29-11 show, the West and North Central regions display similar responses, while the South and the Northeast regions diverge substantially from the national pattern and from each other. A much larger proportion of respondents in the Northeast express the view that ability should be taken into account than is the case for all other regions. Only one-third of the respondents in the Northeast are willing to extend assistance to all students, compared to nearly one-half in the other regions.

TABLE 29-11

TAXES FOR COLLEGE STUDENTS WITHIN REGION
(PERCENTAGE DISTRIBUTION OF SPENDING UNIT HEADS)

Taxes for college students	Region				All spending unit heads
	Northeast	North Central	South	West	
Tax support should go to:					
students with ability	17	14	8	14	13
students with need	15	17	23	12	18
students with need and ability	23	14	11	12	15
everyone	33	46	45	49	43
no one	4	2	2	2	3
other responses; do not know; not ascertained	8	7	11	11	8
Total	100	100	100	100	100
Number of spending unit heads	645	855	1,044	453	2,997

Regional differences in the existing role of public support for education, in income, in religious preferences of the population, and the proportions of the population who are nonwhite all appear to help to explain the contrasts observed. Nonwhites and Fundamentalist Protestants mention need more frequently and ability less frequently than whites and non-Fundamentalist Protestants and Catholics do. Thus, the combination found in the South, that is, low average income, a comparatively low level of tax support for education, a large proportion of the population which is Fundamentalist Protestant, and a large proportion of nonwhites, explains the responses for this region of the country. Similarly, underlying characteristics of the population in the other regions account for the observed differences in views expressed.

If there is anything surprising in the findings about attitudes toward tax assistance for college it is that a large proportion of all heads of spending units favor helping everyone. This may be because of the fact that selection of a criterion for assistance, such as need or ability, requires considerably more thought on the part of the respondent than does the "everyone" response. In addition, the phrasing of the question clearly suggests a positive answer rather than offering a free choice as to whether or not *anyone* should be supported. A different distribution of responses might have been obtained if the ordering of the choices suggested in the question had been reversed, with "everyone" appearing first and the ability criterion last. It appears, however, that there is a tendency to favor general support rather than selective aid.

The extent to which presumed self-interest shapes people's attitudes is much smaller than one might have expected. It is not only those with something to gain who favor more support, nor those with nothing to gain who oppose it. Furthermore, the fact that there is no general feeling that tax funds should support students in college solely on the basis of need or ability may indicate little sympathy for selective scholarships as opposed to a general subsidy for all students. The costs of a system which does not attempt to be selective are, of course, larger relative to its output in terms of trained manpower than one which uses need, merit, or both in giving selective aid.

Summary

Because the future demand for public colleges and universities looms so large, it is obvious that the current level of tax support for higher education will not meet the future needs. In response to questions about increasing public support of higher education, a large proportion of spending unit heads expressed the view that a larger part of the costs of higher education should be borne by the government. As incomes and education levels increase, the proportion favoring more tax support decreases. However, self-interest plays a surprisingly small role in determining this attitude; in fact, spending unit heads who expect their children to go to college are less in favor of increased tax support than are heads who do not expect to send children to college. Geographic differences and differences in the current level of per capita tax support by states are reflected in attitudes toward increasing tax support of colleges.

Likewise, almost half of all spending unit heads favored the use of tax support to help all college students, regardless of the students' abilities or needs. Income and education of the spending unit head affect his attitudes toward whether students should receive help from tax funds, and what the criteria for assistance should be. Apparently there is no strong opposition to the increased use of tax funds for public education, and there is even a tendency to favor general support.

PART VII

Other Plans for The Future

Chapter 30

PLANNING FOR THE FUTURE
AND THE FAMILY'S FINANCES

Poverty may result from inability to plan for the future. Many of the economic problems of poor families could have been avoided by planning. Life insurance and other savings might have provided adequate income for widows and retired persons. Some poorly educated persons could have received more education if they and their parents had made more realistic plans and implemented them by adequate savings. Of course the causation may be partly circular—people with low incomes may find it more difficult to plan ahead. Lack of planning would then have a cumulative effect in the long run as it led to poorer economic circumstances and even greater difficulty in planning.

Because the impact of events on the family can be affected by their planning horizon, a portion of this book is devoted to findings that are related to the families' planning behavior.

The data here relate both to the general attitudes of families toward planning ahead and to specific instances of planning, such as planning for retirement, planning for the children's education, and planning for taking care of parents. Moreover, they include some objective evidence of plans carried out. Information is available about the extent to which the family has been able to save, whether some provision has been made for retirement, and whether the family has savings or insurance for educating its children. This chapter deals with these plans and their results. The data offer modest support for the hypothesis that planning is an intermediary mechanism through which highly educated, highly motivated families manage to move up the socioeconomic scale and increase their income.

Attitudes toward Planning

Slightly over half the spending unit heads expressed the belief that they were able to plan ahead. The question asked was, "Some people feel that they can make pretty definite plans for their lives for the next few years.

Others feel that they are not in a position to plan ahead. How about you? Do you feel able to plan ahead or not? Why?"

Among the heads who felt able to plan, the most frequently given reason was financial position. This category includes people who gave as reasons for their ability to plan such factors as "My job is steady," or "My wife is going back to work next week and we'll be able to save some." One respondent who felt able to plan reported, "Financially I'm in a stable position. Not that I have a savings account, but I'm able to meet financial obligations." Many responses in this category referred to job security. People who attributed their planning ability to their life situation said such things as "We're young and we have a lot to look forward to," or "I'm retiring next year, and then I'll be able to do some of the things I want to."

Another important reason offered by people who feel able to plan was desires for the future. "I'm paying for insurance now so I can send my daughter to college" or "We're planning on buying a home as soon as we can get the money."

Several respondents gave moral or normative reasons for their ability to plan, indicating their attitude that planning was a good thing in itself: "The Lord helps them that help themselves."

TABLE 30-1

FEELING OF ABILITY TO PLAN AHEAD AND REASONS
(PERCENTAGE DISTRIBUTION OF SPENDING UNIT HEADS)

Reasons [a]	Feeling of ability to plan ahead					
	Feel able to plan	Feel able to plan, qualified	Do not feel able to plan, qualified	Do not feel able to plan	Depends, do not know	All spending unit heads
Feel able to plan ahead because:						
financial position	48	26	3	0	4	24
life situation	18	7	3	0	1	9
world conditions	2	1	1	0	0	1
desires for future	14	11	1	0	0	7
planning is good	6	10	0	0	4	4
other reasons	3	1	1	0	1	1
Do not feel able to plan ahead because:						
financial position	0	8	37	32	4	15
life situation	0	3	17	25	3	10
world conditions	0	3	12	11	1	5
past failure	0	3	6	6	1	3
planning is not necessary	0	0	4	9	5	4
other reasons	0	3	9	7	1	3
Number of spending unit heads	1,225	323	181	1,122	146	2,997

[a] Detail does not add to 100 per cent because some persons gave no reasons; other gave two.

The largest number of reasons given by people who felt that they were unable to plan also concerned their financial positions. One man who felt unable to plan said, "We just live from hand to mouth—there's never enough to put anything away." Another reported, "We try to save, but we've had so many medical bills that we just can't."

Some respondents cited their life situations as the reason for their inability to plan. Such statements as "I'm too old to make plans," or "We're thinking about moving and we just don't know" reflect this attitude. World conditions were cited by more people who felt unable to plan than who felt that they could plan. One person who felt unable to plan stated, "Governments keep bickering back and forth and you can never tell what's going to happen."

Of the three per cent who felt unable to plan because of past failures, most said, "I used to plan but the plans never worked out," or "Things happen that you didn't count on."

Many of the statements about the ability to plan, both by those who felt able to plan and those who did not, reflect short range views and situations, rather than long range plans or lifetime expectations. Current job situations or expenses at the time of the interview seem to have a much greater effect on this attitude than do long range goals. Many people of course spoke in terms of long range goals such as buying a house or sending the children to college, but the most noticeable characteristic of the replies in general was their failure to look beyond current situations and feelings, and to think of planning in terms of immediate activities and needs.

Those who reported they were able to plan also said they planned specific purchases twice as often as those who said they were not able to plan. The question from which this finding is drawn was, "Do you plan ahead as to what your next major expenditures will be, or do you buy things when you have to have them?" The alternatives in the question are not mutually exclu-

TABLE 30-2

PLANNING OF PURCHASES WITHIN FEELING OF ABILITY
TO PLAN AHEAD
(PERCENTAGE DISTRIBUTION OF SPENDING UNIT HEADS)

| Planning of purchases | Feeling of ability to plan ahead | | | |
	Feel able to plan	Do not feel able to plan	Depends, do not know	All spending unit heads
Plan purchases	34	14	14	24
Plan purchases, qualified	9	5	4	7
Sometimes plan, sometimes do not plan	5	2	1	4
Do not plan, qualified	2	2	0	2
Do not plan	47	70	52	57
Not ascertained	3	7	29	6
Total	100	100	100	100
Number of spending unit heads	1,548	1,303	146	2,997

sive. People with low incomes are likely to postpone purchases until they have to have them even though they plan some purchases. Thus answers to the question may reflect both the family income and its planning horizons.

TABLE 30-3

HOSPITALIZATION INSURANCE COVERAGE WITHIN FEELING
OF ABILITY TO PLAN AHEAD
(PERCENTAGE DISTRIBUTION OF SPENDING UNITS)

Hospitalization insurance coverage of spending units	Feeling of ability to plan ahead			
	Feel able to plan	Do not feel able to plan	Depends, do not know	All spending unit heads
Hospitalization insurance	78	60	58	70
No hospitalization insurance	22	40	35	30
Not ascertained	0	0	7	0
Total	100	100	100	100
Number of spending units	1,548	1,303	146	2,997

Spending units whose heads feel able to plan are more likely to be covered by hospitalization insurance than spending units whose heads do not feel able to plan.

Spending unit heads who feel able to plan ahead also report significantly higher savings than those who feel unable to plan ahead. This relationship may imply that savings are the result of successful planning in the past; or it may be that persons with savings have an economic cushion which makes discretionary action possible.

TABLE 30-4

SAVINGS WITHIN FEELING OF ABILITY TO PLAN AHEAD
(PERCENTAGE DISTRIBUTION OF SPENDING UNITS)

Savings	Feeling of ability to plan ahead			
	Feel able to plan	Do not feel able to plan	Depends, do not know	All spending unit heads
Less than $500	40	61	47	50
$500 or more in past 5 years	16	14	13	16
less than $500 in past 5 years	18	34	25	25
amount in past 5 years not ascertained	6	13	9	9
$500–999	14	10	11	12
$1,000–4,999	26	18	16	22
$5,000 and over	18	7	16	13
Not ascertained	2	4	10	3
Total	100	100	100	100
Number of spending units	1,548	1,303	146	2,997

Because it is possible that the apparent relationship between saving and planning is the spurious result of their common correlation with income, the relationship was plotted along the income distribution. This was done only for spending units whose heads were between thirty-five and fifty-four, in order to eliminate the effect of age on planning and to provide a group in which all members had similar periods of time over which to accumulate

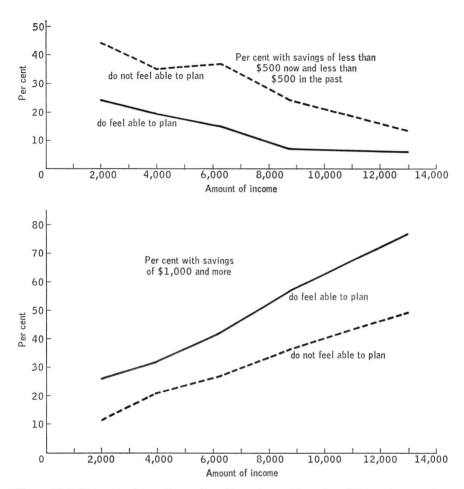

Figure 30-1. Per cent of spending units with savings of less than $500 and more than $1,000, within feeling of ability to plan and gross disposable income (for spending units with heads aged thirty-five to fifty-four).

savings. Figure 30-1 indicates that, while income affects both saving and planning, the relationship between saving and planning is still quite powerful.

The positive relationship between savings and planning reiterates itself for planning purchases. Spending unit heads who plan purchases have greater savings than spending unit heads that do not plan purchases.

Differences in foresight thus perpetrate differences in economic status.

Those with assets tend to have the foresight necessary to keep their assets. Those without assets tend to be without insurance or plans, and so are likely to continue without any.

Characteristics of Planners

Feeling able to plan ahead appears to be related to the spending unit head's age and his stage in the life cycle. In general, younger persons more frequently feel able to plan than do older persons. About half of those under thirty-five feel able to plan, while less than a third of those sixty-five and older express this attitude. The decline in feeling of ability to plan results both from increasing realism and from a narrowing of the alternatives available to persons as their age increases. Older people may find that their plans miscarry and report that they are unable to plan as a consequence; younger persons have less experience and have seen fewer of their plans succeed or fail. It is also likely that the expression of feeling able to plan is the concomitant of life situations in which the respondent feels that he has many alternatives open to him and can make a choice. As he grows older career lines become set; definite retirement circumstances and retirement income develop; sickness and disease restrict physical capabilities.

Feeling able to plan is not a function of age alone, however. Married couples with children are less likely to feel able to plan than married couples without children. Least able to plan are single persons with children. This may reflect the generally low incomes of that group, and the difficulty in arranging employment and child care jointly. However, more persons in that group reported that they planned their purchases than would be expected from their generally negative feelings about being able to plan ahead. In fact the proportion of single parents who plan purchases exceeds the proportion planning purchases in any other of the life cycle categories including those where heads or wives are forty-five and older. The relationship between life cycle and planning purchases parallels Table 30-5 closely for all other groups.

Table 30-6 shows that spending unit heads who have incomes in excess of their estimated needs feel much more able to plan than spending unit heads whose incomes are barely sufficient to meet their budget requirements.

Those whose incomes exceed their needs also report more frequently that they plan purchases. Twelve per cent whose welfare ratio is less than .9 and 32 per cent whose welfare index is 1.7 and over report that they plan purchases. In general those whose incomes are high relative to their requirements also accumulate savings, are covered by hospitalization insurance, and have security against unemployment which is not typical of the poorer groups.

It is relatively clear that income differences tend to be perpetuated by the dynamic relationship between present plans, present income, and future income. Those with little present income have the greatest need for planning ahead and are least likely to do so. One would expect this failure to plan to

TABLE 30-5

FEELING OF ABILITY TO PLAN AHEAD WITHIN STAGE IN LIFE CYCLE
(PERCENTAGE DISTRIBUTION OF SPENDING UNIT HEADS)

Stage in life cycle

Feeling of ability to plan ahead	Unmarried heads — Heads under 45 — No children	Married heads — Wives under 45 — No children	Wives under 45 — Children under 6	Wives under 45 — Children 6 or older	Wives 45 or older — No children	Wives 45 or older — Children	Unmarried heads — Heads 45 and older — No children	Unmarried heads — Heads 45 and older — Children	All spending unit heads
Feels able to plan	48	55	49	47	45	40	29	20	43
Feels able to plan, qualified	8	11	15	12	8	12	6	11	10
Do not feel able to plan, qualified	5	5	5	8	6	9	6	5	6
Do not feel able to plan	33	26	29	29	34	35	52	59	36
Depends, do not know	6	3	2	4	7	4	7	5	5
Total	100	100	100	100	100	100	100	100	100
Number of spending unit heads	285	211	729	352	542	225	468	185	2,997

TABLE 30-6

FEELING OF ABILITY TO PLAN AHEAD WITHIN FAMILY WELFARE RATIO
(PERCENTAGE DISTRIBUTION OF FAMILIES)

Feeling of ability to plan ahead	Family welfare ratio					All families
	0.8 or less	0.9–1.2	1.3–1.6	1.7–2.2	2.3 and over	
Feels able to plan ahead	20	31	44	51	67	43
Feels able to plan, qualified	8	11	12	13	9	10
Does not feel able to plan, qualified	8	8	6	5	4	6
Does not feel able to plan ahead	57	44	32	27	16	36
Not ascertained	7	6	6	4	4	5
Total	100	100	100	100	100	100
Number of families	788	507	469	534	502	2,800

be reflected in their future incomes. Failure to plan may be symptomatic of a situation in which the family income is low now or it may be a direct cause of low income, or both.

Planning Index

An index was developed to measure the extent to which spending units planned and are concerned with providing for the future. A score of one was given for each of the following attributes: (1) head of the spending unit feels able to plan ahead (53 per cent), (2) head of the spending unit plans purchases (31 per cent), (3) someone in the spending unit is covered by hospitalization insurance (70 per cent), (4) spending unit has more than $500 in liquid assets (47 per cent), (5) head of the spending unit reported a definite age at which he plans to retire (62 per cent of the nonretired over 30 years of age), (6) head is enrolled in a private pension program (40 per cent of the nonretired over 30 years of age). The total score obtained for the spending unit forms the index of evidences of planning and foresight. The index includes only those items which are generally applicable to spending unit heads who were over thirty and not retired. For this reason the index does not include evidences of planning associated with plans for sending children to college and the age at which the head's eldest living child was born, which are only applicable to persons with children.

The index correlates with those evidences of foresight which were not included. Heads of spending units whose eldest living child was born while he was between the ages of twenty and twenty-nine exhibit significantly more instances of foresight and planning than persons whose first child was born earlier and less than those whose first child was born later.

The index is normally distributed and increases with both education and the need-achievement score of the spending unit head. Planning, in the forms included in the index, thus may be one of the intermediate mechanisms whereby high levels of need-achievement are translated into financial success.

TABLE 30-7

MEAN PLANNING INDEX WITHIN ATTITUDE TOWARD HARD WORK,
AND NEED-ACHIEVEMENT SCORE
(FOR SPENDING UNIT HEADS 35 AND OLDER IN THE
LABOR FORCE OR STUDENTS)

Attitude toward hard work, need-achievement score	Number of spending unit heads	Mean planning index
Hard work is equal to or more important than luck; need-achievement score is:		
high range	388	3.8
middle range	589	3.4
low range	286	3.0
Hard work is less important than luck; need-achievement score is:		
high range	76	3.0
middle range	161	2.6
low range	96	1.8
Need-achievement score was not ascertained	64	2.7
All	1,660	3.2

TABLE 30-8

MEAN PLANNING INDEX WITHIN EDUCATION
(FOR SPENDING UNIT HEADS 35 AND OLDER IN THE
LABOR FORCE OR STUDENTS)

Education of head	Number of spending unit heads	Mean planning index
0–8 grades	577	2.3
9–11 grades	361	3.2
12 grades	239	3.5
12 grades and nonacademic training	148	3.7
Some college	153	3.8
College, bachelor's degree	131	4.3
College, advanced degree	51	4.2
All	1,660	3.2

Summary

Heads of spending units differ widely in their attitudes toward planning. Feeling of ability to plan is correlated with having savings and hospitalization insurance. The correlation suggests that planning ahead perpetuates differences in income and the well-being of families. Families who do not plan are likely to become poor and dependent when they are faced with a financial crisis, such as extended unemployment of the breadwinner or serious illness in the family. Families that plan ahead will have a financial cushion to prevent dependency.

Planning ahead is measured by a number of different questions in this study. A simple index of evidences of planning is highly correlated with the education, the need-achievement score, and the attitude toward hard work held by the head. The correlation suggests that planning may be a mechanism by which motivation to achieve success is translated into high levels of income. Further studies in which attitudes are measured prior to, rather than after, the fact are necessary to prove this suggestion.

Planning is related to the future income and success of this generation; it is even more clearly necessary for the success of the next generation. The analysis in Chapter 23 shows that the level of education which people attain is likely to be an important factor in their careers and lifetime incomes. Obtaining education beyond high school, in turn, requires some advance planning by parents.

Chapter 31

PLANNING FOR RETIREMENT

The reality and clarity of spending units' plans for retirement offer many clues to the unit's foresight and its future economic situation. Other studies of retired people have shown that many people did not plan to retire but were forced to do so by ill health or compulsory retirement rules. The studies also indicated that those who had not planned to retire were more likely to be in poor economic circumstances after retirement.[1] In this study information was collected on the age at which the head of the spending unit plans to retire, his eligibility for benefits under social security or private pension programs, and how well he feels he will be able to manage on his retirement income. This information was obtained from all nonretired spending unit heads aged thirty and older. Dependent adult units are excluded from the analysis.

This analysis will examine each kind of planning for retirement and assess the reality of this planning in terms of the assets and pension rights available to the spending unit after retirement.

Most nonretired spending unit heads thirty and older plan to retire before they are seventy years old. Only 12 per cent reported that they did not know when they would retire or had not thought about it. However, 25 per cent reported that they did not plan to retire. Indefinite postponement of retirement is unrealistic for most people; more than four-fifths of all workers who have retired, did so either because they become unable to work or because of involuntary retirement programs.[2]

[1] Floyd Bond and others, *Our Needy Aged: A California Study of a National Problem* (New York: Henry Holt and Company, Inc., 1954); Peter O. Steiner and Robert Dorfman, *The Economic Status of the Aged* (Berkeley, California: University of California Press, 1957); Wayne E. Thompson, "Pre-Retirement Anticipation and Adjustment in Retirement," *The Journal of Social Issues*, 14, No. 2 (1958), 35–45.

United Kingdom Ministry of Pensions and National Insurance, *National Insurance Retirement Pensions: Reasons Given for Retiring or Continuing at Work* (London: Her Majesty's Stationary Office, 1954).

[2] See Henry D. Sheldon, *The Older Population of the United States* (New York: John Wiley & Sons, Inc., 1958), pp. 44, 49; Steiner and Dorfman, *The Economic Status of the Aged*, p. 49.

Definite plans for retirement and plans for retiring before age sixty-five are closely associated with the earning potential of the spending unit head. Those with college education plan to retire earlier than those who have not completed high school.

White farmers report significantly fewer plans to retire than do others in the sample. Lack of plans stems from farmers' self-employment status, their general exclusion from compulsory retirement programs, and their irregular hours of work. The failure of nonwhites to report retirement plans is harder to explain, except in terms of the low economic position of nonwhites and the instability of their employment.

TABLE 31-1

PLANNED RETIREMENT AGE WITHIN EARNING POTENTIAL
(PERCENTAGE DISTRIBUTION OF NONRETIRED
SPENDING UNIT HEADS 30 AND OLDER)

| Planned retirement age | Earning potential of spending unit heads | | | | | All nonretired spending unit heads 30 and older [a] |
| | Nonwhite | White farmers | White nonfarmers | | | |
			0–11 grades	12 grades	Some college	
30–59	4	4	4	5	9	5
60–64	9	8	9	11	14	11
65–70	40	27	48	51	43	46
71 or older	1	0	1	1	2	1
Not ascertained	14	17	13	11	10	12
Do not plan to retire	32	44	25	21	22	25
Total	100	100	100	100	100	100
Number of spending unit heads	270	155	748	399	382	1,967

[a] includes 13 nonretired spending unit heads for whom earning potential is not ascertained

Those who plan to retire are much more likely to say that they will be able to get along financially during retirement than the group who say they will never retire. Seventy-eight per cent of those who plan to retire before sixty-five thought that they would be able to get along financially during retirement. Those who plan to retire between sixty-five and seventy are slightly less optimistic. Among those who do not plan to retire or are uncertain about the age at which they will retire, 54 per cent feel they could manage financially.

This finding is emphasized by the experience of persons who have already retired. Spending unit heads who have already retired report much greater dissaving since retirement if their retirement was not planned than if they had planned to retire. Included among those who did not plan to retire are some spending unit heads who became disabled and were forced to retire, and for these persons the problem of discontinued earnings may have been accentuated by unusual medical expenses. The group of spending unit heads who

TABLE 31-2

AMOUNT OF DISSAVING SINCE RETIREMENT WITHIN WHETHER
HEAD'S RETIREMENT WAS PLANNED
(PERCENTAGE DISTRIBUTION OF RETIRED SPENDING UNIT HEADS)

Amount of dissaving since time of head's retirement	Whether head's retirement was planned		All retired SU heads [a]
	Planned	Not planned	
Had savings at time of retirement; have used			
less than one-fourth	14	6	9
one-four to one-half	4	8	7
one-half to three-fourths	3	6	4
more than three-fourths	6	20	15
amount not ascertained	9	6	7
Have not dissaved; had no savings at time of			
retirement, have none now	51	37	42
Has saved since retirement	13	17	16
Total	100	100	100
Number of spending unit heads	104	177	304

[a] includes 23 cases for whom planning was not ascertained

have not dissaved includes persons who had no savings at the time they
retired.

Spending unit heads who reported that times would be difficult during retirement mention more plans to take a part-time job after retirement than
heads who felt they would be able to get along. The latter groups mention
more plans to travel. Differences in plans suggest a considerable variation in
the retirement income available to those who will get along and those for

TABLE 31-3

RETIREMENT PLANS WITHIN GENERAL RETIREMENT OUTLOOK
(PERCENTAGE DISTRIBUTION OF NONRETIRED SPENDING
UNIT HEADS 30 AND OLDER)

Retirement plans	General retirement outlook			All nonretired spending unit heads 30 and older
	Things will be all right	Things will be difficult	Depends, do not know, not ascertained	
Get another job	5	9	5	5
Start business or farm	4	4	1	4
Work on hobbies; other unpaid work	4	3	4	4
Travel	8	0	3	6
Move to another location	4	4	1	4
Other plans	6	4	3	5
No plans	67	74	64	67
Not ascertained	2	2	19	5
Total	100	100	100	100
Number of spending unit heads	1,276	270	421	1,967

whom retirement will be difficult. However, these findings apply to a small group of spending units. Two-thirds of all spending unit heads thirty and over mentioned no plans about what they will do during retirement.

Naturally the financial resources available for retirement affect spending unit heads' retirement outlook. Most of those who are eligible for social security report that things will be all right during retirement. Less than a quarter of those who are not eligible for any old age pensions express optimistic retirement outlooks.

TABLE 31-4

GENERAL RETIREMENT OUTLOOK WITHIN ELIGIBILITY FOR PENSIONS
(PERCENTAGE DISTRIBUTION OF SPENDING UNIT HEADS
30 AND OLDER, NOT RETIRED)

General retirement outlook	Eligibility for pensions			All spending unit heads 30 and older not retired [a]
	No pensions	Only social security	Social security and private pensions	
Things will be all right	22	63	76	66
Things will be difficult	17	16	8	13
Depends	2	6	5	5
Not ascertained	59	15	11	16
Total	100	100	100	100
Number of spending unit heads	136	1,098	710	1,967

[a] includes 23 spending unit heads who will receive only private pensions

Savings have a similar effect on reports that the unit will get along during retirement. The larger the liquid assets held by the spending unit, the more likely the head is to expect good times during retirement. However, even spending units who have had less than $500 in the bank for the past five years are more likely than not to report they will get along during retirement. Some increase in the awareness of financial problems of old age occurs as the spending unit approaches retirement. Nine per cent of spending unit heads between the ages of thirty and forty-five foresee hard times in retirement; 16 per cent of spending unit heads aged forty-five and older foresee economic difficulties after they retire.

Financial Provisions for Retirement

Persons may accumulate assets for their retirement in a number of ways. Perhaps the most common is investing in a home. The family may also accumulate liquid assets, real property, stocks and bonds, an interest in an unincorporated business, or pension rights.

For most persons, the primary source of income during retirement is from Federal social security benefits. Ninety-four per cent of spending unit heads reported that they or their wives will be eligible for social security benefits.

The two-fifths of the population who report that both the head and the wife are covered by social security are likely to collect benefits close to the legal maximum. Table 31-5 shows that both private pensions and coverage of the wife under social security tend to complement the basic coverage of the head under social security. Very few heads of spending units who are not covered by social security are eligible for other types of pensions or acquire social security coverage through their wives.

TABLE 31-5

ELIGIBILITY FOR SOCIAL SECURITY AND PRIVATE PENSIONS
(PERCENTAGE DISTRIBUTION OF SPENDING UNITS
WITH HEADS 30 AND OVER, NOT RETIRED)

| Eligibility for social security | Eligibility for private pensions | | Total |
	Eligible	Ineligible	
Head	21	33	54
Wife	0	0	0
Head and wife	18	22	40
Neither head nor wife	1	5	6
Total	40	60	100
Number of spending units	733	1,234	1,967

Generally, the ownership of assets which will provide retirement income accompanies coverage under social security or other pension plans. Spending units with both public and private pensions have more net equity in their homes and greater liquid assets than spending units with less coverage. Families with no pension coverage are a somewhat heterogeneous group. A substantial minority have less than $500 of liquid assets and no real investments, and are ill-prepared for retirement. A few have substantial savings and investments which will provide income.

A lack of foresight carries over to provisions for medical expenses. Less than half of those who are not covered under any pension program have hospitalization insurance which covers all members of the spending unit. More than two-thirds of those who are covered by social security have this type of insurance.

The profile of other assets held by spending unit heads forty-five to sixty-four is given in Table 31-8. Few persons have no real or financial assets by the time they reach middle age. However, the fact that more than a third have less than $5,000 of assets suggests a financial problem for a large number of persons who will retire during the next twenty years.[3]

Data collected in another independent survey of people's plans about retirement conducted by the Survey Research Center in May, 1960 complement the findings presented here. Nonretired adults were asked to report the amount

[3] These data are from *1960 Survey of Consumer Finances,* Survey Research Center Monograph Series, No. 20 (Ann Arbor, Michigan: Survey Research Center, 1961), pp. 123ff.

TABLE 31-6

SAVINGS WITHIN AGE AND ELIGIBILITY FOR PENSIONS
(PERCENTAGE DISTRIBUTION OF SPENDING UNITS
WITH HEADS 30–64, NOT RETIRED)

Savings	Age and eligibility for pensions			
	No pensions	Only social security	Social security and private pensions	All [a]
	30–34			
Under $500	61	64	48	57
$500–999	11	13	15	14
$1,000–4,999	16	18	27	22
$5,000 and over	5	5	8	6
Not ascertained	7	0	2	1
Total	100	100	100	100
Number of spending units	24	172	111	308
	35–44			
Under $500	58	55	34	47
$500–999	11	14	15	14
$1,000–4,999	18	20	33	26
$5,000 and over	13	9	15	11
Not ascertained	0	2	3	2
Total	100	100	100	100
Number of spending unit heads	38	351	249	648
	45–64			
Under $500	65	49	28	41
$500–999	8	12	13	12
$1,000–4,999	9	21	30	25
$5,000 and over	18	14	27	19
Not ascertained	0	4	2	3
Total	100	100	100	100
Number of spending unit heads	58	540	334	936

[a] includes some spending unit heads who are eligible for private pensions only

of income they would receive from assets and pension rights after retirement. Even among the respondents over fifty-five, less than half of the nonretired were able to estimate the amount of income they would obtain from their retirement program insurance and social security. Moreover more than two-fifths of the spending unit heads over fifty-five were unable to estimate their income requirements during retirement. Those who estimated needs during retirement were rather unrealistic about the amount of income required. Among respondents with a current income of more than $10,000, 19 per cent expect to need more than $5,000 a year after retirement and 22 per cent less than $5,000, while 59 per cent could not give such information. Among respondents with a current income between $5,000 and $7,500, 14 per cent expect to need more than $3,500, and 18 per cent less than $3,500.

In the same study a general question was asked about current behavior.

TABLE 31-7

HOSPITALIZATION INSURANCE COVERAGE WITHIN ELIGIBILITY
FOR PENSIONS
(PERCENTAGE DISTRIBUTION OF SPENDING UNITS
WITH HEADS 30–64, NOT RETIRED)

| | Heads' eligibility for pensions | | | |
Hospitalization insurance	No pensions	Only social security	Social security and private pensions	All spending units with heads 30–64, not retired [a]
All members covered	43	63	82	70
Some members covered	7	9	7	8
No one covered	50	28	10	22
Not ascertained	0	0	1	0
Total	100	100	100	100
Number of spending units	120	1,063	694	1,892

[a] includes 15 spending unit heads who are eligible for private pensions only

TABLE 31-8

OWNERSHIP OF ASSETS
(PERCENTAGE DISTRIBUTION OF SPENDING UNITS WITH HEADS 45–64)

Value of assets	Total assets	Liquid assets	Corporate stock	Equity in home	Other real estate	Unincorporated business
Do not own	12	22	84	35	79	93
Own	88	78	16	65	21	7
Less than $1,000	10	33	4	1	2	1
$1,000–4,999	14	28	5	12	4	1
$5,000–9,999	22	9	2	20	5	2
$10,000–24,999	26	6	2	29	5	1
$25,000 and over	14	2	3	3	4	2
Not ascertained	2	0	0	0	1	0
Total	100	100	100	100	100	100
Median, all spending units with heads 45–64	$8,000	$800	0	$5,500	0	0
Median, holders only	$9,400	$1,100	$4,200	$9,900	$9,000	$8,800

SOURCE: *1960 Survey of Consumer Finances,* Survey Research Center Monograph Series No. 20, p. 132, Table 7-6c.

The question, "Do you now do anything to add to your retirement income?" was asked of all nonretired people, irrespective of whether they thought that they have or do not have enough for retirement. About half of the nonretired people said that they are doing nothing or cannot do anything. The other half gave two kinds of answers frequently: that they contributed to social security or a pension plan, or that they were saving money. Altogether 25 per cent of nonretired people mentioned voluntary saving for retirement. The higher the income, the more frequent was this answer.

Summary

There are many families who approach retirement with vague notions about their retirement income and indefinite plans about the age at which they will retire. The most concrete plans for retirement are participation in retirement programs and social security, which will supply the bulk of retirement income for most families. In a majority of cases participation in these programs is not voluntary. A substantial minority of families have less than $5,000 of real and money assets in the twenty years preceding retirement. Nearly all are covered by social security, while two-fifths are covered by private pensions. Clearly those few persons who are not covered under social security or private pension plans are the worst prepared for retirement. They are unlikely to have either savings, substantial equity in their homes, or protection against medical expenses. It would appear that many in this group will become dependent on others when their present earnings cease.

Other studies at the Survey Research Center indicate that most people find it very difficult to think ahead and to estimate how much income they will need when they retire. Most of them do not know what income to expect from social security, other pensions, or their own savings. While expectations become somewhat firmer among those over fifty-five years old, the general impression is that most people have only a vague idea whether their retirement will be financially difficult or not.

Previous sections had shown that education appeared to be the mechanism for upward mobility as well as for the transmission of level of economic status from generation to generation. Education affects a man's earnings and his progress during his lifetime, as well as the education of his children. This is not just a matter of skills and training. Foresight and planning, which are essential to getting ahead and assuring the education of one's children, are affected by formal education as well as by the attitudes and achievement motivation of the head.

The plans and provisions currently being made for retirement have been analyzed in this chapter. It appears that aside from the automatic and largely compulsory retirement systems, and the accumulation of equity in a home, most people are making little other provision for retirement. The vast increase in retirement systems, particularly the Federal social security system, makes this less of a problem than it has been in the past. The question remains whether people, most of whom expect to retire by the time they are seventy years old, will find themselves dissatisfied with their economic situation when they retire.

In general then, the evidence is consistent in showing a pattern by which education determines income and ability to plan ahead, which in turn affects the family's future income and the education of its children, and in turn the children's income and propensity to plan ahead.

PART VIII

Future Research Needs

Chapter 32

FUTURE RESEARCH NEEDS

Research is a continuing process. Each step forward logically leads to new problems to be solved and new ideas to be tested. The present work is no exception.

While the statistical procedures used in this analysis represent some advance over previous practice, they still fall short. The sequential nature of causation, involving logical priorities by which one factor can change a second but not the reverse, needs to be included more directly. Complex interaction effects by which particular combinations of factors lead to extremely variant behavior or outcomes need more chance to show up in the results. All this requires not so much new statistics or theory as it does new data processing programs and procedures.

In many facets of behavior reported here, further analysis is needed which can be done with the data already at hand. A series of articles is already under way doing some of this. More important, however, is the explanation of the many problems which the data have disclosed but could not resolve.

The apparent independence of different forms of mobility and change leaves unsolved many questions about mobility and progress. Different forms of movement and change appear to be motivated by different forces. Much more study of the reasons for movement and change is called for. Change in a man's place of residence or in his occupation may be the result of outside forces beyond his control, or a reaction against an unsatisfactory situation rather than the positive lure of a new opportunity. A study of the reasons for movement, and in particular an analysis of purposeful positive reasons for mobility, is called for.

Such study is doubly important because the economic growth of a country is in large measure a function of purposeful movement by individuals to better jobs, new and better ways of doing things, use of new products, and the ancillary tendencies to plan for the future, accumulate capital, work hard, and provide education for children. Hence, studies need to be conducted in the less well-developed countries of the world, incorporating some of the behavior variables used in the present work, and some, like purposeful mobility, still to be done here. Such studies would provide both useful description and international comparisons, and detailed analysis which could be used to facilitate economic development within each country.

It should be possible to discover the forces that keep some individuals or communities from doing the things that contribute to economic growth and motivate or allow others to do them. Economic development programs can then be focused on the most promising programs and the most promising areas and subgroups in the country. The implementation of such programs can be made more effective by discovering the problems of the individuals and understanding their behavior.

Comparative studies with the mature economies of Western Europe are also called for in the analysis of redistribution mechanisms and attitudes and behavior under these systems. Countries with more advanced social security systems can provide useful contrasts and some insight into future problems the United States may face.

Such international comparisons can serve as a substitute for longitudinal studies. Comparisons now between countries in different stages of economic development and with social security and tax systems of differing complexity and sophistication should provide useful insights into historic processes as well as into cultural differences. What is needed is not over-all comparisons of one country with another, but comparisons of causal processes and relationships in different settings. Do the same forces which lead wives to work in the United States seem to apply to West Germany, Yugoslavia, Mexico, the Philippines, and Brazil? Is the intergenerational pattern of educational transmission different, or similar except for the over-all level of education? If such comparative studies focus on individual behavior which contributes to economic growth, they will shed light on whether differences are largely attributable to the situations people face, or to the decisions they make in those situations.

The present study would have benefited if data had existed describing the situation in this country at an earlier period. Both economic facts and people's attitudes have been changing rapidly, with the development of income maintenance programs and other powerful redistributive mechanisms, with higher levels of real income and of educational achievement and with the separation of families into nuclear units. Comparisons with other countries at earlier stages in their economic development or with more advanced social security systems are the only way now open to provide comparison studies. The situation in this country is changing rapidly enough, however, so that in ten years or even sooner a follow-up study to see which group's attitudes or practices have changed, would vastly increase our understanding of the dynamics of change.

Appendix A

SAMPLING, SAMPLING ERROR, WEIGHTING

Sampling

This study required a sample which would provide reliable data on low income families, also provide data on middle and high income families for purposes of comparison with low income families, and represent all families in the United States in order that distributions of income, property taxes, and other measures could be determined.

The sample design included a cross section of the noninstitutional population in the United States and a supplementary sample of low income families. The cross section sample was selected from the Survey Research Center's national sample of dwelling units. It is a multistage area probability sample that gives equal chance of selection to all noninstitutional dwelling units in the conterminous United States.

For added efficiency, per dollar spent, the sample was clustered geographically at each stage and stratified with interlaced controls.[1]

The supplementary sample consisted of a group of families with heads under sixty-five and low per capita incomes. Low per capita incomes were defined as follows:

Number of family members	Income
1, 2, or 3	under $2,000
4 or 5	under $3,000
6 or 7	under $4,000
8 or more	under $5,000

The low income families were selected from the 1960 Survey of Consumer Finances, which also used a cross section from the Survey Research Center's

[1] Roe Goodman, and Leslie Kish, "Controlled Selection—A Technique in Probability Sampling," *Journal of the American Statistical Association,* 45 (September, 1950), 350–372;

Leslie Kish, "Efficient Allocation of a Multipurpose Sample," *Econometrica,* 29 (July, 1961), 363–385.

449

national sample.[2] About one out of every eight families was selected from the Survey of Consumer Finances sample. Low income families are represented about twice as frequently as nonlow income families in this study's sample; thus estimates regarding low income families are subject to smaller sampling errors than are estimates regarding other families. Low income families were assigned lower weights than other families in order to prevent bias in statements about the entire population.

This sample design resulted in interviews with the heads of 2,997 spending units in 2,800 families with 3,396 adult units. Of the 2,800 families, approximately 300 were low income families selected from the Survey of Consumer Finances sample. Table A-1 shows the actual numbers of interviews and noninterviews for families and spending units in the cross section and supplementary samples.

[2] For developmental history see James N. Morgan, "Repeated Surveys of Consumer Finances in the United States," *Family Living Studies, A Symposium* (Geneva: International Labour Office, 1961).

TABLE A-1

SAMPLE SIZE, INTERVIEWS, AND NONINTERVIEWS BY SPENDING UNIT
AND FAMILY CLASSIFICATION FOR THE CROSS SECTION
AND SUPPLEMENTARY SAMPLES

	Cross section sample		Supplementary sample	
	Number	Per cent	Number	Per cent
Spending units	3,390	100.0	390 [b]	100.0
Interviews	2,692	79.4	305	78.2
Noninterviews	698	20.6	85	21.8
Refusals	360	10.6	26	6.7
Respondents not at home, and noninterview for other reasons	338	10.0	59	15.1
Families	3,095 [a]	100.0	427 [b]	100.0
Interviews	2,513	81.2	296	69.3
Noninterviews	582	18.8	90	21.1
Refusals	326	10.5	36	8.4
Respondents not at home, and noninterview for other reasons	256	8.3	54	12.7
Families not selected in the sample	—	—	41	9.6

[a] Includes eight cases which have double weights because they were selected at half the sampling rate. Includes one case which was eligible for both the cross section and supplementary samples. Thus the actual number of families interviewed is only 2,800, i.e., $[(2,513 - 9) + 296]$.

Forty-three spending units who were interviewed are nonresponses because interviews with other spending units in the family were not completed. Failure to complete interviews with all spending units in a family made it impossible to estimate the family income and several other critical financial variables.

[b] Supplementary sample response rates shown for family units include an estimate of the number of low income families who were not contacted during the first wave of interviewing on the 1960 Survey of Consumer Finances. These families could not be selected for the reinterview sample because no information was available.

Weighting

When, because of different sampling rates or different response rates, one interview represents a larger fraction of the population than another, unbiased estimates are still possible if one weights each interview according to the proportion of the population it represents, i.e., by the inverse of the product of its sampling and response rates. The adding of the supplementary sample amounted to approximately doubling the sampling rate for low income families.

Therefore, low income families were given weights approximately half the size of weights for other families to compensate for the fact that low income families were sampled at twice the rate used for other families.

To determine differences in response rates, interviews were stratified by rent level, population of city, race, and age of head. Strata with lower response rates were given correspondingly higher weights. Thus the results of the study are not distorted by the fact that some segments of the population are more likely to be interviewed than are others.

One result of this weighting procedure is that the proportion of the population represented will be different from the number of interviews. Where estimates of aggregates might be of interest, the proportion of the sample has been given. Where the significance or stability of the finding is more important, the number of cases has been given.

Sampling Error

As with all survey data, the statistics in this study are subject to error arising from sampling variability. The sampling error is a measure of the chance deviation of a sample statistic from the corresponding population value. The sampling error does not measure the actual error of a particular sample estimate; rather it leads to statements in terms of confidence intervals that are correct in a specified proportion of cases in the long run.

In this study, the most interesting figures are differences between two subgroups, and Table A-2 presents approximate sampling errors of the differences between percentages. The sampling errors in Table A-2 were computed for statistics from the 1953 and 1954 Surveys of Consumer Finances, which used samples similar to the one used in this study. They are conservative estimates, somewhat on the high side, and most differences beyond these values may be considered significant at the 5 per cent level. For tables which include data about region, the sampling errors are closer to this limit than for other data because a regional subsample is clustered in a limited number of sample points rather than being spread over many sample points in the region.

No general purpose table of sampling errors of means is possible, and sampling errors of complex statistics such as the multivariate coefficients can only be estimated from repeated split half-sample estimates. When the latter procedure has been tried, the estimated sampling errors of multivariate coefficients are frequently close to those of simple random sampling. Hence, a simple F test has been used for sets of these coefficients, and the standard deviation of the dependent variable has been given for those who desire crude tests of individual coefficients. (See Appendix E.)

TABLE A-2

SAMPLING ERRORS

Number of spending units	Number of spending units				
	200	300	500	700	1,000
	For percentages from about 35 per cent to 65 per cent				
200	14	—	—	—	—
300	13	11	—	—	—
500	12	10	9	—	—
700	11	10	8	8	—
1,000	11	9	8	7	6
2,000	10	9	7	6	5
	For percentages around 20 per cent and 80 per cent				
200	11	—	—	—	—
300	10	9	—	—	—
500	9	8	7	—	—
700	9	8	7	6	—
1,000	9	7	6	6	5
2,000	8	7	6	5	4
	For percentages around 10 per cent and 90 per cent				
300	8	7	—	—	—
500	7	6	5	—	—
700	7	6	5	4	—
1,000	6	6	5	4	4
2,000	6	5	4	4	3
	For percentages around 5 per cent and 95 per cent				
300	6	5	—	—	—
500	5	4	4	—	—
700	5	4	4	3	—
1,000	5	4	3	3	3
2,000	5	4	3	3	2

Table A-2 shows the differences required for significance (two standard errors) in comparisons of percentages derived from two different subgroups of the survey. The sampling error does not measure the actual error that is involved in specific survey measurements. It shows that—except for nonsampling errors, errors in reporting, in interpolation, etc.—differences larger than those found in the table will arise by chance only five times in 100.

Validity of Survey Data

There are three ways one can assess the accuracy of survey data. One can estimate aggregates or over-all proportions, such as aggregate income, or the number of people receiving social security benefits, and compare these with aggregates estimated from records by government agencies. There are difficulties in assuring comparable definitions and coverage, and with skewed distributions where survey estimates or means and aggregates are subject to large sampling errors.

Such checks tell little about individual accuracy, which is the crucial problem in analysis of differences between individuals.

Secondly, one can check the accuracy of individual reports if some other source of information about the individual is available. This is difficult with financial information because most such records are kept confidential. With property taxes and house value, validity studies have shown some discrepancies but no particular bias, and in the case of property taxes the discrepancies were generally small. With other financial data, scattered studies show a range of accuracy depending on the item and the method.[3]

Thirdly, one survey can be checked against another done by a different agency or at a different time. It is generally assumed that the underreporting is the main problem so that the survey with more reported is considered better. In general, after taking account of differences in concept and coverage, well-conducted surveys tend to agree rather closely.

Finally, one can rely upon the care and precision with which the survey was conducted. The survey upon which this book was based was patterned after the Surveys of Consumer Finances, and used the same sampling methods, interviewers, procedures, and many of the same questions.[4]

It is probably true that people are more likely to forget items of income, for instance, than to mention items which really belong to an earlier year or never really existed. Hence one expects survey data to underestimate aggregates somewhat.

More important, even the most prosaic economic or demographic facts may have emotional content which affects the way in which they are reported. Hence, people might be expected to exaggerate their giving to church and charity, particularly if those who gave less than $25 were not allowed merely to report that they did not give $25 or more, as in this study.

Finally, it must be kept in mind that the analysis of survey data searches for relationships. Most errors and biases in the data can be expected merely to hide otherwise significant relationships so that they cannot be seen. They are unlikely to produce relationships in the sample data which do not exist in the population.

[3] John B. Lansing, Gerald Ginsburg, and Kaisa Braaten, *An Investigation of Response Error* (Urbana, Illinois: Bureau of Economic and Business Research, University of Illinois, 1961).

[4] For a summary of the history and development of methods of the Surveys of Consumer Finances, see Morgan, *Family Living Studies, A Symposium.*

Appendix B

QUESTIONNAIRE, EDITING, CODING

Questionnaire

Interviews were taken by the Survey Research Center's trained field staff, during March and April 1960.[1] Interviews with cross section respondents were taken using the questionnaire reproduced in this appendix.

Respondents in the supplementary sample had been interviewed one or two months earlier for the Survey of Consumer Finances and had already reported some of the information required by this study. Much of the previously reported information concerned income, a subject many respondents are reluctant to discuss. Therefore the reinterview questionnaire was shortened and most questions about income, as well as some questions about housing, employment, and head's education were omitted. This information was transcribed from the interview schedule of the Survey of Consumer Finances for each reinterview respondent, and was coded as a regular part of this study.

Editing

After interviews were received from the interviewing staff they were edited. This involved checking the responses for consistency, assigning missing data, and calculating financial measures such as net equity in an owned house, net rent, and several income concepts. Calculation of financial variables was simplified by the use of work sheets which indicated clearly what information was required for the calculation and how the calculation was to be carried out.

Coding

A second staff coded the information on the interviews.[2] The information in each interview was summarized by means of numerical codes. The codes for each question were designed to provide mutually exclusive and logically exhaustive categories for describing the answers to each question. A decreasing fraction of interviews was double-coded and differences reconciled in order to assure uniform treatment. Altogether about 10 per cent were check coded. The editing process was checked in a similar fashion.

The codes were key punched, after which some of the complex variables were built by machine. Income measures, such as estimated income taexs, which involved synthesizing many of the original responses and taking information from several

[1] See Survey Research Center, *Manual for Interviewers* (Ann Arbor: Institute for Social Research, March 1960, revised).

[2] See Survey Research Center, *Manual for Coders* (Ann Arbor: Institute for Social Research, 1961).

454

places in the questionnaire were calculated during editing; measures which could be derived from the edited and coded data by simple computations were constructed by machine. Several demographic variables were combined by machine to form summary measures such as life cycle, number of children in the family, etc.

Serial Number

Survey Research Center, Project 678
University of Michigan, March, 1960

| Sample Book No. |
| Codes |
| Place |

A

PATTERNS OF FAMILY CHANGE

Interviewer_____Interviewer's Int. No._____Date_____

In this survey we are talking to people all over the country about their families, how they have changed from one generation to the next, and what plans they have for the future.

A1. First I'd like to know who lives here, 18 years of age and over?

(LIST IN SAME ORDER ON ALL FACE SHEETS FOR THIS DWELLING UNIT)

	A2. Relation to Head	A3. Family Unit Number	A4. Sex	A5. Age	A6. Does he (she) usually receive $15 or more per week from any source?	A7. (IF YES) Does he (she) keep his finances separate?	A8. (IF YES) Does he (she) contribute less than one-half of his income?*	A9. Spending Unit Number	A10. Indicate Respondent by check (ALWAYS INTERVIEW HEAD OF SU)
1	Head of DU	1			--	--	--	1	
2.									
3.									
4.									
5.									
6.									
7.									

A11. Does anyone else live here in this dwelling, like roomers or servants? (LIST ABO' E)

Yes   No

A12. Are there any children under 18 living here with you (in SU covered by interview)?

Yes   No

(IF YES)
A13. Are they your sons or daughters or what?

A14. How old are they?

(ENTER DATA ON CHILDREN AT RIGHT)———→

	A15. Relation To Head	A16. Sex	A17. Age
1.			
2.			
3.			
4.			
5.			
6.			
7.			
8.			
9.			

*IF HE (SHE) CONTRIBUTED LESS THAN ONE-HALF, HE (SHE) IS A SEPARATE SPENDING UNIT. IF "NO", HE (SHE) IS NOT A SEPARATE SPENDING UNIT. THE MAIN SPENDING UNIT SHOULD BE NUMBERED "1". PLEASE NUMBER ALL SPENDING UNITS. FILL OUT ADDITIONAL COVER SHEETS (FORM A) FOR EACH SECONDARY SPENDING UNIT.

(ASK EVERYONE)

A18. Are you single, married, widowed, divorced, or separated?

Single ⎰ (IF CHILDREN IN SU, SKIP TO PAGE 4, B16)
⎱ (IF NO CHILDREN IN SU, SKIP TO PAGE 6, B40)

(SPECIFY WHETHER
FIGURE INDICATES
AGE OR YEAR)

Married	A19. When were you married?	_____
Widowed	A20. When were you widowed?	_____
Divorced	A21. When were you divorced?	_____
Separated	A22. When were you separated?	_____

B. EDUCATION

B1. Do you (HEAD) have any (other) children who don't live here, that is, including
grown sons and daughters?

Yes   (SKIP TO PAGE 3, B4)

No   ⎰ (IF CHILDREN IN SU, SKIP TO PAGE 4, B16)
⎱ (IF NO CHILDREN AT ALL, CONTINUE WITH B2)

(IF NO CHILDREN AND WIFE UNDER 40 - See Face Sheet)

B2. Do you expect to have any children?   Yes   No

(IF YES) B3. Do you think they will go to college?

(SKIP TO PAGE 6, B40)

(IF YES, HAS CHILDREN WHO DON'T LIVE HERE - See B1)

	I	II	III
B4. Is that a son or daughter?	Son	Son	Son
	Daughter	Daughter	Daughter
B5. How old is he (she)?	Age:_____	Age:_____	Age:_____
B6. What is he (she) doing now?			

(IF CHILD IS NOT IN COLLEGE - See B6)

	I	II	III
(IF WORKING) B7. What kind of work does he (she) do?	_____	_____	_____
B8. What kind of business is that in?	_____	_____	_____
B9. How many grades of school did he (she) finish?	_____	_____	_____
(IF COMPLETED 12 GRADES) B10. Did he (she) go to college?	Yes No	Yes No	Yes No
(IF YES) B11. Did he (she) get a college degree?	Yes No	Yes No	Yes No

(ASK ABOUT ELDEST SON - See B4, B5)

B12. Roughly speaking, about how much income do you think your eldest son earns each year?

Under $3000	$3000 - 5000	Over $5000

(IF CHILD IS IN COLLEGE - See B6)

	I	II	III
B13. Is the college a state or city supported college or a private one?	Public	Public	Public
	Private	Private	Private
B14. About how many months was he (she) in college in 1959?	_____	_____	_____
B15. During 1959, about how much do you think it cost you for his (her) education, including tuition, books, living expenses away from home, and transportation?	$	$	$

{ (ASK ABOUT ANYONE UNDER 18 IN THIS SU - See A12)
{ (ASK ABOUT ADULT SONS AND DAUGHTERS OF THE HEAD IN THIS SU - See Face Sheet)

You said you had ___ children living here . . . . A

| IF ANY CHILD 5-25 YEARS OLD | B16. How many of the children living here are in grade school or high school? _____ B |
| | (IF ANY) B17. How many are in public schools? _____ |

| IF ANY CHILD UNDER 7 YEARS OLD | B18. How many have not started school yet? _____ C |

IF B + C ACCOUNTS FOR ALL CHILDREN SKIP TO PAGE 5, B34

		I	II
IF ANY OTHER CHILDREN* ASK B19-33	B19. (What about the others), what are they doing now?	_____	_____
	B20. Which of your children would that be?	Son _____ Daughter Age: ___	Son _____ Daughter Age: ___

(IF CHILD IS NOT IN COLLEGE - See B19)

(IF WORKING)	B21. What kind of work does he (she) do?	_____	_____
	B22. What kind of business is that in?	_____	_____
	B23. How many weeks did he (she) work last year?	_____	_____
(IF NOT WORKING)	B24. How is it that he (she) is not working?	_____	_____
	B25. Did he (she) do any work for pay last year?	Yes No	Yes No
	(IF YES) B26. How many weeks did he (she) work?		
	B27. How many grades of school did he (she) finish?	_____	_____
	(IF COMPLETED 12 GRADES) B28. Did he (she) go to college?	Yes No	Yes No
	(IF YES) B29. Did he (she) get a college degree?	Yes No	Yes No

*SONS OR DAUGHTERS OF HEAD OVER 25 YEARS OF AGE, OR CHILDREN UNDER 25 WHO ARE NOT ACCOUNTED FOR IN B + C.

(IF CHILD IS IN COLLEGE - See B19)

	I	II
B30. Is the college a state- or city-supported college or a private one?	Public / Private	Public / Private
B31. Does he (she) stay at home or live at the college or what?	_____	_____
B32. About how many months was he (she) in college in 1959?	_____	_____
B33. During 1959 how much do you think it cost you for his (her) education, including tuition, books, (living expenses away from home), and transportation?	$	$

(ASK IF   1) CHILDREN 20 OR UNDER IN THIS SU [B16, 18, 19])
          2) CHILDREN OF HEAD, 20 OR UNDER, IN SECONDARY SU'S   [See Face Sheet]
          3) CHILDREN OF HEAD LIVING ELSEWHERE, 20 OR UNDER [B6])

(IF   B34. How much education do you expect your boy(s) to have before they
BOYS)   stop going to school

(IF   B35. How much education do you expect your girl(s) to have before they
GIRLS)   stop going to school?

(IF ANY   B36. How do you expect their (his, her) college education will be
CHILDREN   financed?
MAY GO
TO   B37. Do you think your children (son) (daughter) will go away to
COLLEGE)   college, or will they (he) (she) live at home, or both?

               B38. Do you think any of your children (your son) (your daughter)
                    will be going to a state-supported college?

                                        Yes How many? _____
                                        No

               B39. To what extent do you expect your children (your son)
                    (your daughter) to support themselves (himself) (herself)
                    in college?

(ASK EVERYONE)

B40. How much education do you think children ought to get these days?

B41. Why is that? (What does it depend on?)

B42. Part of the costs of college are now paid for out of tax funds, and part by college students and their families. Do you think that tax funds should cover more of the costs than they do now, or less, or what?

B43. Should tax money be used to support only those with ability, only those who have financial need, or should everyone be supported?

B44. We're interested in how people compare occupations. How do you think most people would feel if a boy of theirs chose each of these types of work?

SHOW CARD I

	Not Happy 1	Wouldn't Mind 2	Happy 3	Very Happy 4	Delighted 5
a. Carpenter					
b. Social Worker					
c. Doctor					
d. Night Watchman					
e. Mail Carrier					
f. Bookkeeper					
g. Bus Driver					
h. High School Teacher					
i. Auto Mechanic					
j. Drug Store Owner					

C1. Now I have a few questions about your home. Do you (SU) own this home or pay rent or what?

Owns or is buying	(CONTINUE WITH C2)
Pays rent	(SKIP TO C7)
Neither owns nor rents	(SKIP TO C11)

(IF OWNS OR IS BUYING)

C2. Could you tell me what the present value of this house (farm) is? I mean about what would it bring if you sold it today? $_____

C3. About how much do you think it would cost you to rent a house about like the one you live in? $_____

C4. How much do you pay in property taxes on this house every year, including city, county, and school taxes? $_____

C5. Do you have a mortgage, a land contract, or any other debt on this property?   Yes   No

(IF YES) C6. Approximately how much do you owe on this property altogether? $_____

(SKIP TO PAGE 8, C17)

(IF RENTS)

C7. About how much rent do you pay a month? $_____

C8. Do you pay for water, electricity, gas, or heat?   Yes   No

(IF YES) C9. How much did they cost you last year altogether? $_____

C10. Do you rent this place furnished or unfurnished?   Furnished   Unfurnished

(SKIP TO PAGE 8, C17)

(IF NEITHER OWNS NOR RENTS)

C11. How is that?

C12. Do you help with the mortgage payments, or pay some of the utilities or anything like that?   Yes   No

(IF YES) C13. How much did you pay last year? $_____

C14. Who pays the property taxes? _____

(IF R [SU] PAYS) C15. How much did you pay last year for property taxes? $_____

(IF PRIMARY SU)

C16. Could you tell me about what this house (apartment) would rent for? $_____

(ASK EVERYONE)

C17. Did you spend any of your own time repairing or improving this house (apartment) last year?

Yes   No

    (IF YES)   C18. What did you do?

                 C19. How much do you think you saved by doing it yourself? $_____

C20. How long have you lived in this house (apartment)?_____

C21. Do you feel that you have settled down to stay here in this house (apartment), or do you plan to move?

    (IF PLANS TO MOVE OR MAY MOVE)

         C22.   Why is that?   (What does it depend on?)

(IF INTERVIEW WITH A SECONDARY SU, SKIP TO PAGE 9, C27)

(ASK ONLY IN INTERVIEW WITH PRIMARY SU - See A9)

     C23. Not counting bathrooms, how many rooms are there in this house (apartment)?   _____

    (IF ADULTS OTHER THAN HEAD AND HIS WIFE LIVE IN THIS FAMILY - See A3)

         C24. Do you receive any rent from the others in your family who live here?

Yes   No

            (IF YES)   C25.   How much is it a month? $_____

         C26. Do the others in your family living here pay for their own food, or what?

(SKIP TO PAGE 10, E1)

(ASK IN ALL INTERVIEWS WITH SECONDARY SPENDING UNITS - See A9)

C27. Do you share your living and eating arrangements with others in this house (apartment)?

      (IF YES) C28. Tell me about it.

      (IF NO)   C29. How do you get to your room - do you have a private or separate entrance, or do you have to pass through some other rooms?

              (IF PASSES THROUGH OTHER ROOMS)

              C30. Is there cooking equipment here for your own private use?   ☐ Yes   ☐ No

Now I'd like to ask a few questions about your experiences in past years.

E1. Where did you grow up?_____
                                (Specify State, if U.S.; Country, if Foreign)

E2. Was that on a farm or in a large city or small town or what?

  Farm   Small town   Large city   Other _____
                                                              (Specify)

E3. How many brothers and sisters did you have? _____ Brothers _____ Sisters

E4. How many grades of school did you finish?

  None   1 2 3 4 5 6 7 8 9 10 11 12

E5. Have you had other schooling?   Yes   No

  (IF YES) E6. What other schooling have you had?

            Type of schooling:_____
                                (College, secretarial, business, etc.)

         (IF ANY COLLEGE)

            E7. Do you have a college degree?   Yes   No

E8. Were your grades (marks) above or below the grades of most of your classmates?

E9. How old were you when you left school?_____
                                            (SPECIFY WHETHER AGE OR YEAR)

E10. After you left school, when did you get your first full-time regular job?

                                _____
                                (SPECIFY WHETHER AGE OR YEAR)

            (IF HEAD NEVER WORKED, SKIP TO PAGE 11, E15)

(IF HEAD HAS WORKED)
_____
| E11. What kind of a job was it?   (What did you do?) |
| |
| |
| E12. Since you got your first regular job, how many states have you |
| lived in (not including your experience while in military service)? |
| |
| _____ |
| |
| (IF ONE) E13. Since your first regular job, have you ever |
| lived more than 100 miles from here?   Yes   No |
| |
| (IF TWO, OR MORE) E14. Where was that? |
| |
| |
|_____|

            (IF HEAD NOT MARRIED SKIP TO PAGE 11, E21)

(IF <u>NOW</u> MARRIED - See A18)

E15. Now about your wife
where did she grow up?_____
(Specify State, If U.S.; Country, if Foreign)

E16. Was that on a farm or in a large city or small town or what?
| Farm | | Small town | | Large city | | Other |
(Specify)

E17. How many grades of school did she finish?
| None | | 1 | | 2 | | 3 | | 4 | | 5 | | 6 | | 7 | | 8 | | 9 | | 10 | | 11 | | 12 |

E18. Did she have other schooling? | Yes | | No |

(IF YES) E19. What other schooling did she have?

Type of schooling:_____
(College, secretarial, business, etc.)

(IF ANY COLLEGE)

E20. Did she get a college degree? | Yes | | No |

(ASK ABOUT HEAD'S FATHER)

E21. Where did your father grow up?_____
(Specify State, if U.S.; Country if Foreign)

E22. How many grades of school did he finish?
| None | | 1 | | 2 | | 3 | | 4 | | 5 | | 6 | | 7 | | 8 | | 9 | | 10 | | 11 | | 12 |

(IF NONE, OR   E23. Could he read and write? | Yes | | No |
<u>DON'T KNOW</u>)

(IF COMPLETED 12 GRADES) E24. Did he go to college? | Yes | | No |

(IF <u>YES</u>) E25. Did he get a college degree? | Yes | | No |

E26. What would you say his usual occupation was while you were
in grade school?

E27. Did he work for himself or for someone else or what?_____

E28. Was his church preference Protestant, Catholic, or Jewish?
| Protestant | | Roman Catholic | | Jewish | | Other |
(Specify)

(IF <u>PROTESTANT</u>) E29. What denomination was that?_____

(IF <u>JEWISH</u>) E30. Was that orthodox,
conservative or reform?_____

E31. Did he attend religious services regularly, occasionally, or not at all?
| Regularly | | Occasionally | | Not at all |

Now we would like to ask you some questions about your job.

G1. What is your occupation?   What sort of work do you do?

Employed _____ (SKIP TO PAGE 13, G17)——————
(Specify job)

Unemployed   **G2.** What kind of work do you do when you work? _____
(Specify job)

G3. What kind of business is that in? _____
(SKIP TO PAGE 14, G39)

Retired   **G4.** What kind of work did you do when you worked? _____
(Specify job)

G5. What kind of business was that in? _____
(CONTINUE WITH G6)

Student   **(CONTINUE WITH G6)**

Housewife)   **(SKIP TO G8)**

(IF HEAD IS RETIRED OR A STUDENT)

G6. Did you do any work for pay in 1959?   Yes   No   (SKIP TO PAGE 16, G52)

(IF YES)   **G7.** What did you do?

(SKIP TO PAGE 15, G46)

(IF HEAD IS HOUSEWIFE)

G8. Have you ever had a (regular) job?   Yes   No

(IF YES)

G9. What did you do? _____

G10. How many years did you work altogether (including years that you worked before you got married)? _____

(IF HOUSEWIFE UNDER 65 - See Face Sheet)

G11. Do you think you would be able to find a job easily?   Yes   No

G12. Why is that?

G13. What about the future, do you think that you will go to work sometime at a regular job?   Yes   No

G14. Why is that?

G15. Did you do any work for pay in 1959?   Yes   No   (SKIP TO PAGE 18)

(IF YES)   **G16.** What did you do?

(SKIP TO PAGE 15, G46)

(IF HEAD IS WORKING)

G17. What kind of business is that in?_____

G18. Do you work for yourself or someone else or what?

                    MAIN JOB: [Self]   [Someone else]
                    (See G1)

G19. Do you have more than one job?   [Yes]   [No]
   (IF YES)

     G20. What is the other job?_____

     G21. What kind of business is that in?_____

     G22. On your second job, do you work for yourself or someone else, or what?

             SECOND JOB: [Self]   [Someone else]
             (See G20)

(IF SELF-EMPLOYED IN ANY JOB)

     G23. Do you employ other people?   [Yes]   [No]

     (IF YES)

        G24. About how many? _____

     G25. How long have you been in this kind of work? _____
                                       (Specify months or years)

     G26. Does it bring in a steady income, or does it vary from year to year?

        (IF INCOME VARIES)

          G27. Why is that?

         (IF SELF-EMPLOYED ON MAIN JOB, SKIP TO PAGE 15, G46)

(IF HEAD IS TENANT FARMER SKIP TO PAGE 15, G46)

(ASK ABOUT HEAD'S MAIN JOB, IF WORKS FOR SOMEONE ELSE - See G18)

G28. About how many other people work where you do?

              [1 - 3]   [4 - 9]   [10 - 99]   [100 or more]

G29. Do you supervise other people?   [Yes]   [No]

G30. About how long have you been with your present employer? _____
                                              (Specify months or years)

G31. Does your work bring in a steady income or does it vary from year to year?

   (IF INCOME VARIES)   G32. How is that?

G33. What would you say are your chances for promotion or getting ahead?

    G34. Why is that?

(ASK ABOUT HEAD'S MAIN JOB IF WORKS FOR SOMEONE ELSE - See G18) (continued)

G35. If they had to cut down in your organization, would you be among the first to be laid off or the last or what?

G36. If you should lose your present job, what would you say were your chances of finding another job that paid about the same?

G37. Why is that?

G38. Have you been unemployed in the last 5 years?   Yes   No

(CONTINUE   WITH G39)

(IF HEAD ⎰IS UNEMPLOYED OR
         ⎱WORKS FOR SOMEONE ELSE - See G1, G18)

G39. Some people are out of work for a time every year, others are unemployed every few years, and for still others unemployment is quite unusual. How has it been in your (HEAD'S) case?

(IF NEVER UNEMPLOYED, SKIP TO G44)

(IF UNEMPLOYED AT SOME TIME IN PAST 5 YEARS - See G1, G38)

G40. Did you receive unemployment compensation at some time during the past 5 years?   Yes   No

(IF NO)

G41. How did it happen that you didn't get it?

(IF YES)

G42. Did your unemployment benefits run out at any time during the past 5 years?   Yes   No

(IF YES) G42. When was that?_____
                                        (Months and years)

G44.   Do you think unemployment compensation payments should be higher, lower, or the same as they are now?

G45. Why do you think so?

(IF HEAD IS: <u>EMPLOYED NOW</u> ⎫
                          ⎬ [See G1])

or UNEMPLOYED NOW ⎭

or WORKED LAST YEAR ["Yes" to G6 or "Yes" to G15])

G46. In 1959, how many weeks did you work full time (including paid vacations and sick leave)? _____

(IF LESS THAN 49 WEEKS)

G47. How about the weeks you didn't work full time, were you working part-time, unable to find work, ill, or what?	G48. How many weeks were you (working part-time, unable to find work, etc.)
Reasons	Number of Weeks
_____	_____
_____	_____
_____	_____
_____	_____

(IF WORKED AT ALL)

G49. About how many hours a week did you usually work last year (while you were working) (at all jobs)? _____ hours per week

(IF HEAD IS MARRIED, SKIP TO PAGE 16, G52)

(IF SU CONTAINS ONLY ONE ADULT, ADULT IS WORKING, AND THERE ARE CHILDREN UNDER 12, ASK G50-1) —————————————

(ALL OTHER SU'S SKIP TO PAGE 18)

G50. What arrangements do you have for taking care of the children while you are at work?

        G51. (IF NOT CLEAR) How much does this cost you per month?

                                                     $_____

(SKIP TO PAGE 18)

(IF HEAD IS MARRIED, EVEN IF HEAD IS RETIRED)

G52. What about your wife, is she working or earning any money now?

> Yes
>
> No (SKIP TO PAGE 17, G61)

(IF YES, WIFE WORKS)

G53. What sort of work does she do?

G54. What kind of business is that in?

G55. How many weeks did she work either full-time or part-time last year? _____

G56. How many hours a week did she usually work when she was working last year? _____

> (IF SU HAS CHILDREN UNDER AGE 12 - See Face Sheet)
>
> G57. What arrangements do you have for taking care of the children while you and your wife are both at work?
>
> G58. (IF NOT CLEAR) How much does this cost you per month? $_____

G59. How many years has she been working altogether (including years before she got married)? _____

G60. What are her plans, how long will she keep on working?

(SKIP TO PAGE 17, G69)

(IF NO, WIFE DOES NOT WORK - See G52)

G61. Did she ever have a job?   [Yes]   [No]

   (IF YES)

      G62. What did she do?

      G63. What kind of business was that in?

      G64. How many years did she work altogether (including years that she worked before she got married)?   _____

G65. If she wanted to work would she be able to find a job easily?
                                             [Yes]   [No]

      G66. Why is that?

G67. What about the future, do you think she will go to work sometime at a regular job?   [Yes]   [No]

      G68. Why is that?

(ASK IF HEAD IS MARRIED)

   G69. There are many wives who have jobs these days. Do you think it is a good thing for a wife to work, or a bad thing, or what?

      G70. Why do you say so? (What does it depend on?)

      (IF CHILDREN MENTIONED IN G70)
      G71. What if there are no children at home to be cared for?

In this survey all over the country we are trying to get an accurate picture of people's financial situation. One thing we need to know is the income of all the people we interview.

(IF HEAD IS NOT A FARMER ASK H7)

(IF FARMER - See G1)

H1.	Did you receive any income from crops you placed under commodity credit loans, or from soil bank payments?	
	Commodity Credit Loans Soil Bank Both Neither	
H2.	What were your total receipts from farming in 1959 (including commodity credit loans and soil bank payments)?	$_____
H3.	What were your total operating expenses, not counting living expenses or income taxes?	$_____
H4.	Does that include any investments in things that will last for a while, like tractors, trucks, equipment or buildings?	Yes No
	(IF YES) H5. How much went for things like that?	$_____
H6.	How much is the livestock and equipment that you own on this farm worth?	
	(SHOW CARD II)	
	A Less than $500 B $500 - 999 C $1000 - 4999 D $5000 - 9999	
	D $10,000 - 24,999 F $25,000 and over	

(ASK EVERYONE)

H7. Did you own a business any time in 1959, or did you have a financial interest in any business enterprise?

Yes   (CONTINUE WITH H8)   No   (SKIP TO PAGE 20, H24)

(IF YES)

H8. What sort of business is it?
H9. Are you the sole owner, or is it a partnership, or what?
(IF A PARTNER - H10-17 REFER TO HEAD'S SHARE ONLY)
H10.Is it a corporation or an unincorporated business or do you have an interest in both kinds?
Corporation   (IF CORPORATION, SKIP TO PAGE 20, H24)
Unincorporated business
Both kinds   (CONTINUE WITH H11)
Don't know

(ASK ALL UNINCORPORATED BUSINESSMEN)

H11. Did your business make a profit or a loss in 1959?

| Profit or broke even | | Loss |

(I PROFIT OR BROKE EVEN)

H12. Did you (or your wife) take anything out of the business as salary or living expenses or profit in 1959? | Yes | | No |

    (IF YES) H13. How much did you take out in 1959? $ _____

H14. In addition, did you leave any profit in the business? | Yes | | No |

    (IF YES) H15. How much did you leave in, I mean profits before deducting income taxes? $ _____

(SKIP TO H19)

(IF LOSS)

H16. How much was your loss in 1959? $ _____

H17. Did you (or your wife) take anything out of the business as salary or living expenses in 1959? | Yes | | No |

    (IF YES) H18. How much did you take out in 1959? $ _____

(CONTINUE WITH H19)

H19. Does the business owe any money for business improvements, new equipment, new buildings and things like that? | Yes | | No |

H20. Did you pay off any money in 1959 that you owed on things like that? | Yes | | No |

    (IF YES)

H21. Some people think of money used to pay off business debts as part of the expenses of their business and some think of it as profit used to increase the value of their business. Did you count this money you paid off in 1959 as a business expense or as part of profit? | Business expense | | Profit |

    (IF BUSINESS EXPENSE)

H22. How much did you reduce your business debt during 1959? $ _____

H23. How much is your share in the business worth? (SHOW CARD II)

A | less than $500 | B | $500 - 999 | C | $1000 - 4999 | D | $5000 - 9999 |

E | $10,000 - 24,999 | F | $25,000 and over |

(ASK EVERYONE)

H24. How much did you (HEAD) receive from wages and salaries
in 1959, that is before deductions for taxes of anything? $_____

H25. In addition to this did you have any income from bonuses,
overtime, and commissions?   [Yes]   [No]

   (IF YES)   H26. How much was that? $_____

H27. Did you receive any (other) income from:

(IF "YES" TO ANY ITEM)

H28. How much was your income from (SOURCE) after allowing for expenses?

a) professional practice. . $_____

b) a trade . . . . $_____

c) farming or market
gardening . . . . $_____

d) roomers and boarders . $_____

(ENTER AMOUNT AT RIGHT)⟶ e) any other
self-employment . . . . $_____

f) rent . . . . $_____

H29. How about:

a) interest . . . . $_____

b) dividends . . . . $_____

c) trust fund or royalties . . . . $_____

d) veteran's pension, veteran's school
allotment, serviceman's family allotment . . . . $_____

e) unemployment compensation . . . . $_____

f) Social Security . . . . $_____

g) other retirement pay,
pensions, annuities . . . . $_____

h) alimony, regular contributions
from family or others . . . . $_____

i) public welfare, other
government aid . . . . $_____

NOTE TO INTERVIEWERS: LEAVE NO BLANK SPACES, ENTER ZERO IF NO INCOME FROM A GIVEN SOURCE

(IF SINGLE PERSON SU SKIP TO PAGE 23, H53)

(ASK ABOUT WIFE OF HEAD)

| H30. Did your wife have any income during 1959? | Yes | No |

(IF YES)

	SOURCE:	A	B	C	D
H31.Was it from wages, salary, a business or what?					
H32. How much was the income for 1959?		$_____	$_____	$_____	$_____

(IF NO ONE ELSE LIVING IN SU, SKIP TO PAGE 23, H53)

(ASK ABOUT ANYONE UNDER 18 IN THIS SU - See A12)
(ASK ABOUT ADULT SONS AND DAUGHTERS OF THE HEAD IN THE SU - See Face Sheet)

	I	II	III
AGE:	_____	_____	_____
RELATION TO HEAD:			
H33. Did_____ have any income in 1959?	Yes No	Yes No	Yes No
(IF YES) H34. Was it from wages, salary, a business, or what?			
H35. How much was the income for 1959?	$_____	$_____	$_____
H36. Did he (she) have any other income during 1959?	Yes No	Yes No	Yes No
H37. What was it from?			
H38. How much was it for 1959?	$_____	$_____	$_____

(IF NO ONE ELSE LIVING IN SU, SKIP TO PAGE 23, H53)

(ASK ABOUT ANYONE ELSE IN SU - See Face Sheet)

	I	II
AGE:	_____	_____
SEX:	_____	_____
RELATION TO HEAD:	_____	_____
H39. How long has _____ been living with you?		
H40. Is he (she) working now?	Yes No	Yes No

(IF YES, IS WORKING NOW) (See H40)

	I	II
H41. What is he (she) doing?	_____	_____
H42. What kind of business is that in?	_____	_____
H43. How many weeks did he (she) work during 1959?	_____	_____
H44. How much did he (she) earn during 1959?	$_____	$_____
H45. Did he (she) have any other income during 1959?	Yes No	Yes No
(IF YES)		
H46. What was it from?	_____	_____
H47. How much was it during 1959?	$_____	$_____

(IF NO, IS NOT WORKING NOW)   (See H40)

	I	II
H48. How is that?	_____	_____
H49. When did he (she) last have a full-time job?	_____	_____
(IF IN 1959 ASK H43-47)		
H50. Did he (she) have any income in 1959?	Yes No	Yes No
(IF YES) H51. Was it from a business, a pension, or what?	_____	_____
H52. How much was it for 1959?	$_____	$_____

(ASK EVERYONE)

H53. Did you (SU) grow any of your own food in a vegetable plot or anything like that? [Yes] [No]

(IF YES)

> H54. Do you think you saved more than $50 on your food bills this way? [Yes] [No]
>
> > (IF YES)
> >
> > H55. About how much did you save by growing your own food?
> >
> > (IF DON'T KNOW) $_____
> >
> > > H56. Approximately what fraction of your food for the year did you grow?
> > >
> > > _____

H57. Did any of you (SU) get any medical care at reduced fees, as a veteran or in a free clinic or some other way during 1959? [Yes] [No]

(IF YES)

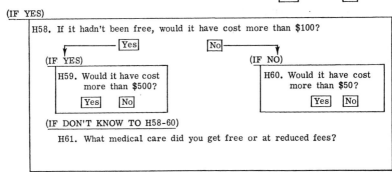

> H58. If it hadn't been free, would it have cost more than $100?
>
>   [Yes]   [No]
>
> (IF YES)   (IF NO)
>
> > H59. Would it have cost more than $500?   H60. Would it have cost more than $50?
> >
> > [Yes] [No]   [Yes] [No]
>
> (IF DON'T KNOW TO H58-60)
>
> > H61. What medical care did you get free or at reduced fees?

H62. Did you (SU) get more than $50 of food and clothing or large gifts free in 1959? [Yes] [No]

(IF YES)

> H63. Tell me about it.
>
> H64. Where was it from?
>
> H65. Did you get any thing else? _____
>
> H66. What would you say it added up to in dollar value altogether? $_____

H67. Did you (SU) use up any of your savings last year? [Yes] [No]

(IF YES) H68. How much did you use up? $_____

H69. Have you (SU) ever inherited any money or property? [Yes] [No]

(IF YES) H70. When was that? _____

(SPECIFY WHETHER YEAR OR YEARS AGO)

H71. What was it worth? $_____

H72. Was there a time when you (HEAD) earned more than in 1959? [Yes] [No]

(IF YES) H73. In what year did you earn the most? _____

H74. About how much did you make then? $_____

H75. Did you (SU) ever get anything like welfare or other aid from government agencies? [Yes] [No]

(IF YES) H78. Tell me about it.

(ASK EVERYONE)

H77. Have you had an illness, physical condition, or nervous condition which limits the type of work or the amount of work you can do?

(WORK REFERS TO JOBS OR HOUSEWORK) [Yes] [No]

(IF YES)

H78. How would you describe this condition?

H79. How does it limit your work?

H80. Were there some public or private agencies which helped you get ready for a job after you became sick or injured? [Yes] [No]

(IF YES)

H81. What kind of help did you receive?

H82. Are you satisfied with the help you received? _____

H83. From what agencies did you receive help? _____

(IF SINGLE PERSON SU, SKIP TO PAGE 26, I1)

H84. Is there anyone else living here whose work or schooling is limited by some illness, physical condition, or nervous condition?

(SKIP TO PAGE 26, I1)

(WORK REFERS TO JOBS OR HOUSEWORK) [Yes] [No]

(IF YES)

	I	II
H85. Who is that? SEX: AGE: RELATION TO HEAD:		
H86. How would you describe his (her) condition?		
H87. How does it limit his (her) work (for schooling)?		
(IF AGED 18 OR OVER)		
H88. Were there some public or private agencies which helped him (her) get ready for a job after he (she) became sick or injured? (IF YES) **H89.** What kind of help did he (she) receive? **H90.** From what agencies did he (she) receive help?	[Yes] [No] ____ ____ ____	[Yes] [No] ____ ____ ____
(IF UNDER 18 YEARS OLD)		
H91. Is he (she) now receiving a special education or training program because of his (her) condition?	[Yes] [No]	[Yes] [No]

Now we have some questions on the ways people use their money.

I1. Did you pay out any money to help support anyone in 1959; that is, friends, parents, children, or relatives, or did you pay alimony or anything like that?　　　　　　　　　　　　　　　　　　　　　[Yes]　　[No]

(IF YES)

> I2. Who was it? I mean how are they related to you?
>
> I3. How much did this amount to in 1959?　　　　　　　　　　$_____
>
> I4. Is anyone not living here depending on you for more than half of his support?　　　　　　　　　　[Yes]　　[No]
>
> 　　(IF YES) I5. Is it just one person, or two or what?　_____

I6. Did you give your friends or relatives more than $50 of food, clothing, or large gifts?　　[Yes]　　　　[No]

(IF YES)

> I7. Who was it, I mean, how are they related to you?
>
> I8. How much would you say this was worth?　　　　　　$_____

I9. Now, what about the church or religious organizations, would you say that in the course of the year you contributed more than $25 altogether to the church or religious organizations?　　[Yes]　　[No]

(IF YES) I10. About how much did you contribute?　　　　　　$_____

I11. How about donations to other organizations, did you give more than $25 altogether to things like Community Chest, schools, cancer or heart associations, and so forth?　　　　　　[Yes]　　　　　[No]

(IF YES) I12. About how much did you contribute altogether to such organizations? $_____

J1. Do you people (SU) have Blue Cross or other hospitalization insurance?

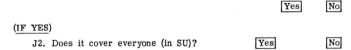

(IF YES)

    J2. Does it cover everyone (in SU)?   [Yes]   [No]

J3. How about savings in banks or savings and loan associations or government bonds, do you people (SU) have as much as $1,000 altogether in savings?

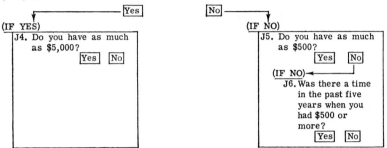

J7. Some people feel that they can make pretty definite plans for their lives for the next few years. Others feel that they aren't in a position to plan ahead. How about you? Do you feel able to plan ahead or not?

    J8. Why?

J9. Do you plan ahead as to what your next major expenditures will be, or do you buy things when you have to have them?

J10. Some people say that people get ahead by their own hard work; others say that lucky breaks or help from other people are more important. What do you think about this?

J11. Some older people move in with their children, others try hard to keep a separate household even when it means pinching pennies. Do you think it is a good idea or a bad idea for older people to live with their children?

    J12. Why is that? (What does it depend on?)

J13. If the older people don't have enough money, do you think their relatives should support them, or should the government take care of them, or what?

    J14. Why do you say so?

K. RETIREMENT

(IF HEAD IS RETIRED - See G1)

Now I'd like to ask you a few questions about your retirement.

K1. How long has it been since you were last working full time at your regular job?

        _____
          (Years)

K2. Had you planned to retire then, or did you have to change your plans?

    (IF CHANGE) K3. Why was that?

K4. When you retired, did you have more savings than you have now, or less?
    [More]   [Same]   [Less]

    (IF MORE) K5. What fraction of your savings have you used? _____
                        (SKIP TO PAGE 30, L1)

(IF HEAD <u>NOT</u> RETIRED - See G1)

K6. A few years from now, would you think you and your family will have a better income than you have now, or will you be in about the same situation, or in a less satisfactory situation?

(IF "BETTER" K7. Why do you say so?
OR "WORSE")

K8. Do you think you may have to help take care of your parents (or your wife's parents), or do more for them, sometime in the future? [Yes] [No]

(IF YES) K9. What do you think you might do?

(IF HEAD UNDER 30, SKIP TO PAGE 30, L1)

(IF HEAD IS 30 OR OVER - See Face Sheet)

K10. What about retirement, when do you think you will stop working altogether? (Give year or age.) _____

K11. Will you get Social Security, Railroad Retirement, or some other government pension? [Yes] [No]

(IF HEAD IS MARRIED - See A18)

K12. Will your wife be eligible for Social Security benefits from her own work? [Yes] [No]

K13. What about other pensions or annuities, will you (or your wife) have anything like that? [Yes] [No]

K14. Do you think you will be able to get along all right when you retire, or do you think things may be difficult or what?

(IF NOT CLEAR) K15. Will your income be enough to live on?

K16. Do you have any other plans for what you will do when you retire? [Yes] [No]

(IF YES) K17. Tell me about them.

L1. Is your church preference Protestant, Catholic or Jewish?

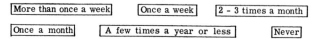

(IF PROTESTANT) L2. What denomination is that?_____

(IF JEWISH)   L3. Is that orthodox, conservative or reform?

L4. About how often do you usually attend religious services?

| More than once a week | | Once a week | | 2 - 3 times a month |

| Once a month | | A few times a year or less | | Never |

L5. Generally speaking, do you think of yourself as a Republican, a Democrat, an Independent, or what? _____

(IF REPUBLICAN OR DEMOCRAT)

    L6. Would you call yourself a strong (Republican) (Democrat) or a not very strong (Republican) (Democrat)?

| Strong Democrat | | Not very strong Democrat | | Not very strong Republican | | Strong Republican |

(IF INDEPENDENT OR OTHER)

    L7. Do you think of yourself as closer to the Republican or Democratic party?

| Yes, Democrat | | No, neither | | Yes, Republican |

L8. Do you belong to a labor union? union?   [Yes] [No]

L9. Is anyone here a veteran?   [Yes] [No]

    (IF YES)

       L10. Who?

M1. Race: White   Negro   Other _____
                                                        (Specify)

M2. Length of interview: _____
                              (Minutes)

M3. Number of calls:_____

M4. Who was present during the interview?

M5. How would you describe the interior (furniture, draperies, paint)?
     | Well kept up and | Fairly well kept up | Not kept up and |
     | in good condition | and in fair condition | in poor condition |

M6. How would you describe the outside of the dwelling, the yard, etc.?
     | Well kept up and | Fairly well kept up | Not kept up and |
     | in good condition | and in fair condition | in poor condition |

M7. This is a | single D.U. | | two-D.U. structure | | structure originally |
                 | structure | | or duplex | | built as an |
                                                               | apartment house |
                 | converted house with |
                 | 3 or more D.U.'s, or |
                 | a rooming house | trailer   other _____

M8. Does the head speak English?
                        | Haltingly, or with marked accent |
            Fluently | (difficult to understand) | Not at all

M9. Is the head alert and able to answer questions easily, or does he have difficulty
     understanding and answering?
     | Alert, answers | Has slight difficulty in | Has considerable difficulty |
     | easily | understanding or answering | understanding and answering |

M10. Did you notice any member of the family with a handicap not mentioned in the
     section on work limitation?   Yes   No

         (IF YES) M11. Who was it?

                   M12. What was the handicap?

Do you have any impressions, aside from what has already been stated in the interview as to how hardworking and intelligent this family is, whether they are trying
to get ahead financially or socially, and whether they have a set of realistic plans
for the future?

THUMBNAIL SKETCH:

Appendix C

ESTIMATES AND IMPUTATIONS

Budgetary Requirement

An estimate of annual cost of food, housing, clothing, and medical care for the unit based on average expenditures of low-to-moderate income families in New York City.[1] Table 16-1 shows the estimates which were used in calculating the budgetary requirement for each unit.

Income Taxes

The estimated Federal income tax liability of the unit. In estimating the liability it is assumed that all husbands and wives file joint returns. Minors in the unit are assumed to file separate returns if they received $600 or more of taxable income. Deductions were estimated equal to the average deduction as a per cent of income used by persons in that income bracket who filed income tax returns.[2] Special deductions and tax credits were calculated for units with over $500 of dividend income, but no estimate was made of the tax credit due retired persons from their property income.

Index of Need for Achievement

A measure of a supposedly enduring personality trait—a disposition to strive for success. Attitudes and behavior interact with one another in ways difficult to untangle. Psychological factors which might be related to behavior, when classified according to their stability, range from volatile moods at one end of the scale to stable personality dispositions at the other. In a single cross section study, it is only the stable personality dispositions which can be assumed to affect behavior rather than to be determined by current behavior. It is also profitable to see whether certain attitudes are related to behavior, without prejudging the causal directions.

Among the various personality dispositions it is necessary to select a few, because with limited resources it is not possible to measure and test a large number of such variables. Recent work in the field of personality and motivation has pared down the long lists of motives to a few in the interest of quantifying them and testing

[1] The Community Council of Greater New York, Budget Standard Service, *Annual Price Survey and Family Budget Costs, October, 1959* (New York: 1959), pp. 11, 12.
[2] U.S. Department of Treasury, "Individual Income Tax Returns for 1957," *Statistics of Income, 1957* (Preliminary) (Washington, D.C.: 1959), 12.

hypotheses about them. The three most commonly used are the needs for affiliation, achievement, and power. Reasonably reliable measures of these motives have been developed using Thematic Apperception Test protocols, and have been used on a national probability sample.[3]

Even measurement of three motives would have strained the resources of this study for interviewing time and analysis—they must be adjusted for different numbers of words in the replies and other factors.

The need for achievement was selected as the most important motive likely to affect economic activity. This motive is defined as a propensity to strive for success in situations involving an evaluation of one's performance in relation to some standard of excellence. A person with a high need for achievement tends to derive satisfaction from overcoming obstacles by his own efforts. He takes calculated risks, rather than playing long shots or being overly cautious. As compared with a desire for affiliation—to give and receive affection—or for power—to be in control of the means of influencing the behavior of others—the need for achievement seems mostly likely to be associated with upward mobility, long hours of work, desires to educate one's children.

In addition, there was reason to believe that an indirect measure of achievement motivation could be derived from a relatively simple procedure. Direct questions about the importance of achievement had been shown to be uncorrelated with the indirect measures which predicted behavior.[4] The method was suggested by John Atkinson. Laboratory research had shown that individuals with high achievement motivation made strong distinctions between difficult and easy tasks, and placed high reward values on difficult tasks. Also, college students' estimates of the proportion who could succeed at different occupations were correlated $-.85$ with the prestige rankings of those occupations.[5] Furthermore, an examination of various occupational prestige rankings found them all correlated with one another at levels between .88 and .98 providing "strong evidence that the occupational prestige system, for at least some thirty years past has been perceived in a highly similar manner by Americans from every stratum of society." [6]

An index of achievement motivation should, then, be provided by the extent

[3] John Atkinson (ed.), *Motives in Fantasy, Action, and Society* (Princeton: D. Van Nostrand Company, Inc., 1958);

Joseph Veroff and others, "The Use of Thematic Apperception to Assess Motivation in a Nationwide Interview Study," *Psychological Monographs*, 74 (1960), 12.

[4] Richard C. deCharms and others, "Behavioral Correlates of Directly and Indirectly Measured Achievement Motivation," in David C. McClelland (ed.), *Studies in Motivation* (New York: Appleton-Century-Crofts, Inc., 1955);

David C. McClelland and others, *The Achievement Motive* (New York: Appleton-Century-Crofts, Inc., 1953);

Bernard C. Rosen, "The Achievement Syndrome: A Psychocultural Dimension of Social Stratification," in Atkinson (ed.), *Motives in Fantasy, Action, and Society,* where achievement motivation is correlated with school grades, but expressed value of achievement is not.

[5] Harry J. Crockett, Jr., "Achievement Motivation and Occupational Mobility in the United States" (unpublished Ph.D. dissertation, The University of Michigan, 1960), p. 33;

Charles H. Mahone, "Fear of Failure and Unrealistic Vocational Aspiration" (unpublished Ph.D. dissertation, The University of Michigan, 1958).

[6] Crockett, "Achievement Motivation and Occupational Mobility," p. 30.

to which an individual places high values on succeeding in the difficult, high prestige occupations, and low values on succeeding in the easy occupations. In order to reduce biases connected with the respondents' own occupations, we asked the following question about "most people": "We are interested in how people compare occupations. How do you think most people would feel if a boy of theirs chose each of these types of work?" Respondents were given a choice between: not happy, wouldn't mind, happy, very happy, delighted. Table C-1 gives the occupations used, together with National Opinion Research Center rankings,[7] the scale rankings this study used, and the average rankings which actually came from this sample.

TABLE C-1

OCCUPATION PRESTIGE RANKINGS FROM NORC STUDY,
USED IN BUILDING THE ACHIEVEMENT INDEX
AND DERIVED FROM THIS STUDY

Occupation [a]	NORC score	Scale score used for index	Average score in this study [b]
Night watchman	47	1	1.25
Auto mechanic	59	2	2.31
Carpenter	65	3	2.30
Mail carrier	66	4	2.15
Bus driver	68	5	1.75
Bookkeeper	68	6	2.54
Drug store owner	69	7	3.33
High school teacher	80	8	3.19
Doctor	93	9	3.96

[a] "Social worker" was also included, not to use in deriving the index, but to see how people evaluated the occupation. The average evaluation for social worker fell in the middle, at 2.41.

[b] using an index ranging from 1 for "not happy" to 5 for "delighted"

It is clear that changes have occurred since 1950 in the rankings of auto mechanics and carpenters, who moved up, and bus drivers and high school teachers, who moved down. It is possible that shifts resulted from differences in questions but likely that they reflect real changes.

The index of achievement motivation was based on the scale score in the central column of Table C-1, derived from the NORC rankings. A better index could presumably be developed by using the rankings from this study.

The extent to which an individual differentiated between occupations on the basis of their prestige was measured by the slope of the regression of the evaluation index (1 for "not happy" to 5 for "delighted") on the prestige scale score (1 to 9). The regression coefficient indicates the increase in the evaluation index as one increases the prestige of the occupation.

Table C-2 provides information on the spread of the evaluation scores and the relation of the scores for each occupation to the education of the spending unit

[7] Bernard Barber, *Social Stratification* (New York: Harcourt, Brace and Company, Inc., 1957). This is based on a 1950 study by the National Opinion Research Center.

TABLE C-2

OCCUPATION EVALUATION

(MEAN SCORES WITHIN EDUCATION OF HEAD AND DISTRIBUTION BY OCCUPATION)

A. Mean score for each occupation within education of the head

Education of head	Night watchman	Auto mechanic	Car-penter	Mail carrier	Bus driver	Book-keeper	Drug store owner	High school teacher	Doctor
None	1.86	2.90	2.97	2.48	2.25	2.82	3.10	3.29	3.71
1–8 grades	1.02	2.52	2.55	2.42	1.92	2.70	3.28	3.20	3.82
9–11 grades	1.36	2.30	2.31	2.10	1.72	2.56	3.38	3.14	3.94
12 grades	1.42	2.29	2.31	2.13	1.76	2.53	3.41	3.20	3.99
12 grades and nonacademic training	1.28	2.17	2.20	2.26	1.61	2.47	3.39	3.20	4.06
College, no degree	1.31	2.16	2.06	2.00	1.61	2.37	3.28	3.29	4.08
College, bachelor's degree	1.25	2.02	1.92	1.83	1.54	2.30	3.25	3.14	4.14
College, advanced degree	1.15	1.88	1.72	1.75	1.52	2.15	3.18	3.16	4.27
All	1.25	2.31	2.30	2.15	1.75	2.54	3.33	3.19	3.96

B. Distribution of evaluation scores within each occupation

Evaluation scores	Night watchman	Auto mechanic	Car-penter	Mail carrier	Bus driver	Book-keeper	Drug store owner	High school teacher	Doctor
Not happy	66	19	17	22	43	9	5	4	2
Wouldn't mind	22	38	43	43	35	38	18	18	8
Happy	7	30	29	25	14	40	33	39	20
Very happy	1	6	4	4	2	7	22	22	26
Delighted	0	2	3	1	1	2	18	11	40
Do not know; not ascertained	4	5	4	5	5	4	4	6	4
Total	100	100	100	100	100	100	100	100	100

head. It is clear that the differences between mean scores are significant, and that while those with more education make stronger distinctions between occupations, the occupational differences persist through all education groups.

The correlation between education and the need for achievement index, raises a question of whether the need-achievement index measures anything beyond the effects of formal education, a question which can only be resolved in the multivariate analyses where both are used jointly to predict behavior. The theory, however, is that achievement motivation is fixed early in life and helps determine the amount of education an individual completes.

In a sample of 73 pretest interviews the index of need for achievement was related to a score indicating the number of evidences (mostly in attitudes and plans) of upward mobility, and a low but significant positive correlation was found. A better measure of actual striving would presumably have been more highly correlated with the need for achievement.

In a class of sixty-four psychology students at the University of Michigan, the need-achievement index proved to be uncorrelated with a Thematic Apperception Test as a measure of achievement motivation. There were some problems with the administration of the protocols, and it is possible that the range of occupations used, relevant for a cross section of the population, was largely below the interest range of college students. The actual index measures for the students were much higher than for the cross section sample, twice as many in the group over .35, and no students in the group under .15.

The theory relating achievement motivation to behavior involves two other intervening variables. These two variables are the incentive value of the expected outcome and the expectancy (subjective probability) that a particular course of action will lead to that outcome. Behavior is thought to be a joint result of the levels of all three.[8]

Variations in the incentive value of economic success are uncontrolled, difficult to measure, and perhaps not so different from one person to another within one culture. The major factor affecting a person's desire for more income might be the number of other persons dependent upon him, which was used as a separate predictor in many of the analyses.

The subjective probability that working hard, or getting more education, or accumulating capital, would pay off, can vary from individual to individual, and the theoretical model says that it may interact with the motive value to determine actual behavior. Hence, a measure of the expectancy was attemped, and a joint classification of individuals on both motive and expectancy was used in much of the analysis. The measure of expectancy was based on a single question: "Some people say that people get ahead by their own hard work; others say that lucky breaks or help from other people are more important. What do you think about this?"

The theory was that those who had a high need for achievement, *and* believed that hard work would result in success, would work the hardest. The problem remains that the expectancy is an attitude which can change as a result of experience. The joint motive-expectancy mix should affect current behavior. However,

---

[8] John Atkinson, "Motivational Determinants of Risk-Taking Behavior," *Psychological Review,* 64 (November, 1957), 359–372.

past behavior, or current situations which result from that past behavior, resulted from the combination of the stable motive and whatever expectancies existed when the behavior took place. Thus, if income from capital, resulting from saving and accumulation, is related both to our index of need for achievement and to the belief that hard work pays off, the causal direction is relatively clear for the motive, but could go in either direction or both for the belief that hard work pays off. The belief in hard work reinforced by successful application remains, but a man who believed in hard work and failed many have lost his confidence that work is rewarded.

It is useful to remember that minority groups, particularly the visible minorities like Negroes or Jews, are more likely to feel that luck or help from friends makes a difference, and for them perhaps this reflects reality. In general, however, the belief that hard work will be rewarded is predominant in this country.

It is quite possible that in other countries, reliance on luck may be more wide-spread, the incentive value of economic success as compared with success as a priest or general or scholar, may be lower, and the proportion with high achievement motivation may be different. Only carefully designed comparative studies will tell.[9]

Net Intrafamily Transfers

Any money payments or food and housing donations which the unit received from other members of the family less any such contributions which the unit made to other members of the family. Information on money payments within the family was taken from the questionnaire. Value of food was estimated from the Department of Agriculture's data on mean expenditures on food according to income and family size.[10] Value of housing was allocated according to a formula which gave more than proportionate weight to the husband and wife of the primary adult unit. Husbands and wives of the primary adult unit were given a weight of two each; all others were given a weight of one; allocation of housing expense for each unit was then determined as the ratio of weights of the unit to the total weight for all occupants of the dwelling. The value of other transfers within the family was not estimated. Net intrafamily transfers is a meaningful concept only for adult units and spending units; it equals zero for any family, since benefits contributed equal benefits received within any family.

Planning Index

An index of the extent to which the spending unit appeared to be thinking ahead and planning for the future. It is based on whether the spending unit has hospitalization insurance, savings of $500 or more, whether the spending unit head feels able to plan ahead, plans for purchases, whether the spending unit head has plans for the age at which he will retire, and whether he will have pensions other than social security. The value ranges from six for those who display each of these characteristics to zero for those with none of these characteristics.

[9] For a start on this assessment, see David McClelland, *The Achieving Society* (Princeton: D. Van Nostrand Company, Inc., 1961).

[10] U.S. Department of Agriculture, "Income and Household Size: Their Effects on Food Consumption," *Household Food Consumption Survey* (Washington, D.C.: 1959).

Property Taxes for Renters

The estimate of the property taxes paid by renters in their rent. It assumes that renters bear the full burden of property taxes levied on their dwellings, and that the effective tax rates are the same for rented dwellings as for owner-occupied homes.

Home owners were asked for the value of their homes, the amount it would cost to rent a similar home, and the amount of property tax they paid. The first two figures were used to estimate relationships between house values and rents. (See Table C-3.) The relationships differed significantly among the four regions of the country, perhaps owing to different rates of population growth and climatic factors. From the regressions it can be seen that the rule that houses are worth 100 times gross monthly rent (eight times annual rent) is approximately correct for houses valued around $5,000 and renting for around $600 per year. The rule understates the value for more expensive houses.[11]

[11] Paul F. Wendt, *Real Estate Appraisal* (New York: Henry Holt and Company, Inc., 1956), pp. 89ff.

TABLE C-3

MEAN AVERAGE ESTIMATED ANNUAL RENT EQUIVALENT
WITHIN HOUSE VALUE AND REGION
(FOR HOME OWNING FAMILY UNITS)

Value of house	Region			
	Northeast	North Central	South	West
Less than $3,000	$ 519	$ 629	$ 317	$ 501
$3,000–5,999	746	733	553	685
$6,000–8,999	945	894	789	825
$9,000–11,999	1,109	1,022	1,005	1,180
$12,000–14,999	1,337	1,289	1,324	1,366
$15,000–17,999	1,596	1,503	1,324	1,465
$18,000–20,999	1,965	1,698	1,557	1,602
$21,000 and over	2,351	1,818	1,848	2,056

Weighted regression of average estimated annual rent equivalent
on house value within regions

Northeast	$R = .0809\,H + \$301$
North Central	$R = .0560\,H + \$495$
South	$R = .0654\,H + \$288$
West	$R = .0665\,H + \$391$

Significance of the effects of individual regressions

	Sum of squares	Degrees of freedom	Mean square	F	$F < .05$
Variance of residuals from the pooled regression	585,145,828	27			
Variance of residuals from the four regressions	329,173,445	24	13,715,560		
Contribution of the individual regressions	255,972,383	3	85,324,128	6.2	4.7

Home owners, in estimating the rent for houses similar to their own, were undoubtedly referring to rent exclusive of payment for furnishings and utilities, because that is the way in which single family houses are usually rented. To make rent paid by renters comparable to the rent estimated by home owners, the rent paid to the landlord was reduced by 20 per cent if the dwelling was rented furnished. Any amount which the renter paid directly for utilities was added to this adjusted rent. The total rent bill was then reduced by another 20 per cent to eliminate utility payments made by the landlord or the tenant.[12]

The resulting figure was taken as a rental payment comparable to the rentals estimated by home owners. This figure was used with the regressions in Table 18-1 to estimate a house value for each renter. The minimum value which was assigned was $1,000 with all lower estimates being raised to this amount. This eliminated the few negative and very low estimates of property value which would have resulted from low rental payments.

The next step was to estimate an effective ratio of taxes to house value. The effective tax rate for each of twenty areas was derived from the mean house value and the mean property tax bill reported by home owners in each area. The ratios of means are reasonable approximations of mean ratios because tax rates do not vary appreciably within areas. The rates for various areas ranged from 0.8 per cent to 2.7 per cent.

Multiplying the estimated house value for each renter by the tax rate in his area resulted in an estimated tax bill for each renter. This is the estimate that was used throughout Chapter 19.

Public School Benefits

The cost of the education being received currently by the unit's children in primary and secondary public schools. Questions were asked about the number of children currently going to public schools. This number of children was multiplied by an estimate of the current expenditure per pupil for public schools in the area.[13] The necessity for averaging school districts in concentric area bands around the metropolitan areas and for blocks of rural areas reduces the precision but also reduces spurious differences resulting from consolidated schools, particularly high schools.

Real Capital Income

For self-employed businessmen and farmers, real capital income was increased by an amount equivalent to a reasonable return on the capital invested in the

[12] For some comparable estimates of the fraction of rents going for services other than space, see Louis Winnick, "Long Run Changes in the Valuation of Real Estate by Gross Rents," *Appraisal Journal,* 20 (1952), 484.

[13] U.S. Bureau of Census, *1957 Census of Governments,* vol. III, no. 1, "Finances of School Districts" (Washington, D.C.: U.S. Department of Commerce, 1958), 21–367; also vol. III, no. 6, "Local Government Finances in Standard Metropolitan Areas" (1959), 10–49;

U.S. Office of Education, *Biennial Survey of Education in the United States, 1954–56,* Chapter 3, Section I, "Statistics of Local School Systems, 1955–56, Cities" (Washington, D.C.: U.S. Department of Health, Education and Welfare, 1959), 42–239; also Chapter 3, Section III, "Statistics of Local School Units, 1955–56, County Units," 23–65.

enterprise. Capital income was estimated as 6 per cent of capital in businesses; 6 per cent of the investment in livestock and equipment; 5 per cent of investment in land and buildings for farms. The remaining income realized by the enterprise was considered to be wages. Where earnings of the enterprise did not cover a reasonable return to capital, wages are considered to be negative.

For home owners, an estimate of the value of "free housing" received by living in a home which one owns was added to real capital income. The value was taken as 6 per cent of the owner's equity in his home.

For units which have received inheritances, self-accumulated capital income was calculated by subtracting 4 per cent of any inheritance from real capital income. The calculation assumes that 4 per cent represents a minimum annual income that could be received from investing the original inheritances in low yield, low risk assets such as bonds and not accumulating the interest. Any capital income in excess of 4 per cent of the inheritance may be attributed to savings of the unit. Any deficit represents dissavings of the unit.

Missing Information

Most large surveys are characterized, at least to some degree, by the problem of missing information. Even when interviews have been obtained, the information is not necessarily complete. Some information is missing because interviews were never taken with the designated respondent. There are usually some respondents who do not know the answers to some of the questions; there are others who have the necessary information but refuse to give it to the interviewer.

Missing information in this study was dealt with in three ways: [14]

1. In cases where information on house value, weeks worked, *and* earned income were all missing, the interviews were discarded before analysis and considered to be nonresponses. The bias inherent in discarding some interviews and failing to contact the respondent at some sample addressess was minimized by means of weights. Interviews with demographic characteristics similar to the missing interviews were given higher weights so that each type of interview would be represented in the sample in the proper proportion. (See Appendix A.)

2. When minor pieces of information were missing from an interview, they were coded as "not ascertained." Thus many tables show a separate line for cases where information was not ascertained. The reader is left to decide for himself how such cases should be interpreted. In some cases it may be appropriate to assume that cases where answers were not ascertained are distributed among possible categories in the same proportion that the known cases are distributed. However, incomplete and uncodable answers are more likely to appear in interviews with poorly educated, nonverbal respondents.

3. Missing information was filled in or "assigned" for a few cases for each of many economic and demographic variables about which data were available from other studies. Using characteristics of the individual family, editors made assignments on the basis of relationships shown in other data. This method of assigning missing information takes account of the fact that the not ascertained cases might

[14] For a discussion of the problem of handling missing data, see John B. Lansing and Thomas A. Eapen, "Dealing with Missing Information in Surveys," *Journal of Marketing,* 24 (1959), 21–27.

come from only certain demographic and economic groups within the sample. It allows one to manipulate financial data without the complications which arise when one attempts to separate missing data from the known cases. This same procedure is used in the Surveys of Consumer Finances. It is particularly necessary where multivariate analysis is involved, or where new variables are to be built as a combination of several variables. In these cases, a few not ascertained cases in each variable will cumulate and eliminate from the analysis many cases in which only one minor bit of information is missing.

The variables for which editors made assignments and the variables which were used in making the assignments are as follows:

Assigned variable	Assigned from [a]
Age of each adult	Marital status, age of spouse
Education of head	Occupation
House value	Size of city, age and education of head
Income—head's wage and salary	Race, occupation
wife's wage and salary	Race, education, number of weeks worked
farm or business	Farm or business value
rent, interest, dividends	Wage and salary income of head, age of head
transfer	Wage and salary income of spending unit, age of head
Mortgage debt	Number of years family has owned house, house value
Rent	Size of dwelling, income, family size
Value of free medical care	Number of days in hospital
Value of home-grown food	Family income, farm or nonfarm, fraction of food grown
Value of home improvements	Number of years family has lived in house, whether family owns or rents
Weeks head worked in 1959	Income, age, education

[a] The data on age were taken from Paul Glick, *American Families* (New York: John Wiley & Sons, Inc., 1957); the data on value of home-grown food were taken from *United States Department of Agriculture Household Food Consumption Survey* (Washington, D.C., 1959); and the data on value of medical care were taken from the Survey Research Center's Michigan Medical Study. The remaining data for assignments were taken from the Survey Research Center's 1959 Survey of Consumer Finances.

The number of assignments was small, involving well under 5 per cent of the sample for any particular variable.

It should be kept in mind that the choice is not between assigning and not assigning. Omitting a case with some bit of information missing implicitly assigns it the average of the rest of the population, not only on that variable but on all others. The use of assignments vastly reduces the biases at the expense of a very small exaggeration in the strength and significance of interrelationships.

Appendix D

A GLOSSARY OF CONCEPTS

ADJACENT AREAS   See Belt Code.

ADULT UNIT   A person eighteen or older, his spouse if he is married, and any children under eighteen who live with him and for whom he is responsible.

Dependent Adult Unit   Any adult unit which does not contain the head of a spending unit. Any adult unit which does not contain the major earner in the spending unit.

Extra Adult Unit   An adult unit which does not contain the head of a family. All dependent adult units are extra adult units; in addition, adult units containing the heads of related secondary spending units are extra adult units.

Head of Adult Unit   The single adult in the adult unit or the husband in the case of a married couple.

AVAILABILITY OF COLLEGES IN AREA   Whether public colleges, private colleges, both, or neither are located in primary sampling unit.[1]

BELT CODE

Central Cities   Central cities of standard metropolitan areas. If a standard metropolitan area has two or more central cities, the largest and any others of 250,000 population in 1950 are designated as central cities.

Suburban Areas   All urbanized areas in the primary sampling unit and the remainder of any county which includes a central city.

Adjacent Areas   All territory beyond the outer boundaries of suburban areas but within fifty miles of the central business district of a central city.

Outlying Areas   All territory more than fifty miles from the central business district of a central city.

BETA COEFFICIENT   A measure of the relative importance of variables used in multivariate analyses. (See Appendix E.)

BLUE COLLAR WORKER   See Occupation.

BUDGETARY REQUIREMENT   An estimate of annual cost of food, housing, clothing, and medical care for adult units and families. (See Appendix C.)

CAPITAL INCOME   Money income from rent, dividends, interest, trust funds, and royalties.

---

[1] U.S. Office of Education, *Education Directory, 1959–1960,* Part 3, "Higher Education" (Washington, D.C.: U.S. Department of Health, Education, and Welfare, 1959), 15–180.

Real Capital Income Capital income plus an imputed return on capital invested in owner-operated businesses and farms, and an imputed return on the investment in owner-occupied homes (estimated as 6 per cent of net equity). (See Appendix C.)

Self-accumulated Capital Income Real capital income less 4 per cent of any inheritance received by the unit.

CENTRAL CITIES See Belt Code.

CONTRIBUTIONS—NONFAMILY Gifts to friends and relatives living elsewhere, contributions to churches and charitable organizations, support of children in college, regular support of others outside the dwelling.

DEEP SOUTH See Region.

DISABILITY A condition, physical or mental, which, according to the spending unit head, limits the type of work or the amount of work a spending unit member can do. Work is taken to include school attendance for children and housework for housewives.

DISPOSABLE MONEY INCOME Money income of the unit less an estimate of Federal income taxes paid by the unit.

DWELLING UNIT In general, a dwelling unit is a group of rooms or a single room occupied, or intended for occupancy as separate living quarters, by a family or other group of persons living together or by a person living alone.

Head of the Dwelling Unit Head of the spending unit which owns or pays rent for the dwelling unit.

EARNING POTENTIAL For the head, a nonsymmetrical classification by race, age, education, whether he is retired, and whether he is a farmer. The most important factors known from other studies to affect earnings. (See Table D-1.)

EARNINGS

Hourly Earnings For heads and wives who are not self-employed businessmen or farmers, the ratio of wage and salary income to hours worked. For self-employed businessmen and farmers, wages and salaries were imputed by deducting a reasonable return on the capital investment in the enterprise from the business or farm income. (See Appendix C.) Earning rates were calculated on the basis of these imputed wages and salaries. If the business or farm did not earn enough to cover the imputed return on capital, earning rates may be negative. For those with more than one job, hourly earnings are a weighted average of all wage rates.

Peak Earnings Largest annual amount ever received by the head of the spending unit from wage and salary income, business or farm income. Peak earnings may be less than 1959 earnings if the respondent's definition of earnings does not coincide with the survey definition.

Real Earnings Wage and salary income plus mixed wage-capital income, less an imputed return on capital, plus money saved by home production.

EXTENT OF UNEMPLOYMENT Proportion of workers covered by unemployment insurance who were unemployed in 1958 in state.[2]

FAMILY All occupants of a dwelling unit who are related to each other by blood, marriage, or adoption.

[2] U.S. Bureau of Employment Security, *Handbook of Unemployment Insurance Financial Data, 1938–1959* (Washington, D.C.: U.S. Department of Labor, 1960).

TABLE D-1

EARNINGS OF SPENDING UNIT HEADS WITHIN EARNING POTENTIAL
(PERCENTAGE DISTRIBUTION OF SPENDING UNIT HEADS)

	Earning potential of spending unit heads									All spending unit heads [a]
	Nonretired									
				White, nonfarmer						
				18–34 years old			35 or older			
Earnings	Retired; disabled	Nonwhite	White farmer	1–11 grades	12 grades	Some college	1–11 grades	12 grades	Some college	
Less than $1,000	87	30	45	11	6	7	19	10	6	24
$1,000–1,999	4	16	16	11	9	9	9	3	4	8
$2,000–2,999	2	11	9	11	13	9	12	4	4	8
$3,000–4,999	5	28	16	38	33	27	27	23	17	24
$5,000–7,499	1	12	7	22	32	33	25	36	28	23
$7,500–9,999	1	2	4	6	6	9	7	17	17	8
$10,000 and more	0	1	3	1	1	6	1	7	24	5
Total	100	100	100	100	100	100	100	100	100	100
Number of spending unit heads	312	378	170	250	220	211	759	365	314	2,997

[a] Includes 18 cases for whom earning potential was not ascertained

499

Families with Inadequate Incomes Families whose gross disposable incomes are less than nine-tenths of their budgetary requirements.

Head of Family The major earner in the spending unit who owns the dwelling unit or pays the rent for it. In the case of a married couple, the head of the family is always the husband.

Poor Families Families with less than $5,000 in savings and gross disposable incomes which are less than nine-tenths of their budgetary requirements. Families with inadequate incomes and less than $5,000 in savings.

F RATIO A measure of significance of multivariate analyses results. (See Appendix E.)

GROSS DISPOSABLE INCOME Disposable money income plus nonmoney transfers plus money saved by home production plus 6 per cent return on investment in owner-occupied home. An alternate definition: gross factor income plus total nonfamily transfers less income tax. Total money and nonmoney income available to the unit after taxes.

GROSS FACTOR INCOME Real earnings plus real capital income. Total money and nonmoney income available to the unit through its work and investments. This measure excludes all transfer income.

HOME PRODUCTION Labor which the unit expended growing some of its own food and performing repairs and improvements in the home. The value of home production is the spending unit head's estimate of the money that the unit saved by doing this work itself.

HOURS WORKED An estimate of the total number of hours worked during 1959. It is based on an estimate by the spending unit head of the number of weeks worked multiplied by his estimate of the average number of hours worked per week when working. It thus includes the effects of overtime, second jobs, unemployment, or part-time or part-year work.

HOUSE VALUE For home owners, the present market value of the dwelling unit and surrounding land. If the owner-occupied building also contains other dwelling units, the value of the building is apportioned among the various dwelling units and the value of one dwelling unit assigned to the owner as his house value.

INCOME TAXES The estimated Federal income tax liability of the unit. (See Appendix C.)

LABOR FORCE PARTICIPATION Whether adult was employed at any time during 1959. Does not include unpaid family workers.

LABOR FORCE STATUS Whether an adult was employed, unemployed, retired, a student, a housewife, had never worked, or was disabled and not working at the time of interview.

LIFE CYCLE Whether the head is married, the age of his wife, the number of children he has, and whether any of them are under age six. This describes the stages through which the normal family goes and has been shown to be superior to using the component factors separately.[3]

LOCAL LABOR MARKET CONDITION Lowest monthly rating of county during 1959 according to labor supply-demand situation, ratio of unemploy-

---

[3] John B. Lansing and Leslie Kish, "Family Life Cycle as an Independent Variable." *American Sociological Review,* 22 (October, 1957), 512–519.

ment to total labor force, net nonagricultural labor requirements for next two to four months, effects of seasonal or temporary factors on labor supply-demand situations. B is highest rating; F is lowest rating.[4]

MIXED WAGE-CAPITAL INCOME   All money income from enterprises which involve capital and labor inputs. Money income from farming, unincorporated businesses, roomers, and boarders.

MONEY INCOME   Wage and salary income plus mixed wage-capital income plus capital income plus regular money transfers.

MOVEMENT OUT OF DEEP SOUTH   See Region.

NEED-ACHIEVEMENT SCORE   A measure of the extent to which spending unit heads differentiate in favor of high status, high reward occupations, thought to be a measure of need-achievement. (See Appendix C.)

NET REAL INCOME   Gross disposable income less nonfamily contributions. The net income available to the unit including all sources of income in kind and deducting Federal income taxes and contributions.

NORTH CENTRAL   See Region.

NORTHEAST   See Region.

OCCUPATION   A classification of jobs in general parallel to 1950 Census classifications.

White Collar Workers   Professionals, technical workers, managers, officials, self-employed businessmen, clerical and sales workers.

Blue Collar Workers   Craftsmen, foremen, operatives, laborers, service workers, government protective workers.

Skilled Workers   Craftsmen and foremen.

Semiskilled Workers   Operatives.

Unskilled workers   Laborers, service workers, government protective workers.

OLD AGE ASSISTANCE PAYMENTS PER INHABITANT IN STATES   Amount expended for old age assistance from July 1, 1958 to June 30, 1959 averaged over total population of state.[5]

OUTLYING AREAS   See Belt Code.

PER CAPITA TAX SUPPORT FOR HIGHER EDUCATION   Per capita state and local tax support for publicly controlled colleges and universities in 1955–56 by states.[6]

PER CENT OF AGED IN STATE WHO RECEIVE OLD AGE ASSISTANCE OR SOCIAL SECURITY   Persons sixty-five and older who received Old Age Assistance or social security benefits as a per cent of persons sixty-five and older in June, 1959 by states.[7]

PER CENT OF CLAIMANTS EXHAUSTING UNEMPLOYMENT COMPENSATION IN STATES   Claimants of unemployment compensation exhausting

[4] U.S. Bureau of Employment Security, "Area Classification," *The Labor Market and Employment Security* (Feb., Apr., June, Aug., Oct., Dec., 1959).

[5] Social Security Administration, *Research and Statistics,* Note #4—1960 (Washington, D.C.: 1960).

[6] U.S. Office of Education, *Biennial Survey of Education in the United States,* Chapter 4, Section II, "Statistics of Higher Education—Receipts, Expenditures, and Property" (Washington, D.C.: U.S. Department of Health, Education, and Welfare, 1959), 92–105.

[7] Social Security Administration, *Research and Statistics,* Note #4—1960.

benefits as a per cent of persons receiving first payments in 1958 by states.[8]

PLANNING INDEX   Measure of degree to which spending unit plans and provides for future. (See Appendix C.)

POOR FAMILIES   See Family.

PRIMARY SAMPLING UNIT   One of sixty-six areas chosen at the first stage of sample selection. Each of the twelve largest metropolitan areas forms a primary sampling unit; fifty-four additional units, each consisting of a county or a group of adjacent counties, are chosen from outside the metropolitan areas.

PROPERTY TAX   For home owners and those who neither own nor rent, amount paid in property taxes on homes including city, county, and school taxes. For renters, estimated amount of property taxes included in rent. (See Appendix C.)

PUBLIC SCHOOL BENEFITS   Number of head's children in public primary and secondary schools multiplied by the current expenditure for public school per enrolled pupil for the area where he lives. (See Appendix C.)

Potential Public School Benefits   Number of head's children in primary and secondary schools (including those in private schools) multiplied by the current expenditure for public school per enrolled pupil for the area where he lives.

RANK AND PROGRESS IN SCHOOL   Spending unit head's evaluation of the level of his grades and number of years that head was behind his age group when he completed his schooling. The measurement of progress assumes that head started first grade before age seven and can be determined only for heads who had some education but did not go beyond high school. It was computed as age when left school minus highest grade completed minus six.

RATIO OF COLLEGE ENROLLMENT TO LOCAL POPULATION   Ratio of enrollment in colleges in primary sampling unit to total population of primary sampling unit in 1958.[9]

REGION   Four areas of the United States, according to U.S. Census definition.

Northeast   Connecticut, Maine, Massachusetts, New Hampshire, New Jersey, New York, Pennsylvania, Rhode Island, Vermont.

North Central   Illinois, Indiana, Iowa, Kansas, Michigan, Minnesota, Missouri, Nebraska, North Dakota, Ohio, South Dakota, Wisconsin.

South   Alabama, Arkansas, Delaware, District of Columbia, Florida, Georgia, Kentucky, Louisiana, Maryland, Mississippi, North Carolina, Oklahoma, South Carolina, Tennessee, Texas, Virginia, West Virginia.

West   Arizona, California, Colorado, Idaho, Montana, Nevada, New Mexico, Oregon, Utah, Washington, Wyoming.

Deep South   Alabama, Georgia, Kentucky, Louisiana, Mississippi, North Carolina, South Carolina, Tennessee, Virginia.

[8] U.S. Bureau of Employment Security, *Handbook of Unemployment Insurance Financial Data, 1938–59* (Washington, D.C.: U.S. Department of Labor, 1960).

[9] U.S. Office of Education, *Education Directory 1959–60*, Part 3, "Higher Education" (Washington, D.C.: U.S. Department of Health, Education, and Welfare, 1959); U.S. Bureau of Census, *1950 Census of Population*, vol. I, "Number of Inhabitants" (Washington, D.C.: U.S. Department of Commerce, 1950).

Movement out of Deep South   Whether head grew up in Deep South, whether he now lives in South. Heads who have always lived in Arkansas, Delaware, District of Columbia, Florida, Maryland, Oklahoma, Texas, or West Virginia grew up outside the Deep South, now live in the South; yet, they did not move. The crucial group is made up of those who grew up in the Deep South and moved out, not to other Southern states, but to the North or West.

RELIGIOUS PREFERENCE   The expressed preference of the spending unit head for a particular religious denomination. Denominations were grouped according to the average income and education levels of members rather than according to theology, although the more fundamentalist groups tend to have lower incomes and less education. Table D-2 shows the variety of income distributions represented, and Table D-3 the variety of education levels.[10]

SEMISKILLED WORKERS   See Occupation.

SKILLED WORKERS   See Occupation.

SOUTH   See Region.

SPENDING UNIT   All members of a family who pool their incomes for major items of expense.

Head of Spending Unit   The major earner in the spending unit. Always the husband in the case of a married couple.

Primary Spending Unit   The spending unit which owns or pays the rent for the dwelling unit.

Related Secondary Spending Unit   Any persons who belong to the same family as the primary spending unit but who earn more than $15 a week and keep their finances separate and contribute less than half of their earnings to the primary spending unit.

Unrelated Secondary Spending Unit   A spending unit who does not own or pay the rent for the dwelling unit, and whose members are not related to members of the primary spending unit.

STANDARD METROPOLITAN AREA   A county or group of contiguous counties (except in New England) which contains at least one city of 50,000 inhabitants or more in 1950. In addition to the county or counties containing such a city or cities, contiguous counties are included if according to certain criteria they are essentially metropolitan in character and sufficiently integrated with the central city. In New England standard metropolitan areas have been defined on a town rather than on a county basis.[11]

SUBURBAN AREAS   See Belt Code.

TRANSFERS

Net Intrafamily Transfers   Any money payments or food and housing donations which the unit received from other members of the family less any such contributions which the unit made to other members of the family. (See Appendix C.)

Nonmoney and Irregular Transfers   Any large gifts of food, clothing, plus irregular money gifts plus free housing, plus free medical care plus free child care plus net intrafamily transfers.

[10] Bernard Lazerwitz, "A Comparison of Major United States Religious Groups," *Journal of the American Statistical Association,* 56 (September, 1961), 568–579.

[11] U.S. Bureau of the Census, *Statistical Abstract of the United States, 1956* (Washington, D.C.: U.S. Department of Commerce, 1956), p. 4.

TABLE D-2

GROSS DISPOSABLE INCOME OF SPENDING UNITS, WITHIN RELIGIOUS PREFERENCE OF SPENDING UNIT HEADS
(PERCENTAGE DISTRIBUTION OF ALL SPENDING UNITS)

Religious preference of spending unit heads

Gross disposable income	Baptist	Other Fundamentalist Protestant	Catholic	Lutheran	Non-Christian; Non-Jewish	None; not ascertained	Other Non-Fundamentalist Protestant	Presbyterian	Jewish	Episcopalian	All spending units
Less than $1,000	7	6	2	3		2	4	5	2	2	4
$1,000–1,999	13	16	7	9		14	12	9	3	6	11
$2,000–2,999	15	13	11	10	too few cases	10	13	5	9	7	12
$3,000–4,999	27	28	24	22		29	23	17	18	19	24
$5,000–7,499	24	24	30	30		29	23	25	26	22	26
$7,500–9,999	9	8	16	18		10	13	22	14	22	13
$10,000–14,999	4	5	8	6		5	9	13	13	15	7
$15,000 and more	1	0	2	2		1	3	4	15	7	3
Total	100	100	100	100		100	100	100	100	100	100
Number of spending units	703	336	610	191	14	89	719	174	79	82	2,997

TABLE D-3

EDUCATION WITHIN RELIGIOUS PREFERENCE
(PERCENTAGE DISTRIBUTION OF SPENDING UNIT HEADS)

Religious preference of spending unit heads

Education	Baptist	Other Fundamentalist Protestant	Catholic	Lutheran	Non-Christian; Non-Jewish	None; not ascertained	Other Non-Fundamentalist Protestant	Presbyterian	Jewish	Episcopalian	All spending unit heads
None	3	2	1	1		2	1	0	3	0	1
1–8 grades	41	36	30	29		41	26	14	7	5	30
9–11 grades	24	25	23	22	too few cases	8	20	15	12	16	21
12 grades	12	14	19	15		11	18	13	21	16	16
12 grades and nonacademic training	5	10	11	10		5	10	13	7	20	9
College, no degree	9	8	9	15		11	14	20	21	15	12
College, bachelor's degree	5	4	6	6		15	8	19	20	21	8
College, advanced degree	1	1	1	2		7	3	6	9	7	3
Total	100	100	100	100		100	100	100	100	100	100
Number of spending unit heads	703	336	610	191	14	89	719	174	79	82	2,997

505

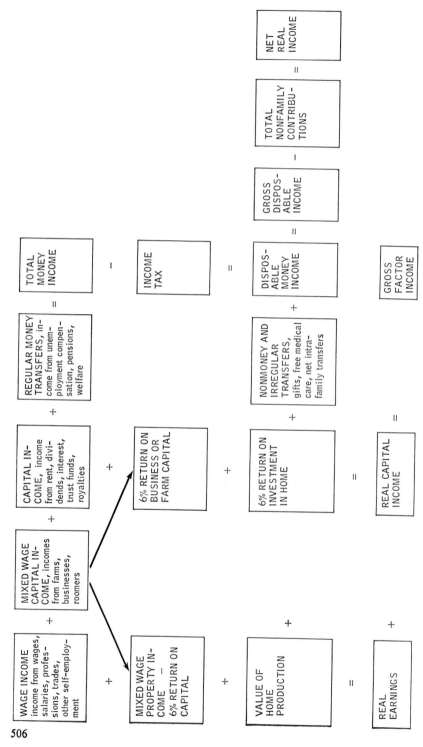

Figure D-1. Schematic representation of income.

Nonpublic Transfers   All money and nonmoney transfers received from individuals not in the family such as gifts, support or alimony payments, nongovernment pensions.

Public Contributory Transfers   Money payments in the form of veteran's benefits, social security, unemployment compensation. All of these benefits are contributory in the sense that part of the employee's wage is contributed for insurance or other benefits which are the right of the beneficiary without means tests or other tests of financial need.

Public Noncontributory Transfers   Money and nonmoney transfers from public or semipublic agencies which are primarily assistance to persons unable to support themselves. Public assistance, gifts from private charities, free medical care.

Regular Money Transfers   All money transfers received at regular intervals from sources other than members of the family.

Total Nonfamily Transfers   All money and nonmoney transfers received from sources outside the dwelling unit. Public contributory transfers plus nonpublic transfers plus public noncontributory transfers.

UNSKILLED WORKERS   See Occupation.

WAGE AND SALARY INCOME   All money received in the form of wages, salaries, bonuses, overtime, commissions, income from professional practice, a trade, self-employment in enterprises too small to be termed businesses.

WELFARE RATIO   Gross disposable income as a per cent of budgetary requirement. Calculated for adult units and families.

WEST   See Region.

Appendix E

MULTIVARIATE ANALYSIS

Because of the complex relationships which often exist between sets of character-istics related to a particular phenomenon, it is sometimes best to examine the rela-tionship through a multivariate analysis. The technique is a relatively simple extension of multiple correlation to the situation where the explanatory factors are membership in subclasses like age, rather than numerical variables.[1]

Any regression equation is essentially a formula for predicting the dependent variable for each individual, making use of information about the individual on a number of factors simultaneously. The estimating procedure has the characteristic that the summed squared errors of these predictions are smaller than for any other equation using the same factors and the same additive model.

The new feature in the analysis is that it converts each explanatory classification into a set of "dummy variables," which take the value one if an individual belongs to a particular subclass of each factor, and zero if he does not. Instead of a single regression coefficient for a numerical variable like age, we have a set, one attached to each age group, constrained so that their weighted sum is zero.

In practice dummy variables were used even when it might have been possible to form a numerical scale of the explanatory factor. This has the advantage that we make no restrictive assumptions about the linearity of the effect. If both extremes of the age range, for instance, are below average, such a curved effect of age appears in the data but would not be discovered in regression using age as a numerical variable.

The actual means of the dependent variable for each subclass of each explana-tory classification are presented in the form of unadjusted deviations from the grand mean, as well as the adjusted coefficients—adjusted simultaneously for the effects of all the other factors and intercorrelations among them. One can then see, for example, whether those whose fathers had a college degree themselves achieved a higher level of education than the average, and secondly whether this

[1] Daniel Suits, "Use of Dummy Variables in Regression Equations," *Journal of the American Statistical Association* 52 (December, 1957), 548–551.

For another example of this type of analysis and a mathematical interpretation of it, see T. P. Hill, "An Analysis of the Distribution of Wages and Salaries in Great Britain," *Econometrica* 27 (July, 1959), 335–381.

difference persists in an analysis that also takes account of age, race, and other factors.

In addition, the differences between the unadjusted and the adjusted deviations provide evidence about the extent to which intercorrelations among the explanatory factors required adjustments, and hence the extent to which the unadjusted deviations were biased as the result of these intercorrelations.

The predicting formula permits estimation of expected value for each individual by starting with the over-all average, and adding or subtracting the adjusted deviation for each explanatory factor, depending on which subclass he belongs to in each. In other words, the prediction for an individual uses only one "adjusted deviation" from each set. For example, to predict the number of grades of school completed by the head of a particular spending unit the process is as follows, using Tables 24-2 to 24-12.

Over-all average ------------------------→ 2.82 (3 = high school graduate)

Adjustments

1. Father graduate from high school	.70	
2. Head is forty years old	.25	
3. Father was a skilled worker	.12	
4. Head had four or more brothers and sisters		−.20
5. Head believes hard work pays off, and scored in the middle range on need-achievement	.05	
6. Head grew up in a small town in the Deep South		−.27
7. Father was a Baptist	.00	
8. Head is white	.02	
9. Head's father grew up in the South		−.05
10. Head is male	.01	
11. Head's father was self-employed	.04	
	1.19	−.52

Expected level: 2.82 + 1.19 − .52 = 3.49

The most important restriction on this type of analysis is the assumption that each explanatory factor affects the dependent variable in an independent manner, regardless of the values of the other explanatory factors. For example, it is assumed that education of the father always affects education of the spending unit head in the same way, no matter what the age, sex, or other characteristics of the head may be.

The assumption that the effects of various factors are independent (additive) is only an approximation of reality. Where interactions seemed likely to exist, two alternatives were available.

If two factors were likely to be interacting with each other, but not affecting any other factors, combination variables were formed. Religious preference and church attendance, attitude toward hard work, and need-achievement score were treated in this way.

Where several factors were likely to operate differently for a particular subgroup, the analysis was done separately for that subgroup. This was done for hourly earnings of white, male, nonfarmer spending unit heads, for example.

It is possible to imagine an individual for whom the multivariate coefficients will produce a predicted value absurdly large or absurdly small. Methods of adjusting the data so that the predictions can be used in a iterative simulation process have been suggested by Orcutt.[2]

Vernon Lippitt and the General Electric Company developed this multivariate analysis program.

Measures of Importance and Significance for the Multivariate Results

The importance and significance of the sets of coefficients are of greater concern than the importance of one particular subgroup. Selecting the largest single adjusted coefficient or the largest difference between any two requires special tests which take account of the number of possible things one could have selected. However, the reader who would like to know the order of magnitide of the sampling error of an adjusted deviation could take three times the standard deviation of the dependent variable divided by the square root of the number of cases on which the deviation is based. (This is two standard errors plus an adjustment for losses due to the clustered sample.)

There is no precise test for heterogeneity of a whole set of adjusted deviations, since they are themselves complex results of the whole multivariate process. However, a rough approximation to a test can be made by treating the adjusted deviations like a set of means, each representative of some subpopulation, and applying a simple one-way analysis of variance.

$$F = \cfrac{\cfrac{\text{Weighted sum of squares of adjusted deviations}}{\text{Number of subclasses} -1}}{\cfrac{\text{Unexplained sum of squares}}{\text{Number of interviews} - \text{number of subclasses} + \text{number of sets of subclasses} -1}}$$

The clustering in the sample has the effect of leaving fewer degrees of freedom than there are interviews; however, there are a large number of interviews. The resulting F test is relatively robust if the basic distribution departs from normality.[3] Most of the distributions are reasonably symmetrical and do not suffer from extreme kurtosis.

A test for heterogeneity of a set of means does not test for pattern of direction in the differences, and in some cases results appear which are unlikely to arise by chance even though they produce nonsignificant F ratios.

A more important question than significance of pattern or significance of heterogeneity among a set of subclass deviations is importance of differences. Important differences are those which allow one to reduce the summed squared errors in predicting the dependent variable. Again there is no exact and precise way to determine importance with respect to a set of adjusted deviations in a multivariate analysis, except by redoing the analysis, omitting only the classification in question. Assessing the importance of each of fourteen factors would then involve rerunning the multivariate analysis fourteen times, an impossibly expensive procedure.

[2] Guy H. Orcutt and others, *Microanalysis of Socioeconomic Systems: A Simulation Study* (New York: Harper & Brothers, 1961), pp. 229–231.

[3] G. E. P. Box, "Non-Normality and Tests on Variance," *Biometrika* 40 (December, 1960), 318–344.

The measure of the contribution to error reduction used here is:

$$\text{beta} = \sqrt{\frac{\text{Weighted sum of squares of adjusted deviations}}{\text{Standard deviation of the dependent variable}}}$$

It is analogous to the partial beta coefficient in the ordinary multiple regression using numerical variables. The following imaginary experiment should explain why this measure is referred to as a partial beta coefficient.

Consider the set of coefficients for one explanatory factor, say age, as a single bit of information, the importance of which is to be measured. For each individual there is one bit of information for each of the explanatory factors, in the form of the adjusted deviation for the subgroup in which he falls. Treat these adjusted coefficients as numbers. This amounts to defining a new set of variables (one for each factor) which can be treated numerically. Compute a new multiple regression which uses these new "variables" to explain the dependent variable.

It can be shown algebraically that the regression coefficient for each of the new variables will be 1.0. The character of the estimates of the adjusted deviations in the original analysis makes this so.

The formula for the partial beta coefficient in ordinary numerical multiple regression to be found in the statistical textbooks is: [4]

$$\frac{\text{Partial beta coefficient}}{\text{for factor } A} = \frac{\begin{array}{c}\text{regression coefficient} \\ \text{for explanatory variable } A\end{array} \times \begin{array}{c}\text{standard deviation of} \\ \text{explanatory variable } A\end{array}}{\text{standard deviation of the dependent variable}}$$

The upper left term becomes 1.0, the upper right term is the square root of the weighted sum of squares of the adjusted deviations, since they *are* the variable, and have a weighted mean of zero. Hence the formula reduces to the one given previously.

The one difference from ordinary beta coefficients is that these will all be positive, because the different directions of effect were already accounted for by the signs of the adjusted deviations.

The partial beta measure of importance so calculated is invariant with respect to the standard deviation of the dependent variable, and is adjusted for the variability of the predictor, hence provides an index of the importance of an explanatory factor relative to other factors in the same analysis or in other analyses.

It is possible to compute beta coefficients for the unadjusted deviations, representing the gross effects of that factor (the simple correlation coefficient if the factor were numerical rather than a classification). The difference between this beta coefficient and the beta coefficient for the adjusted deviations represents the extent to which intercorrelations among the different predictors have attenuated the apparent influence of that factor. The formula is the same as given above except that the unadjusted deviations are used. Such a comparison is particularly useful where the factor has a logical priority so that a case can be made that the adjustments for other factors attribute to them influence which is originally the result of the factor being considered.

[4] Mordecai Ezekiel, *Methods of Correlation Analysis* (New York: John Wiley & Sons, Inc., 1941), p. 217.

Appendix F

ESTIMATING AGGREGATES

Extrapolations from the Bureau of the Census data for 1959 show that there were approximately 57.4 million spending units in the United States during March and April, 1960. Using this number, and the proportions shown in tables in this report, means and percentages can be expanded to national aggregate estimates. However, several limitations on this process should be borne in mind.

1. All estimates are subject to sampling error (deviation of estimate derived from a single sample, from true value, although the average estimate from many samples would contain no error). Each of the three statistics used in estimating an aggregate is subject to sampling error: the estimate of number of units in the population, the estimate of the proportion of units relevant, and the estimate of the mean or percentage. When an aggregate is based on a mean or a percentage for a small subgroup, the cumulative effect of the three types of sampling error is substantial. See Appendix A.

2. The data also contain biases (systematic errors) arising from errors on the part of respondents and from the fact that everyone who fell into the sample was not interviewed. The method of weighting responses attempts to compensate for nonresponse biases but all such biases may not be remedied.

3. All aggregates derived from this survey apply only to that portion (96 per cent) of the United States population which resides in private dwelling units. This excludes inmates of institutions, people who live in college dormitories, hotels, military bases, Y.M.C.A.s, and similar places.

4. There are conceptual differences which complicate comparisons between these data and other presentations of national aggregates.

INDEX

The symbol *n.* indicates a footnote, *t.* a table.

513